A CHILD WENT FORTH

There was a child went forth every day,
And the first object he look'd upon, that object he became,
And that object became part of him for the day, or a certain part of
    the day,
Or for many years or stretching cycles of years.

The early lilacs became part of this child,
And grass and white and red morning-glories, and white and red
    clover, and the song of the phoebe-bird,
And the Third-month lambs and the sow's pink-faint litter, and the
    mare's foal and the cow's calf,
And the noisy brood of the barnyard or by the mire of the pond-
    side,
And the fish suspending themselves so curiously below there, and
    the beautiful curious liquid,
And the water-plants with their graceful flat heads, all became part
    of him.

—Walt Whitman, *Leaves of Grass*

A CHILD WENT FORTH

REFLECTIVE TEACHING
WITH YOUNG READERS AND WRITERS

JANINE CHAPPELL CARR

HEINEMANN • PORTSMOUTH, NH

Offices and agents throughout the world

The author and publisher wish to thank those who have generously given permission to reprint borrowed material:

Cover Photo:

Cover image from Sharon, Lois & Bram's *Mother Goose* copyright © 1985 by Sharon, Lois & Bram. Published by Groundwood Books/Douglas & McIntyre.

From the cover illustration by Barry Moser of *When Birds Could Talk and Bats Could Sing* by Virginia Hamilton. Published by The Blue Sky Press, an imprint of Scholastic Inc. Illustration copyright © 1996 by Barry Moser. Used by permission.

Cover image from *Piggie Pie!* by Margie Palatini. Copyright © 1995. Published by Houghton Mifflin Company. Reprinted by permission of the Publisher.

Cover image from *The Big Book of America* © 1994 by The Templar Company plc. First published in the United States by Courage Books, a promotional imprint of Running Press Book Publishers, Philadelphia and London.

Cover image from *Meet Felicity* by Valerie Tripp. Copyright © 1991. Published by Pleasant Company Publications. Printed with permission of Pleasant Company, 8400 Fairway Place, Middleton, WI 53562.

Excerpt from "The Boa" from *Beast Feast*, copyright © 1994 by Douglas Florian, reprinted by permission of Harcourt Brace & Company.

Jack Prelutsky's autobiographical sketch appears by courtesy of Jack Prelutsky and Greenwillow Books, a division of William Morrow & Co., Inc.

Library of Congress Cataloging-in-Publication Data
Carr, Janine Chappell.
 A child went forth : reflective teaching with young readers and
writers / Janine Chappell Carr.
  p. cm.
 Includes bibliographical references and index.
 ISBN 0-325-00171-5
 1. Language arts (Elementary)—United States. 2. Reading
(Elementary)—United States. 3. English language—Composition and
exercises—Study and teaching (Elementary)—United States. 4. Carr,
Janine Chappell. 5. Elementary school teachers—United States
Biography. I. Title.
LB1576.C31714 1999
372.6'044—dc21   99-29498
                                                     CIP

Editor: William Varner
Production: Elizabeth Valway
Cover design: Jenny Jensen Greenleaf
Cover photo of Victor Ventura by Janine Chappell Carr
Manufacturing: Louise Richardson

Printed in the United States of America on acid-free paper
03 02 01 00 99 RRD 1 2 3 4 5

For Michael,
and for Matthew

I love you.

CONTENTS

BECOMING WRITERS

APPENDIXES

FOREWORD

A Child Went Forth is an invitation, a challenge, and a gift to all teachers. Janine Chappell Carr invites us into her classroom and shows us how to give children the foundations of literacy, in a caring, nurturing, consistently clear way. She sets up a learning environment with a meticulously organized framework that allows children to become independent, responsible learners, while still valuing, and explicitly teaching, vocabulary, the conventions of language, spelling, and sound systems.

Janine challenges us to be what we teach, by reading and learning from other educators, from poets, from fiction and nonfiction writers, and from our children. She is a reader in the most professional sense, grounding her teaching strategies and philosophies in the ideas and theories of the most respected educators and writers: Marie Clay, Don Holdaway, Frank Smith, Regie Routman, Nancie Atwell, Don Graves, Lucy Calkins, Annie Dillard, Cynthia Rylant, Katherine Paterson, and Georgia Heard. The careful structure with which Janine frames her teaching is so effective because she is a reader, writer, and researcher. She knows what good readers and writers do, and she teaches that to her children. She knows good books. She knows her children, their families, and the community in which she teaches.

She knows how each student learns because she tracks reading with anecdotal and running records for the two years she keeps each child. She has equally impressive writing samples that document the growth of her students as writers. She keeps full, rich literacy portfolios that inform her, her children, and their parents, documenting their learning by describing what they did, and how they did it. Through her journal, where she captures conversations, discovers problems, thinks, draws, and plans "all in the swirl of children," she has brought the notion of *reflective practitioner* to a new level, a practical level. Each chapter and the appendixes are so rich with detailed instructions that they could be used by primary teachers or adapted for the middle school classroom. *A Child Went Forth* gives other teachers a responsible structure in which to make the complicated work of teaching our own. This book is a study in how to research as insiders, in our own classrooms, in a practical moment-by-moment way.

The gift is in how thoughtfully and thoroughly Janine documents the what and how of her language-rich learning environment, where all children are taught not only how to read and write, but how and why to *become* readers and writers. Each chapter is rich with the details of sound reading and writing instruction grounded in Janine's broad classroom experience and her own continual development as a teacher who believes learning is for life.

I teach seventh and eighth graders, yet I have eagerly awaited Janine's book. I have read the products of her classroom: the writing, art, responses to books, science projects, journals, and literacy portfolios. I have seen the eager, involved, purposeful, happy faces of the children she teaches. From her organizational strategies I've learned how to reshape my classroom. She reminds me again and again to set high standards for all my students. When I see these first and second graders working so hard to meet her high expectations, I ask myself, how can I challenge my thirteen- and fourteen-year-olds in similar ways?

What is particularly ironic to me is that Janine gives little mention to the constraints under which she taught these first and second graders: always more than thirty children in the class, the majority of whom came from low socioeconomic conditions, and many of whom spoke English with limited fluency. She never saw these reasons as an excuse for doing anything less than what she believes involves the most rigorous academic work. At the center of all she does, is her deep respect for children and equally deep respect for their individuality.

In their first child Matthew's room, there are several pieces of artwork, all professionally framed and hung with great care to be a focal point, as Janine and Michael's son lives in this room. The art is vivid and rich, splashed with intense, bold colors: yellows, pinks, reds, purples, and black. All the images are varying interpretations of the sun, yet each is sophisticated in pattern and design. I bend in to look more closely, realizing that each artist has chosen a different medium. Chalk. Oil pastels. Watercolor. Tempera. Sometimes the artist has experimented and mixed media. Each piece is unique and truly aesthetically pleasing. Despite all the baby furniture, picture books, and stuffed animals, my eyes keep going back to the art.

"Who's the artist?" I ask. "These are amazing."

"Artists," Janine says. And she names them. "Eddie. Snow. Rosanna. Nhi. Mary."

These are Janine's first and second graders. All artists. And all so respected by their teacher that their art hangs in the most important room in the house. It is with such deep respect and trust in children that Janine models, teaches, and inspires the best practices that lead to the most profound products. What we give children *first* is what they become.

I turned the last page of this book thinking, the *best teachers* should be teaching first grade. Ones who teach with compassion, with humor, with kind words, with intelligence, with high expectations, and with the belief that all children want to learn, and all children can learn. Teaching six- and seven-year-olds is perhaps the most difficult, most complicated, yet most rewarding age level to teach.

As Janine sets up the environment and then awaits her children, she asks herself the question we should all ask ourselves as teachers, "Would I enjoy being a child in my own classroom?" Peek into Janine's room. Listen to the hum of real work. Page after page, you'll admit, "I would certainly enjoy being a child in *this* classroom."

LINDA RIEF

ACKNOWLEDGMENTS

Gratitude is the fairest blossom which springs from the soul.
—Henry Ward Beecher

First and foremost, *A Child Went Forth* is a book about children—about my love, humility, and joy of teaching, living, and learning with young children in a primary classroom; about my fascination with observing children; and about my admiration of children and their many and varied ways of becoming readers and writers. To this end, my first expression of thanks and gratitude goes to the children, and their families, who became my "Room 12" community and extended family at Bobier Elementary. My special thanks to parents Amber Anderson and Vicky Rowland, who gave countless hours of time and care to all Room 12 children and supported and extended my efforts fully and graciously. Their commitment is unmatched and unforgettable. This book exists because of these children, their stories, their learning lives, and their diverse paths to literacy.

I would also like to thank several of my primary colleagues at Bobier Elementary who were dedicated to the art of teaching a diverse group of children in a supportive environment. First, Janet Hatfield, who, despite a love of teaching second-grade children, graciously handed me the "second-grade green track position" at the eleventh hour so that I could continue with my work and research with Room 12 children. Cathy Smith, a Reading Recovery teacher, spent weekly lunches with me, sifting through children's lives and learning nuances, and eventually the proposal for this book. I continue to admire her dedication to Bobier children. Andrea Holmes, Mary Wadleigh, Beth Hatten, Larry Dovenbarger, Carol Grimes, Peggy Duffield, Suzanne Stremmel, Jess Gadsby, Meg Jepsen, Gwen Smith, and Sal Cordero are all teachers with whom I enjoyed many short and long before- and after-school conversations about children, literacy, and schools. JoAnn Camarino was my capable and caring assistant teacher during my last year at Bobier. Kevin Nicholas, Rose-Yvonne Urias, and Leo Urias, wonderful bilingual teachers, were generous with both time and conversation about bilingual children and were patient with my frustrations at dismantling classroom community in the name of teaming. They were gracious beyond belief.

Last among my Bobier colleagues, I would like to thank my principal, David Lacey, with whom I've had many philosophical and practical discussions and letters about "best practices and decisions" for children—practices and decisions that embrace equality, diversity, integrity, responsibility, caring, and kindness. I am immensely appreciative of his active participation in our Room 12 learning community while I taught at Bobier and of the many hours he has since given to tracking permissions, discussing the Bobier neighborhood and community, and reading and responding to drafts of the introduction.

Before Bobier Elementary, I worked with "Room 6" children and their families at White City Elementary in Southern Oregon, and even though this book is not directly about those children, it *is* about them because many of my beliefs and practices evolved as I worked within that community. My special thanks to one of those parents, Sheila Mapes, who gave an inordinate amount of time, love, and care to Room 6 children and again, understood and supported the teaching of reading and writing in real and meaningful ways. Along with this, my thanks go to my principal, Bill Jones, and my many teaching friends at White City Elementary who shared laughter and practices with me for six years; among them: Barbara Schack, Pat Higgins, Bonnie Abramsson, Jan Wood, Lynn Scott, Georgia Davison, and Jay Sparks, my teaching partner.

To the extent that this book is a "child-watcher's guide to literacy" (Holdaway 1979), I would like to thank my mentors who have supported, guided, and influenced my form of child-centered teaching from the early days to the present.

- Sherry Vaughan—my mentor while I was an undergraduate student at Washington State University. She was one of the first voices I heard that advocated immersing children in good books and purposeful writing. Together, we started the WSU-NCTE affiliation on campus. I view teaching the way I do because of this start.
- Karen Dalrymple, currently director of education of Ashland Public Schools in Ashland, Oregon, has had a profound influence on my teaching. After finishing my first year of teaching, I attended a two-week summer institute taught by Karen, who at that time was an elementary teacher in Colorado, and in the course of two weeks, I could finally envision the implementation and management of a thoughtful, integrated language arts program. Karen's classroom was a world that captured the bright minds of young learners through inquiry studies; a world of exploring fine books and not managing reading groups; a world of engaging children as real writers; a world of empathy for the complexity of young lives; a world where the rewards of learning and belonging to a caring community were the only rewards in the classroom; a world of rigorous and reflective teaching. To this day, I regard Karen as one of the most intelligent, articulate, and compassionate teachers I have ever met. She has left an indelible mark on my teaching soul.
- Linda Rief—whom I first met at Regis University while I was a graduate student in the Master's in Whole Learning program. It is a privilege to be one of Linda's students, and her teaching cemented my primary workshop approach to the teaching of reading and writing and my belief in

the importance of developing the democratic voices and lives of five-, six-, and seven-year-olds. It was Linda who told me to "write" that summer, and so, trusting her, I have. It was also Linda who later reminded me that writing is an arduous process and to stay with it; I give tribute to her for saving this book. I continue to admire and appreciate Linda's intelligence, craft, respect for teachers and learners, and dedication to public schools. She is a true *teacher.*

- Bea Lasky, director of the Master's in Whole Learning program; Brenna Isaacs, my mentor; and Robyn Platt, Eileen Pennington, Dan Seger, Glenn Bruckhart, and Kathy Escamilla—all thoughtful and inspiring teachers while I was a graduate student at Regis University.
- Mike Dilena—with whom I've enjoyed friendship and correspondence for ten years. One of the highlights of my teaching career to date was visiting South Australian primary schools and having the opportunity to observe in action and talk with several creative and compassionate primary teachers. Being included in Mike's circle of educators felt like being "home." Mike was another person who told me to "write" and who read drafts of my lengthy first manuscript, then sent continual email encouragement throughout the writing of the second manuscript, which helped me through the sometimes rough and tired waters of writing.
- Ann Van Horn, currently director of professional development at Rigby, challenged me to think and rethink my classroom practices and biases during the two weeks I spent studying and talking late into the night with her one summer in Pacific Grove, California. I also discovered that we have a similar taste in professional and children's literature, and I still think of Ann when choosing books for my library.

I also have blossoms of gratitude for colleagues, who are also dear friends, who have supported my work with children and shared laughter, tea, their homes, their philosophies, and their visions, all of which have enriched my life:

- Nellie Edge, an educator in Salem, Oregon, continues to sound the battle cry for "schools worthy of our children." Nellie was yet another person who told me to "write" and has supported my classroom and me professionally for several years.
- Nancy Leigh Davis, a special-education preschool teacher in Seattle, Washington, has emailed countless words of encouragement, while never forgetting to write about the simple, wonderful details that make up "living."
- Linda Foglia, a gifted primary teacher in Vancouver, Washington, visited my classrooms in both Southern Oregon and Southern California and is the quintessential lifelong teacher, learner, and friend.
- Paula McDonald, whom I taught with at Bobier, is now my long-distance teaching friend and a kindred spirit with home and garden. I have appreciated her "I can't wait to read your book!" calls and letters of encouragement.

- Cliff Jones, who is both family friend and an extraordinary kindergarten teacher in San Diego City Schools, built classroom furniture for me, spent time in my classroom, talked children and literacy for hours on end, and now gathers kindergarten samples and stories for my work with primary teachers. I extend my love, thanks, and appreciation to him.

Two recent experiences with teachers have shaped my teaching life in a different way for which I owe thanks. For one intense year, I worked closely with teachers in their classrooms at McKinley Elementary in Tracy, California, after several years of summer inservicing with them. Their willingness to open their classroom doors and allow me to teach beside them and reflect with them was a wonderful learning experience.

During the past three years, I have worked closely with Sharon Shanahan, curriculum director, and the primary teachers and principals of Ceres Unified School District. The Ceres' early literacy project, developed with and led by teacher leaders, has been a comprehensive effort to help primary teachers implement sound early literacy teaching and assessment practices in their classrooms so that all children learn to read and write with skill and confidence. Throughout my time on the project, I have been challenged in different ways beyond my teaching life within my four classroom walls, and I have learned a great deal working alongside this group of teachers. They prevail in difficult times and I thank them for continuing to help me view teaching and learning in dynamic ways.

Both experiences have helped me understand the complexity of change, the need to respect individual teaching differences, the need for kindness and tolerance, the need for standards and expectations, the need for true teaching mentors to work alongside their colleagues in their classrooms, the need for assistance as part of evaluation, and the need to think clearly and solve problems cooperatively. Ultimately, both experiences have made me a better teacher of children and teachers.

In addition to children, colleagues, mentors, and friends, I would like to express my thanks to the team at Heinemann for assisting me with this work. My journey started with Maureen Barbieri, who gave critical assistance during the proposal phase of the manuscript and read first drafts of the beginning chapters. I appreciate her belief in the voices and learning lives of these children and the nudge to share their stories. Linda Allen's editorial talents were immensely helpful as I worked through the process of tightening my manuscript, and Elizabeth Marzoli's impeccably detailed final edit allowed me to bring my composing process to completion. I also have great appreciation for Elizabeth Valway for her patient, prompt, and careful assistance; and for seeing my manuscript through the maze of production, and the countless hours and details I'm envisioning that work entailed so that *A Child Went Forth* could go forth in both beautiful and articulate ways. And to Bill Varner, a wonderful editor, who reminded me that even T. S. Eliot endured setbacks as a writer, and who subsequently gave patient direction, time, and care throughout the second writing of my manuscript. I am honored to work with such a professional and caring team.

I also have blossoms of gratitude for everyone who falls somewhere between my grandparents and my nieces and my nephews in my families, the Chappells, the Millers, and the Carrs. "Families are our shelter from the storm, our oldest and most precious institution and our last great hope," writes Mary Pipher (1996, 10). Thank you all for providing purpose, hope, shelter, and words of encouragment when needed.

And finally, I save the fairest blossoms of my gratitude for my son, Matthew, and my husband, Michael. Already I delight in Matthew's path to literacy, and his wonder and delight in the world; he is now the crown jewel of my child watching and child admiration. There are no better moments than those I spend with him in my lap in the rocking chair, a pile of favorite books on the ottoman, with only the ticking of the kitchen clock for company.

Michael is the essence of endurance without complaint, and knows, more than anyone, how much *A Child Went Forth* has been a late-night labor of love. Michael has been my faithful reader, editor, listener of ideas, and sorter of confusions from the beginning. He has read and responded to every word of every draft, and his suggestions have been invaluable. For both Michael and Matthew, my gratitude, appreciation, and love springs from deep within my soul.

Thank you.

INTRODUCTION

I have come to believe that a great teacher
is a great artist. . . . Teaching might even be
the greatest of the arts since the medium
is the human mind and spirit.

—*John Steinbeck*

I am convinced. Children love to learn, regardless of their circumstances. I believe that with close instruction, sustained effort, and a caring classroom community, all children can succeed in becoming proficient readers and writers.

Teaching young children, particularly low-socioeconomic children, requires constant vigilance, dedication, and attention to detail. Why? Because these children generally enter school with fewer language skills and learning experiences than their middle-class peers. They are also more likely to encounter instability, social problems, and low academic expectations at home (Graves 1998). The generalizations continue: Low-socioeconomic children live in tougher neighborhoods, have tardy and attendance problems, and move often with their families. Low-socioeconomic children may not arrive clean for school, complete their homework, or return their schoolbooks on a regular basis. Low-socioeconomic children are more difficult to teach.

However, despite the media's insistence that American schools typically are inept at teaching children from low-income neighborhoods and that some educators think it is unreasonable to expect low-socioeconomic children to reach high academic levels (Graves 1998), I believe that *all* children possess a deep desire to learn and can attain the same levels of academic excellence. What makes it possible? Knowledgeable, loving teachers who take the time to establish strong classroom communities and make connections with children's families.

Knowledgeable teachers are successful in teaching young children how to read and write well when they orchestrate a blend of meaningful and interesting reading material and early writing, speaking, and direct instruction practices (Ransom 1998). Loving teachers, who care deeply about the future lives of children, establish relationships with their students so that optimal learning occurs. "The relationship between children and their teachers isn't incidental," writes Mary Pipher in her book *The Shelter of Each Other* "but rather it is the central component of their learning. Human development occurs within the context of real relationships. We learn from whom we love" (1996, 87).

My ten-year teaching career has found me teaching first- and second-grade children in low-socioeconomic neighborhood schools: six years at White City Elementary in Southern Oregon and four years at Bobier Elementary in Southern California. At the time I taught at each of these, both schools were—and still are—considered the toughest schools in their districts. Although I moved from one state and district to another, the similarities between them were striking: many, many children who needed a great deal of help amidst difficult home lives; hardworking colleagues; and schoolwide efforts to define a common philosophy for communication, curriculum, discipline, and management. The differences between the two schools were glaring, as Bobier grappled with a year-round schedule, bilingual and cultural issues, large class size, controversial state-curriculum frameworks, and restricted budgets. Although my teaching life took shape in Southern Oregon among wonderful children and families, my four years at Bobier Elementary impacted me even more deeply as a teacher.

Bobier Elementary is one of thirteen elementary schools in Vista Unified School District, which is located in North San Diego county. An open-campus school, Bobier is a bit drab in appearance—tan buildings with dark brown trim—and is situated between a diverse working-class neighborhood on one side and a busy four-lane avenue on the other. The original classrooms are of average size with banks of windows along one of the walls; however, portable classrooms continue to overtake precious playground space as the school strains to accommodate more and more children. Bare dirt lies everywhere, although some shrubbery lines the walks and the areas in front of the original classrooms. When you approach the school from the front, an eight-foot-high chain-link fence greets you. It is a barrier that reminds everyone of the rough neighborhood surrounding this school.

Built in 1963, Bobier Elementary was designed to house 450 students. However, during the 1995–1996 school year, the last year I taught at Bobier, it served approximately 1,075 children. Vista has experienced growing pains as newcomers continue to settle in the district. With a tremendous increase in school enrollment, and a community unwilling to pass a bond to build new elementary schools, it became necessary to adopt a multitrack, year-round school calendar in 1990. Bobier, like other schools in the district, operates on a three-track system with two tracks—totaling approximately 750 children—on at one time and one track off. This "modified concept 6" plan, which school districts in California are no longer even allowed to adopt as a year-round plan, results in only 163 student school days per year, although thirty-five minutes were added to each student day to compensate for lost school days. Particularly for Bobier children, this schedule simply does not give students enough days in school. The longer school day doesn't compensate for this; it just produces weary primary children, especially at the beginning of the year.

In 1995, 60 percent of the children attending Bobier were Hispanic; 26 percent were white; 10 percent were African American; 2 percent were Filipino; 2 percent were Pacific Islander; 2 percent were Asian; and 1 percent were Native American. Nearly half of the students had limited or no English language skills.

Bobier has a moderate transiency rate, but nonetheless, instability often affects the children's school-attendance rates. During the 1995–1996 school year, the school had increased its attendance rates from 92.34 percent to more than 95 percent; however, unexcused (nonillness) absences still plagued the school, averaging about 2,263 days per year. In addition to student absences, tardiness was a problem, with approximately 4,000 instances per year. The tardiness problem has since improved because Bobier now starts at 8:45 A.M., which seems to help families get their children to school on time.

Bobier Elementary draws children from single-family homes in the immediate neighborhood, as well as children who live in two large apartment complexes and ride the bus to school. Nearly all children come from low-income families and are therefore eligible for free and reduced-cost meals. Bobier receives the greatest percentage of Title I money in the district, based on the new poverty index. During the 1995–1996 school year, 73 percent of the school's families lived within the poverty level, based upon the federal government's standards.

The schoolwide average class size was twenty-nine students during my tenure, but I always had thirty-two children in my classroom. At that time, California ranked fiftieth among all states in the nation relative to "acceptable" student/teacher ratios. Since my departure, kindergarten through third-grade classes have been reduced to twenty students.

In a staff letter, our principal, David Lacey, described Bobier's population in this way:

> Our students are lovable, affectionate, and have many social and interpersonal needs. [A sampling of some of the difficulties various children in my classroom had experienced within their families included divorce, drug-related problems, separation from parents, foster care, prostitution, physical and emotional abuse, gun violence, being home alone before and after school, teen pregnancy in the family, gang-related issues, and frequent moves.] One of their greatest needs is family cohesion. As I visit their homes, it is common to see single-parent households, households with numerous unrelated people living jointly, and households lacking basic furniture such as beds, couches and dining tables.

It is a daunting school profile. Bobier Elementary has become a low-socioeconomic school in what was once a quiet, middle-class rural community. "Vista is now a multieconomic area," my principal said to me recently, "and Bobier Elementary happens to be located near the center of the community, in an older part of town. I've heard it referred to as Vista's inner city."

Despite the reference to Bobier as being "Vista's inner city," I never felt that it was an unsafe school while I taught there. In fact, when I parked my car in the back parking lot and walked to my classroom in the middle of the campus, I was always struck by the serenity of the neighborhood off to the distance—green, rolling hills, with red-tiled roofs and palm trees dotting the landscape. This sense of security didn't stop my principal from conducting intruder drills—in which we pulled the curtains, locked the door, and hunkered down in our classroom library—along with the standard fire and earthquake drills. Occasionally children reported sounds of gunfire in their neighborhoods.

While I taught at Bobier, I often had to remind myself that many parts of this school neighborhood were quite different from the neighborhood in which I had grown up. I had to learn not only about different ethnic cultures, but about different neighborhood and family cultures as well. I grew up in a middle-class family, so when I began teaching at Bobier, I had to examine how I viewed and lived in my world in contrast to how many of these children lived in their worlds. Despite this, I didn't have different expectations for their capacity to learn—I believed they were as eager as other children to become readers and writers and to explore and construct knowledge about the world—but I did have to revise my viewpoints and perspectives. I already knew how to look at the world from the eyes of five-, six-, and seven-year-olds, but I also had to learn how to look at the world from the vantage point of those children in my classroom who lived in poverty.

There also seemed to be some quiet, underlying racial tensions at school during the four years I taught at Bobier, although not to an overwhelming degree. Kids playing soccer on the playground divided themselves into teams of the "Mexicans versus the Americans." A few of Bobier's families stopped attending Family Math Night because there were "too many Hispanics." Other families requested transfers to different schools because they didn't feel comfortable having their children attend a "minority-majority" school. The manner in which the bilingual program was implemented was accepted by some staff members, but questioned by others, and was a difficult issue to solve.

When I first interviewed at Bobier, staff members told me that parents had a reputation for missing school functions, not returning nightly reading books, and not doing homework with their children. When I started teaching, I discovered that families were also in various states of mental and emotional health. In my classroom, families ranged from those like Jana's and Rachael's, who were typical hardworking families trying to make ends meet and raise responsible children, to families like Cynthia's, in which the mother was a diagnosed paranoid-schizophrenic receiving marginal medical attention.

Given all of this, how was I to meet the needs of thirty-two first-grade children and their families? How would I engage these children, make connections with their families, manage classroom and discipline issues, *and* teach reading and writing in responsive, meaningful ways? More worrisome than the social, community, and home issues that faced me when I started teaching at Bobier was the large class size—thirty-two first-grade children in one classroom seemed inhumane.

In her new edition of *The Art of Teaching Writing*, Lucy Calkins writes:

> It's often hard to imagine how we can make time to study what our students do when they write. When our classes are filled (as they often are) with thirty or more students, it's difficult to find ways to take our cues from

students. We need to petition and work for more humane class sizes, but in the meantime, we need to remember that we have no choice but to teach responsively . . . and, as writing teachers, we must let students show us how to teach them. (1994, 54)

Despite the difficulties, I was determined. Even with thirty-two children, on a fast-paced, year-round schedule, I wanted to delve into the lives of these students and create a classroom where they were valued. I knew my biggest challenge would be to find ways to come together as a community of readers, writers, and learners who trusted, supported, cared for, and taught one another while also respecting individual and cultural differences. And even though I hadn't grown up in the same way that most of these children were growing up, I believed in their capacity to live well and learn deeply.

THERE WAS A CHILD WENT FORTH EVERY DAY

I felt compelled to write *A Child Went Forth* to capture the many voices, both the ordinary and the brave, of Bobier children. Daily, I listened to their stories and examined how these affected their learning lives. Mild stories of sibling annoyances were contrasted with the aches of children like Lee, who longed to live with her real mom and dad. I still recall her trembling voice as a first grader when she told me that she was trying to remember the good times when she had lived with her mom and dad, but that she missed them so much and wished she could live with them again; her only good news was that she had asked her dad to stop drinking and she thought he had. I listened to Jana share wonderfully "normal" stories about life in a large family, but I also remember holding Priscilla's hand one day as we walked to lunch and she told me she'd offered to give her mom "half of a hundred dollars" because her mom had run out of money.

In the midst of these children's lives, I wanted my classroom to be an opening for their young voices, my curriculum, the children themselves, and the world in which they lived. I wanted to show them how passionate I was about my own reading, writing, and learning, expecting they would become enthusiastic readers and writers themselves, regardless of whether their homes had scads of books like my own.

In the first section of *A Child Went Forth*, I describe and explore my process for getting my classroom environment and materials ready for a new school year. I also describe a "typical" first day of school, as well as how I spend the first two months of school establishing the routines and structures for learning in my language arts program.

In the second section, I describe and explore the structures in my language arts program, both at school and at home, that assist young children in becoming proficient readers; it is my primary reading workshop in action. I offer my perspective on approaches that are now becoming commonplace in American classrooms, e.g., shared reading, and describe how I have constructed and changed them with the children I've taught. I also describe ways in which I monitor the progress of young readers and assist those who are struggling. I present my practice of looking at the teaching of reading in a "slightly deeper way, not a different way" (Mooney 1997). As I teach young readers, I reflect upon what I enjoyed the most in my childhood book world at home and what I disliked in my reading life at school. My book world must be alive in my classroom because that is what I value as I help children become readers.

In the third section, I describe and explore the structures in my language arts program, both at school and at home, that help young children become proficient writers and spellers; it is my primary writing workshop in action. It is my attempt to offer a perspective on how the children and I work together in our "writing studio" (Graves 1983). I describe the ways in which I monitor the progress of young writers and assist those who are struggling. I also explore how diagnostic and student-kept literacy portfolios are a helpful way to document a student's literacy history. As I reflect on how to help five-, six-, seven-, and eight-year-olds learn how to write so that they may "hold their lives in their hands and make something of them" (Calkins 1994), I examine whether there is a good balance between teacher instruction and individual exploration. I consider what I enjoyed the most in my writing life as a young girl against the backdrop of the hard work that I now know writing requires. My writing world must be alive in my classroom, for that is what I value as I help children become writers.

In her thoughtful book *A Stone in My Shoe*, Lorri Neilsen writes,

> Nourishing the spirit of learning for a future global awareness is not merely a social or cognitive or spiritual enterprise; it is also an ethical and moral one. We are ready now, I think, to look out at the horizon and the days stretching before us and ask larger, deeper questions: How can I help human beings grow and learn in this world, now and for tomorrow? And what kind of person do I provide as an example? (1994, 141)

I continue to ask myself the larger, deeper questions as a teacher, knowing that regardless of children's home lives or socio-economic status, I wouldn't change how I teach. I didn't teach Lee or Priscilla, who coped with difficult home situations, any differently than I taught Rachael, who went home to an intact, loving family every day. All of these children deserved the gift of literate, democratic lives. I believed our classroom was the place to nurture this gift.

The many anecdotes that I share about my Room 12 children as readers, writers, and learners, and the stories that I share about their lives are from my last two years teaching at Bobier when I had them for both their first- and second-grade years. I hope that within these chapters, you find children and stories of young learning lives similar to those you have in your own classroom. I also hope that this book provides an opportunity for you to reflect, and ask the questions that are important to you and your own teaching of reading and writing. Lastly, I trust that the many diverse answers that you discover, as well as the further questions those answers lead to, will continue to deepen your passion for reflective teaching with young children as you encourage them to go forth into the world.

BEGINNINGS

You must think of those . . . steps not as preparation for the beginning but as the beginning itself.

—E. L. Konigsberg, The View from Saturday

FIGURE I–1
A view of Room 12

1 | CREATING AND READYING

Our best hope is to provide environments where everyone is given the opportunity, support, and freedom—to think.
—*Frank Smith,* to think

The beginning of the school year hands me the thoughtful work of creating my classroom environment, along with readying forms, folders, journals, and other assorted materials fundamental to my program. No detail is too small to consider as I contemplate how to put into motion the type of classroom that I believe will nurture the young readers and writers in my care. At Bobier, I only had one month between the end of one year and the start of the next. I reserved at least two of the four weeks to clean out and reassemble my classroom for a new group of children. The following describes my process for preparing my room for the upcoming year.

First, I stand back and reassess my classroom environment. What changes do I want to make? How do I make this room feel fresh not only for the children, but also for me? I love creating a "home" in my classroom, particularly for children who may not have a stable or orderly home.

Then I turn my attention to readying materials. What do I need to prepare before the year begins so that this classroom will house children, teacher, and resources in a way that allows us to live, learn, and function together in the most effective way possible (Jackson 1993)? Every year is a new beginning. I love the look and feel of a clean slate.

CREATING THE ENVIRONMENT

Structuring a literate, artistic, organized, resourceful classroom environment is important work because it supports what is involved in a day, a week, a month, and a year of learning. I want to greet my class on the first day of school with enough structure in place to get started, but not so much that there aren't still nooks, crannies, and displays left to negotiate with the children. I recall Tracy saying during our first few days of school, "I like this classroom. It's different than other classrooms I've been in. It's neat and tidy and there's room for the kids."

Donald Graves writes that if the classroom is not carefully designed and structured and continually adapted to meet the shifting social and learning needs of the community, then children's natural urge to express themselves will be thwarted. He calls on teachers to prepare for the entrance of children with a predictable classroom (1991, 33). The highly structured classroom is a functional classroom. He poses two questions to consider when designing the classroom environment: What is this for? and How does it enhance the quality of classroom living for learning (45)?

I have settled on several essential areas in my classroom that lead to a balance of organization, efficiency, and beauty. I create the following areas in my classroom before the children arrive so that the structure of the classroom will allow us to work together cooperatively:

- whole-group gathering area
- classroom library area
- science/discovery area
- art area
- writing supply area
- teacher/student storage shelf unit
- computer/listening center area
- unit study display area
- math area
- teacher area
- children's work table area
- children's storage area
- display lines/wall space for children's work

Whole-Group Gathering Area

I simply couldn't teach without a large gathering area on the floor in which all the children are able to sit comfortably. We assemble in this area often. I always choose floor space next to a wall, rather than in the center of the room, because I need the wall space to hang resources that we consult frequently during our class meeting, shared reading, book talks, and sharing time. I locate several resources in this area, including large world and U.S. maps; our "What's in the News?" chart, where we post current news clippings; song and poetry charts on skirt hangers; a pocket chart that displays our daily schedule; a "Reminders" clipboard perched on the ledge below the pocket chart; the children's written sharing clues along with a "Who, What, Where, When, Why, and How" question chart; and a small, erasable white board. A chalk ledge in front of the maps allows me to display the books I've chosen for read-alouds. I arrange my chair, an easel with tape player and tapes underneath, and a supply basket with Post-its, markers, and pens at the corner of this area, providing a break between this space and the entrance to our classroom library.

Above this area, I post a large alphabet. Every year the children and I create a new alphabet together. Some years ago, I cut apart a commercial alphabet that I had, saved the letters, ditched the pictures, photocopied the letter formation parts, and glued them onto construction paper. Every year one of my first projects with a new class is to brainstorm and illustrate a new alphabet, which is then displayed with the upper- and lowercase letters, pictures, and words that I've written on sentence strips. It's one of the many ways I help children make sense of the alphabetic principle of our language. Figure 1–1 shows an example of my whole-group gathering area at Bobier.

Classroom Library Area

The classroom library area holds approximately thirty tubs of books—about 800 titles—categorized by beginning-reader books, fiction, nonfiction, and author sets. I describe my book organization system in Chapter 4. Other items located in the classroom library include two small, metal book display racks, pillows, bigbook racks with skirt hangers to hold bigbooks, a small rocking chair, and indoor plants that are situated on a window ledge. I also displayed several items on the bulletin board in this area, including our collection of "What's in the News?" chart papers (with two holes punched at the top and held together with metal rings), spelling minilesson charts, information about authors, my weekly letters written to my husband when we do family journals (on chart paper), and my teacher-made classroom library key. An example of this wall area is shown in Figure 1–2.

FIGURE 1–1
Our gathering area

Science/Discovery Area

At Bobier, I set up the science/discovery area along the wall that has the large bank of windows. A window ledge is a perfect display area. I place one of the children's wooden cubby units against the wall to add to the display space for the treasures children bring in throughout the year such as leaves, rocks, sticks, and even a bump on a leaf that Eric suspected was a caterpillar egg. "Eric's egg," his card read. "Do not touch. It's a kind of a egg and it might be a caterpillar." Throughout the year I display my finds along with the children's, as well as add interesting items that relate to our current unit study. Other permanent items in this area include a globe, Geosafari computer, a large photograph of planet Earth from space, a microscope, magnifying glasses, display dishes, and a basket with small pieces of tagboard for the children to write labels and comments about the items they display.

Art Area

The art area contains supplies as well as a paint easel that I situate on a blue plastic tarp to protect the floor. I like to have art supplies out in the open, right at hand so the children and I have easy access to glue, scissors, paint-brushes, paint, markers, colored pencils, colored chalk, oil pastels, rulers, fabric, yarn, and construction paper. Before the children use the materials, I introduce each item as we delve into beginning-of-the-year projects, teaching them how to use, clean, and put away the materials properly. I monitor this area carefully throughout the year, always giving the children enough cleanup time at the end of projects so they don't put materials away haphazardly. I've discovered that if children are shown how to use and respect materials, they will do so. There are times when we do have to solve materials

FIGURE 1–2
*Wall area in classroom
library*

problems, but I believe it's important to keep the supplies out for children, and I do the hard work of teaching them how to be responsible for them. In her book *Creative Display & Environment*, Margaret Jackson writes,

> It is also possible that when children (like adults), cease to care about their environment, or feel detached from it, we are faced with additional social problems such as thoughtlessness, litter and even vandalism. Surely children who feel responsible for and value their surroundings, are more likely to care for it (1993, 13).

Writing Supply Area

Our writing supply area holds different types and sizes of writing paper in baskets and trays, along with pencils, erasers, paper clips, tape, staplers, staple removers, Post-its, an electric pencil sharpener, a letter-writing tub, and a small book-making tub with blank "little" books. Like the art area, it is a self-service area for the children, and I give several use, care, and storage minilessons before I allow them to use the materials independently. Again, I monitor this area carefully, solving problems with the children when the need arises. The children keep their writing notebooks and "work-in-progress" folders in their individual cubbies.

Teacher/Student Storage Shelf Unit

The teacher/student storage shelf unit holds various tubs and trays that we rely on to keep us organized throughout the day and week. I reserve the top of the shelf for my items: current chapter book read-aloud, timer, my dictionary and thesaurus, and a tub with my conferencing/assessment clipboards that I use daily. The shelves underneath house bins for the children's family journals, journals to me, spelling folders, and classroom job clipboards, along with two trays to turn in work and four trays that hold forms we use frequently: class rosters, sharing reminders, book talk letters and forms, and writing conference checklists. On the bottom shelf is a large, red tub where the children store their school folders, which are double-pocket folders that they carry between school and home every day. The children and I use this area a lot throughout the day. It's our classroom's version of a central processing area. Like the art supply area and elsewhere in the room, everything is clearly labeled with a black permanent marker.

Computer/Listening Center Area

Our classroom computer and listening center area is located next to the storage shelf unit. I love having a computer for publishing the children's writing, composing a classroom newsletter, and so forth. The listening center unit next to the computer has six bins, each one holding a small Sony cassette player, book, and tape. Children can take these to another area in the room to enjoy them. Over the years I have acquired a nice collection of books and tapes through book clubs, and I change the selections in the listening center every two weeks.

Unit Study Display Area

To the right of the listening center is a bulletin board area that I use for unit study displays. The children and I post photos, artwork, posters, vocabulary charts, question charts, and any other items that relate to our current topic of study here. We use a chalk ledge to display books that relate to our study and store additional unit study books and resources we've collected in tubs on the floor. Above this area, I mount my roll-up screen, which I pull down over the display when I use the overhead projector. I keep my overhead projector in a small, wooden rolling cart so that it is easy to roll out and use, which I do frequently. I assemble the children around me on the floor, and I sit on one of the children's small chairs next to the overhead when I teach from this space. I find that keeping the children close to me prevents many management and discipline problems.

Math Area

The last area along this wall is the math area. The calendar is situated on a bulletin board space, and two wooden cubby units hold bins of math manipulatives and supplies. Other items in this area include a bathroom scale, estimating jar and clipboard, and a tub for "calendar update supplies" that two of the children use every morning when updating the calendar, which is one of our classroom jobs. In the math area, all storage bins have labels written with black permanent marker on orange construction paper to distinguish them from other supply tubs.

FIGURE 1–3
Joseph listening to a story tape

Teacher Area

My teacher area is the smallest space in the classroom. I abandoned the luxury of a teacher's desk when I moved into my Bobier classroom because it simply took up too much space. Besides, I am never at my desk, and when I do need to sit down to work, I sit alongside the children at their tables. A large paper/chart storage cabinet with five drawers is part of my work area. I sometimes use this as a desktop. I keep the paper cutter on top of this cabinet.

Above the cabinet there are two shelves where I organize my office supplies as well as my planning and curriculum notebooks and two tubs for the children's early literacy portfolios. The children's "student-kept" math and language arts portfolios are located on the floor in this area also.

Children's Work Table Area

I prefer tables instead of desks in a primary classroom. I usually have four rectangular tables that seat eight students each. The children work throughout the room, so individual desks are not necessary; we simply need a work space. A plastic bin in the center of each table holds resources that are helpful to them as young readers and writers: a smaller version of our class-made alphabet ($8\frac{1}{2} \times 11"$, which I re-create and photocopy), letter/number formation card, the first one-hundred high-frequency words organized alphabetically, and a punctuation resource card. (See Appendixes 1–1 and 1–2.) I laminate these resources to withstand the wear and tear of many little hands

FIGURE 1–4
Teacher-Student storage shelf/computer-listening center/unit study display area

throughout the year. Another, smaller bin holds pieces of scrap paper that the children use when they scrounge for the conventional spelling of a word in the room.

Children's Storage Area

The children all have their own bins in the wooden cubby units in the classroom. They store various items in these bins including pencils, book bags, journals, dictionaries, money (in film canisters that I provide), library books, and any other materials that are necessary to our classroom life. The children clean out their cubbies every Friday morning after they finish with their housekeeping and classroom job responsibilities so that the contents inside remain under control. It's amazing what five-, six-, and seven-year-olds can collect in the space of a week!

I always make sure there is a suitable space for the children's coats, backpacks, lunch boxes, and sharing bags. I've had both hooks and hangers for coats in my classrooms. Either is fine as long as coats have a proper place. Hooks are nice because children can hang both backpacks and coats on them. In Room 12 at Bobier, we used large, plastic laundry baskets to store backpacks and usually placed them right outside our door. We also had a laundry basket to store lunch boxes. Each basket was a different color and labeled for easy identification.

Display Lines/Wall Space for Children's Work

Clotheslines for display purposes crisscross the room and are also strung in front of the windows. I am careful about how much goes on the clotheslines, although the children and I are prone to having a full and vivid classroom. I aim for a balance between too much and just enough so that the display lines don't take away our feeling of openness.

Creating and re-creating a classroom environment with the children is a dance of negotiating a space that we must live and work in together, starting on the first day of school. In his book *Build a Literate Classroom*, Donald Graves writes:

> Classrooms need careful structuring so that children can function more independently. Structure also helps integrate the enormous range of differences among children in any classroom. Structure and responsibility must be carefully developed through the school year: what is possible in January may not be possible in September. You will find that you and the children grow in your ability to make the room function more effectively. (1991, 35)

My work is to go beyond the merely decorative in structuring our classroom. Spending long hours on teacher bulletin boards or simply putting up children's work to fill space sorely misses the full potential a classroom should have for both the children and me. I work from the premise that children must have the appropriate print, picture, and object resources available so they can be resourceful in their learning. Print-rich is not simply viewing pleasure for the eye. Print-rich means having distinct, predictable places in the classroom environment to display the many print resources children will ultimately need in their work as serious young readers and writers: alphabets, number words, high-frequency word cards, dictionaries, spelling mini-lesson charts, unit study vocabulary charts, my weekly family journal letter, newspaper articles/summaries, classroom job sheets, and material labels. I encourage children to consult these resources frequently.

Our room is a workshop space and must allow for the hum of our daily lives, our learning, our work. Graves calls this a "studiolike atmosphere" and writes, "In a room where I want to demonstrate, conduct conferences, and convene small groups of children, I need a class that knows how to operate without my immediate attention" (1991, 35).

I aim for a classroom that embraces and displays the individuality of the children as well as our units of study and investigation. I do not display commercial work, other than an occasional reading poster, art poster, or something of that nature. Having separate spaces allocated for display, storage, and work allows us to change these areas efficiently throughout the year as we move through our studies. Margaret Jackson writes:

> Impressions made in childhood are often with us for life, therefore children should be encouraged to share in the organization and development of their environment. Children often have very definite ideas, with strong likes and dislikes, sometimes without understanding why they feel so strongly. By discussion and by working together, they can learn to develop ideas, to compromise (one of the most important lessons we can teach them), to understand, progress and find solutions to practical problems concerning their immediate environment and other wider issues. (1993, 13)

Finally, I reflect on these questions as the children and I create and re-create our classroom environment together:

- Is our classroom interesting?
- Does it show who the children are as learners and people?
- Is it clean and organized?
- Am I proud of the look of our classroom?
- Do I observe and hear that the children are proud of our classroom also?
- Does it show a focus of study, of reading, of writing?
- Do I observe the children being able to use all of the classroom's resources throughout the day?

Ultimately, I ask myself if I would enjoy being a child in my own classroom.

READYING MATERIALS

In addition to creating a workshop environment, I also take time to prepare materials, folders, and forms for the first few weeks of school. It's much easier to do this before school begins because the unpredictable whirlwind of children will soon require all of my available time and energy.

Letters, Folders, and Portfolios

First, about two weeks before school begins, I write two letters that I send to all of the children and their families. I introduce myself and invite my new students to be part of my classroom. (See Appendixes 1–3 and 1–4.) I know that many of these children—first graders more than second graders—will carry this letter around with them like a security blanket as they prepare for their first day of school.

I also prepare the school folder labels, which I create on my computer, and a "Family Help" survey. (See Appendix 1–5.) In my before-school letter, I ask children to bring two double-pocket folders to school; one for their school folder, the other for their "work-in-progress" writing folder. I have extras on hand for those who forget or are unable to bring any. One of our jobs on the first day is to attach the school folder labels and insert the Family Help survey. This folder becomes somewhat tattered and worn because the children carry it between school and home every day. When the folders are in a state of disrepair, we replace them.

I send the Family Help survey home on the first day of school so I can find out which family members will be able to do home projects. For instance, several folders and journals need to be assembled at the beginning of the year, and if possible, I rely on home project helpers to do this. I've never been disappointed, nor have I had to scrounge for help.

I gather, create, copy, and prepare forms for several folders, notebooks, and journals before the start of the school year, which I've listed below. I explain the forms and assembly process (if applicable) in the chapters indicated.

Reading Forms and Materials
- I Can Read anthologies—Chapter 4
- nightly reading/partner reading folders—Chapter 5
- book talks—Chapter 6

Writing/Spelling Forms and Materials
- writing tablets/notebooks—Chapter 9
- journal materials—Chapter 10
- writing conference checklist—Appendix 11–1
- spelling folders—Chapter 14

Assessment Forms and Materials
- early literacy assessment portfolios—Chapter 15
- reading assessment clipboard—Chapter 7

I gather the materials before school starts, butI don't assemble the actual folders and journals. Instead I rely on my home family helpers to do this for us once the year begins. I send project bags home to volunteers with a sample folder or journal and the necessary supplies to complete the project. Many working family members, who are unable to assist in the classroom during the day, like being a part of our classroom world in this way. I am careful to note with the children and in our classroom newsletter whose families helped with home projects, not only to express appreciation, but also as a way to extend our classroom community. Besides, all of the folders and journals we use require a mountain of preparation that would take endless hours if I were to do it myself.

I also set up two tubs for the children's individual math and writing/art portfolios that they keep throughout the year. Inside each tub are hanging file folders, one for each child, and inside each of these, two file folders: one for math, the other for writing and art. I wait to write names on the files and folders until we are well into our first week because it seems there are always changes in the class roster.

School and Home Connections

In terms of school-home connections I concentrate on preparing three items: a daily homework letter, a weekly homework form, and materials for our Note Books, a correspondence book I keep with the children's families. By the end of the first week I will have prepared our first classroom newsletter also. (See Appendix 1–6.) During the first two weeks of school, I type a short, daily homework letter to the children and their families that the children take home each day in their school folder. In the letter I include a brief explanation of their homework as well as brief snippets of how our classroom life is evolving. I discovered this helps children and families get into a routine of having nightly homework responsibilities, which is new for families with first-grade children, while also providing a beginning connection to me and our classroom. At the start of the year, I keep the homework responsibilities light for both first- and second-grade children, e.g., simple family graphing activities, nightly reading, going through the first book club order together. (Samples of first- and second-grade daily homework letters can be found in Appendix 1–7.) By the end of the first month, we work into a full homework schedule, which is when I start a weekly homework form. I give this form to the children on Mondays and they return it to school on Fridays with their families' signatures indicating they have completed their responsibilities. Samples of first- and second-grade weekly homework sheets can be found in Appendix 1–8.

I also gather materials for our communication Note Books, which are blank journals assembled by family volunteers. This letter is taped to the inside front cover:

Dear Families,

This marks the appearance of our official Note Book. Instead of writing back and forth to each other on separate pieces of paper, the purpose of the Note Book is for us to keep a record of our correspondence throughout the year. When you write to me, I will respond in the book and send it back home to you. I will do the same when I need to be in touch with you. It is important for your children to carry this book between home and school each day so that our correspondence isn't interrupted. I look forward to corresponding with you in this way. It may also serve as a "memory book" when our year is over.

I look forward to notes big and small—earth-shaking news, progress you are noticing, concerns you may have, stories you want to share about your child, or simply questions you may have when something is unclear to you. I will be sending the same sorts of writings home to you.

Thank you for your time in keeping in touch with me regularly. Your child's success continues to depend on how well we work together as a team.

After I introduce the Note Book to families at our Back-to-School Night, some families correspond frequently and others don't write much at all. A communication book like this is helpful to me, as I prefer not to spend a great deal of time on the phone. It never replaces conferences, but it does keep communication open and clear between the children's families and me throughout the year.

The last piece I prepare is a two-page curriculum overview sheet that I distribute to families at our Back-to-School Night, which takes place during the second week of school. (See Appendix 1–9.)

Housekeeping Forms

In the housekeeping department, I prepare classroom job sign-up forms, as there are certain jobs that need to be delegated starting the first week of school. I use large lettering so that the title of the job can be clearly read, with enough space to write the children's names in big print. I also make copies of these forms so they can be used throughout the year. I consider the following to be the essential "beginning-the-year" jobs, which I delegate on the first day of school:

- table helpers
- classroom library
- general room cleanliness
- lunch card duty
- ball carriers
- door duty
- school folders
- room host/hostess
- lunch menu
- science/discovery area
- art area
- sharing sign-up

- homework check-in
- class meeting leader

Another housekeeping form/clipboard that I prepare is a three-column to-do list for myself. The columns are Home, Classroom/School, and Children. I like this three-column list because it helps me keep track of three significant areas in my teaching life. I always have something to do at home or bring from home, so when those items come up, I jot them down in the Home column. The same is true for classroom and school responsibilities, so as things surface or are brought to my attention, I mark them in the Classroom/School column. The last column is reserved for children, and generally it is a running list of small concerns I have as I observe my students at work. I have several other formal places where I jot notes about children, e.g., my reading assessment clipboard, but this column is a catchall for little things, such as "Heidi still reversing her 6's," or "Brenda needs to write a letter of apology to another child." Every Friday, when I go through spelling checks, I list the children's names and the words they missed in this column, then create my word-study chart from this for the following Monday. I go through pages and pages of this form during the school year. When I run out of room, I place a fresh sheet on top. Occasionally I look back through the columns to see if there is a pattern in children's behavior, in missed spelling words, or if there are items that I may have missed in the daily shuffle of teaching and kids. My reminder system simply helps me keep track of the many details that fall under the heading of teaching.

Teaching Journal

The final piece that I tend to before the starting bell rings is my teaching journal. I am particular about my journals. They are small notebooks ($9\frac{1}{2} \times 5\frac{1}{2}$"), and I wrap the front covers with an Italian gift wrap that I love. "Your journal covers are beautiful," Brenda used to say to me. Once the year begins, my journal never leaves my side. Everything that I observe and can possibly write in my journal, I do. I capture conversations, announcements, and problems, make plans, think, and draw pictures, and I do all of this right in the swirl of the children. I have learned how to examine the children and our classroom life "on the go." I rarely find time to sit down and write reflectively at the end of the day; rather, I do this on my feet as I listen in to children, sit in the back of our group during class meeting announcements, or capture two or three precious minutes at the start of our quiet-writing time. I have learned the art of reflection in the moment, sifting through discussions, events, and experiences as we live them, so I can make decisions about what's next. This journal becomes part of how I teach. I refer to it often in our conversations and our work. My kids become used to seeing me with my journal and often make sure that I have it in hand if they discover it somewhere in the room. In the time since I've come to this place of needing journal in hand as I teach, I've discovered it is the way that I make sense of the children and my teaching world.

Even though I often feel that I'm never quite ready for the first day of school, and rarely sleep a wink the night before, with my classroom structure in place, materials ready, and plans on paper, it's time to roll up my sleeves and dig deeply into a new year. All that I need are the children. I can't wait to meet them.

2 | PLANNING AND STARTING

I have been looking into schedules. . . .
How we spend our days is of course, how
we spend our lives. . . . A schedule defends
from chaos and whim. It is a net for
catching days. It is a scaffolding on which
a worker can stand and labor with both
hands at sections of time.

—*Annie Dillard,* The Writing Life

I call the first two months of school "Establishing the Crucial Structures and Routines for Learning." This is a big, capital-letter task that I take seriously. The first few weeks of school are critical for establishing productive literacy routines so that the rest of the year is about sustaining learning. Nothing can be left to chance. My goal is to establish predictable routines, particularly when I know that some of my students have unpredictable home lives. Before the year begins, I find a quiet place, hunch over my notebook paper, and begin charting out the first day and the first weeks of the school year.

My plans for the first day are detailed as I sift through what is important. How do I introduce myself? How should the children introduce themselves? What events will be interesting not only for them, but also for me? How do I show my new class what I value? Even more important, how do I show them that part of what I value is discovering what they value?

I plot out the remainder of the first week on another piece of paper. My plans are broad strokes. What reading, writing, and other organizational pieces do I need to put into place? I then do the same for the rest of the first month, pulling out my school calendar to consider such items as assemblies, Back-to-School Night, fund-raisers, PTA drives, school pictures. The list of "extras" seems endless at the start of the year.

I extend my broad framework to include the second month as I continue to chart out reading and writing structures. I know I have to take it slowly. If I do too much too soon, I will overwhelm us all. If I introduce routines slowly, and give the children time, I know we will come to live and learn deeply within these structures.

In this chapter, I describe and explore a typical first day of school, the routines I establish with a new class during the first week, and the framework I use for implementing my language arts program during the first two months of school.

THE FIRST DAY

The first day always feels awkward to me. The children and I don't know one another yet, and everything feels new—the classroom itself, routines, even getting up early. I am in "talk and show" mode all day, which is so different from the workshop atmosphere we'll eventually work in, but the time spent setting expectations and putting routines in place during the first weeks of school is necessary. Two "first days" that I've enjoyed the most were with second-grade children whom I had taught the previous year as first graders; our first day together was a matter of picking up where we had left off. It felt easy in comparison to typical first days.

Before school begins, I plan a simple, clear day. On a piece of notebook paper, I create two columns for my planning: Events/Structures and Supplies. I actually continue with detailed plans like this for at least the first month of school, sitting down at the end of each day to draw up the next day's schedule while referring to the broader framework I created before school started. Figure 2–1 shows typical first-day plans for my classroom.

First Day of School

FIGURE 2–1
First day of school plans

Events/Structures	*Supplies*
Beginnings: • introductions • housekeeping/room tour	• attendance clipboard • name cards for children • school folder / name labels • family help surveys • daily homework letter • school registration forms
Class Meeting	• announcement board prepared • classroom jobs forms
Recess Preparation: • playground expectations • bathroom use • tour of the playground • where to line up	• morning snacks out for recess • chart with playground expectations
Shared Reading	• "I Am Janine" book • favorite bigbook • favorite read-alouds on chalk ledge
Name-Card Project: • create names for cubbies and calendar area	• 3 × 8" sentence strip cards— 2 per child + extras • permanent marker • sponge-painting materials: small paper plates, sponge cubes, paint

Events/Structures	Supplies

Lunch Preparation:
• lunch expectations
• tour of the lunch area
  • cafeteria use
  • picnic table manners
  • where to place baskets
   for lunch boxes
• walking to the
  playground after lunch
• bathroom use
• where to line up after
  lunch recess
	• lunches/lunch cards out
	• chart with lunch expectations

Sharing	• my artifact for sharing (in bag) • chart paper and markers

Math—Calendar Walk:
• create calendar pieces
• introduce calendar
  routine
	• $4\frac{1}{2} \times 5\frac{1}{2}"$ calendar pieces
	  with numbers
	• crayons
	• *Chicken Soup with Rice* bigbook
	  and tape

P.E.	• none—cooperative games
Closing: • distribute items to go home • gather belongings • chapter book read-aloud	• chapter book

Going Home:
• sorting out transportation
  by bus, car, or walking
• walking children out to
  buses and pickup area	

FIGURE 2–1
(cont.)

Meeting the Children

On the first day, I meet the children on the playground and look at the line of small faces, taking in the details of who they are. Whose hair is combed? Whose face is washed? Whose eyes sparkle? Who wants to hold my hand? I also introduce myself to any family members who have made the first-day journey, and start making connections. It's my first opportunity to glimpse the diversity of the children's families—families who will become my context for understanding each child in my classroom.

After greeting the children and walking to the classroom, the hard work begins. Generally first graders' new shoelaces are as long as the children are tall, and that in itself is often the major preoccupation of the day. Second graders are considerably more independent and have a distinct, grown-up air to them in contrast to their first day of first-grade uncertainties. On this first morning, I invite any family members who are able to stay until recess to do so. I appreciate the extra hands, especially when we tackle housekeeping items like unpacking school supplies and putting name labels on school folders.

Organizing the Children

I gather the children on the floor, then excuse a few at a time to find a chair at a table to store their backpacks and lunch boxes—I don't create name labels on tables until the end of the first week—hang sweaters or coats in the hanger area, take a walk around the classroom, and find their name tags on the corkboard placed on my easel. I use this first literacy task to note who can and cannot locate their names. The way we handle these beginning tasks sets the tone for how our classroom will work. I don't underestimate the power of giving clear directions and showing children how I expect things to be accomplished, which I do repeatedly during the first weeks of school. I consider it time well spent.

Introducing Ourselves

Now that the children's hands are free of their belongings, we can concentrate on introductions. I enjoy singing, and I know that children enjoy music, so I like to have the children introduce themselves through song. One of my favorite introduction songs is an innovation on "Mary Wore Her Red Dress." I ask the children what they are wearing that they would like us to sing about and we compose the verse together. With my last group, Chris wore his cowboy vest and boots on the first day, and of course we had to sing about that. We sang,

> "Chris wore his boots and vest,
> boots and vest,
> boots and vest.
> Chris wore his boots and vest,
> All day long."

Even though he was quite shy while we sang to him, he loved having us sing about his cowboy vest and boots. I sing this song with the children throughout the first week, helping them make connections to one another. Already during our introduction song, I begin observing the children. How do they introduce themselves? Who seems shy? Who acts silly? Who appears confident? Who is embarrassed?

After introductions, it's time for movement. It's difficult for the children to sit still for long during the first weeks of school, so we play a game called "Back-to-Back" that gets the children moving and interacting with one another. We pair up, and I call out "back to back"; they put their backs together. Then I call out, "elbow to elbow" and they put their elbows together. I continue with various parts of the body until I say "back to back" again, which is the children's cue to find a new partner. This game provides another opportunity for me to observe the children.

Housekeeping: Organizing Belongings

Housekeeping is next. This is when I can use the extra hands of family members if there are any. Children retrieve their backpacks, and we form another circle. Circles work well this time of year when I have to show them so much. First, children take out their school folders that I asked them to bring in my before-school letter—I distribute folders to those who don't have any—and they adhere the school folder label as well as a name label. I write name labels for first graders; second graders write their own names on blank labels I provide. This is the first of many times the children will be involved in preparing their own materials. Then I introduce the three items that need to be tucked inside their folders: Family Help survey, daily homework letter, and school registration packet. Next I show the children how to place these papers in their folders without getting them caught and bent in the middle crease. I do this now, while the children are fresh, versus waiting until the end of the day when they are tired. Folders are placed right back inside backpacks so they are ready when it's time to go home.

Holding Our First Class Meeting

I lead the class meeting on this first morning, but begin handing this over to the children on the second day of school. Mainly, I want to introduce my class to the idea that after they take care of their belongings each morning, which is a process I call "housekeeping," we gather for a class meeting. On the first day, I use this time to discuss the "who, what, when, where, why, and how" of classroom jobs and answer any questions the children may have about them. Then I begin delegating. I call out jobs; choose from the sea of hands, and record names clearly on the job sheets I prepared earlier. As the year progresses, the children will take over this responsibility of signing up people for new classroom jobs. I don't set a specific time limit for jobs, rather the change takes place when the children decide they are ready for new responsibilities. The children and I negotiate changes to classroom jobs throughout the year, adding or changing responsibilities to fit our needs. I delegate early, but follow up with a considerable amount of teaching and daily monitoring so the children learn how to do their jobs thoroughly. Our classroom runs smoother if children know how to do their jobs well.

My goal for our shared-reading time on this first day of school is to share more of who I am as well as books that I love. The first book that I share with my new class is one that I've created, *I Am Janine*. I've compiled my story into a photo/storybook that shows my growing-up years, my family, my friends, and what I love. The kids seem to enjoy seeing my grade school pictures, particularly my first- and second-grade photos. I like to do this because I know it's hard for them to imagine that grown-ups, especially their teachers, were once kids. I leave this book displayed on the chalk ledge so the children can return to it during future quiet-reading times, but interestingly enough, it's a book that parents seem to enjoy looking through during Back-to-School Night.

I always enjoy reading one bigbook with the children and one or two favorite read-alouds during this first shared-reading session. *Franklin in the Dark* (Bourgeois 1986) is a bigbook I love to share with first graders; *Strega Nona* (dePaola 1975) with second-grade children. Favorite first-day read-alouds include

> *The Friends of Emily Culpepper* (Coleridge 1983)
> *Kylie's Song* (Sheehan 1988)
> *The Jewel Heart* (Berger 1994)
> *Lilly's Purple Plastic Purse* (Henkes 1996)
> *Mama Don't Allow* (Hurd 1984)
> *Harry's Stormy Night* (Leavy 1994) (See Appendix 3–4.)

I place my selections on the chalk ledge, explain to the children they are favorites of mine, then decide with them which ones to read. On this first day, I want to plant the seed that one of the nicest things in life is to have a pile of favorite books and the time to read them.

Completing Two First-Day Projects

Two projects we tackle on the first day are the name-card project and the calendar-walk project. Both tasks need to be completed, as they are necessary to the life of our classroom. The name cards are needed for cubbies and our calendar area, and the calendar pieces are necessary for our August/September math calendar.

I have used various mediums with the children on their name card projects, but one that I find most manageable on the first day is sponge painting. The children sponge paint the background of their cards with two or three colors, then I write their names on top in black permanent marker. The project is active and quick—paint plates and sponge cubes can be thrown away after use—and it produces colorful name cards.

Our math time is devoted to making calendar pieces. I do something called a "calendar walk," (first inspired by Glen and Elaine Olsen of the Heritage School in Salem, Oregon) and we create the calendar pieces in this way:

With a black marker, I write the numbers for the month on separate squares of white drawing paper ($4\frac{1}{2} \times 5\frac{1}{2}$"), e.g., for the month of September, there are thirty calendar pieces. With the children standing in a large circle, I place the calendar pieces on the floor around the inside of our circle. We discuss what is happening during that month; for instance, a new season starting or an upcoming holiday. The children who have birthdays that month always receive their birthday calendar pieces to illustrate, so these pieces are not placed in the calendar walk. If two children share the same birthday, we have two calendar pieces for that day. Now for music. Strains of *Chicken Soup with Rice* (Sendak 1962) reverberate from the tape player, and the children begin to walk, dance, and sing around the circle until I stop the music. At this point, I ask the children to look at the piece in front of them, and if that is the number they want to illustrate, they pick it up and take it to their table to begin work. If not, they stay in the circle and the musical game of calendar walk continues until all the pieces are in the children's hands. One child illustrates the month card I've written and that completes the calendar.

I introduce the illustration work to a new class by showing them samples of calendar-piece illustrations that children have done in previous years. Along with this, we discuss expectations for this project:

1. Write your name on the front of the calendar piece so we know who the artist is.
2. Use markers for outlining only; color with crayon. Markers were not in use for this project at the start of first grade.
3. Work carefully. Do your best.

We redo calendar pieces at the start of every full month that we are in school. Often we use a permanent marker to write special events, guest speakers, assemblies, field trips, etc., on the calendar pieces to keep us organized.

Breaking for Outdoor Time

Toward midafternoon on the first day, and for several weeks thereafter, the children usually get tired and restless, and play time is helpful. I try to include a short P.E. session outside so children can stretch, wiggle, and get some fresh air. I continue daily P.E. for the first two months of school with first-grade children because the days are so long for them.

Learning the Closing Routine

The last piece of our first day is establishing our closing routine. I like to start this process twenty to thirty minutes before dismissal time. It is important to make sure that backpacks, coats, lunch boxes, and any other belongings are in the right hands. It is also crucial at this point to go through how children are getting home. We sit in a circle so I can see that everyone has his or her belongings and is ready to go home. I like to complete this task with time to spare at the end.

If we do finish early, I read aloud to the children from the first chapter book I've chosen for the year. (I've listed favorite chapter book read-alouds in Appendix 2–1.) This helps us relax for a few minutes before saying good-bye.

Ralph Peterson, in his book *Life in a Crowded Place*, writes about how ceremonies like this pull the day together:

> When teachers use a touch of ceremony to make the day complete, the working rhythms of the day are slowed; loose ends are tied. Students are brought together to end on a harmonious note. . . . Regardless of how ceremony is incorporated, the intent is to establish a feeling of completeness before the students return to the everyday world beyond the classroom walls. (1992, 20)

With my closing ceremony, I always wait to start the read-aloud until we have everyone and everything ready to go home and we're comfortably gathered on the floor. First we acquaint or reacquaint ourselves with what's going on in the story, then I begin reading slowly, not getting into the flow of the words until we're settled into our book world. The words of the story float through the air and rest on the children's heads. This is my way of giving the children a bedtime story at the end of the day. Words to complete our day and go home on.

FIRST-DAY REFLECTION

All first days don't go as smoothly as the one I plan so carefully on paper or picture in my head when I can't sleep the night before. Problems inevitably occur. Behaviors get in the way. Lunch boxes end up in the wrong basket, children fall asleep, don't listen well, poke at each other and ask, "When is it lunchtime?" at morning recess and "When is it time to go home?" at lunch. It all seems to happen in the course of a first day. However, if my work has led to a day where we are able to enjoy one another and also accomplish a few things vital to our classroom life, then it has been preparation time and a first day of school well spent.

THE FIRST WEEK

My goal for the rest of the first week is to continue to add routines and structures to our day so that we are moving toward having a full daily/weekly schedule in place. It actually takes almost two months for me to put "a typical day and week" into place with young learners.

Projects I like to have completed by the end of the first week include

- name projects
- book bags tie-dyed
- journal covers painted

The book bag project is discussed in detail in Chapter 5 and journal covers are explained in Chapter 10.

Routines that I like to have in place by the end of the first week include

- housekeeping
- classroom jobs
- morning-work routine
- student-led class meetings
- children's sharing
- shared reading
- math
- writing time started
- closure
- chapter book read-aloud

Learning Our Morning Work Routine

During the first week, we establish our morning routine. Deciding on arrival routines requires a balance of ceremony and routine. Our morning-work routine, which includes housekeeping, classroom jobs, and choice time will eventually take place within the first twenty minutes of school. Ralph Peterson writes:

> Routines and jobs, more mundane and ordinary than other elements in the learning community, are nonetheless necessary if living space is to be kept orderly and if students are to have ready access to tools for learning. . . . The contributions routines and jobs make to life and learning in the community cannot be overemphasized. When a large number of people share a crowded place, productive life is possible only when the place is orderly. Routines and jobs are a necessary part of community life. (1992, 61–63)

In my classroom, the daily housekeeping routine includes putting lunch money, coats, lunch boxes, recess snacks, school folders, homework, book bags, and Note Books (starting the second week of school) in their proper places. During the third week of school, I add "gathering quiet-reading materials" to this list of responsibilities. Sharpening pencils also falls under the umbrella of arrival responsibilities. Housekeeping and recess are the only times the pencil sharpener may be used. I make a word and picture chart that lists the responsibilities so the children can consult this in the morning instead of relying on me. I hang this on my easel, gather the children when they first come in the door, and show them how they are to take care of their responsibilities.

There are several classroom jobs that need to be handled in the morning also and children who sign up for these jobs do them directly after they finish their housekeeping responsibilities. These jobs include lunch card duty (sorting cards by table for quick lunch lineup), lunch menu (writing the lunch menu for our class meeting announcement board), sharing sign-up (signing up one person each day for the next day's sharing and giving that child a reminder note after we've created it), and eventually calendar update, and book talk sign-up. I give beginning guidelines as to how to complete the jobs and check in with these children frequently. I am always curious as to the variety of ways children complete and extend their classrooms jobs.

Ralph Peterson makes a distinction between routines and jobs. Whereas routines become automatic and require limited judgment, jobs require students to exercise judgment in carrying them out, which is a contribution to the classroom community and part of the learning experience.

Taking care of arrival responsibilities in this manner takes at least the first twenty minutes of the day during our first week, often extending to a half-hour. However, eventually this routine becomes automatic and we no longer need to gather at my chair to review responsibilities. The children know how to begin once I greet them at the door. During this time I monitor everything from how children use the pencil sharpener to how they stand in line to place their school folders in the tub (right sides up with labels showing). I am particular because I don't want routines to waste our time.

Generally during the second week of school, some children begin to finish their responsibilities quickly and have a few minutes to spare between housekeeping and the start of our class meeting. When this happens, I introduce morning-work choices. At the beginning of the year these include

- Legos
- Lincoln Logs
- building blocks
- quiet reading
- science/discovery area
- ABC games (first-grade children)

As the year progresses, I add:

- paint easel
- quiet writing
- letter writing
- computer
- other choices the children and I negotiate

To help the children, I create another word and picture chart with morning-work choices, similar to the housekeeping chart, so that they can consult this when making a decision about how to use their time. I introduce the choices and materials to the children, establishing expectations for use, care, and cleanup with them. I don't limit numbers of children per choices; rather, I ask them to use their best judgment. We problem solve when necessary. If we eventually have to go to "numbers of children allowed at these materials," then that's what we do. It depends on the group of children. Some manage and work together better than others. I would rather negotiate and problem solve this with the children than operate from "my rules."

I structure the beginning of our day in this way because I don't want idle minutes. When all of my children come in the door at the same time, I am bombarded with stories, questions, lost lunch money, "I left my journal/book at home," notes from parents—more things than I could possibly imagine when I wake up in the morning—and I don't want children waiting for me as I sift through everything at the beginning of the day. I need a few minutes to breathe, settle in with the children, adjust to the pace of the day ahead of us, and take attendance. At the same time, I want the children to arrive, handle their housekeeping responsibilities, and begin the day with purpose.

Managing Transition Time

Managing transition time with a new class is as complicated as structuring new reading and writing routines with them. I like to make them as "tight" as possible, so that children know what's expected of them. I actually plan for transition within each reading and writing routine that I put into place. In reflecting upon a "typical" day in my classroom, I discovered there are approximately thirteen transitions that the children and I have to manage in order to clear our minds for the next task at hand.

In my classroom, the first major transition I teach during the first two weeks is moving from our morning-work routine to our class meeting. Children are scattered throughout the room handling arrival responsibilities, completing classroom jobs, or enjoying one of the available choices, so I have to bring the group together from the four corners of the room. In teaching any new management or curriculum routine, I start with a discussion time in our whole-group gathering area before we embark on the task at hand. In this case, I have to "talk and show" what I mean by finishing responsibilities, putting away materials, then gathering on the floor in front of the easel—all in a timely manner. Literally, I have the children follow me with their eyes or with their bodies, showing and discussing with them what I

FIGURE 2–2
Morning work

expect. I aim for instructional conversation because often the children will add their own details for cleanup that I haven't considered.

After the children seem clear on how to handle their responsibilities, I excuse them a few at a time to finish and return to our gathering area on the carpet. I watch closely. If someone needs help, I ask another child who has finished to assist. If a bigger problem seems to be brewing, I stop the entire class and we discuss how to solve it before it takes on a life of its own. For the most part, I can anticipate the problems—e.g., not putting tubs back in their proper places, not hanging coats properly—and I work to include those issues in our beginning discussion. I encourage the children to work efficiently and come together as a group as quickly as possible, without being rushed or silly. It's a fine balance with primary children. Some of them "go over the edge" easily, and I have to be firm but caring in the beginning weeks of school.

Eventually, when it feels like children understand how to work through this time, I ask one of the children to go around and initiate cleanup. This allows me to situate myself at the easel and add another layer to transition time: singing or reading. I wait until cleanup is well under way and a few children are already gathered at the easel before I begin either. If I sing with the children during this time, I place large charts of favorite songs on my easel and sing and gather them quickly in this way. Other times I read aloud a brief segment from a nonfiction book that correlates to our current unit study, reading from it each morning until we've made our way through the entire book. During our ocean study with my second-grade class, I did daily readings from a book titled *Ocean: The Living World* (Greenaway, Gunzi, and Taylor 1994), which was a perfect format for this short reading time. The book contains a wealth of picture and print information that was impossible to tackle in one sitting but perfect over a period of weeks as we steeped ourselves in our ocean study. Any of the Dorling Kindersley *Eyewitness Juniors, What's Inside?,* and *Eye Openers* books or other nonfiction books with the same format would work just as well.

I begin reading as soon as I have a little group on the floor, but before I start, I ask those children who are still finishing, cleaning, or completing jobs to soften their voices so they won't interrupt the start of our reading time. After we are in the routine of doing this, I only have to remind occasionally. I continue to read until all the children are gathered on the floor and find that there is as much discussion as reading during this time. I like this manner of transitioning and bringing my group together. The key is choosing a wonderful book that children are anxious to revisit every morning.

Introducing Student-Led Class Meetings

Whereas morning-work time is an informal opening to our day, class meeting is our formal beginning. In the years that I have been doing a class meeting with my class, I have come to look on it as not only an important opening ceremony, but also the center of our classroom life. These meetings are a forum for taking care of classroom business while also providing an opening for the children's voices. It is a time for children to talk, learn how to listen, and be heard. In his book *a sea of talk,* John Dwyer advocates the need for children to have time and opportunity to talk in their classrooms. He writes:

> Through talk children negotiate not only their own learning but also their place in the classroom world and beyond. Accordingly *all* children must be given opportunities to develop the ability to talk in a variety of settings, for their own benefit and for the general good of our society. (1989, 6)

I establish the routine for this meeting during our first week of school, assisting the class meeting leaders until they are able to lead the meetings by themselves. At this point, I take my place at the back of the group, journal in hand, ready to capture the important points of the meeting as well as the children's voices.

Our class meeting announcement board is set up in this way:

- Sharing: name of person sharing that day; written and posted by person with that job
- Book Talk: name of person giving a book talk that day; written and posted by person with that job
- Janine's Announcements: written by Janine before school starts
- Lunch Menu: daily menu written and posted by person with that job
- Children's Announcements: clipboard with class roster; children write "yes" by their names if they have announcements for that day

After my poetry reading—and eventually the children's poetry readings— the class meeting leader stands by the announcement board and conducts the meeting following the order on the announcement board. The following describes how Lisa led one of our class meetings during the first week of our second-grade year together.

Lisa: Today's sharing is Rosanna. Today's book talk is Tracy. Other things of interest: Do you have any announcements, Janine?

Janine: Yes, I do. (I sat in my chair at the back of the group and read the list of announcements I had posted earlier.) Today is Friday so you don't have any homework tonight. (Everyone smiled.) We have a three-day weekend because it's Labor Day weekend, so we won't be back at school until next Tuesday. (Everyone *really* smiled!) That's all I have for today, Lisa. Thank you.

Lisa: Brenda, would you please read the lunch menu?

Brenda: Um . . . I can't read it very well. I think I need some help.

Lisa: You should have practiced it before class meeting or asked someone else to read it for you.

Brenda (looking uncomfortable): I just didn't have time. It took me the whole time just to get it written and then I didn't get to practice. (During our morning-work time, Brenda had written out Friday's menu and posted it on the announcement board, because this is what her job required. She had consulted the monthly cafeteria menu, found the correct day, and written the menu on a sheet of paper [$8\frac{1}{2} \times 11$"]. I had done this last year until one of the children was ready to take over the responsibility, which was about a month into the school year.) Several children began reading the menu, and Lisa pointed to each word as they read:

> Deli Sub
> Chips
> Carrots and Celery Sticks
> Apple
> Jungle Animal Cookie.

Lisa: Timmy, we're ready for announcements. (Timmy, clipboard in hand, now assumed responsibility for this segment of our class meeting. Consulting his clipboard, he called out the names of the children who had announcements. One at a time, these children walked to the front of our gathering area to give their announcements.)

Class meetings are one way for the children to make sense of the world as well as participate in a democratic classroom. We do take care of classroom business during this time, but the announcement portion of the meeting is always the most intriguing. My announcements always include daily homework information; our daily schedule, particularly if there's anything out of the ordinary that day; interesting newspaper clippings; and any other classroom or school business that I think is important for the children to be aware of.

The children's announcements range from family news ("my dog ran away"), to classroom problems ("crayons aren't being put away properly"), to school issues ("why does the cafeteria menu say lettuce when we never have any?"), to local events (4th of July fireworks at Brengle Terrace Park), to state headlines ("a newspaper article describing the 'Street of Killers' in L.A. where a little girl was shot and killed"), in addition to any national and world events or just about anything else they feel they need to report. I learn a great deal about the children during their announcements—their lives, their feelings, their dreams, and what affects them, captures their attention, or causes them to pause, listen, and think.

We limit our announcement time to approximately ten minutes and if time runs out, those who didn't give their announcements can sign up again the next day if it's still important to them to share their news. My last class devised a system whereby one day they started at the top of the class list, the next day at the end of the list, so that everyone had a fair shake at giving their announcements.

Some of the announcements and discussion time the children had during the first week of our second-grade year together, which I wrote in my journal, follow.

On Tuesday, Nhi, a beautiful Vietnamese girl, informed us her hamster had gotten out of its cage.

Eddie: Where do you think it went?

Tracy: How do you think it got out?

Nhi: (smiled a little and shrugged her shoulders at the questions before she tentatively replied) My mom says there's a hole in the door. (She was still self-conscious about speaking English, as Vietnamese was her first language, but she was becoming more comfortable and confident in front of our group.)

Janine: Nhi, please keep us posted. We'll wonder how he's doing outside his cage.

Nhi had another announcement on Friday.

Nhi: My brother gave me these gemstones. They're like my necklace.

Brenda: What kind of necklace is that?

Nhi: It's a jade, and that's a gem.

Eddie: Why would they name them after a man?

Janine: Oh, I know what you're thinking, Eddie. Like the man's name, Jim. They sound the same, *gem,* and *Jim,* but they are spelled differently, and obviously mean something different.

Eddie: How do you spell it?

Janine: I'll show you on my whiteboard. (I walked to the easel and put my little whiteboard on the ledge. I keep it handy for these teaching windows.) *Gem* is spelled g-e-m and those are like Nhi's gems. I'll draw a little picture by this to remind us. The man's name, *Jim,* that you were talking about, Eddie, is spelled J-i-m. I'll draw a little man by this spelling. So, do you see the difference? (I had not planned on teaching the difference between Jim and gem that morning, but it was a window of opportunity for a meaningful phonics lesson. I listen and watch for just these moments.)

Brenda felt this announcement was important on Friday also.

Brenda: You know why I was gone yesterday? I needed to get an X ray on my tooth. (The group was quiet and the children were not responding. I sat quietly in the back and waited.)

Brenda: Are there any questions about that? (Wow, I thought to myself, she picked up on the pause. She wanted to keep this going, and she knew how to do that.)

Lisa: Why do you need an X ray on your tooth?

Brenda: I bit into a plum and hit the seed. My mom was worried so she wanted to take me to the dentist.

Kayalani: Oh, I know what you did. You were, like, taking a bite out of your plum, and when you bit down, your tooth went deep into the plum really fast, and you hit that big seed in the middle.

Brenda: It doesn't hurt anymore.

Joseph: Are you OK?

Brenda: Yes. There's nothing wrong with it. It's not cracked or anything.

During class meetings, I sit in the back of my group with journal in hand and listen to the voices of the children, interjecting only when necessary, demonstrating what is involved in "good listening." I participate in the children's announcements and discussions, but I am not an overriding voice. I want the children to learn how to listen and respond to one another, solve problems, offer empathy, and participate in the workings of the classroom. They learn to do this without raising their hands or relying on me to facilitate them. I help them learn the subtleties of handling discussion, but my goal is for them to learn how to do this for themselves. My job is to help them get there. I am impressed with the intelligence and care that first- and second-grade children demonstrate when they are given the opportunity to talk, listen, and respond to one another during class meetings.

THE FIRST TWO MONTHS: A FRAMEWORK

The detailed planning for the first day and first week of school is only the beginning of at least two months of this type of work. Ultimately I work toward a daily schedule that devotes approximately two-thirds of the day to language arts. The rest of the year is built on this work. It's eight weeks of foundation building that must support the complex workings of an entire year.

Figure 2–3 shows typical first- and second-grade daily schedules:

First-Grade Schedule

FIGURE 2–3
First- and Second-Grade Daily Schedule

Time	Structure/Children	Janine
8:00–8:30	Morning Work • housekeeping • choices	• housekeeping • time for one guided reading group if I choose to do this with a group of readers
8:30–8:45	Class Meeting • poetry • announcements	• gathering read-aloud • poetry • announcements • note-taking: Journal
8:45–9:10	Quiet Reading	• quiet reading: 5 minutes • individual reading conferences/ anecdotal notes: reading assessment clipboard
9:10–9:30	Partner Reading • nightly reading books	• status-of-the-class • reading observation conferences: anecdotal notes

First-Grade Schedule

Time	Structure/Children	Janine
9:30–9:50	Reading Workshop • choices	• time for one guided reading group if I choose to do this with a group of readers
9:50–10:05	Morning Recess and Snack	
10:10–10:45	Shared Reading	• bigbooks, read-alouds, mini-lessons
10:50–11:35	Writing Workshop • quiet writing • individual or whole class writing projects	• check-in conferences during quiet writing • mini-lessons for individual or whole class writing projects
11:40–12:25	Lunch and Recess	
12:30–12:50	Sharing/Book Talk	• journal: note taking
12:50–1:45	Math Block	
1:45–2:20	P.E./Unit Study Projects	
2:20–2:35	Closure/Novel Read-Aloud	
2:35	Dismissal	

FIGURE 2–3
(cont.)

*Tuesday through Friday schedule; Spelling Folder Set-Up on Mondays (no Partner Reading)

Second-Grade Schedule

Time	Structure/Children	Janine
8:00–8:20	Morning Work • housekeeping • choices	• housekeeping • time for one guided reading group if I choose to do this with a group of readers
8:25–8:45	Class Meeting • poetry • announcements	• gathering read-aloud • poetry • announcements • note-taking: journal

Second-Grade Schedule

FIGURE 2–3
(cont.)

Time	Structure/Children	Janine
8:50–9: 20	Quiet Reading	• quiet reading: 5 minutes • individual reading conferences/anecdotal notes: reading assessment clipboard
9:25–9:50	Partner Reading • nightly reading books	• status-of-the-class • reading observation conferences: anecdotal notes
9:50–10:05	Morning Recess and Snack	
10:10–10:45	Shared Reading	• bigbooks, read-alouds, mini-lessons
10:50–11:35	Writing Workshop • quiet writing • individual or whole class writing projects	• check-in conferences during quiet writing • minilessons for individual or whole-class writing projects
11:40–12:25	Lunch and Recess	
12:30–12:50	Sharing/Book Talk	• journal: note taking
12:50–1:45	Math Block	
1:45–2:20	P.E./Unit Study Projects	
2:20–2:35	Closure/Novel Read-Aloud	
2:35	Dismissal	

*Tuesday through Friday schedule; Spelling Folder Set-Up on Mondays (no Partner Reading)

The framework in Figure 2–4 shows how I spend the first two months of school working toward having a daily schedule like this in place. Previous routines are sustained as new ones are added each week.

Establishing the Structures for Learning: Language Arts Program

Day 1	Week 1	Week 2	Week 3
Housekeeping Introductions Shared Reading • bigbook intro of teacher Class/School/Recess/Lunch Routines Math Journal Cover Artwork My Message: "Welcome to this classroom" • before-school letters sent prior to first day	Morning Routine: • housekeeping • classroom jobs • class meeting Shared Reading • I Can Read Anthology–Friday Quiet Reading Book Bags Sewn and Tie-Dyed Writing Tablet or Notebook Journal Covers Painted Portraits Under Way Second-Grade Writing Project: Auto-biographical Piece Math End-of-Day Routine in Place Begin Introducing Independent Activities Available	Nightly Reading Partner Reading Reading Logs Writing: Family Journal Sharing Routine Back to School Night Begin Early Literacy Assessments/Portfolios First Classroom Newsletter Continue Introducing Independent Activities	Quiet Reading • begin individual reading conferences Journal to Janine Spelling Program: 2nd grade Correspondence • Note Books started with families Continue Introducing Independent Activities
Week 4	**Week 5**	**Week 6**	**Weeks 7/8**
Book Talks Writing Project: Letters Continue Introducing Independent Activities	First Unit Study Begins Writing Project • little books Continue Introducing Independent Activities	Writing Project: Guided Writing—First Story Continue Introducing Independent Activities	Writing Workshop • with structured choices Guided Reading Groups if applicable Spelling Program: 1st Grade Continue Introducing Independent Activities

FIGURE 2–4   *Framework for the first two months of school*

REFLECTION

Attending to the first two months in a careful manner has become ingrained in me. I discipline myself to be thorough and pay attention to the details of the classroom, our schedule, the children, and their families. My thoughts and work center on organizing classroom environment and curriculum, establishing a community, observing children at work and play, and reflecting on needed changes. It is a time when I observe either first- or second-grade children begin to grow, learn, make decisions, and solve problems. I expect a lot but I know that the children will learn how to live in a classroom that operates like a workshop because of my high expectations and the caring community we create together. It takes consistency, focus, clarity of purpose, problem solving . . . and patience.

BECOMING READERS

I believe that as teachers we must look at what we do in a slightly deeper way, not a different way. I believe our work must be about "more learning" vs. "new learning."

—Margaret Mooney, Presentation at Year of the Young Reader Conference

FIGURE II–1
*Elizabeth, Tracy,
and Roni reading*

3 | SHARED READING

Learning to read and write ought to be one of the most joyful and successful of human undertakings.

—*Don Holdaway,* The Foundations of Literacy

"Who told you! Who told you," my second graders read exuberantly as we neared the end of our rereading of the bigbook *Rumpelstiltskin* (Parkes 1990). We were gathered for shared-reading time and my group was gleeful yet again because Rumpelstiltskin had been outsmarted by the Queen. We had enjoyed the book several times during the three weeks we had been reading and comparing folktales, fables, and fairy tales. For the most part, the children knew the story well enough that they were able to choral read while I led with my pointer, my reading voice having faded to the background. However, the Queen's guesses at Rumpelstiltskin's name were still posing a bit of a challenge, as well as three verbs used to describe the King's surprise when he discovered a young girl had been able to turn straw into gold: *astonished*, *astounded*, and *amazed*.

"We've read this fairy tale so many times that you can read most of it by yourselves," I told my group. "But I've noticed that each time we read it, there are three words, which are actually called verbs, that are still tricky for you, and I want to study those with you today. The words are: *astounded*, *astonished*, and *amazed*. Let's go back into the book and find these three verbs so we can read the sentences they're in."

After locating and choral reading the three sentences—*The King was astonished., The King was astounded., The King was amazed.*—I placed my skirt hanger of 12 x 18" paper on the easel and prepared it for our quick verb study. I wrote *Rumpelstiltskin* and the date, 3-13-96, at the top of the paper with a black marker, then wrote *astonished*, *astounded*, and *amazed* with a green marker underneath.

"What do you notice about these verbs?" I asked my group.

"They all start with an /a/," Cynthia said.

I took my blue marker and underlined the /a/ at the beginning of each word. "What else do you notice?" I asked again.

"Astonished and astounded both start with an /a/ and /s/, which is the word *as*," Tracy said.

I underlined the /a s/ at the beginning of both words with my red marker, underneath the blue line I'd drawn previously.

"What about the endings?" I asked my group.

"They all end in /-ed/," several children responded at one time.

"Terrific," I said, and underlined the /-ed/ endings with an orange marker before continuing. "These three words have similar spellings, and I think that's why they're tripping you up when you're reading. You have to follow through to the end of the words with your eyes so you don't misread them. That will help you as readers."

I then wrote out the three words like equations so the children could see that two of the words had an /-ed/ ending, and one word had a /-d/ ending:

astonish + ed = astonished
astound + ed = astounded
amaze + d = amazed

"If you look closely at the ending of each word you will discover a rule for when /-ed/ is added to the end of a verb and when only /-d/ is added. Do you see it?" I asked.

Rachael did. "Astonish ends with an /h/, and astound ends with a /d/ so they have /-ed/ on the end. Amaze ends with a *quiet e* so it just has a /d/ on the end. The /e/ is already there so you don't have to add another one."

I took Rachael's explanation a step further and showed the children that if the verb ends in a consonant, then /-ed/ is added; if it ends with an /e/, then only a /d/ is added for the ending. I knew I could extend the minilesson to listing other verbs, then determining whether they needed the /-ed/ or /-d/ ending, but I decided to wait until the following day to do this. I wanted to stay focused on *astonished*, *astounded*, and *amazed*.

"What other verbs or synonyms could the author have used that would mean the same thing as *astonished*, *astounded*, or *amazed*?" I asked my group. The children talked quietly among themselves for a few seconds before two words were suggested: *shocked* and *surprised*. I wrote their suggestions in purple on the bottom of the chart paper.

"I'll post this chart by the easel for a couple days before adding it to our Word Study Book, so we can review it before we read *Rumpelstiltskin* again," I told the children.

We finished our shared-reading time that day with a discussion about why the author had chosen three different verbs instead of using the same verb each time the King discovered that the straw had been turned into gold. Their consensus was that it made the writing much more interesting; I added the word *skillful* to describe it.

As it turned out, at least three more minilessons that I conducted during future shared-reading sessions originated from the text of *Rumpelstiltskin*. During one minilesson, we brainstormed a list of verbs, then added the /-ed/ or /-d/ ending based on the rule we had discovered earlier. Some of the verbs the children suggested were irregular verbs, which led to another minilesson on irregular past tense verbs. The last minilesson was an exploration of the /ou/ and /ow/ letter patterns, because when we were studying the word *astounded*, Elizabeth commented that the word "sound" rhymes with "astound." These were the kind of teachable moments I listened for and capitalized on every day during shared-reading in my classroom. Like all good shared reading texts, *Rumpelstiltskin* was not only a joyful reading experience, but an informative one as well.

———————————

Shared reading, if done well, convinces children that learning to read is worth it. It is a powerful demonstration of what good readers do when they have good books in their hands. It involves the teacher and *all* children in joyful and informative readings, discussion time, language study, and discovering how readers solve problems. For many young children, shared reading opens the door to a literate life.

Shared reading has its roots in the developmental language learning or "natural learning" model that Don Holdaway explored and wrote about in his groundbreaking book *The Foundations of Literacy* (1979). Some of the major characteristics he attributes to developmental learning include

- The learning begins with immersion in an environment in which the skill is being used in purposeful ways.
- The environment is an emulative rather than an instructional one, providing lively examples of the skill in action.
- What aspect of the task will be practiced, at what pace, and for how long is determined largely by the learner. Practice occurs whether or not the adult is attending, and tends to continue until essential aspects of the task are under comfortable, automatic control.
- The environment is secure and supportive, providing help on call and being absolutely free from any threat associated with the learning of the task.
- Development tends to proceed continuously in an orderly sequence marked by considerable differences from individual to individual. (23)

In searching for ways to apply the model of developmental language learning to the classroom, Holdaway studied the unique characteristics of the bedtime-story setting that takes place with families who have preschool children. He realized that the bedtime story was a way for children and their parents to be involved in a very personal, exclusive literacy act in which the child has close visual and tactile contact with books while becoming increasingly focused on the conventions of print (63). The bedtime story also provided an opportunity for children to see their parents use their reading skills purposefully, and parents could call attention to the fact that the reading process was print-stimulated (65).

Whereas teachers have always read aloud to their students, what Holdaway believed was missing was the visual intimacy with print. Preschool children are able to "experience print" during the bedtime story because they are generally sitting on the laps of family members. He realized that classrooms, with large numbers of children, do not lend themselves to this type of individual, intimate book sharing, so he devised a way to bring this type of reading into the center of the instructional program.

Holdaway and his colleagues enlarged the print of books, poems, and songs that are often favorites with children, making it large enough so the children could see it from a distance. They proceeded to introduce these enlarged books, poems, and songs to the children during their regular story-time hour, involving them not only in joyous readings, but also focusing the children's attention on the print. His goal with this shared-book experience was to find a way for children to engage naturally with print and develop their skills as readers—an instructional practice he believed was supported by the model of developmental language learning. Thus, the "bigbook" and shared reading were born.

GETTING READY AND GATHERING MATERIALS

Items that I find essential for shared-reading sessions in my classroom include

- enlarged print: I use bigbooks, charts, and overhead transparencies.
- easel: I use a small, wooden easel with a solid back and ledge for holding charts and bigbooks. My friend Cliff made mine so it is the perfect height for me to sit at and the children to stand at.
- pointer: Mine is from a nature store. It is made of clear plastic with glitter and stars inside that travel up and down as I move it. My kids love it. A wooden dowel works just as well.
- Post-it notes: I use these to mask out words/letters for minilessons.
- whiteboard/dry erase markers: I use these for minilessons.
- paper/markers: I keep a bundle of 12 x 18" white drawing paper held together by a skirt hanger. I use the paper and markers often for letter/word-study charts.

Bigbooks

When I first started using the shared-reading approach in my classroom, I took my cue from Don Holdaway and created my own bigbooks. At that time, bigbooks were just starting to be published by book companies, there wasn't a large selection to choose from, and I didn't have the budget to buy them. I made a few bigbooks on my own, but soon began doing this with the children. We chose our favorite read-alouds, I enlarged the print—by hand at that time, now on computer—and the children drew the illustrations. It was a wonderful, purposeful way to build a classroom library of bigbooks, and to this day, I prefer many of these books to the commercial ones that have flooded the market. (See Appendix 3–1 for the method I use to construct bigbooks.)

Now, when I do have either the classroom or personal funds to purchase bigbooks, I am careful because they are expensive. I aim for worthwhile and enduring purchases. I look for books that will enhance the whole-group reading experience because of the enlarged format. I'm not interested in having hundreds of bigbook titles. I would prefer to have a collection of carefully selected titles, both fiction and nonfiction, that children will enjoy again and again. (For a list of favorite bigbooks see Appendix 3–2.) I store my bigbooks in one of my large cupboard areas until I introduce them to the children. After that, I use skirt hangers to hang them on two bigbook racks in our classroom library. This way, they are easy to retrieve and reread by both the children and me.

I generally purchase the first book of a series in bigbook form, so I can introduce the children to the character during shared reading. After that, I stock our classroom library with the remaining titles in the series so children can continue to develop a relationship with this book friend. An example of this is Paulette Bourgeois' lovable character, Franklin. First-grade children especially seem to enjoy the bigbook version of *Franklin in the Dark* (1986). By the time we reach the page toward the end where Franklin's mother says, "Oh Franklin, I was so afraid you were lost," the children are completely captivated with this little turtle, who has been off on a journey seeking advice from his friends because he is afraid of the dark. The bigbook, with its large, exaggerated illustrations, gives an even stronger feel to the reading experience. By the end of the reading, children know Franklin is a friend with similar cares and worries as their own. After I introduce Franklin in this enlarged format, children immerse themselves in many readings and rereadings of every Franklin book in the series. It does what a bigbook is supposed to do: captures the attention of young readers enough that they want to read on their own.

In addition to purchasing the first book of a well-loved character series, I look for these qualities in bigbooks before I buy:

Bigbook Purchases: Elements I Consider

Quality of the Story

- fiction: Is it a "jewel" of a story that will capture children and beg for rereadings? Will the story endure over time?
- nonfiction: Is the information presented in a clear manner with language and vocabulary appropriate for young children to understand? Is it a format where we can review and reread easily before starting the next section of text?

Quality of the Illustrations

- fiction: Do they extend the story?
- nonfiction: Do they clarify facts, procedures, and concepts? Are there photographs?

Style of the Illustrations

- fiction: Can we study the illustrations as artists?
- nonfiction: Are there models of scientific drawings?

Size of the Print

- Is the text large enough to be seen from a distance so children can read along when they are ready?

Quality of the Book Construction

- Will it hold up to the handling from both my hands and the children's hands throughout many rereadings?

Quality of the Production

- Has care been taken with the printing of the text as well as the printing and color of the illustrations?

Format of the Pages

- Do text and illustration match on each page?
- Are sentences completed on each page or are they left hanging on one page and finished on the next? If possible, I like to read and study both pages before I have to turn to the next page. This isn't always possible with an older book, e.g., *Corduroy* (Freeman 1976) because the original version has incomplete sentence page breaks also.

During the first month of shared reading time with first-grade children, I introduce a wonderful set of read-and-sing bigbooks developed by my friend and colleague Nellie Edge. She has created bigbooks for many of the traditional songs, rhymes, and chants that young children love. These big-books are particularly good for beginning readers because they incorporate the elements of rhyme, rhythm, and repetition. They are short, inviting, joyful, and memorable, which are the characteristics children need in bigbooks during these early reading demonstrations.

The bigbooks are printed in black and white and I've had numerous parents color them with colored pencils for home projects. As a way to show appreciation for their contribution to our classroom, I acknowledge their work on the front of the bigbook by writing, e.g., Colored by: Juanita's Family, 1995–96 School Year. Included with Nellie's bigbooks are black-line masters for little books of the songs and rhymes, which, with parent help, are copied and assembled for the children so they have their own books after I've shared the bigbook. After the children color them, they store these little books in a Ziploc bag in the back of their anthologies so that they always have access to them.

Nellie's *I Can Read Colors* (1988) bigbook is one that I've used on the first day of first grade for many years. This is a simple song about familiar colors and objects, and has a patterned text, e.g., *Orange is an orange. Yellow is the sun.* The last page of text reads: *I can read. Listen to me.* Before I introduce the bigbook, I sing the song with the children and have them pull cards that go with the items in the book from colored pockets that I've sewn onto an apron. After we've enjoyed the song and the bigbook several times and the children know it by heart, the children color their own little book copies. While they are coloring, I go around and read the little book with the children, taking their hands to help them track each word, saying to them, "You're reading!"

This little book goes home with the children at the end of the day so they can share it with their families. Yes, it's a way to start nightly reading on the first day, too. Prior to the first day of school I make a "pocket certificate"— folded construction paper with a handmade certificate on the front that reads, "I can read on the first day of first grade" with space to write the child's name—and the children tuck their little books into these certificate folders to take home with them.

This is just one of the ways I begin planting and nurturing "I am a reader" seeds in the children. My goal is for first-grade children to go home feeling and behaving like readers on the first day of school, which is ever so important to them. I know from experience that if you ask first graders what they want to learn during their first-grade year, most will say without hesitation, "I want to learn how to read and write." They come to school expecting it. Their families have been telling them, "You're going to learn how to read and write this year." I don't wait for a month to get into reading. I start on the first day during shared reading.

Once our year gets under way, and the children and I begin developing a history together, I listen closely to them for book possibilities. When a child loses her tooth, I know I must read Tom Birdseye's *Airmail to the Moon* (1988). When our classroom is invaded by ants, I pull out *"I Can't," Said the Ant* (Cameron 1961). However, I don't choose all books in this manner. Not everything connects to the lives, conversations, and discoveries of first and second graders. I save my collection of folktales, fairy tales, and fables until we have two to three weeks to devote to a ministudy of this genre of story. I wait until we are between unit studies, so that we can devote the heart of our shared-reading time to enjoying, then comparing and contrasting these stories. It's too difficult to juggle content-area reading with a genre study.

I've also earmarked other bigbooks for sharing at particular times of the year. I love to share *Mary Wore Her Red Dress* (Edge 1988) during the first

FIGURE 3–2
Roni and Jana: conducting their own shared-reading time

week of school because it lends itself to a wonderful innovation in which the children create a page about themselves, using the same pattern as the book, that we can publish as our first class-made bigbook. I start building resources like this early.

Content-area bigbooks are saved for shared reading until we are immersed in our units of study. Not all inquiry studies are the same every year; however, most of these bigbooks make their way into the classroom. Even if we don't tackle a study as a whole group, I find that either small groups of children or individuals are interested in these topics, so I share these bigbooks as a way to further their knowledge and understanding of a particular area. The rest of the group may not be quite as devoted to the area of study, but I have never found a time where they didn't enjoy reading the information together.

Songs and Poems

I select songs and poems from several resources when I create enlarged charts for our shared-reading sessions. In addition to making charts for a number of traditional, folk, and patriotic songs, I have several favorite song resources. Raffi, Charlotte Diamond, Rory, Jim Valley, and Sarah Pirtle are noteworthy. Favorite cassette tapes of theirs, from which I create song charts, include

Raffi
Bananaphone
Singable Songs for the Very Young
Rise and Shine
Baby Beluga
Raffi in Concert

Charlotte Diamond
10 Carrot Diamond
Diamond in the Rough
Diamonds & Dragons

Rory
I'm Just a Kid!

Jim Valley
Friendship Train

Sarah Pirtle
The Wind Is Telling Secrets

Because I love children's poetry, I have a large collection of poetry books and poetry charts for shared reading in my classroom library. (Favorite poetry resources that I consult often when creating large poetry charts for shared reading are marked with an * in Appendix 3–3.) I store my poetry and song charts in one of the drawers of my large paper table and attach skirt hangers to the top of the charts so I can hook them on the easel when I want to share them with the children. As I introduce and reread these poem and song charts with my group, I store my growing collection behind one of the wooden cubby units in our whole-group area; this way I have easy access to them when I am gathering materials for our daily shared-reading sessions. The children don't have access to these charts for rereading like they do with the big-books. Instead, small copies are made for their anthologies (see Chapter 4).

ORGANIZING A SHARED-READING SESSION

In my classroom, shared reading usually occurs after morning recess. Prior to that, the children have been involved in morning-work time, class meeting, quiet reading, and partner reading. In terms of the overall flow of my language arts time, it's a good place to come back together as a whole group; we've been engrossed in a workshop atmosphere and now I like to draw in my community of readers.

Daily shared-reading sessions generally include these elements:

- gathering with favorite songs, poems, bigbooks
- introducing/reading/discussing a new bigbook OR reviewing/reading/discussing a content-area bigbook
- conducting minilessons

Gathering

As children come in the door from recess, I greet them, then remind them to set their writing tablets/notebooks and pencils at their tables. I do this because immediately after shared reading, we start our writing workshop time with ten minutes of quiet writing, and often the children choose to respond to what we've read during our shared-reading session. In essence, as we transition into shared reading, we're preparing for the transition into writing after shared reading. It's part of the work I do in thinking through smooth transitions as we ready ourselves for present and future work. Some prefer to call it classroom management; I prefer to think of it as calm, purposeful classroom living.

Once the children are in the door, readying their writing materials and getting a quick drink of water, I take up my position at the easel with pointer in hand. As soon as there are a couple of children on the floor in front of me, I start. At the beginning of the year, I begin with song or poem charts, "hurrying" the children to the floor by enticing them with wonderful language. As the year progresses, we add favorite bigbooks to this gathering phase of the shared-reading session. These bigbooks are chosen and set on the easel during morning-work or quiet-reading time by the two children who are that day's daily helpers. That way every child has the opportunity to choose their favorites for rereading. When the entire group has made its way to our gathering area, I finish whatever we happen to be rereading or "resinging," and move into the next part of the lesson.

As the shared-reading session continues, I introduce a new bigbook to the children, reading, and sometimes rereading it in one sitting; or I read a longer content-area bigbook over the course of several days if we're immersed in a unit study; or I involve the children in several rereadings of favorite books, songs, and poems. In all cases, I have my eye toward teachable points or minilessons to include during the readings.

Introducing a New Bigbook

When I have decided which new bigbook to share for the first time with the children, my work begins at making this introduction and first reading as joyful, interesting, and engaging as possible. I keep the new bigbook tucked away until it's time to share it so there is a sense of anticipation—an expectant air of "What are we going to read today?" Once I've placed the book on the easel, there are standard ways I begin to involve the children in the upcoming book experience. With pointer in hand:

1. I read the title and title page of the book and the names of the author and illustrator to the children.
2. I show the children where to locate the copyright date and read the date the book was published; I ask the children to figure out how many years ago the book was published. Sometimes it takes counting on fingers, noses, and toes to figure it out—but they get it!
3. I read the name of the publishing company and where the book was published and we locate it on our large U.S. map. We have Post-it notes marking Boston, San Diego, Chicago, and New York City on our map because that is where many of the books are published.
4. I point out anything noteworthy about the end pages, including reading the dedication.
5. I share any additional information the author or illustrator may have included at the beginning of the book.

After these details are addressed, I wait for the children to finish shifting and to become ready to be involved with the book. I don't start until I have everyone's attention. I move children who seem to have a hard time settling in closer to me. If need be, I can touch them to refocus their attention during the reading, rather than having to call out their names and wait for them. It's a gentle, but expectant way to work with children who need reminders. As we get into the reading, it's unusual to have to do this to any degree because generally the lure of the book takes over and the children become engrossed in the story.

Once I start, I don't have any preconceived formula for how to proceed other than to become completely engrossed in reading the book to and with the children. Although I always know the book thoroughly before I share it with my class, I don't have a set of questions in mind that I want to ask the children as we go through the reading; I don't structure "the book discussion" in my head before I start. Rather, I set up an atmosphere for discussion and let the story take over. I want this to be not only a reading time, but an active discussion time. I don't want the children to wait until the book is over to respond. I encourage active, full-bodied dialogue the entire time I am reading to them. All the thinking we do in our heads while reading, I want to do out loud. During shared reading, it is often thirty-three readers—myself included—working through a book together, with differing experiences and viewpoints. It's the richness of these different reading voices I want all of us to hear, so we can celebrate the diversity of thoughts, opinions, and avenues of processing. Shared reading isn't just me demonstrating what good readers do, but what all of us are doing as good readers. Choosing the right book is key, but I believe it is the dialogue that transforms the reading into an active, memorable, "I want to learn how to do this myself" process.

When I introduced *Make Way for Ducklings* (McCloskey 1941) to the children at Bobier, there was such good book conversation swirling around that it took almost thirty minutes to get through the initial reading. My introduction of this book was prompted by a newspaper picture that showed a police officer lying on his stomach in a gutter, tenderly holding a little duck.

As I began reading the bigbook to the children, they became quite interested in the size of the ducks and how they were depicted in the illustrations, as well as whether Robert McCloskey had remembered all eight ducks when illustrating Mr. and Mrs. Mallard's family. There was a great deal of concern that he had missed little Quack on some of the pages, as he seemed to lag behind Jack, Kack, Lack, Mack, Nack, Ouack, and Pack. The children managed to locate all eight of them on each page, which was quite a relief to them, and completely unexpected by me. When Mrs. Mallard and her little brood navigated the dangers of busy downtown Boston while making their way to the Public Garden, the children erupted with the sounds of busy cars, honking horns, and the large quacks and little quacks of the Mallard family. Their delight in the story was obvious.

It was a lovely shared-book experience and one that we enjoyed many times over between that April and the end of the year. We reread all of our bigbooks many times during the course of the school year, and each reading adds to a deeper and better understanding of "story" and "language."

Generally, there is so much discussion that takes place throughout the initial reading that we rarely linger over it at the end. Smiles and "Wasn't that a great book?" seem to close the experience for us this first time through. The discussing, pointing out the particulars in illustrations, and making the sounds of animals take at least as long as reading the text. In fact, well-written text and beautiful illustrations are only the starting point. What makes them come alive is the close and warm manner in which books are shared, read, and discussed. There isn't a prescription or formula for doing this. It takes becoming completely involved with the book and the children. It takes good listening for what children are thinking out loud and an eye for observing what the children are saying in response to what is being read.

If the children *do* want further discussion time at the end of a book, we pause for a moment to do so and then continue. There are also times, especially when it's a shorter book, that the children will ask me to read it again. I take my cues from the children. As they learn the format of our shared-reading sessions, they know we will enjoy many rereadings, and that the big-book and at least one copy in the smaller version will be available to them in our classroom library for personal rereadings.

I usually don't do any strategy teaching or word studies during the first reading. I save them for future rereadings. This first time through is for the pure enjoyment of the book. If I do decide to diverge into a minilesson during this initial reading, it's prompted by a remark or observation made by the children, and I keep it short.

Reviewing/Reading/Discussing a Content-Area Bigbook

When the children and I are immersed in a miniexploration—usually prompted by an item someone brings for our science/discovery area—or a major unit study, our shared-reading time is a natural place to incorporate nonfiction, content-area information. I have accumulated a variety of nonfiction bigbooks on subjects ranging from oceans to space, but often I make overhead transparencies or charts for sharing information with the children. I also consult with other teachers to see if they may have something in their bigbook collection that we can borrow for a period of time.

There are differences in how I handle the initial readings of fiction versus nonfiction bigbooks. Fiction bigbooks are generally short enough that we can read them in one sitting and focus on enjoyment. Nonfiction big-books are usually longer, require a period of days to read, and the focus is on concepts and information. However, if the nonfiction bigbook is short, I introduce and read the book in one session. Ruth Heller's books come to mind. I usually save my collection of her books for sharing with the children in the spring when it is a natural time to study an abundance of new life.

I chose to introduce *The Reason for a Flower* (Heller 1983) when I brought a Venus's-flytrap to school and we were scrounging for information about it. That book, as well as transparencies I made of an article featuring carnivorous plants in one of the *Your Big Backyard* magazines, discovered by Brenda during quiet-reading time, provided good information for my young readers at their reading level. While reading the book, we stopped often for our customary discussion, which during content-area reading is much more fact-related than story-oriented. After sharing both the book and the magazine article with the class, I placed them in the science/discovery area by the Venus's-flytrap so the children could reread them if they were interested. With nonfiction books, I observe children searching for clarification or working to make connections to something they know or have experienced in order to make sense of the information, versus their practice of connecting with story and characters during fiction readings. Our reading and discussion time feels more academic. We are grappling with information versus themes and characters.

Reading *The Reason for a Flower* led to introducing *Plants That Never Ever Bloom* (Heller 1984). As I shared this book with my group, there was some confusion over fern spores, so I did a drawing to show the children what spores look like and where spores are located on the underside of the fern leaf. We also talked at length about how ferns spawn more ferns from these spores. Many of the children had never noticed the spores on the back of a fern leaf when it was in that particular cycle of its growth period, so I made a note on my clipboard to bring one of my fern leaves to school the next time it had spores.

It's interesting with Ruth Heller's books that when it's time for a reread-ing, the children often asked me to "do a read-through without any stops." Ruth Heller has such a wonderful way of presenting scientific information poetically, and the children seemed to want to hear and enjoy the melody of the language once they had a chance to discuss all of the information and tid-bits she so cleverly and artistically packs into her writing and drawings.

More often, reading through a content-area bigbook requires several shared-reading sessions. The *Magic School Bus* bigbooks are a perfect exam-ple of this. Each book contains so much information that I find sharing the smaller version of the book is never satisfying with a large group of children. The bigbooks are much nicer because with the enlarged size, the children are able to see and appreciate Joanna Cole and Bruce Degen's close attention to scientific detail, as well as enjoy their sense of humor.

After engaging in the standard introductory items—title, author, illus-trator, copyright, publishing house—we typically make it through about three to four pages of the text during one shared-reading session. We gener-ally have as much discussion time, if not more, as reading time when we dig into a book like this. Again, I read with an invitation for discussion, listening closely for the questions and the "I wonder's that inevitably surface. The first day I introduced *The Magic School Bus Lost in the Solar System* (Cole 1990) to my second graders when we were embarking on our space exploration study, we read three pages in fifteen to twenty minutes. The children's questions centered on two topics: (1) how the Earth's rotation causes night and day, and (2) the Earth's rotation and gravity.

To remind the children what causes night and day, I decided we needed a demonstration with our globe and flashlight. We had explored this concept in first grade, but some of the children still didn't understand it. With our flash-light and globe from our science/discovery area, Timmy positioned the "sun" in the sky and I positioned the globe so that the "sun" was shining on Vista, Cali-fornia. Then I began turning "Earth" on its axis so the children could see how the Earth's rotation causes night and day. After doing this, they still weren't sure how long it took Earth to make one complete rotation, so I reminded them it took twenty-four hours or one complete day on Earth. This was a simple dem-onstration but it helped the children experience an abstract concept.

That demonstration brought up the question, "Why don't we fall off the Earth if it's rotating?" Several of the children knew that gravity keeps our feet on the ground, but they wondered what would happen if gravity weren't holding us on Earth. We also discussed how slowly the Earth actually rotates; so slowly that we can't even feel it as we go about our daily lives. I reminded my group of the Foucault Pendulum at the Natural History Museum at Balboa Park in San Diego. Designed by Jean Leon Foucault in 1851 in Paris, France, this pendulum provides visual proof of the Earth's rotation. Nancy Owens Renner, an exhibit developer at the Natural History Museum, describes the mechanics and the workings of the Foucault Pendulum in this way:

> The hardware holding the pendulum is attached to the roof of the Museum. Once the pendulum is set in motion, it continues to swing back and forth in a vertical plane defined by the track of the ball and cable. Because of air friction and gravity, the pendulum would eventually stop swinging, but a magnet encircling the cable pulls on the cable with each swing. The electric current controlling the magnetism is turned on and off with each swing of the pendulum.
>
> The direction of the swing is constant. The apparent change in direction of swing is related to the perspective of the observer. Since no force is acting to change the direction of the swing—it doesn't change. Instead, the floor, the observer, and the Earth's surface are turning beneath the pendulum.
>
> The pendulum is not a clock, yet the time it takes to go around the circle is predictable. Latitude determines the length of time required for a complete trip around the circle. In San Diego, the pendulum makes its way around the circle in 44 1/2 hours. At the North Pole, the pendulum would complete the circle in 24 hours. (1997)

The exhibit team at the Natural History Museum devised a clever way to show proof of the Earth's rotation (and that the pendulum is not moving around the circle) by arranging wooden pins in various designs on the floor area underneath the pendulum. As the earth rotates, the swinging pendulum knocks down the pins. The day we visited the museum, my second graders were fascinated by this exhibit and watched the pendulum and the falling pins for at least fifteen minutes. Again, it was another terrific demonstration of an abstract concept, and one that clearly helped them understand that our Earth rotates in space.

Questions and discussions like these that occur during the context of our shared-reading time begin to drive our inquiry and study. I listen for and explore these questions with children during our shared-reading sessions and afternoon unit study times because I like to begin with what they understand. My work becomes extending their understanding with more information or with eye-opening demonstrations.

Including longer content-area bigbooks during shared reading allows me to demonstrate how a reader holds text and information together when reading it over a period of days or weeks. Each time we stop reading, I mark our start-up page with a Post-it note; however, when we reenter the book during this portion of our next shared-reading time, I return to the beginning of the bigbook so the children and I can do a walk-through of what we've read previously, reacquainting ourselves with the text before reading on. This review is helpful because it allows us to get back into the story in a meaningful, connected way. Each time we skim and review the earlier pages, we relive, we reunderstand, we have more ah-hahs. We've had time to simmer with the information and can bring new understandings to the text.

There are times during unit study shared-reading sessions that I choose to read more than one content-area bigbook at a time. During our space exploration study, I introduced *Postcards from the Planets* (Drew 1988) while I was reading *The Magic School Bus Lost in the Solar System*. *Postcards* is a wonderful science fiction book that follows a family's journey through our solar system. Their communication with "Earthlings" is through postcards written and posted at each of the planets. The text is composed of enlarged postcards that are complemented by real and simulated photos of the sun and the planets. It is not only a good informational text but a nice example of science fiction. I decided the most effective way to share this book would be to match the planet readings from this book to when Ms. Frizzle and her class landed on the corresponding planet in the *Magic School Bus* book. It was an effective way to read and present information in stereo.

Often after shared-reading sessions where we have delved into unit study readings, discussions, or demonstrations, the children respond to the information and discussion in their unit study journals. This takes the place of quiet writing in our writing notebooks at the start of writing workshop, which occurs immediately after shared reading. Periodically we share our journal entries with one another; our understandings, misunderstandings, and questions held up for examination and clarification.

Conducting Minilessons

I view the *entire* shared-reading session as a demonstration of what good readers know and do, but each day, during the course of our readings, I spend a few extra minutes focusing on reading strategies and language principles that are particularly helpful to young readers. In my classroom, these minilessons take place during the rereading of favorite bigbooks or charts, or during the review and reading of longer nonfiction bigbooks, charts, or overhead transparencies. Many times, I conduct several minilessons from one bigbook, as different things seem to crop up each time we reread.

In her second edition of *In the Middle*, Nancie Atwell describes minilessons in this way:

> The minilesson is a forum for sharing my authority—the things I know that will help writers and readers grow. . . . The minilesson is also a forum for students to share what they know and for us to figure out collaboratively what we know—to think and produce knowledge together and lay claim to it as a community. (1998, 150)

During my shared-reading sessions with primary children, I embed minilessons into the readings, rather than teach in a separate forum. I weave in and out of reading and explicit teaching during this thirty- to forty-minute period of time, involving the children in both enjoyable and teachable moments with print. The bigbook, chart, or overhead transparency becomes the meaningful context for pointing out significant information that will help the children develop their skills as young readers.

Where do these lessons come from? First, I read with an eye to what each enlarged text offers in terms of reading strategy and language-teaching opportunities. There may be interesting text/illustration nuances, a play on words, a rhyming pattern, or unusual spellings that I want to point out. Secondly, I read with an ear toward what the children notice in the story and in the print when I read to them. What do they notice about text, illustrations, words, rhymes, or spellings? Are there confusions? Do they lack the language or print knowledge to make sense of something? What words do they stumble over? What strategies do they use to solve word problems? What strategies are missing? What can children teach one another? As I read aloud, I glean information on how to make the reading process and alphabetic principle even more accessible to my young readers. I look for ways to create openings for them to share their developing literacy knowledge with one another.

I search out and listen for these teaching opportunities during shared-reading time, during reading conferences when I listen to individual children read, or when I observe children reading together during partner reading. I keep a Post-it note on my reading assessment clipboard for jotting down any reading strategy/phonic successes or problems children have so I can address them during our shared-reading time. Shared-reading lessons allow me to maximize my teaching time with a large group of children. It's my way of involving children in *daily* lessons, whereas individual conferencing generally only provides a weekly opportunity.

Minilessons fall into five general areas. I work from categories developed by Jan Turbill et al. in their Frameworks program, listed under "what to model in shared reading" (1991, 24). These categories include:

- what reading is
- concepts of print
- phoneme awareness and phonics
- reading strategies
- high-frequency words

What Reading Is Lessons

I find that lessons that fall under the umbrella of showing children what reading is take place naturally during the course of reading and discussing the text—both during initial readings and rereadings. During every reading session I want to model that

- reading is expressive
- reading is enjoyable
- reading is informative

- reading is rethinking
- reading is understanding
- reading is about creating meaning
- reading involves different types of text that are read in different ways: e.g., fiction, nonfiction, poetry
- everyone can learn how to read

These are not necessarily explicit lessons; rather, they are implicit lessons in the way I conduct the reading of the text and engage children in discussion and book talk. "You are becoming good readers" is a phrase I often insert into our dialogue as I fade my voice and let the voices of the children take over during a rereading. I remind them that their job is to become readers and that we must work on this every day in our classroom. Not all children understand that they have to work toward becoming readers; rather, they think it is something that will happen *to* them.

Concepts of Print Lessons

Lessons that are directed toward helping children understand the concepts about print are generally more intensive at the beginning of the year, particularly with first-grade children, and for the most part, are discontinued once the children learn these critical book and print items that are necessary to becoming readers. In my daily discussion with the children, I include items that relate to cover and illustrations, directionality, print conventions, and one-to-one matching. I use my pointer to emphasize directionality, one-to-one matching, and spaces between words. Below is a list of some of the finer points I tend to when drawing the children's attention to the concepts of print during shared reading.

Concepts of Print Minilessons
- Construction of the Book
    - front cover, back cover
    - pages
    - special pages: end pages, title page, dedication page, last page
    - spine
    - page numbers

- Format of the Book
    - title and title page
    - the title tells us something about the text
    - author and illustrator
    - the cover illustrations support the title
    - copyright date
    - publishing house and location
    - dedication page
    - table of contents
    - index
    - glossary

- Illustrations
    - illustrator: other books by that illustrator
    - illustrations support the words on the page
    - illustrations often give us more information than the text by itself
    - style of illustration
    - medium used for illustrations

- Directionality
    - we read from left to right, top to bottom
    - we read the left page then the right page
    - we turn pages as we read
    - how to read texts that vary from left to right, top to bottom, e.g., cartoons or conversation bubbles
    - we read from the front of the book to the back of the book

- Print Conventions and One-to-One Matching
    - we read the print on the page
    - there are spaces between words
    - punctuation helps us as readers
    - punctuation marks: period, question mark, exclamation point, comma, apostrophe, ellipsis, colon, quotation marks
    - pausing for a moment at the end of a sentence or with a comma
    - voice rises when reading a question sentence
    - voice shows excitement and feeling when reading an exclamatory sentence
    - quotation or "talking" marks tell us exactly what a character is saying
    - capital letters indicate people, places, or important things
    - capital letters mark the beginning of a sentence
    - capital letters are used in abbreviations in the middle of sentences, e.g., Mr., Ms., Mrs., Dr.
    - each word we read must match the word on the page

Phoneme Awareness and Phonics Lessons

In lessons that involve phoneme awareness and phonics, I focus on helping the children hear and say particular sounds in words as well as connect these sounds to print. Recent research on phoneme awareness has made it clear that we must pay attention to four aspects of how the sounds of English are represented in print in our teaching:

- Children have to learn to hear the sounds buried within words.
- Children have to learn to visually discriminate the symbols we use in print
- Children have to learn to link single symbols or clusters of symbols with the sounds they represent.
- Children have to learn that there are many alternatives and exceptions in our system of putting sounds into print. (Clay 1993a)

Keeping this in mind, I focus on beginning, middle, and ending letters and letter patterns in words during shared-reading sessions. I pay attention to vowels and vowel patterns. I teach homophones, compound words, and contractions, among other things, in order to help the children understand and cope with our language. I study English through the eyes of a beginning reader and writer; I observe the children wrestling with letters, sounds, letter patterns, words, and word families, then work to explain the nuances of our language so they become insiders to the code. Fortunately for me, I spent two semesters in linguistics classes as an undergraduate, developing a finer eye and ear for our language. Occasionally I do rely on published word lists to help me in my work. Two of my favorite professional resources for lists of words and letter patterns are *Teaching Kids to Spell* (Gentry and Gillet 1993) and *Phonics Patterns: Onset and Rhyme Word Lists* (Fry 1994).

I read aloud titles from my trade book and bigbook collection of "word play" books throughout the year, creating minilessons to engage the children in phonic study. Some of my favorite books that lend themselves to exploring letter and sound patterns with the children are listed in Appendix 3–5.

In choosing which words, letters, or letter patterns to focus on, I study each text for teaching opportunities. Books like those listed in Appendix 3–5 have obvious rhyming patterns that beg for linguistic exploration. Words and letter patterns leap off the page and provide a natural jumping-off point for what I mentally label linguistic dialogue: close inspection and discussion of letters and letter patterns and words and word patterns, which helps the children as readers and writers.

I also listen to the children for phonic-teaching opportunities. When they become "stuck," misread a word, or comment on a rhyming pattern, I know it's the perfect linguistic-teaching moment. During a rereading of *Another Mouse to Feed* (Kraus 1980), the word *enough* triggered an exploration of /gh/, /ph/, and /f/ when some of the children said, "It was hard to tell that word was *enough* because it didn't have an /f /or /ph/ on the end of it." When we were rereading the last page of *Who's in the Shed?* (Parkes 1986), Lee commented that *dare* and *stare* had the same ending pattern. She also pointed out that *bear* rhymed with *dare* and *stare*, but that it didn't have the same pattern. Lee's observations provided the opportunity to explore the /-are/ rime, and our discussion led to creating a chart with words that have /-are/, /-ear/, /-air/, /-ere/, and /-ayor/ rimes.

I keep a skirt hanger with 12 × 18" drawing paper next to the easel for these explicit teaching occasions. I prefer paper because that allows us to keep a record of our letter pattern and word studies. When we have finished a letter or word exploration, I post these sheets next to the easel or hang them on lines in our classroom, eventually adding them to a book titled *Our Word Study Book* for future reference. We refer to this book often throughout the year.

During a rereading of *It Looked Like Spilt Milk* (Shaw 1947) with my second graders, I stopped to explore the difference between *a* and *an*. As the children were reading the lines *Sometimes it looked like an ice cream cone*, most of the children read, "Sometimes it looked like *a* ice cream cone but it wasn't *a* ice cream cone."

"*A* ice cream cone?" I asked the children. "Look closer at the print," I said, using my pointer to show them the word *an*. A few piped up and said, "*an* ice cream cone," but they weren't the majority of the class. I turned back and reviewed some of the other pages with them, asking them to figure out why the ice cream page was different. Two of the children figured it out and said, "Oh, ice cream starts with an /i/. It's a vowel."

We took a moment to discuss when *a* versus *an* is used before we finished reading the book. Then, I hung my bundle of paper on the easel and we did a quick "a/an study." The children brainstormed words, discussed whether each word started with a vowel or consonant, then provided the appropriate preceding article. Our finished chart looked like this:

It Looked Like Spilt Milk
9-25-95

An	*A*
an ice cream cone	a bike
an angel	a turtle
an apple	a foot
an orange	a necklace
an elephant	a shirt
an umbrella	a shoe
(written in green marker)	(written in blue marker)

When we create a chart like this, I always write the title of the book, song, or poem, and the date at the top so the children and I remember what we were reading that prompted the closer inspection. I also write lists in different colors to distinguish letter and word patterns from one another. This is especially helpful when we're comparing letter patterns in words.

In one letter pattern chart that we created, we explored the /or/ pattern. It evolved from a poem titled "The Boa" that I read to the children at the beginning of our class meeting. The poem appears in the book *beast feast* (Florian 1994), which is a terrific collection of poetry about the many animal beasts in our world. The poems and accompanying watercolor illustrations are a nice balance of serious and funny for the ears of young poets. "The Boa" reads:

> Just when you think you know the boa,
> There's moa and moa and moa and moa.

The poem was a perfect invitation to discuss the poet's clever use of language, rhyming boa with "moa," but I waited until our shared-reading time to do this exploration with my group.

I started by listing the words *boa* and *moa* on the chart paper so we could examine the language carefully.

"What is the poet really saying?" I asked the children.

Several understood that it was the poet's own expressive way of saying *more*, only this way was much more entertaining for the reader. I wrote the word *more* underneath *moa* so we could compare the invented and the standard word.

I wasn't expecting to do any further exploration with this, but one of the children noticed the word *more* had the word *or* in it.

"Lots of other words have the little word *or* in them," I reminded my group. "Let's list them."

The children went to work brainstorming with one another while I readied our chart paper for the listing. The chart we created together that day follows:

"The Boa"
Beast Feast
11-29-95

(Written in orange)	(Written in turquoise)	(Written in dark blue)
more	cord	award
bore	Lord	drawer
store	sword	
ore		
core	(Written in purple)	(Written in dark green)
sore	floor	soar
chore	door	board
ignore	poor	Noah

(Written in light green with an asterisk because it didn't fit our pattern)
*knee

We started out linear enough in our listing of words with the /or/ pattern, but soon the children began offering words that had the /or/ sound however the rime portion of the words was spelled differently, which is exactly what I want to discuss and explore with my beginning readers and writers. Margaret Moustafa describes onset and rime in this manner:

> Natural parts of the English syllable have become known as *onsets* and *rimes*. The first part is called the onset and the last part is called the rime. Hence, in *wed* the /w/ is the onset and the /ed/ is the rime. While all spoken English syllables have a rime, not all spoken English syllables have an onset. (1997, 42)

As my group continued to call out words that auditorally fit the /or/ pattern, I changed colors of markers, grouping together "like words" or words that had the same rimes, drawing the children's attention to this as I did. I had to be quick on my toes and study patterns with them. They listed a lot more sounds and patterns for /or/ than I initially expected. At the end of this process, we looked at the many ways that a sound like /or/ can be spelled in our language. The multicolored chart helped them to see this.

As for the *knee* suggestion, I did manage to turn this into a teachable moment by reminding the children it started with that "quiet k" or /kn/ pattern that several readers had wrestled with at one time or another. I study children's responses that don't fit the pattern we are currently studying and brainstorming, which occur often in linguistic explorations like these, for future minilessons or review lessons. I love facilitating this kind of discovery with the children. Our charts provide great review lessons when I encounter children struggling with similar letter patterns in their reading and writing work.

In addition to creating letter pattern/word exploration charts to study the alphabetic principle of English, I use a strategy of sticking Post-it notes over words, folded under so the word underneath can't be seen through it, then having the children predict the words and work through the spellings. I pull the Post-it note off and position it next to the word in question so we can compare our class-created spelling with the standard spelling. Often, spelling patterns become clearer to the children when we do these comparisons.

Often in the course of our daily reading and writing work, we wrestle with vowels, vowel sounds, and vowel patterns. Vowels are tricky for young readers because their sound is dependent upon the consonants that surround them. To help the children distinguish vowels from consonants, I've made up a little song that I teach the children when we are having conversations about vowels in the context of our reading and writing work: "a, e, i, o, u are vowels, and all the rest are consonants." I've created a vowel chart and a vowel overhead transparency that I use to facilitate vowel discussion not only during shared reading, but anytime we are involved in any type of writing lesson. It includes vowels, words, and pictures (where possible). The words I've chosen include the following:

a: *a*lligator, *a*bout, *a*ll, *a*pe
e: *e*agle, *e*nvelope
i: *i*gloo, *i*ce
o: *o*strich, *o*kay
u: *u*mbrella, *u*nifix cube
y: baby

Anytime we are working through a spelling, I have this vowel chart out, along with a picture alphabet chart, so the children have a visual reminder in front of them as we work. When the children were predicting the beginning vowel for the word *all* while we were reading *The Royal Dinner* (Parkes 1990), several offered /o/ for the beginning sound.

"Good choice," I told the children, "but it's another vowel that stands for that sound."

At that point, some offered /a/ and others offered /u/.

"For those of you who said, /a/, you're right; *all* does start with the letter *a*; that's one of the sounds *a* stands for. Let's review the other sounds that the letter *a* stands for."

We reviewed the words *alligator*, *about*, and *ape* and isolated the /a/ sound at the beginning of each word. However, before moving on with the rest of the spelling of *all*, I still wanted to address the *u* that was suggested by some of the children.

"A /u/ wouldn't stand for that sound," I continued. "Let's look at our vowel chart to see what sounds the letter /u/ usually stands for." We read the words *umbrella* and *unifix cube* together and isolated the short /u/ and long /u/ sound at the beginning of each word.

I repeat vowel minilessons like this many, many times a day as I work with the children, especially first graders. I talk explicitly about which vowels would and would not make the sounds they are suggesting. I prod them to offer vowel responses so I can see what knowledge base they are working from before I refine or correct. Little by little, they begin to understand what vowels are and the sounds they represent, and they are able to work with them more accurately as readers and writers.

The list below represents many of the phoneme awareness, phonic, and word-study lessons that I do with the children.

Phoneme Awareness and Phonic Minilessons

- letter and letter sounds: A–Z
- beginning, middle, ending letters/sounds of words
- vowels and vowel patterns
- blends and digraphs at the beginning and ending of words
- rhyming words: onset and rime
- word families
- play on words, particularly in poetry, e.g., "moa" (more) and "boa"
- verb tenses
- verb endings
- segmenting words into parts or syllables: auditorally and visually
- sequencing the sounds of words from left to right when spelling
- words are made up of vowels and consonants

Word-Study Lessons

- reading *a* versus *an*
- homophones
- compound words
- contractions
- acronyms
- abbreviations
- question words: who, what, when, where, why, which, how
- similar words: e.g., *curtain* and *certain*, *quite* and *quiet*, *off* and *of*, *two*, *too*, *to* and *tow* and *toe*
- *a* and *I* are not only letters but also words

It's important to note that shared reading isn't the only time I engage in phonic teaching. I do a great deal of phonic teaching and word segmenting when I help children solve problem words during reading conferences or when they are reading to their partners. It's the first strategy I use with my young readers because often they need explicit help understanding the many letter patterns in our language. I follow up with "now read the sentence to see if that makes sense," to remind the children to always check for meaning. I also focus on letter sounds and patterns anytime the children are working through spellings during our writing time, engaging in both large and small phonic lessons when I conduct our Monday spelling minilesson and when the children are setting up their individual word lists in their spelling folders. Again, it is the context for teaching phonics that matters. It isn't about "knowing phonics," rather it is knowing how to use the letter-sound information to solve a problem.

Reading Strategy Lessons

During reading strategy lessons, I teach the children how to approach their reading and solve word problems when they encounter them. I want them to understand how to orient themselves to their book before they begin reading. I want my readers to have other ways of solving word problems in addition to "sounding it out." I want the children to see themselves as teachers of one another. When Rachael stood at the easel during a rereading of *Henny Penny* (Zimmerman 1996), and pointed out to the class that the author uses rhyming words for the character names and to "just look for the pattern and their names are easy to read," I knew the children were viewing themselves as teachers of reading. Again, the list below represents many of the reading strategy minilessons I incorporate into shared-reading sessions.

Reading Strategy Minilessons

How to Orient Yourself to the Book
- Look at the front and back of the book.
- Read the title
- Look through the entire book—print and illustrations—before trying to read it.
- Figure out what type (genre) of book it is: e.g., fiction, nonfiction, poetry.
- Find someone else who has read the book and ask him or her to help you.

How to Solve Word Problems
- Look at the first letter or letters and the ending letter pattern for sounding it out.
- Segment the word into parts or syllables to sound it out.
- Skip it and come back to it.
- Start at the beginning of the sentence and take another run at it.
- Substitute another word that makes sense.
- Ask someone for help.
- Look at the picture.
- Reread the sentence once you've solved your word problem and check to see if it makes sense.

High-Frequency Word Lessons

The last type of minilesson I do with the children focuses on high-frequency words. The children also study high-frequency words as part of their individual spelling lists (see Chapter 14), but shared-reading time offers one more opportunity to pay close attention to many of these connecting words that don't have meaning, but do hold the text together. Children need to learn high-frequency words so they recognize them automatically when they read and have the words on the tips of their pencils when they write. It makes reading and writing much faster processes. It allows children to hold text together when they are reading and writing because they are not struggling over every word.

I use a Post-it note strategy like the one I use with phonic minilessons to draw the children's attention to high-frequency words. I cover the word before the rereading and ask children to spell it out when we reach the Post-it note (again, folded under to conceal the print underneath). I write their spelling on the Post-it note, then we compare it to the standard spelling in the text. Another way I use the Post-it note is to cover the word—again, before the rereading—and ask the children to spell it once they have predicted the correct word. Instead of writing their spelling on the Post-it note, I uncover the word one letter at a time so they can confirm or correct their spelling as we go.

If it is a word the children need to practice, we quickly "write" the word in the air, on the floor, or in the palm of our hands with our fingers. Sometimes we sing and spell the words. I don't belabor it. These are quick and simple ways to practice, but also effective in committing high-frequency words to memory.

Incorporating Additional Shared-Reading Nuances

In addition to the format I've described above, I include other elements in our shared-reading sessions. Most days I include one or two trade book read-alouds. I have a classroom library full of good books that I love to share and shared reading is a forum for doing this. (My current read-aloud favorites are marked with an * in Appendix 3–4.) I read and recommend trade books that relate to a unit of study, a topic of conversation, an upcoming event or holiday, or the lives of first- and second-grade children. When Kayalani brought in a molted lizard skin that she and her grandmother had found while they were weeding the geraniums, it was an invitation to gather and introduce all the books we had in our library about lizards. When Joseph and his father set up a fish tank in the science/discovery area, I immediately collected every fish book in our classroom library, introduced them to the children during shared reading, then placed them in a tub by the aquarium.

I also share books that encompass several reading levels and interests because I believe that one of my jobs in shared reading is to continually introduce children to good books for the nightly reading they do at home and partner reading they do in our classroom. "This would be a great book for nightly reading," or "Those of you who have younger brothers or sisters at home would love this book," or "If you are interested in ——————, you'll love reading this book," are things I often say to the children when I introduce and read these books to them.

Sometimes I give short book talks during shared reading. I often do this if I know I don't have time to read an entire book but I want to make the children aware that it's in our classroom library. When new book orders arrive, I give book talks on the new titles that have been processed for our classroom library as a way to generate interest in new literature and continually hook the children as readers.

We also use shared-reading time to add pages to our anthologies, which include songs, poems, comics pages, world news, and U.S. news. It takes one entire shared-reading session to organize the pages, add them to our notebooks, then choral sing the songs or read the poems and information together before doing the illustration work. (I discuss anthologies in Chapter 4.)

REFLECTION

Lucy Calkins believes that classroom teachers should treat quiet reading as the "crown jewel" of their reading programs (1994). In primary classrooms, shared reading would have to share that distinction. It provides a forum for inducting children into the "literacy club" (Smith 1988). It is reading and thinking in action. Shared reading is a community of readers, at all levels of development, teaching and learning together.

4 | QUIET READING

. . . I linger alone
In a place of my own
Lost
In a book.
—Karla Kuskin, "Being Lost"

It was quiet-reading time. As I passed by David, he called me over to show me one of the books he was reading about the planets in our solar system. David had been immersed in reading books from our space exploration tub since we had started our study. It was common knowledge in our classroom that David wanted to be a space engineer when he grew up. This was David's third year in my classroom, as he'd had a rocky start with his schooling. He had transferred to Bobier from another elementary school in Vista during his first-grade year, after he had been ridiculed as a learner; his previous teacher had even called him "stupid" in front of his peers. When he started in my classroom, his behaviors were quite immature, and his self-esteem was rock-bottom. At the end of his first-grade year, after a fair amount of discussion, David's parents, David, and I agreed that having a "second" first-grade year would be the most helpful to him as a learner because of his difficult year. Even in my classroom, David's learning journey had had its peaks and valleys, but to his credit, by our third year together, he had grown academically, emotionally, and socially. It wasn't difficult to picture this David as a future astronaut.

"I didn't know the inner rocky core of other planets was the same as ours," David said to me quietly, showing me the page he was reading in his book.

"I hadn't really thought about it," I answered, skimming the illustration and text. "But now that you mention it, that makes sense. I suppose the inner core of the planets would be similar. That's something to remember for one of your journal entries. You may want to mark the page with a Post-it note so you can find it again easily."

Every day, my first- and second-grade children find a nook or cranny in our classroom to lose themselves in a world of good books, enjoy the comfort and quiet of the classroom, and connect with favorite books and book friends. Our quiet-reading time gives children the opportunity to practice what good readers do—read. Daily quiet-reading time is essential to young children becoming good readers.

I know that quiet-reading time means setting aside time for kids to read books—but it's more than that. In exploring how to establish a meaningful quiet-reading time with primary children I've considered many questions:

- What's needed for a sustained, productive quiet-reading time in a primary classroom?
- How do I teach young readers to value this oasis of time in a busy workshop-oriented classroom?
- How much time do I hand over to five-, six-, seven-, and eight-year-olds for exploring their own book choices?
- How do I establish expectations for quiet-reading time?
- How much "quiet" should there be in quiet reading?
- What kinds of books attract the attention of beginning and developing readers?
- How do I organize these books?
- What books should be required reading?
- What books should be choice reading?
- What other reading materials should be available to young readers?
- How much movement should be allowed in the room?
- How much conversation or book talk?
- Should children read by themselves or is it OK to read with a partner sometimes?
- How do I show myself as a reader?
- How do I use quiet-reading time to listen in to young readers?
- How do I help young readers become hooked on books?

Once again, something as simple as "quiet reading" requires a great deal of thought and reflection.

In my own classroom practice, I've narrowed it down to addressing five all-encompassing areas when establishing quiet reading as part of our reading workshop practices. These five areas include

- maintaining a well-organized classroom library
- establishing expectations for the books and materials the children will read
- establishing expectations for a productive, respectful quiet-reading time
- providing time every day for quiet reading
- showing the children that I am a reader

CLASSROOM LIBRARY

I revere the space I carve out for my library. I don't want a little out-of-the-way nook to house my collection of books; rather, I create a large, comfortable, inviting, organized space that shows the children that the library is one of the main hubs in this classroom. The first thing I want children to say when they walk in the door is, "Look at all those books!" If I want to nurture young readers I must have a wide range of interesting and readable books. I want my classroom library to call out to children, "Come in. This is a place for young readers." (I've listed my favorite children's literature for a primary classroom library in Appendix 3–4.)

In addition to enticing young readers to get books in their hands, I want our classroom library to be accessible, organized, and easy to maintain. To that end, I have devised a system for book storage that works well for both the children and me.

The approximately thirty tubs of book—about 800 titles—in my classroom are categorized by beginning reader little books, fiction, nonfiction, and author sets. The beginning reader little books, the bulk of which are published by The Wright Group and Rigby, are separated from the rest of my collection and are housed in separate tubs; fiction books are organized alphabetically, by authors' last names; nonfiction books are organized by subject area, e.g., ocean, space, weather; author sets are organized by author. Each category is coded with a colored adhesive dot, which I buy at an office supply store, and either an alphabet letter or number. My system follows:

- fiction: red dots and alphabet letters
- nonfiction: yellow dots and numbers
- author sets: blue dots and numbers

I place these dots in the upper right-hand corner of each book; I mark book tubs with corresponding colored circles that I cut out of construction paper with alphabet letters or numbers. A system like this allows the children and me to find and return books to the proper tubs with ease. A teacher-made key hangs in the library to help both children and adults who use our classroom library.

All paperback books in my classroom library are covered with contact paper; all hardbound book jackets have protective plastic coverings. (See Appendix 4–1 for resources.) This extends the life of my books when there are many little hands enjoying them each day. I also place computer labels inside the front covers that read: "Please return to Janine Chappell Carr." Each year I have one or two parent helpers who assist with the processing of new books before I add them to the classroom library, which, time-wise, helps immensely.

Five plastic stacking bins house magazines. Each bin has a yellow construction-paper label marked with the name of the magazine and a copy of the cover illustration, which has been reduced on the copier, to further assist the children when putting them away. I subscribe to the following magazines:

- *Ranger Rick*
- *Your Big Backyard*
- *Ladybug*
- *Spider*
- *ZooBooks*

There are several other items located in the classroom library, including

- two small, metal book display racks: We display current favorites on these racks and they are maintained by the two children who have the classroom library job.
- pillows: I've sewn bright blue and purple pillow covers that can be slipped on and off easily for washing since head lice plagued our room more than once during the year.
- two wooden bigbook racks with skirt hangers: We use these for storing the bigbooks we read during our daily shared-reading sessions.
- a small rocking chair: It has back and seat pads so it's comfortable for the children.
- book repair tub: Books in need of "big repair" are placed in this tub for me to tend to; the children handle small repairs, when only tape is needed, on their own.
- indoor plants: At Bobier, I situated these on the window ledge.

There are several pieces displayed on the wall area, which serves as a bulletin board, in my classroom library. These include

- our collection of "What's in the News?" chart papers, with two holes punched at the top and held together with two metal rings
- large word-study charts: I use these for my weekly spelling minilessons before the children set up their individual spelling folders.
- information about authors: I display any current author information I've read to the children.
- my chart-sized letters to my husband, which I write on Thursdays when we work in our family journals
- teacher-made library key

At the beginning of the year, I do several "classroom library/book organization and maintenance" minilessons with my group so they understand how I expect the library to be used and maintained. I've developed these over the course of working with and solving problems with primary children. We review minilessons during the year when we are experiencing classroom library problems. A list of these minilessons appears below.

Classroom Library Minilessons

- how books are organized
- how magazines are organized
- how to consult the library key when searching for a book
- how to return books to book tubs: title and colored dot "up in the air"
- how to return magazines to bins: stacked with covers facing up and in the same direction
- how to do small book repairs: children do repairs that require a simple tape job; Janine does repairs that require more than that
- how to organize classroom favorites on the metal book display racks
- how to stack the pillows so they stay neat and tidy

- when and where pillows can be used in the room
- how to hang bigbooks on the skirt hangers
- how many children can fit comfortably in the classroom library at one time; approximately ten in the Bobier library space
- how the classroom library should look at the end of morning-work time/quiet-reading time, etc.
- how to assist one another in putting away books and not "dumping" everything on the two children who have classroom library jobs

READING MATERIALS EXPECTATIONS

Once the children understand the workings of the classroom library, I move into what my expectations are regarding the kinds of books and reading materials they will be selecting for their quiet-reading time. I think of this as structured choice: the children do get to make book choices but within a structure that I provide. In my classroom the children are expected to gather and have the following materials ready for their quiet-reading time:

- nightly reading book
- guided reading group book (if I am meeting with them in a small group, which is a minority of my class)
- anthology
- school library book
- one or two classroom library choices
- one or two magazines (optional)

FIGURE 4–1
Classroom library

During the course of the year I talk often with the children about the kinds of book choices they make, reminding them not to make ho-hum or hurried choices but to choose books that grab their attention as readers. Book choices make the difference in either having a quality quiet-reading time or one where children never get absorbed in their books. They must be invested in their books. It's that simple. When teachers tell me their kids "don't do well" during quiet-reading time, I ask them what kinds of books their kids are reading. (For further information on how I discuss book selection with children, see Chapter 5.)

To help the children gather the required materials, I create a word and picture chart like the charts listing housekeeping responsibilities and morning-work choices and hang this by the easel in the morning. The children consult with this chart—instead of asking me—until they no longer need to. It's different with every child. Some children rely on this chart longer than others do.

The children gather their materials as part of their morning housekeeping responsibilities. I have them do this for two reasons: (1) so their materials are ready at their tables after our class meeting, making for a smooth transition into quiet reading, and (2) the library cannot accommodate an entire class selecting reading materials at one time, so this gives a fifteen- to twenty-minute window for all children to do this in smaller groups.

QUIET-READING EXPECTATIONS

Once the children understand how the library is organized and what reading materials they are expected to gather, I discuss my expectations for quiet-reading time with them. Choosing a reading space, setting the right tone for the room, deciding which books to read first, and addressing movement are four areas to which I give extra time and attention.

Choosing a Reading Space

In my classroom, children are invited to read anywhere in the room—within reason. I tell the children to look for two things when they are making their decision: quiet and comfort. That means different places for different children. The rocking chair is always a favorite spot and is occupied quickly. Some enjoy sitting at their tables, while others prefer to lie on the floor with a pillow under their head. Since we also do partner reading four days a week, the children do have the opportunity to read and share their books with friends, so I want quiet reading to be an individual reading time. Like Karla Kuskin, I want each reader to realize "I can be anything, any person, anywhere, if I just have my book and chair." (1992, 6)

Setting the Right Tone for the Room

In addition to choosing that "just-right reading spot," I also talk with the children about how the room should sound during quiet reading. This is an interesting item to negotiate with beginning readers because they need to read out loud. I adjust my noise-level scale according to where we're at in our year. The beginning of the year, particularly with first-grade readers, is always much noisier than the middle or the end of the year. The children become progressively quieter until by the end of second grade, when many children have transferred to "reading with their eyes instead of their voices," our classroom is very quiet. At the beginning of a new school year, I ask children to soften their quiet-reading voices. I model a full voice, then a soft voice or a whisper voice. I think it's hard to sustain a whisper so I simply ask the children to monitor their voices and aim for a softened or inside reading voice. For a period of time at the beginning of quiet reading, I ask for a volunteer to model the type of quiet-reading voice that's appropriate for this time. I also model how to talk with a person that may be reading too loudly: "Would you please use a softer reading voice? Right now it's too loud for me and I can't concentrate. Thank you." Along with this I model how to be on the receiving end of this type of request: "OK. I didn't know I was bothering you." I do both because I've observed children politely ask others to use a softer reading voice only to be met with "a look" and an ignored request. I want the children to respect communication with one another as much as they respect communication with me.

One thing that helps with setting a good room tone is the way I excuse children when we start our quiet-reading time. I excuse the children from our class meeting a few at a time to get their books and find a place to read instead of allowing the whole group to go at once. Thus, we don't have a mad rush. I let a few settle in before excusing the next group. It takes only a few seconds longer to do it this way but seems to communicate to the children how we approach our quiet-reading time.

Another issue that we wrestle with is singing during quiet-reading time. Understandably, the children want to sing some of the songs that are in their anthologies during quiet-reading time or sing aloud one of the many read-and-sing trade books in our classroom, so I say to the children, "I know you enjoy our songs, but you must sing quietly to yourself or in your head. We are not ready for a group sing-along during our quiet-reading time. If you want to sing later, make sure you have your anthology with you during partner reading, and you can sing with your partner after you finish reading your nightly reading books."

Deciding Which Books to Read First

After space and voice, I establish two ground rules about which books need to be read first during quiet reading. First, the children must reread their nightly reading book from the previous evening, and second, if they are meeting with me in a small guided reading group, they must read that book also. After that, the children are welcome to read the rest of their materials in any order they choose. I do this because I want the children to spend a portion of their quiet-reading time with instructional-level reading materials. In my classroom, guaranteed instructional-level texts include their nightly reading book, small-group book (if they are meeting with me in a small group), and anthology. The other materials they choose may be easier (so are read quickly) or more difficult (so are "read by pictures"), so this provides a nice balance to our quiet-reading time. In addition to that, partner reading takes place right after quiet reading, so the children will have reread their nightly reading books or a portion of them before they read and share their books with a friend. I am a firm believer in rereading. I have observed over and over how rereading builds fluency in beginning readers.

Addressing Movement

Last, I discuss movement in the room during quiet reading. In fact, I allow *little* to *none*. I purposefully have the children gather several items for quiet reading so that they have enough reading materials to last the entire time. Occasionally a child will get up and ask me or another child for help with a word or they will move to a different spot because they aren't comfortable yet. During one quiet-reading session at Bobier, Lee came over to me because she was stumped on a word in the book *Henry and Mudge Get the Cold Shivers* (Rylant 1989).

"I came up with *rudder*," Lee said, pointing to this vexing word problem on the page. She didn't say, "The word rudder doesn't make sense," but I could tell by the confusion in her voice that this was the problem.

"Those are two /b's/," I told her.

"Oh, *rubber*," she said.

"Does that make sense?" I asked her. Lee immediately began rereading from the top of the page without my prompting her to do so:

> The next morning
> Henry brought Mudge
> some ice cubes,
> a rubber hamburger,
> and crackers.

"Uh-huh," Lee said. "It makes sense."

"Good work," I told her. "I didn't have to help you much this time."

I don't mind interruptions like this in the least, nor do I mind children solving a "comfort" problem. As long as good judgment is involved, it's fine. What I do mind is children getting up and going to the library to search for or exchange books, moving to sit by a friend, heading out to the bathroom, or getting a drink. When these things happen—and they always do—I stop those children and remind them of my expectations. When children realize they are expected to settle in and read, they do—as long as they have good books. Again, I think of Lee, who initially struggled with quiet-reading time until her love affair with *Henry and Mudge* (Rylant) books took over.

"At first I didn't like reading because I couldn't find books I exactly loved that much," Lee said to me. "But now I've found Henry and Mudge and they're just at my level."

"I love *Henry and Mudge* books," I said to her.

"Me too," Lee answered. "When you chose the little books for me, I didn't like them that much. Then I found books I loved."

DAILY READING TIME

Quiet reading is a sacred part of our reading workshop. It is a rare day that we don't gather our books and relax into them for a few minutes. Quiet reading is not an "if we have time" item. When we have to, we even work around head lice checks and fire drills. It's as essential as shared reading and partner reading. It is critical independent practice time that children need in order to develop into skillful readers.

When I start quiet-reading time with beginning first-grade children, I aim for ten to fifteen minutes. Even with beginning readers who are doing more picture reading than word reading, pretend reading than real reading, behaving like a reader versus being a reader, I try for that balance of allowing enough time that it's satisfying, but not too much that they become restless and are twirling their books in the air instead of turning the pages. If children finish quiet reading by asking for a little more time, then I feel it's been successful. I want them to look forward to having quiet-reading time the next day and the next day after that.

As the year progresses, I work toward twenty to twenty-five minutes of quiet-reading time. Remarkably, it happens. Children do indeed start reading, books become longer, anthologies have more pages, and studies get under way which open up a new world of books to be explored, and soon even twenty-minutes or twenty-five minutes doesn't feel like enough quiet-reading time. However, I don't increase the time after that. My second-grade kids at Bobier read for a standard twenty- to twenty-five minutes all year,

FIGURE 4–2
Snow: quiet reading

groaning when they had to put down their chapter books because like all readers the world over, they were "just getting into the good part." However, partner reading, shared reading, and writing workshop, which follow quiet reading, are equally important, and I don't want to hurry through those.

Making the Next Transition

The end of quiet-reading time finds us with lots of books and magazines to put away quickly and neatly. The room becomes quite busy for a few minutes. First, the children are responsible for setting their book bags —with nightly reading book—anthologies, and school library books at their table spaces. This is another management piece. These are the items the children will need for partner reading, which occurs right after quiet reading, so this is my way of "readying children and books" for the next part of our reading workshop. Second, the children need to return their classroom library choices/magazines to the proper tubs and stack pillows neatly. We all work together to do this, myself included. I have to do a lot of showing at the beginning of the year, as well as explaining how to be helpful versus silly when we are working elbow to elbow in a small space, but in time we are able to manage this in about three minutes. I prefer this system to that of individual book boxes, book baskets, or tubs of books at tables. I want children to have daily choice during quiet reading. I prefer to teach them how to manage gathering and putting away materials versus restricting them to a weekly set of materials.

FINAL EXPECTATION: SHOWING MYSELF AS A READER

Of course, the last piece in all of this is making sure that I am not just espousing what good readers do, but that I am also living as a reader among my young readers. I keep my own quiet-reading books on the top shelf of our teacher/student storage unit and read a variety of things during this time. This generally includes professional books and journals, new titles for our classroom library that I'm not familiar with, or books that children recommend to me. While I was reading Eddie's recommendation, *The Castle in the Attic* (Winthrop 1985), he sat next to me during quiet reading every day because he just had to know "what part I was in."

I wait to start my reading time until the children are settled into their books. During the first week, I read the entire time and also tend to any small expectations/management problems that are part of any new routine. Mostly, I want the children to see that I value spending time with a book. After the first week or so I change my practice. I read for about five minutes, then begin peering into the children's reading lives through individual conferences. Thus, quiet reading allows two things: children have that all-important reading time, and I have the time to conference with my young readers—jotting down anecdotal notes and taking running records to assess and evaluate their progress. (I discuss how I monitor children's progress through individual reading conferences in Chapter 7.)

I first encountered the idea of children keeping a reading anthology several years ago when I read Regie Routman's first book, *Transitions* (1988). At the time, I was working through my own literature-based reading program and her newly published book was a wonderful resource.

Regie introduced the concept of children keeping notebooks or folders to compile all of the wonderful songs and poems they had learned throughout the year during shared reading. The poems and songs were typed on $8\frac{1}{2} \times 11"$ paper and copied so the children could have their own pages. Regie also included one teacher's sample letter of introduction to the anthology as well as a page titled "Ways to Help Your Child Read at Home." Through the years I have modified this page as well as crafted my own introductory letter to the anthology (see Appendix 4–2). I place both sheets in a plastic sleeve in front of the notebooks so families can read this information when children bring their anthologies home for nightly reading.

Setting Up the Anthology

I organize anthologies differently with first graders than second graders. In first grade, the notebook is minimally organized: songs and poetry are mixed together and pages are numbered in order as we add them.

Second-grade anthologies are considerably more sophisticated. At Bobier the anthologies I used had five categories, with notebook dividers marking and separating each section:

Section 1: Poems
Section 2: Songs
Section 3: Cartoons/Comics
Section 4: U.S. & World News
Section 5: The Mini-Page—a small newspaper published for children in the *San Diego Union-Tribune* that I reduced and copied for classroom use

Again, family helpers assist with preparing the anthologies by writing the divider tabs and placing them in the notebooks so we can start our anthologies quickly and easily. Both first- and second-grade anthologies have a large three-hole-punched Ziploc bag attached to the back that we use for storing little books and a small dowel the children use for their own individual pointer when reading.

For the first two sections, I type and copy poems and songs that we read and sing during our shared-reading sessions so the children have their own individual copies for rereading. The Cartoons/Comics section developed out of my love for reading the funny papers every morning and occasionally sharing some of the more "literal-humor" cartoons with my kids. When I had enough collected, I taped cartoons onto a sheet of paper, titled it, "Room 12's Comic Page," and made copies of it for the children. We read our comics page during a shared-reading session, and the children added it to the third section of their anthologies.

The U.S. & World News section connects to our "What's in the News?" newspaper clippings and discussions we have during our morning class meetings. After we fill one chart paper with recent news events, I type the summary captions we write as a class when posting the clippings, organizing U.S. News on one side of the paper and World News on the other (see Appendix 4–3.) I also copy U.S. and world maps so the children can locate and highlight with markers "the news" on these maps. We go through this information and add it to our anthologies during one shared-reading session.

The last section is for reduced copies of The Mini-Page. The *San Diego Union-Tribune* publishes this page weekly—many newspapers publish a similar weekly "children's page" that would also work—although I didn't copy it on a weekly basis for the children. I waited until it contained relevant biographical, historical, or scientific information, then made reduced copies for the children's anthologies. (I always bought the weekly Mini-Page to our classroom and gave a brief "newspaper talk" on Friday mornings during my announcement time. We stored these Mini-Pages in a basket in our classroom library so the children could read them during quiet reading.) Again, this kind of information is read together during a shared-reading session before the children add it to their anthologies.

Adding Pages to the Anthology

Before the children add pages to their anthologies, I do the following preparation work:

First, I type the words to the songs, poems, or news items, or I compile cartoons. Then I make front-to-back copies and three-hole punch them so they are ready for notebooks. An interesting issue that I consider when typing these items is the size and type of font that I use. At the beginning of the year with first-grade children, I use a clean, large font, e.g., helvetica or avant garde. Avant garde does not have the funny /a/ and /g/, which is helpful for beginning readers also. The print is easy to read and the large size gives their little fingers room to track the words. As the year progresses, I use different fonts so the children learn how to handle a variety of print types when reading; palatino and technical are later favorites of mine. I have found that children learn to cope with a variety of fonts quite easily.

After typing and three-hole punching, I collate the sheets so I can pass them out to the children easily and efficiently. I also have strips of adhesive hole reinforcers ready, with the exact number the children need for their pages so I can hand these out quickly, too. Placing hole reinforcers on the top and bottom holes of each page prevents the sheets from tearing out of the notebooks. Pages get a lot of wear, tear, and turning throughout the year, and I have found that the extra time and expense are well worth it when initially adding pages to the anthologies.

Once the materials are prepared and distributed to the children, they go to work preparing the sheets for their notebooks. This process includes writing their names on the bottom of each page and applying hole reinforcers to the top and bottom holes of each page.

When everyone has completed these tasks, we number the pages together. Up in front, with my own set of pages, I show the children how to mark the number clearly and neatly in the top right-hand corner of each sheet. Then, I model turning that paper over and writing the next number in the top right-hand corner. This next piece is tricky for some kids and challenges their ability to follow oral and visual directions, but it's a good challenge. I show children they can manage this next part in one of two ways: (1) They can turn this first page back over to the front side and place it underneath the entire stack, or (2) they can lay this page down beside them or in front of them, front side down.

Once children decide which process works best for them, we continue numbering pages until we're finished with the set. My goal is to help children get through this process in an organized way and not get their papers mixed up with one another's—a very real possibility with young learners. I am specific with these processes so the children begin learning critical organizational skills. At the beginning of the year, when I start this routine, the children partner up, as it helps those who are less confident manage this process. It also frees me from being a many-tentacled teacher trying to keep everyone's papers in order—impossible and not enjoyable.

After these three organizational tasks are completed—names written, hole reinforcers applied, pages numbered—I help the children place the pages in their notebooks. When the notebooks have dividers, I have to show the children how to flip the dividers and place the sheets after them, otherwise, I model flipping all the inside pages toward the front cover of the notebook and adding the new set behind. After pages are in notebooks, we choral read poems or cartoons, sing songs, or go through the news or Mini-Page (or similar paper).

Illustrating Poems and Songs

Unless I use a commercially printed piece with black-line illustrations, which I rarely do, I deliberately give the children the poems and songs without pictures so they can draw their own. I prefer that they do their own artwork rather than color someone else's. The prepared drawings may be easier, but I don't think they are as interesting or personal as the children's own work. Even with a small piece like a poem or song, I want the children to give it their own personal mark.

At the beginning of the year, I do an illustration lesson in which I touch on these key points:

1. Draw with your pencil first if you're unsure, then go over your pencil drawing with a crayon.
2. Illustrate around the text with pictures and shading, not on the text. You need to be able to read the words easily.
3. Match your drawings to the song/poem so that your picture helps you remember what it is. This is especially helpful for beginning readers who rely on picture cues to help them with their reading.

4. Take your time and do your best work. This will be an important reading book all year. I want you to be proud of your work.
5. Walk around and see what other children are doing as that may inspire more ideas for you.

I draw my illustrations on each page, enjoying instructional conversation with the children as I show them how to pay attention to the details of their work. I know that saying to young children, "Now illustrate your pages," will not produce the work they are capable of doing. Seeing the illustration process modeled not only increases the time they spend on their own drawings, but also makes for more sophisticated, thoughtful work.

After I complete this illustration lesson and excuse my group to their tables to begin their own work, I move my easel with the illustrated pages closer to their work table area so the children can look at my drawings as they work. This is helpful in two ways. First, the children can look at my pages to help them recall the song or poem if they've forgotten it and aren't reading the print yet, which happens often at the beginning of first grade. Second, if the children don't have their own illustration ideas, they are welcome to use my ideas. Artists learn by imitating their mentors. I treat this concept in a similar way in my classroom. In general, I observe children using many of my illustration ideas at the beginning of the year, then gradually shifting to their own. Toward midyear, I also change my practice and begin illustrating my pages before we meet as a group to add pages to our anthologies so that the children have more time for their illustration work. I don't belabor the "modeling" once they begin doing quality illustration work. I keep a notebook of my illustrated anthology pages so I can reuse them from year to year.

I also encourage the children to look to others in our room for inspiration. With my last group, we came to recognize Kayalani and David as art experts and learned a lot from their artistic insight and perspective, as well as the way they both committed themselves to their work. We also examined the work of trade book illustrators we admired; James Marshall, Eric Carle, Leo Lionni, Tomie dePaola, Marc Brown, Sucie Stevenson, Arnold Lobel, Ruth Heller, Bruce Degen, Jill Murphy, Steven Kellogg, Barbara Cooney, Peter Parnall, Chris Van Allsburg, Lynn Munsinger, and Barbara Firth were favorites.

Adding, Illustrating, and Storing Little Books

In addition to the poems, songs, news, and comics, the children also store their little black-line books in a Ziploc bag in the back of their anthologies. These little books can be awkward for the children to store, so I solve this problem by using large, three-hole-punched Ziploc bags that can be placed on the rings in the back of the notebooks. The Ziploc is easy to open and close at the top, which keeps the little books safe. When the children's bags become worn or ripped, we replace them with new ones. At the beginning of the school year, I ask for donations of large Ziploc bags for this purpose, as it's one more way families can support classroom life on a limited budget. I always find a willing parent to three-hole punch the bags, so again, preparation is manageable.

The little books that I copy and that parents help assemble are made from the black-line masters that Nellie Edge provides with her read-and-sing bigbooks. After we enjoy the bigbook several times during shared-reading sessions, I distribute the little books to the children so they have them for independent reading. The children add these little books to their anthologies at the same time they add other items each week.

The little book black lines that I use include illustrations, so the first time I give a little book to the children, we sit in a circle and color together, either with crayons or colored pencils. The illustrations are small and challenging for little hands to color, but as I model, and we converse and color, the children begin to understand the pace and how to choose colors, and they give their work time and care. I changed to doing an explicit process like this because when I first began using the little books, I was dismayed at how little time the children spent coloring them. More often than not, there would be a smear of one color all over the page, and that was the child's attempt at coloring the pictures. I knew the illustrations were small, but I didn't think the children were valuing the little book enough if they were content with that level of coloring. That's when I decided to gather my group together to color the first little book so they would slow down and value the process. It helped tremendously.

My last group of second graders became so adept at organizing that they even discovered a way to organize their little books inside their Ziploc bags. It started with Joseph, who organized his little books by shape and size one evening when he brought his anthology home for nightly reading. He ended up with three sizes and he held each group together with rubber bands. My group was quite impressed by this; thus began a whirlwind of organizing and rubber banding little books.

Besides the little books, the other item we store in this plastic bag is a small, 6" wooden dowel that children use as a pointer when reading in their anthologies. The children love them. There seems to be something magical about having a pointer instead of using your index finger to track the words when reading. I understand. I am happy with little things, too. The pointers aren't fancy—no glitter or fancy ends—but they work beautifully. I love simplicity.

Organizing Anthology Black Lines

Over the years, I've gathered and typed quite a large collection of songs and poems for anthologies. In terms of my organization, I keep these black lines in two large notebooks. The first notebook has alphabetic dividers for organizing the material alphabetically by title. The second notebook is organized by theme or subject, so when I have a lot of material in one particular area, e.g., trees, I label the divider "trees" and store all the songs, poems, and information in this section. I organize this notebook alphabetically also. This is a quick, efficient system for me and I don't have to go wandering through files searching for pieces when I need them.

Establishing good quiet-reading habits and developing beautiful, yet informative anthologies are two processes that require clear, consistent expectations and time. Helping children slow down in a world that moves increasingly faster is hard work when their tendency is to rush, finish, and move on to the next thing, whatever that may be. It's interesting to watch how long it takes children to settle into quiet reading and their anthology work. I can tell when the majority of the group has turned the corner and has committed to taking more time: the room is settled, we are relaxed, and my reminders and demonstrations decrease in frequency. As a community of readers, we begin valuing quiet time with good books.

As I reflect on quiet reading in my classroom, I realize that more than anything, I am trying to re-create in my classroom the childhood book world that I loved at home. I don't have pink blankets or crocheted afghans for the children to curl up with at school, but we do have pillows, good books, a quiet room, and time.

5 | NIGHTLY READING AND PARTNER READING

We must read in order to read.
—E. L. Konigsberg, "Newbery Medal Acceptance"

Eddie and his dad are both readers. Toward the end of Eddie's first-grade year, he was immersed in *The Castle in the Attic* (Winthrop 1985). At the beginning of his second-grade year, Eddie was ready to delve into C.S. Lewis' *The Chronicles of Narnia*. I found it extraordinary—Eddie's first language was Spanish; his second language, English—but not worrisome in terms of "book level" because Eddie read at home every night with his dad. What Eddie couldn't read, his dad read to him. What Eddie couldn't understand, his dad explained. However, Eddie did most of the reading. His dad and I had a conversation about it during our January school conference because his dad was worried that the books might be too difficult for Eddie; however, he mentioned that when he discussed the book with Eddie he seemed to understand everything so thought he was doing OK. I told Eddie's father that Eddie wouldn't be reading books like *The Chronicles of Narnia* if he wasn't reading with him every night. I still remember his reply, "We do our best," his dad said. "Some nights I'm really tired and we don't read as much, but I know Eddie likes to read."

Eddie's dad was a committed reading parent.

Eddie, and all the other children in my classroom, tucked books into tie-dyed book bags to take home every night to read with their families. Most families don't have the beginning reading books that young children, particularly first graders, need, so providing books for home reading is a necessity. I aim for literacy to be not only part of the fabric of classroom life, but also family life.

At Back-to-School Night, I told families that the children would develop into strong readers if they read every day at school and every night at home. I reiterated that learning how to read and write is a team effort. I reminded parents that with a large class, I couldn't give individual attention to all children every day, but they could. I also asked families to talk with me if there wasn't anyone in their family or neighborhood who read English, because I would be happy to find an older student to read with their child. In my four years at Bobier, I never had to do this. Often, second-language parents learned right along with their children, or there were siblings or cousins at home who helped with the reading. The problem I faced more frequently was with families who were capable of reading with their children but didn't take the time to do it.

At Bobier, I also came to understand that some of these families had not had good experiences with school or reading instruction and were somewhat hesitant to work with their young readers at home. So, during school conferences, I talked with and showed families ways to read with their child, have good book talk, and solve word problems. I told them that it was important for their young readers to see that they valued reading. In her book *Family Literacy*, Denny Taylor writes: "it seems reasonable to assume that if literacy becomes socially significant in the lives of the parents, it is likely to become socially significant in the lives of the children" (1983, 88).

At Bobier, I also had to work from the opposite assumption; that is, I aimed to make literacy significant in the lives of the children so that it would become significant in the lives of their families. My main concern was getting books in the hands of these kids so they could read every night at home.

NIGHTLY READING

In my classroom three items are needed for a nightly reading program: books, book bags, and reading logs. Each of these is critical to the success of the program.

Books

The books in my classroom library, both school and personal, are the ones that children check out for nightly reading. I don't have a separate collection of books; rather, every book is fair game for nightly reading. This includes both paperback books and hardbound books. Teachers often ask me if I allow children to take home my hardbound books, and I do. I don't like to make distinctions between school and home books. I don't like the message that "separating books" imparts. My goal is to build trust and communicate how to respect and care. I trust that my conversations about book care will have an impact on how children will treat books at home. Most of the time I'm not disappointed. When books are lost or damaged—which does happen, but not often—I ask that families reimburse us, if they can, for replacements. I still remember when Christina brought her saved-up allowance money to school one morning, all wadded up in an envelope, and handed it to me with big, soulful eyes.

"I spilled my juice on my book last night when I was reading it at the dinner table," she said. "My mom told me not to read at the table but I didn't listen to her. So I am giving you my allowance."

I was subdued just listening to Christina, and her teary eyes made it even harder.

"You're brave for being honest and for bringing your money to buy a new book," I told her, giving her a hug. "It's hard for me to take it but I think it's the right thing to do, Christina."

I hated taking her allowance money. That was a difficult damaged-book experience.

Book bags

Book bags are made out of pillowcases during our first week of school. In my before-school letter, I ask children to bring one pillowcase and an extra if they have one, and a set of 54" shoelaces to school for our book bag project. I cut pillowcases in two—each pillowcase becomes two book bags—and recruit family volunteers to sew them into book bags.

After the book bags are sewn, I write the children's first and last names in large letters with a black permanent marker along one edge of the book bags. The children then create "ears" with rubber bands all around their bags to prepare them for tie-dying. Choosing which color or colors we should tie-dye our book bags is actually our first math project and involves doing either a favorite color graph or class survey.

Once we decide on colors, I bring four large buckets to school and we do the tie-dying outside. I take the buckets home in the evening, run the bags through a cold-water wash cycle, then dry them. I bring them back to school for the children to pull off any remaining rubber bands (most come out in the dryer), and thread shoelaces through the top casings. I do this type of book bag process for two reasons: (1) so books will be protected as they are carried between school and home, and (2) so children have a hand in making their own book bags, thus increasing their investment in keeping the books safe. Sometimes book bags need repair during the year, which I do or the children's families do. I also make extra book bags at the beginning of the year for those occasions when book bags need to be replaced or a new student arrives.

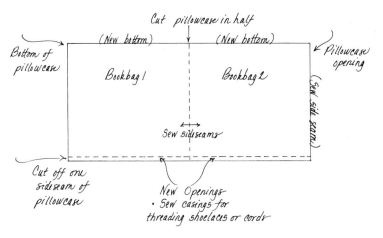

FIGURE 5–1
Cutting and sewing book bags

Reading Logs

Reading logs are small (journal-sized) and assembled by family helpers at home. (See Appendix 5–1 for journal assembly information.) We construct reading logs in this manner:

- cover: artwork by the children
- cover information (written in black permanent marker):
  - "My Reading Journal"
  - child's first and last name
  - school year
  - room number
- first inside pages: letter to families with nightly reading information (Appendix 5–2)
- reading log pages, which include spaces to write date, book title, how many pages read, parent signature, self-evaluation of reading and listening to partner

In my classroom, the reading log serves several purposes. First, it is the way children and I keep track of what they're reading. Second, it is a "book checkout," as it is the only place the children record what books they take home. Third, it is a record of whether families are reading every night with their children, because the reading log must be signed by a family member every evening. And fourth, it is a tool for self-evaluation, as the children rate themselves—with either a happy, straight, or unhappy face—on how well they read and how well they listened to their partner during partner reading. By the end of the year or two years, this reading log becomes a memory book of each child's path to literacy. I hope that families tuck them away for safe-keeping because in essence, they show a literary history.

Book Selection: Getting Started

I handle book selection differently with first-grade children than with second-grade children. With first-grade readers, I keep the beginning month of nightly reading quite structured in terms of book choice. At Bobier, I never had children enter my first-grade classroom who were already reading, so this impacted my practice also. A majority of the children were at the beginning, or emergent stage of reading and needed simple text.

I analyze all emergent and early reading books before adding them to my classroom library, but I do take extra care when I select books for beginning first-grade children to choose from for their nightly reading. The list below represents the items I look for in emergent and early readers:

Text Considerations: Selecting Emergent and Early Readers
Print Characteristics
- clear font
- appropriate size for young readers

- appropriate amount of space between words
- print that is legible on the page—not distorted or difficult to read due to illustration interference

Text Layout
- consistent, predictable placement of print on pages throughout text
- words, phrases, sentences, or short paragraphs are contained to one complete page or two facing pages

Content
- meaning-centered vs. phonic-centered
- story idea/information appropriate, interesting, and appealing to young readers
- story begs for rereading

Quality of Illustration
- illustrations support the text in a complete or partial manner
- illustrations are located above, below, or beside corresponding text—not on the next page
- cartoons are tastefully done, if that style of illustration is used
- illustrations are delightful to children
- illustrations invite further discussion about the story, deepen understanding of the text
- a variety of mediums are used for illustrations in different books
- the medium used complements the text, information, or story idea

The day we begin our nightly reading program, I gather my first-grade readers around me and start the process like this:

"This will be the first evening you take home a book from school to read to your families. I want you to feel comfortable with your book tonight, so I am going to help you with your book choice. I have chosen five different little books and I have eight copies of each book. I'm going to read each book to you and then you can decide which book you would like to check out to take home to read tonight."

After reading each of the little books to the children, I ask the children to think about which book would be best for them. My lesson continues in this manner:

"I want you to choose a book that's 'just right' for you. It needs to be a book that you will enjoy reading to your family tonight. Also, you need to have a second book choice in mind, just in case you don't get your first book choice today. By the end of the week, you'll have had a chance to read four of the books because every day we'll exchange books with each other."

I end this discussion by calling out the book titles and handing out individual copies to the children. Each week after that, I introduce five new sets of books for the children to choose from. At Bobier, we were supported with funds for sets of little books and bigbooks (housed in a central book storage room), which made this type of book-selection process possible at the beginning of the year. When I don't have this resource, I eliminate this process and begin with what I consider the second phase of book selection with first-grade readers, which I describe next.

By the end of the first month, I'm ready to leave this structured book-selection format, and I begin introducing more of the little-book and beginning-reader titles in the classroom library for the children to choose from. This is also the same process I use for beginning second-grade children, except I have a wider range of book levels available for them to choose from. Choosing from a larger selection of books requires more skill on the part of the children, so I talk with my young readers about how to navigate through the decision-making process:

"I would like you to start choosing books from our classroom library now, and that requires a little more thinking on your part. I want to talk through some 'book points' with you before you begin selecting books for yourself."

The next part of my book-selection discussion with the children covers the points listed below.

1. The book needs to capture your eye and make you say, "I want to read this!"
2. You need to open it and see if it is a book you're ready to tackle.
3. You need to check for size of print and how much text is on the page.
4. You need to think about whether the pictures help you as a reader.
5. You need to read the first page or first few pages to see how you're doing with the book:
   - If you're able to read everything on the first few pages, it's "too easy" for nightly reading.
   - If you're having a lot of trouble just reading the first page or so, then it's probably "too difficult."
   - If you can tackle the book but it has a few challenges, then most likely it's "just right" for nightly reading.

After talking through these book points, my conversation with the children continues in this way: "Now, when you're selecting your book, I want you to know that I am always available for a second opinion. We all need different levels of books as readers, and we all like different kinds of books, so you really need to think through this carefully. When you are selecting your quiet-reading books this morning, I would like you to choose your book for nightly reading tonight. I'll come around during quiet-reading time to see what each of you has chosen. I'll let you know if I have concerns, and if I do, I'll help you choose a different book."

Once we enter this world of self-selecting from our classroom library, it becomes a matter of watching and helping children with their book choices each day, or every few days, once they begin to read longer books. After this first book-selection session where I ask the children to choose a book in the morning so I can check it during quiet reading, the children begin selecting their nightly reading books after they finish their partner reading.

As the children become immersed in selecting their own reading books, I do several things to facilitate getting good books into their hands all year long, including

- giving book readings, reviews, and recommendations every day during shared reading: "You will love this book for nightly reading," I say
- becoming a reference librarian, noticing what the children are interested in so I can make book recommendations for their nightly reading
- discussing with the children "living like a reader" and keeping a mental list of book(s) they can't wait to read next
- doing daily check-ins with children to see what books they are choosing for themselves
- discussing with the children that they need to be on the lookout for favorite authors/illustrators because if they enjoy one of their books, they will most likely enjoy other books in the series also
- engaging the children in giving book talks and recommending books to one another (see Chapter 6)
- discussing with the children how they can help one another make book selections

Our classroom becomes very busy each day when children are making their own book selections. It eases up a bit as children begin to develop their reading skills and tackle longer books, and not every child needs to select a different book every day. Inevitably, there are times when children do end up taking home books that are either "too easy" or "too difficult" for them. Sometimes I don't catch it, or other times, I'm not quite sure about the book level myself, and I have to say to them, "Take it home, try it, and see what you think. It may be too difficult for you. Let your family know you're experimenting tonight."

When young readers are intent on taking home books that I know are too difficult for them, I say, "You are welcome to take that book home and have someone in your family read it to you. However, you must also have a book that is 'just right' for you to read. You need to read tonight also." So, the child takes home two books that evening. Everyone wins.

Having self-selection of books at the heart of my reading program requires constant monitoring and observation of children. It's hard work, but I believe in it. I prefer it over small-group instruction where I am choosing the books for the children, although occasionally I do meet with struggling readers in small guided reading groups in addition to their other reading work. With a daily system to check in with children, and a system for individual reading conferences, I know each day what children are reading and whether it is appropriate for them.

I believe there's a lot to be said for challenge and interest with young readers. When children begin developing a keen interest in books and discover there are books about something they're interested in, e.g., Eddie and castles, while also being immersed in a classroom world that revolves around books, it is quite motivating. I observe children become immersed in books that I never would have chosen for them. When Chris decided he was going to read *James and the Giant Peach* (Dahl 1961) at the end of his second-grade year, I never dreamed he would stay with it. He and his mother read together every night. I listened with amazement as Chris read about the adventures of James and his oversized insect friends during his individual reading conferences. Every year, I remind myself to trust the abilities and minds of primary children. My work is to establish an atmosphere for them to make book decisions and be in charge of themselves as readers. Instead of me, the teacher, taking on the sole responsibility of selecting books and matching levels of text to instructional levels of the children, I do this process, with the utmost care, with the children.

Yes, there are children who have difficulty with the self-selection process. However, every year it has been a minority of the class, and it doesn't deter me from having children select their own books. I recognize these children quickly and work with them on selecting appropriate, interesting books for as long as it takes. Some children develop these skills quickly, others need a short period of assistance, and still others require sustained help. With my last group, I had to assist six children for most of the two years I taught them. I kept their names on a Post-it note on the front of my reading assessment clipboard as a reminder to myself to continually check in with them when they were ready for new books. That, and individual reading conferences, were my methods for guiding their reading.

Book Checkout

Once the children have selected their books, they need to record the titles in their reading logs. I make a transparency of the reading log page so I can work at my overhead with the children gathered around me. They have these items with them: book, pencil, reading log, and their anthology, which acts as a "desk" anytime we do work when we're gathered together on the floor. Like with all new routines, the children pair up to help each other. I keep some children closer to me because I know they will need my assistance, too.

First I show the children where to write the date. We write it in what we call "short form" (9-5-96) because the space is small. Next I show them where to write the title of the book. First graders need a lot of help writing the title so I show them:

- how to write the words small because the space isn't very big
- how to write the first two or three words then end with an ellipsis if the title is too long
- that some titles have the funny /a's/ or /g's/, but they can write the /a/ and /g/ the way they normally do
- how to put tiny spaces between words (versus the standard finger space when writing), so the words don't run together

The next space on the page is for families to sign or write their comments after the children read their book to them, so I show children where family members are supposed to sign or write a comment and model how to ask their families to do this: "Would you please sign or write about my reading in my reading log? Ms. Janine likes to see it when she reads with me at school."

The last space is for the children to evaluate themselves as readers and listeners after they've completed their partner reading.

I gather first-grade children around the overhead for a solid two weeks to help them fill out their reading logs before they begin doing this on their own at their tables. Even then, I do a lot of monitoring and teaching for a

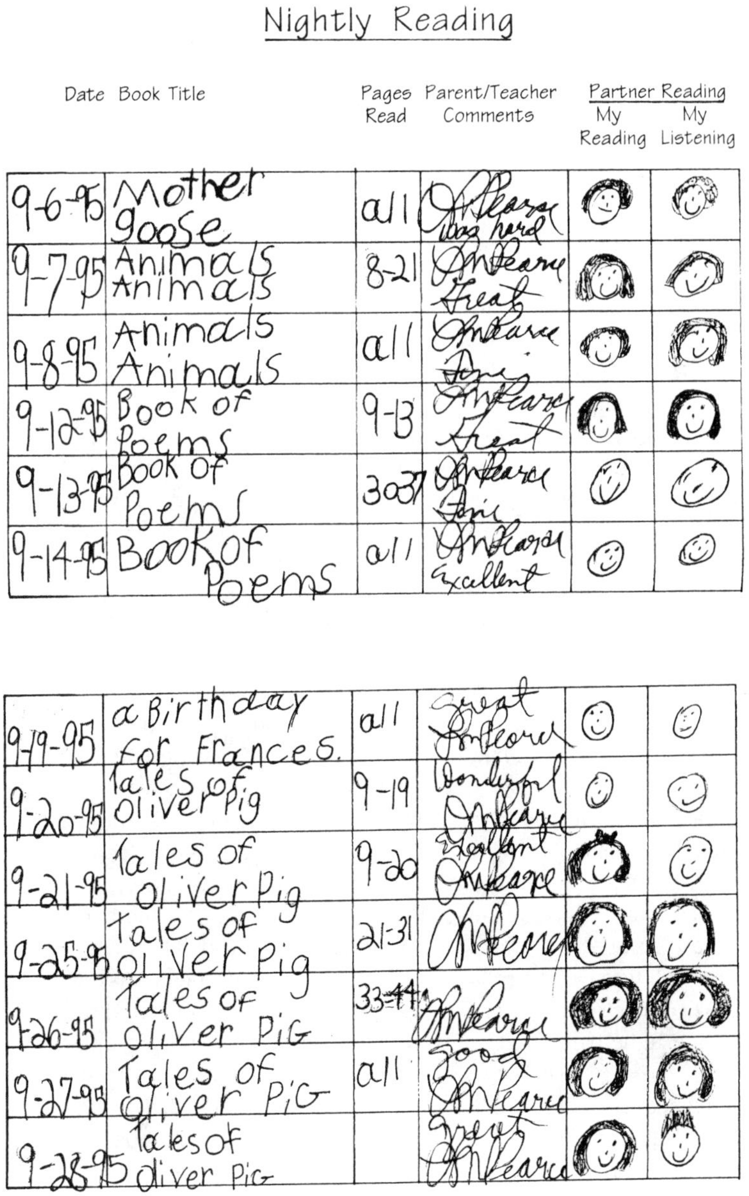

Nightly Reading

Date	Book Title	Pages Read	Parent/Teacher Comments	Partner Reading: My Reading	Partner Reading: My Listening
9-6-95	Mother goose	all	was hard		
9-7-95	Animals Animals	8-21	Great		
9-8-95	Animals Animals	all	Fine		
9-12-95	Book of Poems	9-13	Great		
9-13-95	Book of Poems	30-37	Fine		
9-14-95	Book of Poems	all	Excellent		
9-19-95	a Birthday for Frances.	all	Great		
9-20-95	Tales of oliver Pig	9-19	Wonderful		
9-21-95	Tales of oliver Pig	9-20	Excellent		
9-25-95	Tales of oliver Pig	21-31			
9-26-95	Tales of oliver Pig	33-44			
9-27-95	Tales of oliver Pig	all	Good		
9-28-95	Tales of oliver Pig		Great		

FIGURE 5–2
Lisa's second-grade reading log page

good month before I begin to see a glimmer of independence. Children frequently assist one another and any adults who happen to enter our classroom during this time are put to work immediately. Eventually, the children are able to evaluate their reading and listening, record the date and title of their book, and tuck everything in their book bags to take home with them in a reasonable amount of time. In general, second-grade children are able to do this quickly and efficiently from the start of the year. Even when they are reading longer books over a period of days, I still have them record the book title each day so we have a record of the amount of time they've spent reading one book.

It is a lofty goal to expect that all families will read with their children every night and that all children will want to read to their families every night. I aim for this goal every day, but realistically, when I do my daily check-in, I discover there are generally one, two, or three children who didn't read the previous evening with their families, always for a multitude of reasons: sports practice, family or church events, "I forgot my book bag at school," "I left my book bag at daycare or in the neighbor's car," or "No one had time to read with me." I hear everything. I'm not concerned if it's an occasional occurrence; that's daily life. However, when it becomes a pattern of two or three days in a row, or it starts to seem frequent, then I pursue it with the child's family either through Note Book correspondence, a phone call, or a school conference.

Solutions are different for every family. One year with D'Mitri's family, the only solution that worked was to have D'Mitri's older brother come to my classroom every day after school to read with him before they went home. In my last group, when no one was reading with Leticia at home, I talked with her older sister, a fifth grader, about the importance of doing this, and she began reading with Leticia every night. Timmy's family believed that "school work should be done at school," and that they were "just too busy in the evenings for homework." Timmy was a tentative reader, so I decided to read with Timmy every night after school for fifteen minutes. His older brother, who I'd also taught in first grade, came to my room to finish his homework while Timmy read with me. It made me realize how helpful an after-school homework room would be for some children whose families wouldn't or couldn't spend time working with them in the evenings. It's an increasing problem that schools face.

Brenda's problem was just the opposite. For the most part, her mother or father was willing to fit reading time in, despite her mother working nights as a nurse, but Brenda either didn't want to read with them or conveniently left her book bag at school. The underlying problem was that Brenda hadn't connected to books. Brenda was an active girl and would rather play T-ball or tetherball than curl up with a good book. Reading required every ounce of patience she had. Her father and I went through pages of correspondence regarding the absence of nightly reading and tattered book bags.

Finally, Brenda "fell in love" with books during the early part of her second-grade year. *George and Martha* hooked her. When she discovered James

Marshall's wickedly amusing stories about two fine friends, she began devouring every *George and Martha* book we had in our classroom library. I didn't have as many nightly reading battles with Brenda after that because she finally found book friends that were interesting to her. Those books gave her tremendous pleasure and confidence as a reader.

Brenda is a classic example of a child to whom I will say, "Are you sure you want to read that book? Are you sure it looks interesting enough to you? Do you think you're going to love this? If not, then choose something else. I'm happy to help you. Books need to grab you and say, 'Read me. Discover what's inside my pages.' Don't waste your time on something that doesn't." It's one of the recurring lectures I use as I help children select their own books and shape their own reading lives.

PARTNER READING

In my quest to have children involved in real reading in as many ways as possible, I decided to structure a time for children to read together and also engage in good book talk. I had several thoughts in mind when I began experimenting with partner reading. I wanted the children to:

- have more reading practice
- hear each other as readers
- help each other as readers
- see what other children were reading
- have the opportunity to talk informally about the books they were reading
- begin recommending books to each other

In my classroom, partner reading is connected to nightly reading. The books that the children choose for their nightly reading time are the same books they read to each other during partner reading. Partner reading occurs right after quiet reading and takes place four days a week, Tuesday through Friday. I don't have partner reading on Mondays because the children don't take book bags home on Fridays. I've discovered that books end up in all sorts of strange places when they go home over the weekend, so I tell children to read their own books on those evenings. A Tuesday-through-Friday partner-reading schedule works well because that gives us extra time on Mondays to set up our individual spelling folders for the week.

Getting Started

When I begin partner reading with my class, my first lesson focuses on procedural items and expectations. We form a circle, and the children have these items with them: book bag with nightly reading book, anthology, and school library book.

First, I ask the children to take their nightly reading books out of their book bags so I can jot down what they read on a class grid I prepared for the second section of my reading assessment clipboard. In my head, I use Nancie

Atwell's term, "status-of-the-class" for this conference (1998, 141). Whereas she uses it to check in with her writers before they go their separate ways, I use it to record, every day, what books the children are reading before they begin their partner reading. This conference is critical to the way I monitor children's book choices and how their reading lives are taking shape. It's an opportunity for children to hear what their friends are reading. It becomes a

Room 12: 2nd Grade
Nightly & Partner Reading
Janine Chappell 8.93

	9/14/05	9/16/05	9/19/05	9/20/05	9/21/05	9/22/05
Christie Elliott	The Color Box	The Jng-Prince	Ab.	Ab.	Same	all God's Critters...
Kayalani Evans	Hey Diddle Diddle	Same	Bargain for Frances	Same	Same	Same
Jonathan Garcia	Henry & Mudge: Fun Time	Just Up a Tree	Henry & Mudge	Same	Just Me & My Dad	Thide Mulligan
Brenda Gill	Henry & Mudge: Under Yellow Moon	Same	Same	Just a few words, Mr. Lincoln	Same	Same
Roni Heedinpyle	Mother Goose	Same	Sing a Song of Popcorn	Same	Tales of Amanda Pig	Same
Bianca Huerta	With Grace to School	Same	Same	Same	Same	Same
Tracy Hyman	New Kid on the Block	Same	Same	Same	Same	Mystery of the Blue Ring ch 1-4
Harold Leary	My first book... Space	Same	Same	Nature Search	Same	Days of Jng & Food

FIGURE 5–3
Status-of-the-Class: Nightly Reading

daily moment to connect over a book, share a knowing smile, or offer encouragement. If I treat nightly reading seriously, I believe my young readers will also.

When I do this status-of-the-class, I jot down the titles quickly, using abbreviations or short form to speed up the process. I ask children to listen quietly so that the process will go quickly. If young readers aren't sure of the titles, I ask them to hold up their books so I can read them. Once the children get into the routine of doing this, it takes three to five minutes. I write quickly. After I take a status-of-the-class, my opening lesson follows this format:

> Four days a week we are going to have partner-reading time. I want you to be able to share your nightly reading books with each other so you can find out what other kids in our classroom are reading. I also know that in order to become a good reader you need to read a lot, so this is one more time for you to read in our classroom. It's different from quiet reading where you read by yourself, and shared reading where we read together as a whole group. Partner reading is time for you to read to a friend and help a friend as a reader. It's a time for you to talk about good books.
>
> There are three things that we need to talk about before you start partner reading. The first one is how to find a partner, the second one is how I expect you to read with your partner, and the third one is what I expect you to do after you read with your partner.
>
> In this classroom I want you to choose your own partner each time we have partner reading and I have some expectations for how you will do that. I want you to ask that person politely, "Will you be my partner, please?" You may not refuse anyone in our classroom unless you already have a partner. If that's the case, then say, "Thanks for asking me, but I already have a partner. I'd like to read with you another day." If someone is left without a partner, and she or he asks to be part of your group, please accept that student graciously, saying, "Yes, you may read with us." If you notice someone is left without a partner and that person isn't joining a group, please say to him or her, "You may read with us. We'll make room for you." Each day I expect you to find a new partner.

At this point in my lesson, I ask the children to find their partners and form a new circle. If I were to go through everything involved in partner reading at one time, it would be too much for them to remember. Once the children are partnered, my discussion continues.

"Now that you have your partners, it's time for you to read to each other. This is the procedure I would like you to follow:

1. Decide who's going to read first. That person takes out her nightly reading book from her book bag, and the person listening leaves everything inside.

2. When you are the reader, read as much as you read last night. (When readers occasionally forget their books at home, they choose a "known" classroom library book for partner-reading time.) Hold the book between the two of you so you can both see the book clearly. If you are in a threesome, the reader always needs to sit in the middle so the other two people can see the print clearly. When you are reading, you need to:
   - use your finger to point to the words as you read
   - take your time reading; no rushing
   - point out interesting things in the book or the illustrations to your partner—the things you talked about with your family last night

   When you are the listener, you need to:
   - listen carefully
   - help your partner solve problem words the best you can
   - ask your partner to read a sentence or a page again if she's had several problems
   - take your partner's hand in your own to help him point at the words while reading if this is difficult for him to do

3. If there's still time after you've both read your books, or the part of your book that you read last night, you may reread your books if you'd like, or you may read your anthologies or school library books together. I'll let you know when partner reading is over."

While children are reading, I begin roaming the circle, facilitating the process where needed. I:

- help children solve problem words
- tell them to sit closer together so they can see their books better
- remind children to put their books in their book bags if they're not reading
- show children how to help each other point to the words, in first grade especially
- remind children to talk to each other about their books or interesting things they notice about the books or illustrations

This initial partner-reading time lasts about ten minutes. Mainly I want them to understand the procedure and expectations involved. At the end of this time, I talk with my group about how to close up partner-reading time.

"I think you've all had a chance to finish reading to each other so we need to finish up for today. You need to have a book for tonight, so you can:

- switch books with your partner,
- switch books with someone else in our circle,
- find a new book in our classroom library, or
- continue with the book you're reading if you're not finished.

After you have your book settled for tonight, we'll gather at the overhead so I can show you how to record it in your reading log."

Continuing Partner Reading

As the children become familiar with the procedures and expectations for partner reading, the routine smoothes out, and they get down to the business of reading and sharing good books with each other. Generally it takes about two weeks for the children and me to work through any problems and to feel comfortable with partner reading. Soon, they are able to do the status-of-the-class conference, choose partners, read with partners, select books if they need to, record them in their reading logs, rate themselves on how well they read and listened that day, and tuck everything in their book bags—all in the space of about thirty minutes.

To help the children deepen their work as readers, teachers, and listeners, I often have the children gather around a pair of readers to listen to how they read, teach, and share their books with each other. In my last group, Christina and Lee were far and away the experts in our room when it came to showing kids how to really dig into and enjoy books with each other. By watching them often, the children learned that it was quite fine to interrupt the reading to comment on the text, to study the illustrations, to laugh, or in other words, to simply *enjoy* the book.

As children finish their partner reading, they have several choices in our classroom. These include:

- quiet reading
- computer
- geosafari

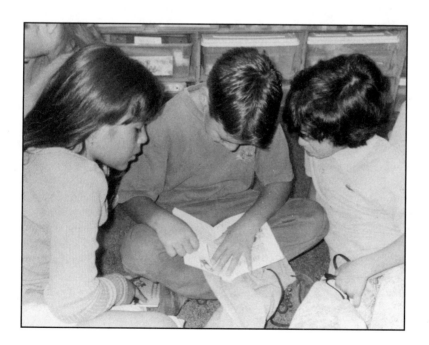

FIGURE 5–4
Mayra, Jonathan, Victor: partner reading

- listening center
- pocket chart: poetry/song charts and line rebuilding
- overhead transparency little books
- letter writing tub
- little book tub
- other choices the children and I negotiate

With first-grade children, I use this choice time at the end of partner reading to meet with a small reading group if I need to.

My job during partner reading is multifaceted. As with quiet reading, it's an opportunity for me to listen to individual readers. I don't call these "reading conferences"; rather, I label them "reading observations." I sit next to a pair of readers on the floor, with my reading assessment clipboard in my lap, and jot down notes on the child I am listening to. Usually, I mark on their sheets whether I am listening to them read during quiet reading or partner reading because I tend not to engage in as much instructional conversation with them when they are partner reading as when they are having a conference with me. Rather, I listen to how they are interacting with their partners and how their partners are helping them. I listen to as many children as I can during this time—a good day is about five—while also giving quick help to children who are stuck on a word, or nodding my "OK" to a book selection a child has made. When I am listening to a reader, children know not to interrupt me. They sit next to me and wait until I can give them my attention. I teach this early and insist on it.

The children and I also readjust our partner-reading routine as needed. One adjustment that occurs both in late first grade and early second grade is when children begin reading longer books. When this happens, we spend time talking about how they need to handle their partner-reading time a little differently. Before they read, they need to bring their listener "into the life of their book." We talk about how to review what's happened in the story up to the point where they're going to start reading, or how to "walk through" the previous pages if it's an informational book.

Some children also begin to transition as readers and no longer need to reread what they read the previous evening. Most first- and second-grade children still benefit greatly from rereading, as it develops fluency, but when I see children ready to make that step to begin reading where they left off the previous evening versus rereading what they read the previous evening, I give them permission to do this. However, I still expect them to "bring their listeners into the story" or review the information before reading to them.

Another adjustment that occurs is in the frequency of the status-of-the-class conference. With first-grade children, I do this quick check-in every day, all year long. I need to keep close tabs on these readers. With my last group of second-grade children, I began reducing this to two times per week toward the middle of the year, and during our last two months of school, I only checked in with them once a week. After two years of being with them, I knew my readers well, and many of the children were immersed in chapter books.

Often, when I work with other teachers, they lament their lack of books for a nightly reading program, saying they feel they can't do partner reading. I have helped several teachers start partner reading in their classrooms when it isn't connected to a nightly reading program. After quiet reading, the children bring their books to the circle, partner up, and take turns reading to each other for ten or fifteen minutes. It still gives the children the opportunity to read and share good books with each other, it just isn't connected to a nightly reading program. I think for beginning teachers, *not* connecting partner reading to a nightly reading program is perhaps easier to manage.

Toward the end of the year with my last second-grade group, I experimented with the format of partner reading and explored having children meet in "small book talk groups" during this time, one or two days a week. My readers were maturing and I felt we needed a change in routine. I took the concept of individual book talks that the children did each day and married it to the concept of small literature groups. Instead of partnering up to read, the children met in small book groups and read and shared their nightly reading books with a group of four or five children. The process was quite successful and was a nice change from daily partner reading.

REFLECTION

It is quite satisfying to hear the voices of thirty-two readers immersed in their books. I love watching the children share their books with each other and teaching each other as readers. I enjoy watching them laugh at stories and illustrations and express awe at the size of planets and ocean animals. I delight in how alive they are as young readers. I also listen to the children so I know how they are teaching each other as readers. I recall Rosanna's words to Tanya during their first-grade year when Tanya hit a trouble spot in her reading: "Tanya, if you want to be a good reader, then go back and start again. That's what Ms. Janine says."

If we are doing our work as readers during shared reading and I am doing my work as a teacher of reading during individual reading conferences, I should hear and see days and days of strategy and phonic minilessons put to use as children's heads are bent over their books during partner reading. It's the best barometer I have for tracking their progress as readers.

Partner reading is one large reading group where everyone has a chance to read and share good book talk with one another. It's an image of Elizabeth sitting close to Lee, lovingly pulling the hair out of Lee's eyes as she read, helping Lee with difficult words when she needed it. For me, this moment captured partner reading: love of books, respectful reading instruction, and friendship.

6 | BOOK TALKS

. . . True books will venture,
dare you out,
whisper secrets,
maybe shout
across the gloom
to you in need,
who hanker for a book to read.
—David McCord, "Books Fall Open"

It was a Wednesday afternoon during the first week of October, and my second graders and I were gathered for our customary book talk after lunch and recess. Adrienne perched on one of the small student chairs in front of the group with *Five Little Monkeys Jumping on the Bed* (Christelow 1990) resting on her lap, and waited for everyone to settle on the floor. I was in my normal spot at the back of the group, sitting on my chair so that I was just above the heads of the children, journal in hand, ready to capture not only Adrienne's book talk, but the children's discussion as well.

Adrienne was a quiet, beautiful girl of Mexican and African American heritage. She was also a terrific reader. She had spent her first-grade year enjoying the rocking chair in our classroom library, reading aloud to an imaginary audience. The *Five Little Monkeys Jumping on the Bed* book that she had chosen for her book talk was actually an easy book for her, but I knew it was a favorite that she loved taking home to read to her baby niece. Adrienne's high school–age sister had recently given birth to a baby girl and was living at home with Adrienne, her mother, her little sister, and an older brother. Adrienne's mother was the sole provider for the family and worked at the local Goodwill center. She had been a single mother since Adrienne and her little sister were babies. In fact, Adrienne's older sister had helped raise the girls, caring for them when their mother worked nights.

Adrienne handed me her book talk form, which she had completed at home the night before, and the children became quiet. She lifted the book so that everyone could see it without having to peer around heads, then began reading aloud while also facilitating the children's discussion. I jotted down some of the children's comments in my journal as Adrienne shared her book:

Tracy: We know this in sign language.
Victor: Is mama monkey gonna jump on the bed?
Jonathan: Maybe.
Victor: That sure is a big bed.
David: Ooo. He fell on his head. He's doing a headstand.
Another child: That's a she.
David: They're all she's?

Tracy: No more monkeys! (Looking at the picture.)

Victor: (interrupting Adrienne's reading) See, I told you mama monkey was gonna jump on the bed.

Several children: We all know!

My husband, Michael, who is also a teacher, was actually the inspiration for starting book talks in my primary classroom. Each day in his middle school classroom, one student would give a five-minute book talk. He started this as a way for students to share their reading lives and recommend books to one another. At the time, I was wrestling with a troubling question in my own classroom: How do I help young children become "librarians" for one another so that I am not the only person in our classroom introducing and recommending books? Daily I mentioned books that tied into our work and discussions, and yet I often felt like I was taking the majority of the responsibility for promoting good books. As I talked with Michael, book talks seemed like the invitation my primary children needed for giving their own book recommendations and to shine as readers.

PREPARING

When I start book talks with children, I prepare the following items:

- book talk letter: This letter (Appendix 6–1) explains book talks to families and gives pointers for preparation.
- book talk form: This form (Appendix 6–2) is completed before the book talk preferably at home the night before, and asks for this information:
- book title
  - author/illustrator
  - what the book is about
  - what the reader's favorite part is
- sign-up clipboard with class roster: This clipboard is managed by the child who currently has the job of signing up children for book talks.
- book talk envelope: A manila envelope with "Book Talk" written on the front in black, permanent marker, illustrated by one of the children; the children carry book, letter, and form home in this envelope for book talk preparation.

DEMONSTRATION: GETTING STARTED

I introduce book talks to the children by giving one myself, following the format I would like them to use:

- reading the title, author, and illustrator of the book
- showing the audience the cover

- telling what the book is about
- sharing a favorite part or parts
- reading a favorite part or parts, or the entire book if it is short

I keep this introduction brief and basic, giving the book talk first, then discussing the process with the children. I know that book talks will take on a different shape and form as the year progresses, but my goal is to give the children a simple structure to follow until they are confident presenting and reading to one another.

In addition to giving the book talk, I do a quick minilesson on the book talk form that is part of this process. When I introduce this form to beginning first-grade children, I ask them to write the book title and author/illustrator, and explain that I will write the remaining information as they give their book talks. With older first-grade and second-grade children, I ask them to complete the entire form to the best of their abilities, then during their book talks, I finish what they are not able to. With my last second-grade group, the day that Tracy handed me her book talk form, fully completed, the children were quite impressed with her level of work. Her form definitely set the standard for the class (see Figure 6–1).

After a child gives a book talk, I write a short note on the bottom of this form, commenting on what I believe was done well, what was interesting to me, or pointers for the next book talk. I send these completed sheets home with the children to share with their families.

I recorded this entry in my journal when Cynthia introduced the book *In a Dark, Dark Room and Other Scary Stories* (Schwartz 1984), and read "The Green Ribbon" to us:

> Cynthia was ready and read beautifully. WOW! Tracy even commented on it at the end. We all knew what the end would be with Jenny's head falling off, but we shuddered anyway. Cynthia kept a straight face the entire reading. At the end, Lisa said,
> "How could you pick such a disgustingly gross story?"

I wrote this note to Cynthia on the bottom of her form:

10-16-95

Dear Cynthia,

You were so well practiced. We were all biting our fingernails wondering why Jenny was wearing the green ribbon. It's a spooky story! You were well prepared. I am proud of you.

Love,
Ms. Janine

When the children first get started with their book talks, I do a great deal of coaching. In essence, I talk them through the book talk using the following prompts:

- "Please tell us the title of your book."
- "Please tell us the author and illustrator of your book. I'll help with the pronunciation of the names if you need it."
- "Please tell us what the book is about."
- "Please tell us your favorite part in the book and why you chose that part."
- "Please read your favorite pages (or the entire book if it's a short book) to us."

As children become familiar with the format of book talks, become comfortable presenting to a group, and become confident as readers, I find

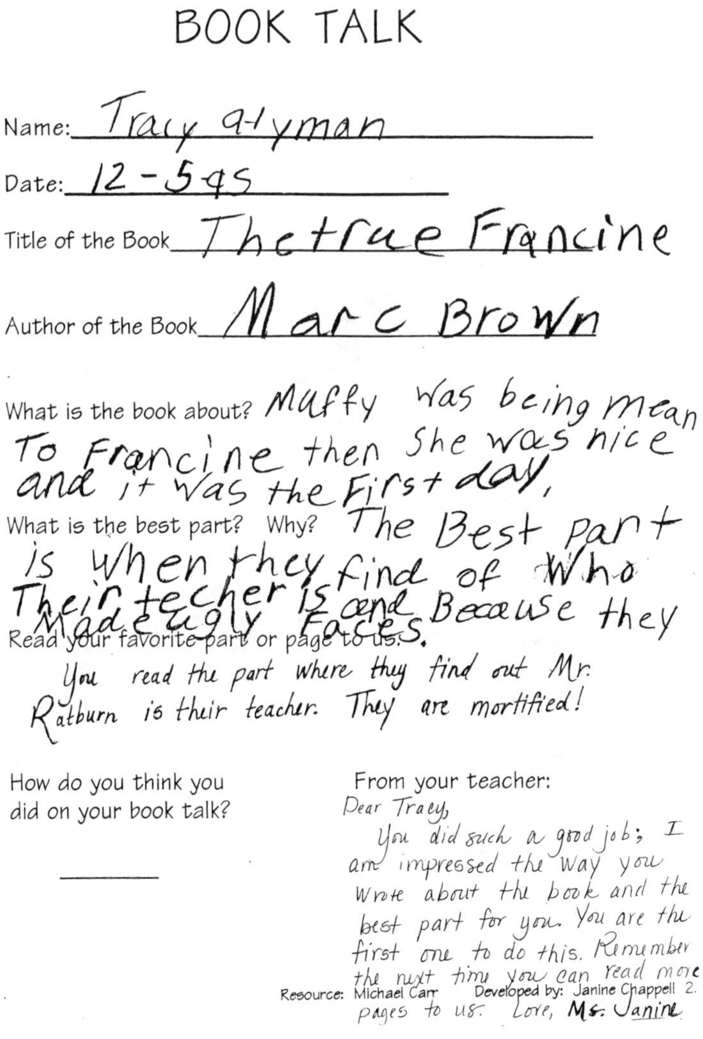

BOOK TALK

Name: _Tracy Glyman_

Date: _12-5-95_

Title of the Book _The true Francine_

Author of the Book _Marc Brown_

What is the book about? _Muffy Was being mean To Francine then She was nice and it was the First day._

What is the best part? Why? _The Best part is when they find of Who Their techer is and Because they Made ugly Faces._

Read your favorite part or page to us. _You read the part where they find out Mr. Ratburn is their teacher. They are mortified!_

How do you think you did on your book talk?

_____

From your teacher:
Dear Tracy,
You did such a good job; I am impressed the Way you Wrote about the book and the best part for you. You are the first one to do this. Remember the next time you can read more pages to us. Love, Ms. Janine

Resource: Michael Carr   Developed by: Janine Chappell 2.

FIGURE 6-1
Tracy's book talk form

that guiding them through their book talks is no longer necessary. Observing and listening, I let the children take the lead. My goal is to hand over this process as quickly as possible so that I am a member of our community of readers rather than the leader. It is the children's job to become the "lead readers" each time they give their book talks.

VALUING THE ROLE OF CONVERSATION DURING BOOK TALKS

One afternoon at the end of our school year when I discovered Leticia was going to share the simple rhyming book *Bears in Pairs* (Yektai 1987), I worried that the book would be too easy.

Leticia's family was bilingual, speaking both Spanish and English at home. When Leticia started in my classroom, it was her second year in first grade. She was socially mature, but had not developed academically; she wasn't reading, and her writing was confined to a few simple words. Leticia was also the quietest child I had ever experienced in my tenure as a primary teacher. I discovered that conversation and "language" in the home was scarce.

FIGURE 6–2
Adrienne; book talk

Knowing this, I often sought out conversation with Leticia because she never initiated "talk" with me.

As the year progressed, and I continued to talk with Leticia about everything from the length of her bangs to the little hummingbird outside our classroom window, I discovered that book talks and class meeting announcements were also openings for Leticia to talk. She had developed into a confident reader, but still chose simple books, like *Bears in Pairs*, for her book talks. It seemed to give her the confidence she needed, so I applauded the fact that she was in front of the group, ready to give a book talk.

After Leticia introduced her book and began reading to us, my group became engrossed with this simple text, listening to and reading with Leticia. They reread pages, played with the rhymes, and commented extensively on the illustrations. How wrong I had been when I had thought to myself that this would be a rather insignificant book talk. I wrote this in my journal as I observed their interactions:

> "It rhymes, Ms. Janine," said Rosanna. Kids are so immersed in the book. I can't believe all the comments. Leticia can hardly read the pages—amazingly enough, they quiet down for her. Leticia is really enjoying this! She smiles a lot as she shares the book.

When I started book talks with my first-grade class, I didn't anticipate the children would have discussion *during* the book talk. I thought they would wait until the end to share comments or ask questions. I soon discovered that my group didn't follow this format at all.

The children completed the introductory phase of the book talk (book title, author/illustrator, favorite part) much as I had expected, but when they started to read their favorite parts, or the entire book if it was short, things took a different turn. My group didn't stay quiet during the readings. They wanted to discuss the book *while* it was being read and shared. I remember sitting at the back of my group thinking, "Should I tell them to listen quietly and let the reader read? That we'll have discussion and questions when the reader finishes? Why is this happening? This isn't what I had planned!"

Since I wasn't expecting this amount of conversation during the book talk, I decided to listen and observe. As the children's discussion continued, I began to see that the interaction between the reader and the audience was quite natural and didn't seem to bother the reader at all. Eventually I made a connection to what was taking place. My group was doing exactly what I had been encouraging every day during our shared-reading time: good discussion and interesting questions. Because I had seen Michael's middle school students handle book talks one way, I thought they would transpire in my classroom in a similar manner. I had to remind myself that our work was to take the seed of book talks and "grow" it to fit our lives as young readers. With that, I relaxed.

My concern about discussion during book talks melted away as over time, I observed the children become adept at handling conversation while also letting the reader move forward with the reading. Their growing ability to handle the dynamics of conversation was wonderfully apparent one day when it was Kayalani's turn to give her book talk.

Kayalani had chosen *The Jewel Heart* (1994), an exquisite book written and illustrated by Barbara Berger, for her book talk. This love story between Pavelle, a dancer, and Gemino, a cellist, is told through a beautifully sculpted text and delicate, wispy paintings. The children knew the book, but it was one that they loved to have reread because it was such an enchanting story.

After introducing *The Jewel Heart*, Kayalani began sharing her favorite parts, which she had marked with Post-it notes, with us. However, in between reading and sharing her favorite parts, she went through each page of the story, showing the illustrations and summarizing what was happening. Her method of doing this was much more effective than reading favorite, but disconnected parts of the book. I sat in the back of my group admiring her thinking and preparation while also listening to the rich, involved story discussion of the children.

"I liked it better when he had brown hair," Lisa told Kayalani as she helped her with some of the difficult words in the text. This was followed by a lengthy discussion among the children about how Gemino's heart was stolen.

"Why does he need a jewel heart?" David asked.

"That's his heart," Kayalani replied. "That's how he's alive." At that point, Lee began retelling the story with Kayalani "because," as Lee explained to the group, "I've read it before." Kayalani didn't seem to mind Lee's interjections and willingly included her in the retelling.

Toward the end of Kayalani's reading and retelling, several wondered why Gemino's hair was "like that," as it was wispy and white.

"It's dandelion fluff," Cynthia told the group. She was right. Gemino's brown hair had been replaced with dandelion down by Pavelle and the forest animals who had tended to him after he had tripped and fallen.

The children ended their discussion by commenting on how the rose seed had become Gemino's new heart and had blossomed at the end. At this point, Kayalani turned back to the beginning of the story so they could compare Gemino's rose bud heart to his former jewel heart. There was considerable discussion about the wood rat taking Gemino's heart, and it became obvious they viewed the wood rat with some disdain.

I listened closely to the children, recording their interactions in my journal. I remained quiet throughout Kayalani's entire book talk, realizing how easily the children engaged in book discussion among themselves. They went back and forth between reading and conversation with such adeptness. Asking my group to wait until the end to give comments or ask questions about Pavelle and Gemino seemed absurd after listening to them delve into good book conversation together.

Now, I see book talks as providing one more opportunity for the children to learn how to handle discussion themselves, instead of relying on the "adult voice" in the room to maintain an appropriate atmosphere. Occasionally, I do step in to redirect and return the focus to the reader if the conversation goes too far afield, but it is the minority of the time. I continue to learn how to appreciate books, and what children appreciate in books, by listening to them in this way.

As I watched the seeds for book talks grow and take shape, my original plan changed in another way. I had wanted the children take on the role of librarians, recommending books to one another, so I had assumed they would introduce *new* books to one another. As it turned out, many, particularly first-grade children, chose books that I had already shared or they had already read. As I observed them sharing these favorite books with one another, they seemed to enjoy the rereadings enormously. I noticed too that the children often chose different "favorite parts" to share, commenting on why those were their favorite part or pointing out things in the illustrations they had discovered that we had missed in previous readings. Like the "no discussion during book talks," I let go of the librarian expectation and instead encouraged children to share books that they enjoyed and that they believed would continue to add to our reading pleasure in some way.

During our second-grade year together, more of the children began sharing new books for their book talks as their reading confidence, ability, and fluency developed. I liked this balance between "old favorites" and "new book friends" and could see the children becoming librarians to one another, relying less and less on me for book recommendations. When Rachael shared her new book, *The Adventures of Snail at School*, (Stadler 1995) from the book fair, I wrote these notes in my journal:

4-24-96

Such fluent and expressive reading. Rosanna told her at the beginning she had a good voice for this book. Kayalani liked the way she said, "Swoosh!" Lots of little discussion as she reads—especially with the Space pages of the book. . . . Rachael gives great commentary on the illustrations that go with the text.

Love her teacher voice for Miss Herby. Rachael said her dad had to help her because she kept reading Miss Harry!

Discussion about why it's light on the planet and dark in space. . . . Conversation about the name "Ed" for a girl. Tracy compared it to Erin and Aaron, Kris and Chris, and decided that the different spellings meant boy or girl. . . .

Lots of discussion about the conductor's baton and triangle. Eddie didn't know what the baton was and Lee reminded him it was like when we went to see Jana's brother in the Marching Band. Rachael was explaining it from a "concert perspective" and he didn't understand.

On the instrument page, Rachael said, "How can they stop? They (the instruments) can't hear. The instruments don't have ears!"

SOLVING PROBLEMS DURING BOOK TALKS

The days when book talks go smoothly are balanced by the days when there are bumps and problems to solve. Problems seem to fall into two categories: reading problems and book presentation problems. Some of the reading problems I have solved with children include

- reader is not prepared and reading isn't fluent
- reader has word difficulties
- read-aloud voice is too soft

A sampling of the book presentation problems I've solved with my class include

- reader doesn't tell the author/illustrator
- reader turns/shows the pages too quickly and children can't see the illustrations
- children who are sitting close to the reader "peek over the page" during the reading which is distracting to the reader and to the group

One problem that I solve quickly with children is what to do when they are not prepared for their book talks. If a reader starts and is struggling, I ask them if they've had enough time to prepare during the previous evening and if not, to stop, take the book home again, or prepare with one of their friends in the classroom during recess, morning work, or partner-reading time. I don't want readers struggling in front of the group. It's painful for the reader and uncomfortable for the listeners. Nothing good comes out of children struggling in front of their peers. As I begin to know my class better, I talk with children who I know have little home assistance, and ask them if they are prepared before we even settle in for book talks. If they're not, together we figure out the best way for them to do this—either with a friend at school if there's time, or at home if they think someone will help them that evening. Tanya was a child in my room who consistently prepared for her book talks during her morning-work time or quiet reading because she didn't have help with them at home.

Another problem that I tackle early on is what to do when a reader doesn't know a word and needs help. With my last group, the children actually decided to institute a "word helper" system and designed it in this way: The person giving the book talk would have a "word helper" sit next to him/her, giving help if and when needed. The student who had the job of signing up children for book talks had a second clipboard with a class roster and kept track of the "word helper" each day, giving every child the opportunity to do this. If neither the reader nor the word helper knew the word—which did happen!—they spelled it out for me, and I helped with the word.

Reading too softly is always cause for concern during book talks and one that we encounter more at the beginning of the year. When Priscilla chose to share two poetry selections from *Talking Like the Rain* (Kennedy and Kennedy 1992), her voice was too soft, and she wasn't enunciating her words clearly. The children became disgruntled with Priscilla, as she was holding the book in front of her face, and they couldn't hear or enjoy the poems. Kayalani interrupted Priscilla saying, "Talk louder, please. Would you start over again?"

"Put it down on your lap and then read it," Rachael added.

"Would you please put it down and read it again?" Lee asked.

At this point, Priscilla said, "No." I sensed she didn't like the way the children had talked to her. I wondered what my group would do as Priscilla still had one more poem to read. This time, Lee asked her once again, *very* politely, to "please read it with the book on her lap." Priscilla obliged, and her second reading was much smoother and more enjoyable for everyone.

Along with soft voices, another common beginning problem involves illustrations: either forgetting to show them or showing them too quickly. With my second graders, the children were insistent that they see every page that was read, and I had to work with them on how to remind one another in courteous ways to show the pictures if the book talk person was forgetting to do this, or in Tanya's case, flashing the pictures at us in a blur of color. When this happened with Tanya, I wondered if the children would problem solve, or if it would take divine teacher intervention. Lisa took it upon herself to work it out with Tanya. In a very deliberate demonstration, she modeled holding the book out, then doing a slow left-to-right sweep with the book so everyone could see it—all without a book in her hands. Tanya took Lisa's instruction willingly and her book talk improved considerably.

Sometimes problems are apparent to me, such as when Priscilla read too softly and we couldn't hear well; other times the children decide something is a problem that I wouldn't necessarily have expected. This was the case when two girls were "peeking over the page" at the illustrations before Lisa showed them to the rest of the class. On this particular day, when Lisa was reading and Juanita and Monica decided to peer over the edge of the book before she held it up for illustration viewing, I wondered what the children would do. Lee spoke first.

"Would you please not look at the pictures first?"

I waited for their response to see how they would respect this type of request from one of their classmates. We had talked about this type of "student request" earlier that morning during our class meeting, as Rosanna had talked with the group about responding appropriately when they were asked by another student "to do or not to do something." Tracy and Brenda had volunteered to do a quick role play to show the children what Rosanna was talking about:

Brenda: Would you please hand me the orange marker?
Tracy: Yes, I'd be happy to.
Brenda: Thank you.
Tracy: You're welcome.

After Lee asked Juanita and Monica not to peek at the pictures during Lisa's book talk, Lisa took it a step further.

"You're a little close," she said. "Would you please find another place to sit?"

She asked gently, but firmly, and Juanita and Monica found another place to sit. They were able to do this without "exchanging looks" between each other or sending "a look" toward Lisa, which I viewed as real progress. Even "looks" during book talks erode classroom community and respect for one another. Problem solved. As I work through specific problems like this with the children, I watch to see if they solve similar problems independently the next time they surface.

REFLECTION

As I reflect on this "ten-minute" time in my classroom, I realize that book talks have cultivated much more than my original goal of the children taking on the role of being librarians for one another. I also see developing in the children:

- a true love of sharing "old favorites" and "interesting new" literature
- a blossoming self-confidence in sharing and reading aloud to their peers
- a multitude of rich, thoughtful book discussion
- an adeptness at presentation skills by preparing for a public speaking, sharing, and reading time
- an adeptness at organizational skills in completing their book talk forms
- an appreciation of different types of literature
- an empathy and/or admiration for those who have different reading abilities than their own
- a gathering of a community of young, supportive readers

These benefits became apparent to me as day after day, I watched first- and second-grade children sit in front of their peers and share books that they loved. Two particular book talks come to mind that I believe show children reading, listening, sharing, and supporting at their best.

The first book talk took place at the end of our first block of school with my second-grade group when Eddie had finally decided he was ready to do a book talk on *The Castle in the Attic* (Winthrop 1985). He was nervous about doing this because it wasn't a picture book. With journal in hand, I was ready.

"I don't have any pictures," he said to us. "Is that OK?"

The children reassured him it was fine. They were curious about his chapter book and I was eager to hear what paths the children's discussion would take once Eddie began reading.

Victor was intrigued from the moment Eddie began retelling the story, then reading the passage he had chosen to share with us. Their conversation began when Eddie stopped to explain "token" to the group.

Eddie: He shrinks people to show them around.
Victor: Does he unshrink them?

Eddie: I don't know yet. I think he shrinks them and grows them back again. (Eddie continued to read more from the passage, stopping to describe who Alistair was.)

Eddie: Alistair was a person who killed the Silver Knight's dad. Alistair told Sir Simon that "There is a price to be paid."

Victor: What happened to the Wizard?

Eddie: I think he's dead. I don't know why he killed him. The wicked wizard put a spell on him.

David: Do you have to imagine what the pictures are in your head?

Eddie: Yeah.

The discussion was intense, the children were absorbed, and in the end, David had captured what it is that readers must do. They must "imagine what the pictures are" in their heads.

The second book talk occurred at the end of our second-grade year when Juanita shared Aliki's *Hush Little Baby* (1968) with us. With Cynthia at her side, she started reading the book, then moved right into singing the lullaby. This last book talk was a shining moment for Juanita. Even though *Hush Little Baby* was a well-known, well-loved "songbook," the children's conversation about the illustrations was rich. I captured only a snippet of it in my journal because I was simply enjoying some of our last book talks together.

> "Janine, is he crying or laughing?" Rosanna asked as she studied the expression on the baby's face. "I just can't tell."
>
> "I think he's laughing," I replied. "I think he likes Juanita singing to him!"

Even though I was lighthearted when answering Rosanna's question, I did believe there was something significant about Juanita being comfortable enough to sing to us. I realized it was an indication of how safe the children felt with one another. We were used to singing together as a group, and I sang to them often, whether it was directions, part of a text, or a song. But to sit in front of one's peers and sing solo was something to celebrate in the life of our classroom. There was only appreciation for Juanita when she finished. The support from the children hung in the air around us. When Juanita finished her last lullaby note, the children gave her a hand.

Book talks create an opening for young readers to share wonderful books and talk about the pictures they imagine in their heads when they read them. It is ten minutes of time for a community of readers to have "inside conversations" about well-loved favorites and "opening conversations" about new book worlds they haven't yet visited. Finally, book talks are a time when every child is seen, heard, and celebrated as a reader.

7 | MONITORING PROGRESS

*The craft of teaching is inextricably
tied to the craft of listening to our kids
and acting on what they tell us.*

—Linda Rief, "Staying Off-Balance and Alive:
Learning from My Students"

"My aunt and our friend next door loved *The Jewel Heart*," (Berger 1994) Lee said to me on a Wednesday morning early in our second-grade year as we settled into quiet reading.

"It's a beautiful book, isn't it?" I said to Lee. It was good to be in one of those weeks where Lee had found a book she loved and was working hard as a reader. Her love affair with reading was still sporadic; however, there was a lot going on in Lee's young life.

Lee was a resilient child. She lived with her aunt and two small cousins because neither her father nor mother were capable of caring for her. As Lee had tearfully explained it, ". . . when I was little they couldn't decide where to live anymore and they split up to live in different houses, so I went to live with my aunt."

Her mom and dad seldom visited her and she missed them terribly. Her conversations and writing were often about how much she wanted to see them. One morning in March during her first-grade year, she had dissolved in a puddle of tears in my arms before school started because she missed them so much.

"My aunt tells me to remember the good times," she had said to me bravely before finding refuge in her tablet, writing, "I miss my mom and dad. And I used to live with them but my mom and dad didn't know where they were gonna live so I had to go live at my aunt's house."

There are times when children's hurts run so deep that it's a wonder they are even able to share books with the next-door neighbor and focus their attention on learning how to read.

After reading quietly for a few minutes myself that morning, I decided Lee would be my first reading conference. I went over to where Lee was sitting at her table and sat beside her. She was used to our reading conferences, as we'd been doing this together at least once a week since the beginning of our first-grade year. Since Lee had already talked with me briefly about her book, I dispensed with my normal, "How's it going?" opening and asked her to start reading to me. I wrote these notes on Lee's anecdotal page on my reading assessment clipboard while she read to me:

Read /called/ for /could/. I asked her if it made sense; showed her the /l/ was quiet in /could/; showed two segments for /on ly/; she does use some phonic strategy—figured out /everyone/ and /whispered/.

At the end of our conference I asked Lee to reread her book that evening because I felt another night of reading would help her fluency.

"I wanted to anyway," Lee replied. "It's a challenging book, but I like it."

"If you really love it, then it's OK to have a challenge," I told her. "You'll do fine with practice."

Conducting reading conferences is only one of the ways I monitor the progress of young readers, although I consider it one of my best practices. Other ways that I track children's reading development include keeping an Order of Concern list, taking running records, and categorizing my readers into three groups: No Concerns, Mild Concerns, and Concerns. I discuss these practices later in this chapter.

Reading conferences are the heart of how I monitor children's reading progress. They are my opportunity to listen to my kids and act on what they tell me. When I sit close to the children either during quiet reading or partner reading and listen to them read, I "dig into" how they are handling themselves as readers, how they are solving problems, what attitudes they are developing about reading, and what kinds of books they are exploring. I listen, question, and engage in instructional conversation with my young readers in the space of approximately five to seven minutes. I revel in the luxury of sitting next to a child for a few minutes, believing these minutes are an integral part of each child's reading program. My goal is to assess quickly their progress, problem-solving abilities, and reading attitudes so that I can nudge them forward as readers. I can only do this by listening closely, meeting with my readers as frequently as possible, and having an efficient record-keeping system for my notes.

READING ASSESSMENT CLIPBOARD: SETUP AND MANAGEMENT

Through reading and experimentation, I have developed a streamlined reading assessment clipboard that serves my purposes well. Since my reading conferences are quick, frequent check-ins with each child, I need an organized documentation system. I organize my clipboard with four sections to assist me in my work.

Section 1: Rating My Young Readers

This first section includes a class roster that I mark after I conference with each child. I use a simple plus, check, or minus system. After I conference with the children, I rate them on how they are doing as readers based on my knowledge about them and their demonstrated reading ability. I rate my young readers in this way:

- A plus indicates the child read fluently, solved problems well, and was enthusiastic about book choice.
- A check indicates the child read with some fluency, solved problems to a certain degree but needed some guidance, and was enthusiastic about book choice.
- A minus indicates the child struggled with this book: the child read with limited fluency, didn't problem solve well, and probably was not enthusiastic about book choice.

This roster, which I keep as the top sheet of my clipboard, also shows me at a glance whom I have and haven't met with for a conference. It usually takes me five to seven days to check in with each of my readers (when I have thirty-two children) before I start the class cycle again; however, I meet with "concern children" two to three times per week. Figure 7–1 is a sample of one of my rating sheets.

Section 2: Reading Log Check-in

This second section of my clipboard contains the same type of class roster as in the first section, only I mark it with a Y (yes) or N (no) when I meet with the children and ask if family members have been signing their nightly reading logs.

Section 3: Status-of-the-Class

The third section of my clipboard contains a different type of class roster that I use to quickly write the titles of the books the children are reading for their nightly reading and partner reading. I do this check-in with the whole group each day before the children start partner reading. I write about this status-of-the-class process in Chapter 5.

Section 4: Anecdotal Notes

The last section of my clipboard includes one sheet for each child, thus thirty-two in total when I began a year at Bobier. I use yellow paper that has a grid marked with 2 x 2" squares. I write each child's name in the upper right-hand square and organize the sheets alphabetically by the children's last names for quick access. I keep the squares small because my anecdotal notes are short and abbreviated. If I run out of room on this sheet, I insert a second page behind the child's first sheet. Figure 7–2 is a sample of one child's anecdotal notes page.

These four sections comprise my reading assessment clipboard. I add rosters and pages to each section as needed. I separate each section with a sheet of paper that has a side tab attached to it with the name of each section, so I can turn to each section quickly. This clipboard becomes an old friend during the year or two years that I am with a group. I review my notes continually as

I meet with my readers. This system helps me monitor closely the reading progress of each child.

I have tried different checklists and prepared forms, but none has assisted me as much in my work as this simpler system. I find that I never

CLASS COMPOSITE SHEET
Assessments

+   No Concerns
✓   Mild Concerns
−   Concerns

Room 12: 2nd Grade Reading Conferences	9/13-9/20/95	9/21-10/1/95	10/2-10/11/95	10/12-10/23/95	10/25-12/1/95	12/1-1/9/96	1/4-1/19/96	1/19-3/13/96	3/13-3/15/96	3/15-4/10/96	4/10-4/15/96	6/01/96
Rachael Anderson	+	✓+	+	✓	+	+	+	+	+	✓	✓+	+
Christina Buhl	✓+	+	+	+	+	+	✓	+	✓+	✓	+	✓+
Chris Bourne	✓	✓	✓+	+	✓+	−	✓	✓+	+	+	✓	+
Priscilla Castaneda	+	✓+	+	+	+	+	+	+	+	+	+	+
Eddie DeCasas	+	+	+	+	+	+	+	+	+	+	+	+
Monica De Casas	+	+	✓	✓	✓	+	✓	+	+	+	✓+	✓
Kaley Ehrig	✓+	✓	+	+	✓	✓+	+	✓	✓+	✓+	✓+	✓+
Christie Elliott	+	+	+	+	+	+	+	+	✓+	✓+	+	+
Kayalani Evans	+	+	+	+	✓+	✓+	+	✓	✓+	+	✓+	+
Jonathan Garcia	+	✓+	+	✓	✓−	+	+	✓+	+	+	✓+	+
Brenda Gill	✓	✓	✓	+	+	✓	✓+	✓+	+	✓+	✓+	✓
Roni Hodenpyle	✓	✓	+	+	+	+	+	+	✓+	✓+	✓+	+
Bianca Huerta	✓	✓	✓+	✓+	✓+	✓+	✓+	✓+	✓+	✓+	+	✓+
Tracy Hijman	✓+	✓+	+	✓+	+	+	+	+	+	+	+	✓+
Harold Leary	✓+	✓	−	✓+	✓+	+	✓	✓+	+	✓+	✓+	✓+
Tanya Luna	✓	✓+	+	✓+	✓−	✓+	✓	+	+	✓+	✓+	+
Elizabeth Meraz	+	+	+	✓+	+	+	+	+	+	+	+	+
Timmy McMahon	✓	✓−	+	✓	✓+	✓+	+	✓+	+	+	+	+
Nhi Nguyen	+	+	✓	+	+	✓+	+	+	+	+	✓+	✓+
Adrienne Palomino	+	+	+	+	+	+	+	+	+	+	+	✓
Edward Paredes	+	+	✓	✓−	✓+	✓+	✓+	+	+	✓+	+	✓+

FIGURE 7–1   *Rading assessment clipboard: rating readers after individual conferences*

have enough time for keeping up checklists. Instead, what I find more helpful is knowing the characteristics of emergent, early, and fluent reading behaviors, then basing my observations and anecdotal notes on those characteristics as they apply to each young reader. Leanna Traill's emergent, early, and fluent reading checklists are excellent resources and can be found in her book *Highlight My Strengths* (1993). I teach by observation and write down those observations. I need a supportive assessment system that I can use *while* teaching every day and that doesn't require hours of after-school maintenance that I don't have time for. My reading assessment clipboard is manageable paperwork.

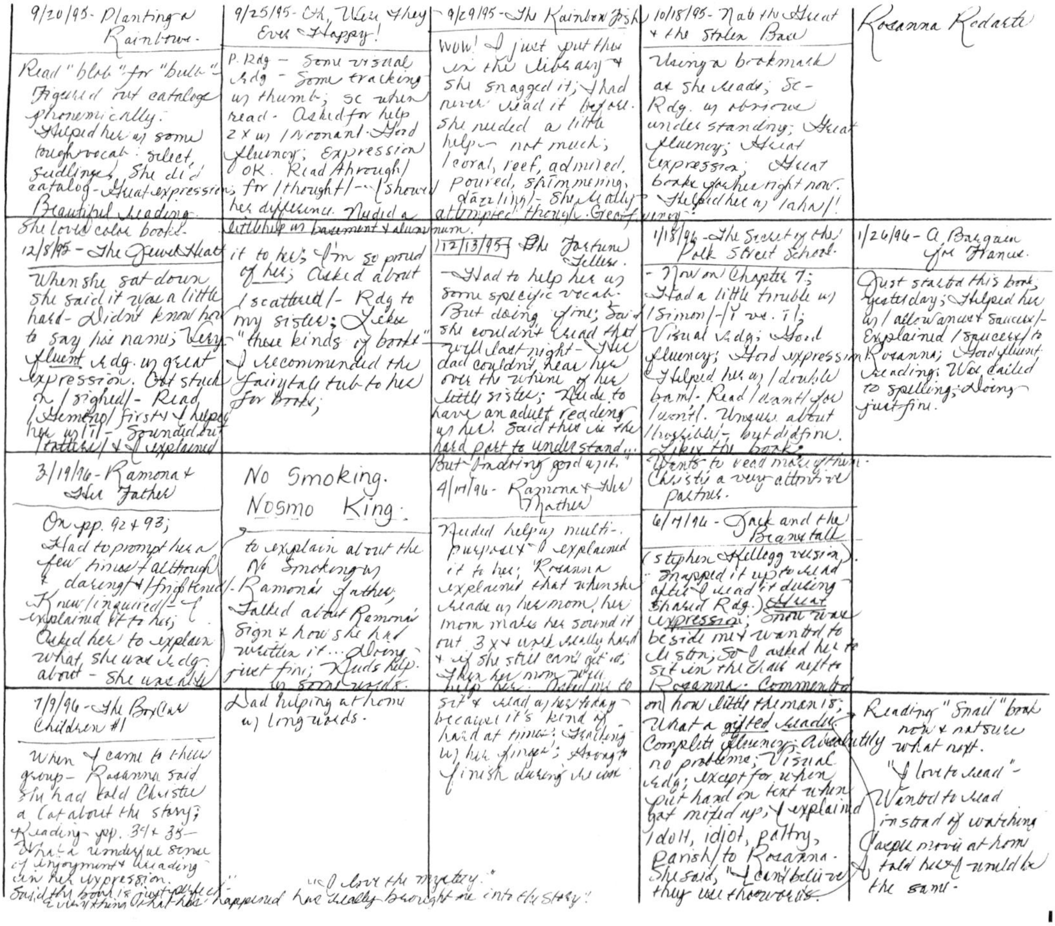

FIGURE 7–2   *Reading assessment clipboard: Rosanna's anecdotal notes page*

I do the bulk of my reading conferences during quiet-reading or partner-reading time in my classroom. If time and opportunity present themselves, I also hold reading conferences during morning-work time, recess, before or after school—basically anytime I can find a few minutes. I wait to start reading conferences until the third or fourth week of school because I want quiet-reading and partner-reading routines firmly in place. When I see children managing themselves productively during these times, I begin my conferences.

In mid-September of our second-grade year, I sat down to conference with Edward. Edward had been in bilingual kindergarten and first-grade classrooms, where his literacy instruction was in Spanish, but his parents had decided to move him to an English classroom for his second-grade year. By the end of first grade, Edward was an early reader in Spanish and an emergent reader in English. During this first conference with him, I listened to Edward read a beginning reader titled *The Monster's Party* (Cowley 1996), which I had helped him select the previous day for his nightly reading. As I talked with Edward, I discovered that he and his mother, who had limited English skills, were working through his beginning books together. When he started reading to me, he seemed to be coping well with this sudden transition from Spanish to English literacy. His reading was quite good; however, I could see that he needed to track the words better because he would often lose his place while reading.

I met with Edward again a few days after this first conference because I was still gathering information about him as a reader. In between conferences, a letter/sound assessment with Edward showed he was able to identify fourteen uppercase letters and the same corresponding lowercase letters. He knew the sounds for fourteen upper- and lowercase letters, although they did not match the letters he could identify. As could be expected, he often responded to the letters and sounds in Spanish. Continued letter/sound work became a natural part of my work with Edward when I helped him solve word problems while reading. I also sent home a set of upper- and lowercase English alphabet cards for Edward and his mother to review together since she was a willing teacher.

For this second reading conference, Edward read *The Little Red Hen* (Parkes 1984). Edward reassured me that his mother was still reading with him in the evenings, although as he began reading, I could tell this text was more difficult for him; however, he was interested and working hard. During this conference, I began to realize how much English story vocabulary was new for him, so I talked with Edward about stopping and asking for an explanation from me or whoever was reading with him when he didn't know a word or understand the story. I also began dividing his book into sections for him because he was doing a great deal of rereading to develop fluency, and he was more successful with a shorter section each evening. After these first two conferences with Edward, I could see he was eager to take on the challenge of reading in his developing second language and was positive about the books he was taking home for his nightly reading. I also knew that it was important for Edward to continue reading familiar stories so that he could draw on his knowledge of the story to solve word problems.

I think of these beginning reading conferences with Edward and the rest of my young readers as "roaming around the known" conferences (Clay 1993b). "The most important reason for roaming around the known," writes Marie Clay, "is that it requires the teacher to stop teaching from her preconceived ideas. She has to work from the child's responses" (13). As I listened to and observed Edward and the other children, I tried to determine what they knew about reading, how they were managing the books they had chosen for themselves for nightly reading, how they were problem solving, what attitudes they were developing about reading, and in Edward's situation, how he was coping with becoming literate in his second language. I try to "get inside" each child as a reader so that I can determine where he or she is starting from, and can make decisions about each individual's reading instruction.

During these beginning conferences, I also remind children that they need to have their nightly reading books and reading logs with them. I always listen to the children read from the book they've selected for their nightly and partner reading. I check reading logs during conferences to see if a family member is signing and/or writing comments each evening. I keep close tabs on this because nightly reading time is critical to the children's development as confident readers. If reading logs aren't signed, I ask the children if someone is reading with them at home. If nightly reading is taking place and the logs aren't being signed, I remind them to ask family members to do this. If nightly reading isn't occurring, I either write a note in the child's Note Book or talk with a family member on the phone or in person to remind them that I expect this process to take place. It varies among the children, so I check reading logs consistently during reading conferences throughout the year.

The Structure of the Conference

Opening Book Conversation

When I sit close to a child to have a reading conference, I start with book questions and conversation. Typical questions include:

- What book are you reading?
- Who is the author?
- When was it published?
- What is happening in the book?
- How is the book going for you?
- Are you interested in your book?
- What challenges have you had? How did you work through them?

When I met with Priscilla for one of her reading conferences, she was exploring new reading tastes with a science book titled *What Is a Fossil?* (Goldfish 1989). As we began our conference, she asked me, "Do I start from the beginning or from the part where I read last night?"

I asked Priscilla to tell me about the first part of the book before picking up with the passage she was going to read to me. When children like Priscilla begin reading longer books over a period of time, I pay close attention to how they converse with me about what is happening in the book. This retelling discussion allows me to see how my readers are "holding the text together" as they read. Besides being an avenue for checking comprehension, it also gives me the opportunity to have real book talk when I meet with them.

Priscilla then began a detailed description of how a fossil is made, pointing to the pictures as she explained the process to me. She had developed into a confident reader even with minimal support at home since her mother worked a night shift. In fact, for her nightly reading, Priscilla read to her younger sister or her older brother if he was home in the evening.

I begin reading conferences with book conversation because as a fellow reader and teacher of reading, I need to connect with the reader and the book before the child reads to me. I want to go beyond performing a check-in duty with my readers. I must have a feel for the book as well as the reader's understanding and reaction so that it is a meaningful experience for me also. In reflecting on this, I've decided it's my curiosity as a reader, developed over many years of finding refuge in a good book, that compels me to begin reading conferences in this way. I savor having "knowing conversations" with the children when they are reading a well-loved favorite, or having "opening conversations" when they are sharing their excitement for a book I haven't yet read.

Reading Aloud and Taking Anecdotal Notes

After this quick introductory discussion, the child reads aloud from the book, reading long enough for me to get a sense of how she or he is doing. This gives me the opportunity to check two items: reading fluency/expression and the strategies the reader uses when encountering a problem word. I find myself balancing two things at this point: listening to the child read and having instructional conversation with him or her if there is a problem and help is needed to solve it. I do far more listening to a child who is reading fluently and far more instruction with a child who is having difficulty solving problem words or who lacks fluency. I write extensively about the role of instructional conversation with struggling readers in Chapter 8.

As Priscilla talked with me and read to me that day, I began writing abbreviated notes on her anecdotal sheet:

10-25-95: *What Is a Fossil?* Q.R.

Visual reading; very fluent reading; asked me if I wanted her to start from beginning or part read last night; told me in her own words how fossil was made after she read it; pointed to pictures and explained.

When I do this type of note taking, I'm the only person that needs to understand the notes, so I keep them short; sometimes one word will capture the essence of what the children are saying or reading. I write just enough that it triggers a memory of the entire conference if I need to review it in my mind. I tell the children at the beginning of the year that I will be recording a lot of what they say and do as readers, writers, and learners, and they quickly get used to me having either a clipboard or my journal in hand.

I start my anecdotal notes in this manner:

- date
- title of the book
- Q.R.: indicates my conference took place during quiet reading
- P.R.: indicates my conference/observation took place during partner reading

If children start with a retelling, I jot quick notes about how well they manage this task. I also try to capture any side questions or comments readers say to me either during the retelling or the actual reading because I often reflect on what they say during this time. I learn a great deal about them as readers in terms of what they notice and what they think about while reading.

Lee was a fascinating reader to listen to because she often commented extensively on what she was reading. At the beginning of one of her conferences when she was reading *D.W. the Picky Eater* (Brown 1995), she said to me, "This is one of my favorite books. D.W. is so funny." When Lee started reading through the vegetables, and read the line in the text, *I hate spinach,* she looked at me and said emphatically, "Same with me. But, I don't know if I'm a picky eater or not." These are the kinds of comments I capture on my clipboard, along with instructional notes about fluency, expression, and strategy, because they tell me how the children are connecting to books, and the attitudes they are developing as readers.

In terms of instructional notes that I write while the children are reading, I generally note these reading strategies and behaviors:

- fluency—including phrasing—and expression
- self-corrections
- tracking the print with finger or eyes
- strategies the reader used to solve problems
- specific word problems that I help the reader with and the way in which I helped him or her solve the problem
- if child is rereading after solving a word problem
- if child is able to recall a problem word later in the text
- if level of text matches level of reading development

I view these as key behaviors that indicate to me how the child is doing as a reader. With a confident, fluent reader like Rosanna, my instructional notes tended to focus more on expression, phrasing, and how she was interacting with the text because she had developed good strategies for dealing with word problems. An entry from her anecdotal sheet follows:

6-7-96—Great expression; Lee was beside me and wanted to listen so I asked her to sit in the chair next to Rosanna; commented on how little the man is; what a gifted reader; complete fluency, absolutely no problems; visual reading except for when put hand on text when she got mixed up. I explained /dolt, idiot, paltry, parish/ to Rosanna. She said, "I can't believe they use those words!" Reading "Snail" book now and not sure what next. "I love to read." Wanted to read instead of watching Casper movie at home. I told her I would be the same way.

Whereas Rosanna was a confident reader, Heidi struggled. When I conferenced with Heidi, my notes focused more on reading strategies and to what extent she was employing them. An early entry from Heidi's anecdotal page follows:

Mrs. Muddle's Mud Puddle (Cowley 1996) Q.R.

9-27-95—Wasn't tracking with her finger on first page and then I asked her to. A little slow at first—then seemed to pick up fluency. Overall, reading rate is slower. Rereads prior word when gets stuck on word. Reads /she/ for /said/ then does SC. Great expression on "Kitty! Kitty!" Helped her with /half way/; she read /hunter/. Really working on it. Used phonics for /an/. Laughed after p. 9 and said, "This is funny!" MONITOR.

There are several ways I help readers like Heidi solve word problems during our reading conferences if they are unable to do this themselves. The problem-solving strategies I model include:

- demonstrating phonic strategies: segmenting words into syllables; showing a common pattern, blending a word if it's "spelled like it sounds"; showing a "word within a word"; looking at the beginning and/or ending letters of the word for help
- demonstrating meaning strategies: looking at the picture for help
- demonstrating rereading strategies: taking another run at the sentence; skipping the word and returning to it

My goal is to zero in on the quickest strategy that will help my readers solve their problems so they can maintain their reading pace. Sometimes this includes me giving a word prompt if it is a word that is difficult or the spelling is irregular.

Whenever possible, I do incorporate a great deal of phonic-level teaching during individual reading conferences because problem words present the perfect opportunity to dissect spellings and letter patterns. When my young readers wrestle with difficult words while reading, I write the words on a Post-it note on the top sheet of my clipboard so I can review them with the entire class during a shared-reading minilesson. One week I gathered these problem words during reading conferences: *buried, yeah, smart, used, Thora, untied, blob* for *bulb, teaspoon, still, roar, why.* Proper names often present difficulties because the spelling can be quite different from the pronunciation, so they appear on my "problem word list" frequently.

When I write anecdotal notes while conferencing with and/or observing children during partner reading, I also note how the children interact with one another as readers in addition to reading attitude, behaviors, and strategies. I recorded a lengthy entry one day on Crystal's anecdotal page when she was reading *Duck and Hen* (Cowley 1996) to Rosanna. I was struck by the level of demonstration and collaboration between these two young readers:

> 9-25-97—Rosanna a great partner. Showing her how to segment words. Remembered /friends/ after read it first time. Rosanna prompting her a lot. Showing her picture cues: "What's this?" Rosanna said as pointed to fence in picture. Also reread Crystal's sentence with expression: "Duck flew over the fence!" Crystal got to /whatever/ and Rosanna said, "It's the same word as on the other page—turn the page." Crystal does remember a word after she has been prompted earlier. Crystal needs to tackle this again. Rosanna pointing at words with Crystal as she reads. /Hen/—Rosanna circles hen in picture to reiterate. Rosanna helped Crystal with bugs, /b-u-g-s/. "All right," said Hen—Crystal stuck a little on /said/; Rosanna showed her /said/ on the other page. Rosanna: /said/ and /said/. Rosanna started to choral read on pages 11–13. Crystal read swimming /lessons/ instead of /feet/ and Rosanna corrected her—does have meaning. P. 15 read /search/ for /scratch/. P. 14 Rosanna got a little distracted and yawned but went right back to it with Crystal.

Closing the Conference

My note taking ends when the child finishes reading to me. At this point, I typically end our conference with comments about his or her reading, how we solved problems, whether I think the child needs to reread more to develop fluency, or a reminder to reread after solving word problems because I'm concerned he or she is losing the meaning of the text by not doing so. Sometimes these comments are woven into the conference, so I don't go through them again. However, I always end a conference with these questions:

- Who's reading with you at home?
- What do you plan to read next?

The first question is my way of monitoring the children's nightly reading life and being reassured (hopefully) that at least one family member is invested in their reading development. The second question is a way to monitor how much this child is living like a reader. In terms of future book selections, I don't call it "choosing instructional-level text" with my young readers. In fact, I don't even think of their book selections in those terms. Rather, I look for them to choose books that will be "just right" first in interest, then in reading level. I know that even beginning readers will not choose "one sentence per page books" for an entire year; they would quickly become bored. Instead, I tap into children's natural drive to be learners and nurture their innate need to choose increasingly more difficult books—not only in reading level but also in concepts and ideas—by immersing them in good books, good talk, and good instruction. In the right environment, and with the right books, children want to become better and better readers. If this isn't happening, I intervene.

I also remind my first and second graders that "real readers are surrounded by stacks of books that they are itching to open," and that they "need to be on the lookout for books they are eager to read." So, my second question, "What do you plan to read next?" also helps me see if this attitude is developing in my young readers. If a child doesn't have a "next book" in mind, I become a reference librarian, either suggesting books myself or referring them to other readers in the room who may have recommendations. While I want the children to enjoy what they are currently reading, I also want to see them developing an internal "must read" list. I worry when children develop a pattern of not having any books "in the wings." It's a red flag showing that they're not developing enthusiasm for books and reading.

ANALYSIS: GROUPING READERS

After I cycle through my class list for reading conferences, I mentally group my young readers into three categories: Concerns, Mild Concerns, and No Concerns. I place those children who struggled during their reading conference on my Concern list. Those children who had a few struggles, but were still moving forward in their reading form my Mild Concerns group. Those children who read fluently, solved problems well, and were clearly successful at challenging themselves make up my No Concerns group.

This type of grouping and analysis is dynamic. I move children among groups from week to week and month to month. I watch for the shifts and patterns. I know that children who frequent the No Concerns list will develop quickly as strong readers; they simply need a constant supply of interesting, challenging books. I watch children who frequent my Mild Concerns list carefully because they generally require consistent instruction/reminders on how to solve problem words during reading conferences, need to reread more to develop fluency, need to hear models of good expression and phrasing, and need reminders to track with their finger instead of with their eyes. Children who frequent my Concerns list are the ones I lose sleep over. For a multitude of reasons that I have to work to uncover, they experience difficulties as beginning readers. I've devoted Chapter 8 to discussing how I work with struggling readers.

I expect some shifting back and forth among lists. When I listen to my readers and rate them with a plus, check, or minus, I always consider various factors: book selection, amount of home-reading time, absence from school, emotional health, and home or school incidents. Any or all could have an effect on the children's reading progress at any particular time during the year. One or two good reading weeks do not mean that children are set for the year, nor does one or two "off" reading weeks mean I am ready to refer them to our Student Study Team. I expect progressions, plateaus, and regressions over the course of the year; what I look for is a consistent pattern of progress over time. Thus, the dual process of assessing every week during reading conferences and grouping readers into three categories is helpful. I can't operate with my lens too narrow or too wide.

Order of Concern List

Of the three lists, my Concerns group is the one that I commit to paper so I can monitor these children carefully. I rank these children in the order of concern that I have about them. For example, I place the child that I am most concerned about in the number one position and rank the rest of these readers in order after that. I write this Order of Concern list on a Post-it note and place it on the front of my reading assessment clipboard to remind myself of these Concern readers every day. I know they will need additional time, instruction, and individual assistance whenever possible. I generally update this list once a month because shifts do occur.

With my last group, I had between ten and twelve children on this list throughout the year. By the end of the year, I still had grave concerns about two, but the rest of the children on the list had graduated to Mild Concerns. A yearlong comparison of my Order of Concern lists follows:

Mid-June, 1996	Early March, 1996	Late October, 1995	Mid-September, 1995
1. Juanita	1. Heidi	1. Edward	1. Monica
2. Heidi	2. Juanita	2. Heidi	2. Crystal (moved)
	3. Edward	3. Juanita	3. Edward
	4. Tanya	4. Tanya	4. Tanya
	5. Elizabeth	5. Monica	5. Kristen (moved)
	6. Nhi	6. Lee	6. Jonathan
	7. Jonathan	7. Elizabeth	7. Leticia
	8. John	8. Brenda	8. Tanya
	9. Leticia	9. Leticia	9. Cynthia
	10. Lee	10. Jonathan	10. Lee
	11. Brenda	11. Cynthia	11. Elizabeth
	12. Monica	12. Nhi	12. Rosanna

RUNNING RECORDS

In addition to writing copious notes during reading conferences, regularly grouping my readers into three categories, and keeping an Order of Concern list, I also take running records to monitor the progress of the children. Marie Clay's book, *An Observation Survey of Early Literacy Achievement* (1993a), provides a clear and thorough section on how to take and analyze running records. Because I write consistent anecdotal notes throughout the year, I only do running records with children at the beginning, middle, and end of the year. When it is time for a running record, I do it during the children's reading conferences. Instead of writing anecdotal notes, I take a running record of the children's reading of their nightly reading books. I cycle through my class in the same manner as before, returning to anecdotal notes when I have completed a running record on each child. These running records are placed in each child's early literacy assessment portfolio. I show how I use running records and additional early literacy assessments in Chapter 15.

COMPARISON OF TWO YEARS' READING GROWTH

At the end of two years with my last group at Bobier, I decided to compare the level of reading development they exhibited at the beginning of their first-grade year to their level of development at the end of their second-grade year. I based their rate of progress on a comparison of their beginning-of-the-year first-grade running record and the title of the last book they read at the end of second grade. Seventeen of my readers were like Chris, progressing from an *emergent* reader at the beginning of first grade to an *early fluent* reader at the end of second grade. These children were reading books that ranged from Jerry Pallotta's *Alphabet* books to *Nate the Great* books (Sharmat) to *The Magic School Bus* books (Cole and Degen). Tracy represented the progress of a smaller group of eleven children: *emergent* readers at the beginning of first grade to *fluent* readers by the end of second grade. These children had progressed to reading chapter books such as *Charlotte's Web* (White 1952), the *American Girls* books, or the *Boxcar Children* (Warner) books, and nonfiction titles such as *Ocean: The Living World* (Greenaway, Gunzi, Taylor 1994). Two of the children had progressed only from *emergent* to *early* readers by the end of their second-grade year and were reading transitional books such as the *Oliver and Amanda Pig* books (Van Leeuwen) or early readers like *My Spring Robin* (Rockwell 1989).

REFLECTION

Over the course of two years, these children developed a great deal of skill and confidence as readers, with some more skilled and confident than others.

After two years of observing and listening to them read, having daily instructional conversations, writing endless notes, and grouping and regrouping them according to how I viewed their progress, I felt like I "knew the insides" of these readers. And except for Juanita and Heidi, whom I discuss in Chapter 8, I believed these readers knew how to select books for themselves, solve problems, recommend books to one another, challenge themselves with more difficult and different types of books, and have grand book conversations with one another.

"Achieving a successful balance of materials and approaches depends on a perceptive and caring teacher," writes Margaret Mooney. "Good first teaching requires a responsive approach where the teacher is aware of what the child can do, what situations will be appropriate to assist the child to meet the next challenges, and what support will be needed. Responsive teaching ensures each step is secure enough to be a springboard for the next learning and that the learner has the resources and confidence for success." (1988, 6).

Even though I believe that one of my most important teaching responsibilities is to monitor the progress of the young readers in my classroom, I also believe a large part of my work is helping children learn how to monitor themselves. My reading conferences are not only vehicles for me to assess, evaluate, and instruct, but also to demonstrate to the children how to assess, evaluate, and instruct themselves. Throughout my one or two years with children at Bobier, I listened for "my talk" to become "their talk." When this happened, I knew they had fully engaged as readers and learners. Margaret Mooney points out that, "the teacher is one who shares responsibility and response ability with the learner. Thus, the teacher becomes a facilitator and respondent, ever mindful that true readers and writers are 'self-winding' and choose to read and write well beyond the care and guidance of the school system." (1988, 1). Marie Clay refers to this taking-over process as becoming a self-managed, self-monitored, self-corrected, and self-extending reader (1991, 345). She describes the roles of teacher and learner in this way:

> The teacher aims to stimulate, foster, support, and reinforce reading work carried out by the learner. The learner must actively search for information, relate this to things known, detect error even if he cannot solve the problem, use all his own resources, initiate his own word-solving of whatever kind, actively relate new discoveries to established knowledge and so on. It is important that the teacher does not narrowly characterize or label what the child is doing because this will reduce her sensitivity to the unexpected links the child is able to make on his own. (343).

As I work to be a facilitator and consultant to each young reader versus a didactic expert, part of "my talk" during reading conferences is that "I trust you." I trust them to learn how to select books for themselves, solve problems, challenge themselves, and share books with fellow readers. My second message to these children is "I will help you." I will help them when they have problems selecting "just-right" books or solving word problems, or when they exhibit reading confusions; and I will work with them to help them solve these difficulties.

Reading conferences, which are the heart of how I monitor children's progress, allow me to listen to my kids, act on what they tell me, *and* help them learn how to act for themselves.

8 | STRUGGLING READERS

*We should start with story and with
poetry . . . with things that enhance
and enlarge life. You learn along the
way the skills you need to manage the
reading. The decoding will come in
large part from the child's desire
to participate in this language feast.*

—Katherine Paterson, *"Share What You Love"*

In the course of teaching young readers, it is inevitable that some children will experience difficulties in their literacy journey. In this chapter I profile three readers, Timmy, Heidi, and Juanita, who needed closer instruction to help them manage the process of reading. I chose these three students because (1) I felt they represented the many children I've worked with who struggle to become readers in different ways, and (2) they show my levels of success as a reading teacher. And even though the particular stories of these children may be different from the stories of other struggling readers, my intent is to show the interactions and close instruction that I used with Timmy, Heidi, and Juanita as a template for working with struggling readers. My goal was to make my classroom reading table inviting and supportive enough so that those children who initially found the transition into literacy hard and confusing (Clay 1991) could indeed participate in the language feast.

TIMMY

Timmy was typical of many of my young readers in the beginning months of first grade. He had good knowledge of concepts of print, was able to identify forty-two out of fifty-two letters, (upper- and lowercase), knew the sounds for thirty-two letters, wrote the alphabet with only minor errors, and read an emergent-level reader titled *Our Granny* (Cowley 1996), when I did his first running record assessment in October. Throughout the year, he continued to read more difficult books and was a solid early reader by the end of first grade. He read the book *Nowhere and Nothing* (Sunshine series, Wright Group) for his year-end first-grade running record, and although his accuracy rate was 87 percent, his errors retained meaning, so I still considered the book at his instructional level. I felt confident he was on his way to becoming a solid reader.

But by the end of Timmy's first month in second grade, he was struggling. When I met with him in mid-September for his first reading conference, he read *Henry and Mudge, The First Book* (Rylant 1986). I wrote these notes on his anecdotal sheet while I listened to him read:

> 9-14-95—P.R. Partner–Jonathan. Tracking with finger; difficulty with book; not doing well; he said he practiced . . . had to redirect on /short/ after prompted previously. MONITOR.

I listened to Timmy read throughout the next two weeks but didn't write notes on his anecdotal sheet until the end of September when he read *Amelia Bedelia* (Parish 1963) to me during his reading conference. My notes follow:

> 9-27-95: Q.R.—3rd day on book; had difficulty with /Cousin Alcolu, coming/; still some visual approximation; read /shower/ for /something/; challenging; SC wait–why; needs continued help with reading and *consistent* practice. MONITOR.

At this point, Timmy's reading regression had lasted a month, and I was concerned. His reading wasn't as fluent, he wasn't using his knowledge of phonics to solve problem words, he wasn't checking for meaning when he did solve a word problem, and he didn't seem to have the enthusiasm for reading that he did at the end of his first-grade year. I called his family to schedule a conference, which is always my first order of business with struggling readers.

When Timmy's father came to school for our early morning conference, I explained my concerns to him and asked if they were still reading in the evening with Timmy. His father explained that the family just didn't have time for homework, and they expected schoolwork to be done at school. I reiterated how important it was for Timmy to have consistent reading time in the evenings, preferably with his mom or dad, but his father insisted that schoolwork needed to be done at school and couldn't promise they would read with him. I was dismayed. I knew that part of Timmy's struggles were due to a lack of nightly reading time with a literate mentor. If Timmy didn't receive extra time, attention, and instruction, I knew he would fall by the wayside on his literacy journey.

Struggling readers like Timmy need more time and individual assistance, both of which are in short supply in a busy school day. Timmy wasn't my only struggling reader, nor did he have the severest problem.

As I considered what Timmy's father said to me that morning, I knew that daily individual reading time was critical for him to get over his bumps, but giving this kind of time to Timmy during the school day was impossible. I decided I would make the commitment to read with Timmy every day after school for fifteen minutes if his father could make arrangements for him to get home safely.

As Timmy and I delved into our reading time together, I discovered that yes, consistent daily reading was helpful, but I also realized he lacked a tool-box of strategies to solve problem words, which is a hallmark of struggling readers. He didn't use typical strategies to help himself, such as applying his letter-sound knowledge to help him figure out words phonetically, looking at pictures for help, skipping over words and coming back to them, or taking another run at the sentence. Often he would guess, not check to see if the word made sense, and keep right on reading.

As I continued to observe Timmy closely, I could see he needed strategy instruction in all areas, especially phonics. Like most struggling beginning readers, he needed to build his working knowledge of letters, sounds, and letter and word patterns so he could tackle problem words systematically. He wasn't paying close attention to the print, and when he hit a problem word, everything fell apart. He would start guessing, go with his first guess, but wouldn't check to see if his guess made sense. At that point he was no longer reading, merely calling out words on the page. Timmy wasn't self-managing, self-monitoring, or self-checking (Clay 1991) as a reader.

With children like Timmy who need more explicit strategy work, I don't dust off an old phonics program or turn to a published, sequential program of reading instruction. I don't believe either is helpful. Yes, these children usually need to build a better working knowledge of phonics for solving word problems, but they also need to learn how and when to employ other strategies and then how to reread to make sure that they are on the right track. This type of strategy instruction needs to take place in the context of real reading. In my classroom, I do strategy work with all readers, albeit more with struggling readers, during writing time and individual reading conferences, or in Timmy's case, during our after-school reading time. The label I use for this type of work is "instructional conversation."

Instructional Conversation

The type of instructive talk, questioning, and strategy prompting that I do with readers like Timmy is critical because my goal is to help them internalize this type of "talk" until they do this for themselves when reading independently. Thus, I call it instructional conversation. As I listen closely to my readers, I make quick decisions on how to question or prompt them in ways that will help them solve their problems. During my instructional reading conversations, I respond to their struggles with the following types of instruction:

- modeling problem-solving strategies
    - "Start at the beginning of the sentence and try it again."
    - "Skip it and come back to it."
    - "Look at the picture for help."
- analyzing problem words phonetically to help them build their phonic knowledge
    - "Look at the first letter/s of the word."
    - "Look at the first and last letter/s of the word."
    - "Stretch the word out a segment at a time."
    - "This word rhymes with _____; it has the same pattern only a different letter(s) at the beginning of it."

- "This word has the little word _____ in it; can you figure it out now?"
- modeling/discussing "holding the story together" strategies after solving problems
  - "Now read from the start of the sentence/page so it makes sense to you."
  - "Reread the entire page so you have the story/information firmly in place before reading on."
  - "Stop and tell me what you've just read so I know you're holding the story together."
- building a large vocabulary of familiar words that they can use to solve unfamiliar words

These are the skills that my proficient readers develop quickly. Struggling readers, like Timmy, need to be engaged continually in this type of dialogue while reading, to develop a storehouse of knowledge and strategies to solve reading problems. They need more strategy scaffolding. They require a longer "handing over" time as they make their way from guided reading practice to being able to handle books independently. These conferences are a critical part of my reading instruction with them.

Timmy and Janine: Transcription of Instructional Reading Conference

I continued to work with Timmy each day after school by first listening to him reread the pages he had read the previous day, then doing a guided reading session with him on the new pages he was going to read that day. I did this same type of work with other struggling readers during individual reading conferences. The following are two excerpts from one of my reading conferences with Timmy when he was reading *The Case of the Two Masked Robbers* (Hoban 1986). The left side is a transcript of the beginning minutes of the actual conference; the right side is the "self-talk" going on in my "reading teacher head" as I listened to Timmy read and made decisions about how to help him solve problems, build strategies, develop confidence as a reader, and begin conducting "reading talk" inside his head.

Text: *The Case of the Two Masked Robbers*	Janine's Self-Talk
Timmy: The Case of the Two Masked Robbers by Lillian Hoban; For Esme **Janine:** Good job, Timmy. OK, p. 16. **Timmy:** The twins tiptoed past the kitchen. The st . . .	

Text: *The Case of the Two Masked Robbers*	Janine's Self-Talk
Janine: /sl/ . . .	Wrong blend; I'm going to prompt with /sl/ to refocus him on blend at the beginning of *slipped*.
Timmy: They slipped into out the front door. **Janine:** Does that make sense? "They slipped into out the front door." This starts with a /qu/ /i/ . . . **Timmy:** . . . quiet out the front door. **Janine:** What's the ending on quiet?	Timmy needs to check for meaning; I'm going to reread what he read so he can decide if it makes sense; I'm going to prompt with the beginning sounds of /quietly/ to refocus him on the word.
Timmy: /ly/. **Janine:** . . . quiet . . . /l/ . . . **Timmy:** . . . quietly out the front door.	Timmy needs to pay more attention to the ending of this word; I'll see if he can solve the problem by directing his attention to it; I'm going to give him the /l/ sound to see if that will get him started.
Janine: OK. Start that sentence again.	I think Timmy has lost the meaning because he's had to stop to solve several problems. He needs to reread to put everything together so it makes sense.
Timmy: They slipped quietly out the front door. They ran through the str . . . **Janine:** /sh/.	Timmy is having difficulty with beginning blends again; I'm going to prompt him with the sound because he's unsure.
Timmy: . . . sh . . . wood. **Janine:** That's a tough one: shad-ow. **Timmy:** . . . Shadow . . . (before I finished the second /ow/ syllable) wood.	Timmy doesn't have the phonic knowledge to work through this one; I'm going to prompt, but do so by showing him the two syllables of the word.
Janine: /e/ (for /-y/ ending sound)—shadowy. **Timmy:** . . . shadowy wood.	I'm going to remind him to add the /-y/ ending by prompting with the sound that the /-y/ ending makes.

Text: *The Case of the Two Masked Robbers*	Janine's Self-Talk
Janine: That's the /e/ sound like at the end of your name. Why don't you read that whole page again just to keep the meaning of the story.	I want to remind Timmy that his name has the same sound as the end of *shadowy* and that it's spelled with the same letter. It's time for Timmy to reread to keep the story together and to build fluency.
Timmy: The twins tiptoed past the kitchen. They slipped quietly out the front door. They ran through the shadowy, shadow, shadow woods.	
Janine: Shadowy woods.	
Timmy: Shadowy woods.	
Janine: That's kind of tricky!	
Timmy: Maybe the real robbers are hiding near here.	
Janine: Good. That's right.	
Timmy: "I hope so," said Arabella. "Grandpa said one robber went west . . ."	
Janine: Check out the beginning letter.	I want to see if Timmy can correct the problem without me giving the initial sound of the word.
Timmy: (SC) . . . east and one robber went west. Now it is dark. They were (SC) will meet back here. They will . . .	
Janine: Three partner letters: /spl/ . . .	Timmy is hesitating on *split*; perhaps if I prompt with the blend at the beginning he will be successful.
Timmy: . . . spli . . .	Perhaps if I segment the word /spl/ and /it/, Timmy will be able to solve it.
Janine: What's the word at the end?	
Timmy: sp – ilt.	Timmy is reading the word *spilt*, which is close; I'm going to blend the /it/ to see if that will help.
Janine: i-t.	
Timmy: it.	
Janine: Now /spl/ . . .	Perhaps Timmy can blend *split* on his own now that he has the two segments.
Timmy: Spilt.	Time to prompt Timmy. This has gone on long enough.
Janine: It's tricky like that. They will spl – it . . .	
Timmy: split up the lost . . .	

Text: *The Case of the Two Masked Robbers*	Janine's Self-Talk
Janine: The loot. Do you know what loot is? The money they got from the robbery, and in this case it's not money, but what is it?	I'm going to prompt to keep the reading going. Plus, I want to check whether he even knows the meaning of loot and to check his comprehension.
Timmy: Turtle eggs.	Great. Timmy's holding the story together. He's on track.
Janine: OK. They will split up the loot . . .	I want to move the reading forward. This time I'm going to reread from the beginning of the sentence and have Timmy pick up from there.
Timmy: . . . and we will be there to catch them.	

I have found that this type of "close reading" with struggling readers like Timmy is my best form of instruction with them. Throughout our "instructional dialogue," I am constantly monitoring how much help is enough versus how much help is too much. Sometimes I err on the side of giving too much help, and I realize that I should have let the reader do more, e.g., I could have probed to see if Timmy could blend the beginning letters /spl/, waited for him to give the /-y/ ending sound before I supplied it, or given more time to answer a question before I press forward. I tend to give more letter-sound prompts when I am first working closely with struggling readers like Timmy because stopping to blend and dissect every word takes too much time and is frustrating. My goal is to balance how much I expect these readers to solve with what I solve for them. As they gain confidence, I pull back, slowly tipping the balance in the other direction, expecting them to solve more problems than I do. It's different with every reader. I listen and observe as closely as possible and work at becoming a better reading teacher to them each time I work with them.

After Timmy finished reading several pages, I asked him to tell me about what he had read. A transcript of our retelling conversation follows:

Janine: Now, you told me yesterday what the story was about when we stopped. And yesterday Grandpa had come to the Raccoon family and said there had been a . . .

Timmy and Janine: . . . holdup.

Janine: And that the eggs that turtle had deposited had been taken . . . had been stolen. Albert and Arabella hatch a plan to dress up because they have masks and they have dark long coats. So they have a plan to go and catch the robber. OK? And that's where we left off yesterday on page 15. You started on 16. They were supposed to have been in bed, right?

Timmy: Hm-hmmm.

Janine: And I would like you to tell me in your own words, I don't want you to read the text, you can look at the pictures if you want, and tell me what you read today? OK? What do Albert and Arabella do first?

Timmy: They tiptoe past the kitchen, went outside.

Janine: Who was outside there?

Timmy: An owl.

Janine: OK. What happened after they tiptoed out? What did they do?

Timmy: They ran past . . . They ran through the shadowy trees.

Janine: All right.

Timmy: Shadowy woods.

Janine: OK.

Timmy: Then they stopped through two trees.

Janine: All right.

Timmy: Then they saw Mondown . . . March . . . Marsh . . .

Janine: Meadow Marsh Bank?

Timmy: Yeah.

Janine: All right. And what are they doing there?

Timmy: Looking for the robbers.

Janine: OK. What happened next?

Timmy: Then they heard something moving . . .

Janine: OK.

Timmy: . . . and Albert ran into a bush and said, "I'm getting out of here."

Janine: OK.

Timmy: And there's a snake. Arabella was afraid to move.

Janine: OK. And that's where you stopped. All right. Any predictions about what's going to happen next in the story?

Timmy: No.

Janine: You don't know? No ideas?

Timmy: Yeah.

Janine: What are your ideas?

Timmy: Arabella's gonna call Albert and Albert's gonna get captured by two crows.

Janine: Oh. Have you looked ahead?

Timmy: (Smiles.)

This type of retelling work with readers like Timmy is meant to help them "rethink" the story and "think ahead" in the story before putting their books away. From experience, I've learned that many young readers need more assistance than just a beginning prompt of "Tell me what you read about," so I provide a "retelling ladder." After they tell me what happened at the beginning of the story or the part they read, I confirm or question that part of the retelling and ask them to go on: "What happened after that?" Sometimes I paraphrase what they say and then ask them to tell the next portion of the story. Often I ask why they think things happened the way they did, or what they think will happen next. This type of retelling conversation seems to give my young readers the scaffolding they need so they can do this independently in the future. The purpose of this "comprehension conversation" is to remind them that what they read needs to make sense, that it's important to keep events in order in the story, that good readers think about what they are reading and connect to it in some way, that they need to think about why something happened the way it did in the story, and last, that they need to anticipate what might happen next.

By the spring of our second-grade year, Timmy's confidence as a reader as well as his ability to solve problem words had developed steadily. Two of the strategies he was using often, without any prompting from me, included going back to the beginning of the sentence or the page to reread after solving a word problem and framing the problem word, then looking closely at the initial and ending letter or letters of the word to help him segment the word so he could solve it phonetically. He was also more engaged as a reader, exhibiting the reading behaviors that I seek to instill in struggling readers, which include showing interest in books, conversing about books, responding to books, and thinking about other readers' interests in the classroom. When Timmy saw the puddle on the cover of *Henry and Mudge in Puddle Trouble* (Rylant 1987) he said, "Lee would love this book!" Then, when he started reading aloud, he said, "I wonder how big Henry's yard is?" Both were spontaneous comments and good signs that he was getting hooked back into reading.

During the week that Timmy read *The Case of the Two Masked Robbers* (Hoban 1986), I was preparing for work with teachers and did several tape recordings of our reading sessions so I could demonstrate the type of work I do with my young readers during reading conferences. The first day, I taped Timmy reading the first few pages of the book after he had read them the night before at home. After that, we reread these pages together. The following day, Timmy reread these same pages for quiet and partner reading, and again, I taped him reading the same pages after school. With approximately three rereadings, the difference in fluency was remarkable. I know that rereading helps all beginning readers, particularly struggling readers, develop fluency, and the tape recordings were solid evidence of Timmy's reading gains. Analysis of the first and second readings follows:

The Case of the Two Masked Robbers: pages 7–15
Running Words: 219

	Reading One	*Reading Two*
Length of time to read pages:	5 minutes	3 minutes
Total # of Errors:	12	7
• errors maintaining meaning	4	3
• errors with same syntax	6	3
• errors with visual similarity	10	4

Total # of Self-Corrections:	7	9
• meaning used to SC	3	5
• structure used to SC	0	3
• visual used to SC	5	6
Accuracy Rate:	94.5%	96.8%
Self-Correction Rate:	1: 2.7	1:1.7

In terms of analysis, based on the research of Marie Clay, the accuracy rate of both of Timmy's readings fell within instructional level, although the accuracy rate had improved in Timmy's second reading. Timmy's self-corrections were in the "excellent range" during both readings, showing that he was actively reading for meaning and correcting his problems to maintain meaning. The key differences between the first and second readings were:

- Timmy's fluency rate had improved by two minutes in the second reading.
- Timmy had five fewer errors in his second reading.
- Timmy had two more self-corrections in his second reading.

Clearly, this type of intervention work had made a difference for Timmy.

Extra Teaching Assistance

Besides my after-school reading time, Timmy received additional individual help. Since our class sizes were high, Bobier had made a commitment to hiring certified teachers to help those children who needed extra assistance. I was fortunate to have a teaching assistant four days a week for approximately an hour and a half per day. JoAnn Camarino, who worked under the title of "Basic Skills teacher" was funded through Title I money, and her assistance provided some relief to the complex task of managing the reading and writing development of thirty-two second-grade children.

Because JoAnn divided her time among several second-grade teachers, we developed a system of planning and communication that allowed her to start her work immediately when she arrived without having to interrupt my work. We set up a notebook with sections for planning, correspondence, and recording student progress in reading, writing, handwriting, letter/sound work, and math. I wrote an overview of the work I felt children needed each day, and after working with the children, she would write about the children's progress or difficulties for me to review after school. I liked this system because the only other time we had for communication was our hurried talks during recess.

Sitting at one of the tables in our classroom, JoAnn did the same type of intervention work with Timmy, and other struggling readers, as I did. This included letter/sound work, instructional reading conferences, and updating assessments so we could monitor progress. We "shared" these children and one person's work needed to support what the other person was doing. When we first started working together, she observed my instructional conferences with the children so that she could learn how to do a similar type of work with them. One problem-solving strategy that we both incorporated into our reading conferences to help our struggling readers with phonic strategy is one that I call "segmenting the word."

Problem-Solving Strategy: Segmenting the Word

"Segmenting the word" is a problem-solving strategy I use often when I am working with all readers, but especially with struggling readers, and am focusing on those words that have common patterns or "words within words" that can easily be solved this way. If it's an unusual word like *sugar*, I prompt from the outset but take the time to explain the unusual features of the word. I tell my young readers, "You just have to remember this word. It's an unusual one in our language."

When children encounter a manageable word problem in their reading, I often start demonstrating the segmenting strategy by covering the problem word with my own thumb or finger, only exposing the initial letter or letter blend. This helps my readers pay attention to initial letter sounds as they work to solve the word. With beginning first-grade readers, I prompt them with the beginning sound of that letter or letter blend if they are unable to do this themselves. As the children's letter/sound knowledge matures, I ask them to produce the sound that letter or those letters make, and engage in the process of turning the work over to them. After we've established the initial sound of the word, I do one of two things:

1. I may continue to help them solve the word phonetically, drawing my finger back to show them the next segment of the word, or completely back to show the end of the word, engaging in whatever linguistic conversation is necessary to help them work out the phoneme segments or syllables in the rest of the problem word. I scaffold as much as I think is needed while pushing them to apply their knowledge of letters and letter patterns. I take my cues from the children when I do this. The more difficult it is for them to figure out sounds, segments, and syllables, the more I help them. OR

2. I go back to context, asking the children to start at the beginning of the sentence if we are in the middle or at the end of the sentence, or the beginning of the previous sentence if it is the first word of a new sentence, and take another run at it. I want them to reread the sentence and try the word based on the initial sound(s) of the word that we have just worked through. If they are successful, I stop to examine the rest of the word with them for a quick moment, now paying close attention to the middle and end of the word, to confirm that the word they chose matches the word in print. I want them to get into the habit of checking themselves as readers in at least two ways, and with my young readers that is often through meaning and phonics. If they are not successful solving the problem word in this way, then I immediately go to the first strategy I listed. Without fail, every time the children stop to problem solve, or I become involved in instructional conversation with them so

they can problem solve, I ask the children to go back and reread after they have solved the word or I have prompted them. They must pick up the flow of the story. Struggling readers need this reminder continually while their more proficient peers incorporate this rereading "meaning work" quickly and automatically.

As I do these individual demonstrations/conversations with this segmenting the word strategy for problem solving, my goal is for these children to incorporate the process into their own toolbox of reading strategies. During one of Timmy's later reading conferences when he was reading *Be Nice to Spiders* (Graham 1967), he used the segmenting strategy independently when he self-corrected from *animals* to *cages* to *camels*. When I begin to see children employ strategies like this without prompting from me, I know they are beginning to internalize how to get themselves out of tough spots when they are reading.

HEIDI

Whereas Timmy's reading struggles began after a successful first-grade year, Heidi struggled from the outset. I didn't have Heidi as a first-grade student, she arrived on my second-grade doorstep with literacy history in hand. Her first-grade teacher reported a year of difficulties in the classroom, socially, academically, and attendance-wise, and had never been able to connect well with Heidi's family. Throughout her first-grade year, Heidi had received daily, thirty-minute, intensive, individualized reading instruction in our school's Reading Recovery program, but she had progressed slowly. Heidi's Reading Recovery teacher said she never felt Heidi received the nightly home reading that would have helped her as a reader. At the end of her first-grade year, our school's Student Study Team finally recommended that Heidi undergo testing for special education, and this testing was scheduled for the beginning of her second-grade year.

At the end of September, I met with Heidi's mother to discuss Heidi's progress during her first month of school. We had been corresponding regularly in Heidi's Note Book as we worked to help Heidi learn the routines of the classroom and remember her school and homework responsibilities every day. However, Heidi was not faring well. I had received this note from her mother in her Note Book:

> Heidi came home tonight upset due to classroom work worried about not keeping up. She says she's having a hard time.

I asked my principal to attend our conference so he could be part of Heidi's support team also. I had compiled beginning assessments and work samples in Heidi's early literacy portfolio so I could share this information easily with her mother, which is my standard practice for any conference. We discussed the progress Heidi had made in reading, spelling, and math, first talking about Heidi's strengths, then reviewing items of concern. During all student conferences, I prefer to discuss strengths before concerns. The following list shows the strengths and concerns we discussed during Heidi's conference:

In reading, Heidi could:

- write her book title in her reading log by herself
- select a book from three choices
- read late emergent-level books
- read with a partner
- quiet read by herself
- recognize all letters and give the corresponding sounds

In writing, Heidi could:

- compose a short message
- draw very elaborate illustrations

In spelling, Heidi could:

- spell thirteen high-utility words in conventional spelling

The following are the items I was concerned about with Heidi. In reading, Heidi had:

- a very slow reading rate
- difficulty recalling basic sight words
- few strategies to cope with problem words in the text
- difficulty applying phonic knowledge to solve problem words

In writing, Heidi had:

- difficulty stretching a word out for sounds in a left-to-right sequence
- difficulty rereading while composing a message
- many reversals in her letter formation
- a very slow rate in forming letters and composing messages

In spelling, Heidi had difficulty:

- remembering high-utility words after practicing them several times

In terms of general learning behaviors, we were concerned about Heidi's rate of learning. Everything took an inordinate amount of time, particularly processing information and completing routines. If she was hurried in any way, or a task seemed too difficult, she would often become frustrated and cry, and any progress became almost impossible. I sensed Heidi felt like the world was just too fast for her and that she couldn't keep up as everything rushed past.

It was also becoming apparent that remembering responsibilities and materials between home and school was another snag for Heidi. She often forgot her journals, her reading book, or her folder at school or at home. Her mother wrote in one of her notes that we were going to have to tie a string around Heidi's finger so she would remember her things. Challenges. How were we going to help Heidi take charge of herself as a learner?

A month later, when we reviewed Heidi's testing results, we discovered that she was essentially performing "at grade level" in all academic areas and showed "good, solid intelligence." Her hearing and vision were within normal limits and her medical record was good. However, she demonstrated auditory processing difficulties; the tester noted that she processed information slowly and needed more time to give responses. I observed the same behavior in my classroom. Other than that, there wasn't a significant discrepancy between specific achievement areas and ability, so we ruled out the possibility of a learning disability. The one outside intervention we decided on was speech and language instruction to see if that would help Heidi with her auditory processing difficulties.

Throughout the year, either JoAnn or I worked with Heidi individually in the form of instructional reading and writing conferences, incorporating the same type of talk, questioning, and strategy prompting that we did with Timmy. As with other struggling readers we worked with, we discovered that rereading helped Heidi develop fluency and retain basic sight words, so part of her instructional program was to reread her books frequently. When she was reading the emergent and early level readers, I fastened four or five of these books together with a rubber band, then marked them with a Post-it note that said "Review Books" to remind Heidi to reread these at home and during quiet reading before working on her new book.

In March, after four months of close instruction, I listened to Heidi read *Ratty-Tatty* (Cowley 1996). Her reading was still slow and deliberate, but she had progressed from reading a late-emergent text like *Ten Little Caterpillars* (Davidson 1993), which she was reading at the beginning of the year, to *Ratty-Tatty*, a solid early level text. I recorded these notes on her anecdotal page:

3-13-96 *Ratty-Tatty* Q.R.

New book; placing her hand on the book to block out the print and tracking along with her right hand finger (index). I asked her if she wanted a card to block it and she said she would use her hand; I need to move her to a table by herself as she is so easily distracted by Kaley. Started to frame the words with her fingers and I asked her to go back to the other strategy; Needed help with /touched/; Needs to read one more night.

3-14-96 *Ratty-Tatty* Q.R.

Started at the middle of the book; Read Snap! with great expression! SC /woman–man/ when it should have been man–woman; prompted with /they/. Fluency seemed improved today; commented on artwork. Didn't cover the page this time as she read.

Despite the small gains, progress remained slow. In April I was still organizing Heidi's book bag for her and feeling frustrated with follow-through at home in terms of nightly reading. There were days when she would arrive at school without her nightly reading book and had no idea where it was. Her mother assured me she was reading with Heidi and helping her organize her book bag, but I couldn't figure out why Heidi would arrive at school so unorganized if she was assisting her.

At year-end, Heidi had not progressed to the point where she was even reading transitional books like the *Henry and Mudge* series, but I was heartened by my last two reading conferences with her at the end of July. During the first of these conferences, she read *How Spider Saved Valentine's Day* (Kraus 1985). My anecdotal notes follow:

7-17-96 Q.R.

She chose this book herself. Has been working on it for 3 days and is now finished; SC /the–my/. Fluency and tracking are *really terrific*. SC /choose–chose/. She loves funny books. Prompted /greedy/. FANTASTIC READING.

During my last conference with Heidi, she read *My Spring Robin* (Rockwell 1989). My notes follow:

7-19-96 Q.R.

Tracking with finger as she reads. Terrific book for her; she chose it herself. Pointed to picture of worm after she finished reading text that referred to it. Said she chooses a book and if it's too hard, then she puts it back and gets something different. This book was terrific. Very fluent!

At the end of July, Heidi's tentative progress did spark my hope for her, but I didn't have an overwhelming sense that Heidi would suddenly take off as a reader and find great success in school. I wondered if she would ever be able to navigate the literacy demands of the adult world. I felt like I had made half the progress with Heidi that I should have and continued to believe that a class with fewer students and more time for individual help in a school on a traditional schedule would have served her needs better.

JUANITA

Like every young reader, Juanita's literacy journey was unique, and in terms of reading struggles, hers were different from either Timmy's or Heidi's difficulties. Like Heidi, she experienced reading troubles from the beginning of her first-grade year. Her struggle was with retention. She would read and reread a text one day, and the next day it was as if she'd never read it before. Juanita's language development was mystifying also. Although Spanish and English were both spoken at home, when she had finally begun talking at about three years of age, she spoke English. However, even with delayed speech development, she didn't seem to experience a second-language difficulty. Although Juanita liked books, reading was hard work for her. After beginning-of-the-year-assessments, she spent a majority of her first-grade year in our school's Reading Recovery program, but her progress was measured and slow.

Even though Juanita struggled as a reader, her struggles were not the same caliber as Heidi's. Juanita was responsible in getting her book to and from school and had good self-esteem as a reader. Even when I didn't feel she was as focused on her reading as she needed to be, she was enthusiastic. She would get tired, yawn, and rub her eyes while reading, but she never seemed defeated by the process.

During Juanita's second-grade year, without the support of our Reading Recovery program, I began reading with Juanita in the morning before school started if her bus arrived early. It was a chance for me to have quiet, individual instruction time with her, in addition to the time she had with JoAnn during the school day.

At the beginning of her second-grade year, Juanita was tackling early level texts like *The Gingerbread Man* (Parkes and Smith 1986) and *The Witch Goes to School* (Bridwell 1992). As with Heidi and my other struggling readers, I had to help her choose a "just-right" nightly reading book each time she was ready for a new book. She read *The Witch Goes to School* during our first reading conference in September. My anecdotal notes follow:

9-20-95—*The Witch Goes to School* Q.R.

Had her read a page and helped her solve words phonetically. Had her then reread the page after that; still needs a lot of help but this seems to increase fluency. Substitutes /of–for/ consistently.

In December she spent a week reading the book *My Sloppy Tiger* (Cowley 1996), which was an increase in difficulty from the books she was reading at the beginning of the year. My anecdotal notes follow:

12-6-95—*My Sloppy Tiger*

Lots of difficulty retaining text even after going over it 3x.

12-8-95

Same book. Much improved fluency. Christina prompting her a lot; doing much better. Asking her to reread from the beginning each night.

12-11-95

Hasn't read it since FRI. Responded to story by talking about cleaning her own room. I prompted with /away/. Hesitated at /lunch/ but got it. I write notes while she problem solves and that seems to prompt her to problem solve her own words. Watching phonic cues—/still, trouble, bounds/. Finally solved /splish-splash/. Most trouble with p. 8. Skipped /water/ and read to end of sentence but didn't come back to it; I had to remind her to do that. Very distracted by everything in the room: door opening, etc. Did figure out /will/ phonetically.

12-14-95

Said she's ready for a new book; still gets stuck on /away/. Told her to skip and return but still difficulty with that strategy. Wanted the prompt instead of problem solving. Taking home for a review and starting new book.

As I continued to read with Juanita and discovered she would wait for my prompt instead of attempting any problem solving, I would say to her, "Work the problem, Juanita. Think about what you could do here. How can you figure out that word?" If she shrugged her shoulders, I would list off different ways she could try solving it. She also had developed a pattern of not paying attention to the ends of words and would guess at the word from the initial letter cue. I showed her how to follow the entire word with her eyes, using her finger to track it to the end, then check herself to see if it made sense. Other than the initial letter, she didn't seem to be using any phonic knowledge to tackle problem words, so I began analyzing the middle and end of words with her, searching out patterns for her to hold onto as a way to help herself when she encountered word problems.

By June, Juanita was reading transitional books like *Days with Frog and Toad* (Lobel 1985) and *Oliver, Amanda, and Grandmother Pig* (Van Leeuwen 1979). I wrote these notes when I listened to her read:

6-17-96—*Days with Frog and Toad*

Doing better than last Friday—doing a lot more problem solving. Not reading for meaning always. Not SC. Not going back and rereading after problems and meaning has been interrupted. Did go back and reread after we got interrupted; much, much improved.

7-5-96—*Oliver, Amanda, and Grandmother Pig*

SC right away at the beginning of Ch. 2 on p. 17. Having trouble with /wake/ reading /wanted/. Finally SC. Reread automatically after had a few problems. Stayed on it until she had the meaning.

Substituting words that make sense. Went back to reread at begin-ning of page and I showed her just to go back to begin. of sentence. Didn't SC /started–set/. Reminded her to use phonics to solve /cups, pots/. Had enough problems that I told her this is a page to read again. Did much better second time through. Confuses Oliver and Amanda. Showed her how to use her bookmark from the top instead of bottom. Is reading for meaning now because does SC. Much better with this book.

At year-end, after two years of reading instruction and ongoing conver-sations with Juanita's mother, we decided to take the next step and refer Jua-nita to our Student Study Team (SST) so that we could review her three-year literacy journey. Juanita had moved forward as a reader, writer, and learner during our two years together, progressing from a nonreader at the begin-ning of first grade to an early reader at the end of second grade, but her rate of progress was our continual concern.

Juanita's Student Study Team Meeting

Preparation: Compiling Two Years' Worth of Information

Juanita's SST meeting was scheduled for the end of the school year, and I spent time gathering and preparing the following items to present to the Stu-dent Study Team:

- Required Student Study Team Paperwork (submitted one week prior to meeting)
  - medical history—completed by family
  - home information sheet—completed by family
  - record of interventions
  - school history
  - documentation of "Triad Meeting" with two other teachers regard-ing concerns about student
  - student interview—conducted by staff member other than teacher
- First- and Second-Grade Assessment Information
  - letter/sound knowledge
  - running records—including taped readings, running records and retelling of pp. 26 and 27 in *Tales of Oliver Pig* (Van Leeuwen 1979)
  - anecdotal notes
  - first-grade reading recovery information
  - writing samples
- Taped Interview with Juanita: "How do you feel about yourself as a reader?"

Meeting with the Team

Present at our early morning meeting were Juanita's mother, our assistant principal, our school nurse, one of our special-education teachers, Juanita's first-grade Reading Recovery teacher, and me. Bobier has a standard format for conducting this formal team meeting, so we studied Juanita as a learner in the following manner, listing information on a chalkboard under each category:

1. Strengths: home and school
2. Known Information: medical, home, and school histories
3. Known Modifications: home and school
4. Concerns Prioritized: home and school—focused on literacy struggles
5. Strategies: brainstormed as a group
6. Actions: prioritized
7. Responsibilities: who and when

After we finished this process, Cathy Smith, her Reading Recovery teacher, and I presented a more detailed description of Juanita's reading development and struggles. Cathy presented her anecdotal/running record information from her first-grade year of reading intervention instruction with Juanita, and I did the same with my two years' worth of information. I also brought tape recordings of Juanita reading and rereading the same two pages in the *Tales of Oliver Pig*—her current nightly reading book—so the team could assess her first and second readings, since one of the characteristics we were studying about Juanita was an apparent difficulty in holding information in short- and long-term memory. In addition to the tape recordings, I brought running records of these two readings so the team could follow along with the taped readings. I prepared the running records with both the text and the marking of Juanita's readings, so it would be easier for the group to study.

The following grid compares Juanita's first and second readings of this passage:

Title: "Bad Oliver" (pp. 26 and 27) from *Tales of Oliver Pig*
Running Words: 88

	Reading One	Reading Two
Errors:	6	1
Self-Corrections:	1	4
Accuracy Rate:	93%	98.8%
Self-Correction Rate:	1:7	1:1.25

There were obvious differences between Juanita's first and second readings in all areas. However, as helpful as rereadings were to Juanita, she had difficulty holding this information and wasn't able to read fluently if one or two days passed before reading the same pages again. Often, she couldn't remember problem words between the first reading and the subsequent rereading, even when the second reading occurred right after working through the problems. This difficulty of holding print in short- and long-term memory was the part the team needed to look at most closely.

After studying Juanita's readings, we listened to Juanita give a retelling of the pages she had read, as well as what happened in the rest of the story since she had read all of it by that time. Juanita's retelling interview follows:

Janine: Juanita, I just want to ask you a couple things about your reading. OK? All right. Would please tell me in your own words what you just read on pages 26 and 27? What happened?

Juanita: It's about that um, she, um like, um, she, um, played a trick on her um, grandmother. She hided her um, eyeglasses on her tiger, on his tiger because um, because he was um, he didn't want her to um, um, find them because he was bad.

Janine: What happens at the end of the story, Juanita? You've read the whole story. What happens at the end?

Juanita: Um, he gets in trouble.

Janine: OK. What does he do after he gets in trouble?

Juanita: Um . . .

Janine: What happens to Grandmother's eyeglasses?

Juanita: Um, Oliver gives um, Grandmother's eyeglasses back, and then um, Ol . . . um, Grandmother talks about when she was a little girl.

Janine: What does she say to Oliver?

Juanita: She said that um, she used to play tricks and that kind of stuff but now she doesn't do it again 'cause she's big now.

Janine: How does Oliver feel at the end of the story?

Juanita: Sorry.

Janine: How does Grandmother feel at the end of the story?

Juanita: Um, kind of sad because he did that.

Juanita needed scaffolding questions to do her retelling, like many young readers, but she was able to give an accurate retelling of the story. The pattern of "um"s in her speech was typical. Nervousness? I didn't know if she was searching for a word, an idea, or a way to express an idea, but whenever Juanita spoke with me individually, or in front of our group, this was a significant and noticeable pattern. For the listener, it was sometimes difficult to follow her flow, but Juanita did seem to be able to hold everything together to get to the end of her thoughts. It was interesting to study and I thought it needed closer scrutiny.

The last item I presented to the team was the taped interview I conducted with Juanita after the readings and retelling. The purpose of this last interview was to give the team an idea of how Juanita perceived herself as a reader. Since we were studying Juanita, I wanted the team to actually hear Juanita at this meeting. Excerpts of my taped interview with Juanita follow:

Janine: I want to ask you a couple questions about reading, OK? How do you feel about reading?

Juanita: Good. I love this book.

Janine: And what in reading is easy for you? What do you think is easy when you sit down to read?

Juanita: Sound the words out.

Janine: What is challenging for you in reading when you sit down to read?

Juanita: Like, Grandmother is like, uh, a hard word, is longer, the hard, um, if a um, um, letters, like, um, a different kind of hard word, I can't . . . I have to sound it out.

Janine: What kinds of ways do you solve problems when you're reading?

Juanita: Ask you or um, asking people and my friends, or um, sounding them out.

Janine: Juanita, how do you think I, as your teacher, or teachers that you have coming up could help you more as a reader?

Juanita: Helping me solve the words or . . . or . . . sounding it out . . .

Janine: How do you think you can help yourself as a reader as you go into third grade? How do you think you will be able to help yourself as a reader?

Juanita: Solve my problems that I have or I can um, ask one of my friends that are by me.

Janine: How do you think your mom and your dad could help you as a reader?

Juanita: Sounding it out.

Janine: Thanks, Juanita.

As I listened to this taped interview and reflected on the two years I had been Juanita's reading teacher, I still believed that she perceived herself as a reader. She hadn't lost confidence in her ability or in the process, but it was evident, by listening to her answers to my questions, that she had very limited problem-solving strategies as a reader. "Sounding it out" seemed to be emphasized as the primary problem-solving strategy when reading at home, which carried a lot of weight in her school reading world. Where the other children in the classroom had a toolbox of strategies after two years of reading, conferencing, and working together, Juanita's strategies were minimal with a heavy reliance on the phonic system, and "mastering" our phonic system was posing difficulty for her. Her answers to my questions stayed focused on the word or letter level versus the meaning level. She seemed to have the perception that reading was about "sounding out words" instead of creating meaning and solving problems in order to hold the story together.

The final recommendation of the team was careful third-grade placement, as well as administering a battery of assessments to further study academic areas and speech and language development. Juanita's complete literacy history was passed on to her next teacher so that this process could continue at the beginning of her third-grade year. Monitoring Juanita's progress, as well as maintaining this literacy history, were critical to helping her develop as a learner.

REFLECTION

In my experience, struggling readers need explicit strategy instruction more frequently and for a longer period of time than those readers who seem to "instruct themselves." It takes struggling readers longer to "break the code" and manage the process of reading. It seems to take longer for them to develop a desire to participate in the language feast. My challenge is finding the time to provide the kind of individualized instruction that I know these readers need. Marie Clay addresses the issue of struggling readers in this way:

> My special plea would be that we recognize that some children need extra resources and many more supportive interactions with teachers to get them through the necessary transitions of reading acquisition to the stage where they can pick up most of the different kinds of information in print. As they read familiar texts or are challenged to engage in reading work on novel texts their literacy 'systems' which generate (a) correct responding and (b) effective problem-solving, provide them with feedback on the effectiveness of the strategies they used. Success encourages more risk-taking which, in turn, is likely to extend the range of strategies they try. Meanwhile, more and more encounters with 'known' words gives them rapid and 'direct access' to a wider vocabulary of words that require little or no solving. Literacy activities can become self-managed, self-monitored, self-corrected and self-extending for most children, even those who initially find transitions into literacy hard and confusing. (1991, 345)

In reflecting upon my work with struggling readers, I find that my path for instruction always depends on what I know about them from previous conferences and observations. Although there are similarities in my instructional conferences with these children, the focus, the questioning, the prompting, and the strategies are determined by what each child needs. No two conversations are exactly the same. I—not a book or a program—am teaching a reader. The differences are vast. The idea that a "program" can do this fine, fine work of teaching children, particularly struggling children, to read is a mystery to me. Programs do not "know" individual readers. Teachers do.

BECOMING WRITERS

*But I became a writer instead. And used my pen like a little
pink comb, and got quiet, and thought good thoughts, and
twirled and curled and rolled words into good stories . . .
There are many ways to learn to be a writer.*

—Cynthia Rylant, "My Grandmother's Hair"

FIGURE III–1
*Timmy and
Brenda: writing
together*

9 | QUIET WRITING AND WRITING NOTEBOOKS

In a pencil
noisy words yell for attention
and quiet words wait their turn.
—Barbara Esbensen, "Pencils"

I go to scool to lrn I do not go to scool to wiyn are missbehav I go to
scool to lrn and lisin and you shod to
    P.S. Scool is not for playing
    (I go to school to learn. I do not go to school to whine or misbehave. I
go to school to learn and listen and you should to.
    P.S. School is not for playing)
                            Rosanna's writing notebook entry, 9-1-95

My decision to have children keep a writing notebook and have daily quiet-writing time actually occurred while my husband, Michael, and I were on a five-week backpack trek across Europe. We were celebrating the completion of my graduate work.

During our travels, my journal became a collection of everything we experienced. Sometimes I wrote lengthy narrative entries, other times I jotted quick snippets of information. One day I did a quick sketch of a patch of houses along the Rhine River. Another day I taped a grape leaf from an arboretum in the Mirabel gardens in Salzburg, Austria, onto a page. Train tickets, bus tickets, postcards, and other scraps found their way into the pages. As I thought about my journal during this time of exploration, I realized I was viewing the world as a writer and historian—my journal provided the place to record my life.

Could young children live as writers in this way? I wanted to find out. Georgia Heard writes,

> So much of the delight teachers feel when they teach Kindergarten and first grade is born of the kids' natural curiosity, their everyday discoveries and transformations, their original way of looking at the world. (1989, 121)

It was these very things—the natural curiosity, the everyday discoveries and transformations, their original way of experiencing the world—that I wanted to help my young writers capture on paper. I knew they were there.

I collected their stories every day in my own school journal as I listened to the children and observed them going about their work in our classroom. Every day these children poured in the door, stories dripping off them, and I felt like I needed a bucket to catch all of them. Now I knew the perfect bucket: individual writing tablets. I wanted to invite the children to catch the splashes and drips of their own lives in the pages of their writing tablets. I envisioned this tablet as being a holding place for ideas until one little drop became a river of thoughts, ready to be ladled into a story, poem, informational book . . . any type of writing project.

PREPARING

Because of the differences in children's writing development, I prepare a writing *tablet* for first-grade children and purchase writing *notebooks* for second-grade children. Writing tablets for first-grade children consist of twenty pages of blank white paper bound at the top with a $4 \times 8\frac{1}{2}$" piece of construction paper folded in half and stapled together. Assembling writing tablets is a home project for one of my family helpers. I prepare blank tablets in this way because I want beginning writers to have space to write, draw, and explore without the confines of lines. Lines will come soon enough during the course of the year when children show they are ready to cope with them. When I introduce tablets, the first task the children do is to write their names and the date—neatly—on the strip of construction paper, first in pencil, then in black permanent marker, so they can lay claim to them as their own.

Second graders are ready for lines—even if they choose to disregard them at times while composing or drawing. I purchase wide-ruled notebooks at a local office supply store for my second-grade writers, using part of my classroom supply money to do this. I like to provide the first writing notebook, and for most of my children at Bobier, it was necessary that I do this. When children finish their first notebooks, I talk with them about buying their own if they prefer different shapes, sizes, or colors. However, I always have notebooks available in the classroom when a second one is needed. With my last group, several children wrapped their covers with gift wrap because they liked the way I covered my school journals and they, too, wanted "fancy covers." At recess one day, I helped Rosanna cover hers with an impressionist art wrap that she loved. Others, like Tracy, did theirs at home. Mainly, I want these notebooks to become a comfortable place for gathering thoughts, experimenting with words, and planning for writing projects—a notebook that the children will come to respect and love. I've discovered that when children see me treating my journal with care, it goes a long way toward encouraging them to do the same with theirs.

First-Grade Writers

With first-grade writers, I start quiet-writing time during the first week of school because I want the children to develop good writing habits early and learn the routine of starting our writing workshop time with ten minutes of quiet writing. Because the first session generally requires about an hour, I don't start on the first day. There are too many housekeeping items to address, and we haven't had time to settle in with one another.

When I'm ready for our initial writing session, I gather my group around the overhead projector. First, I show them how to set up their paper for writing an entry. I have the children choose which direction they want to write in their tablet, showing them that their tablets can be turned so the binding is either at the top or on the side. Once each child makes a decision, I demonstrate how to divide the page in half by drawing a line across the middle of the paper. I introduce rulers early!

Next, I explain to my young writers that I would like them to draw their illustrations on one half of the page—with pencil only, we don't use crayons in our writing tablets or notebooks—and write on the other half. I let them choose which half they would like for drawing, and which half for writing. The half-page they choose for writing is where they write the date in short form.

After this initial setup, I model writing an entry on the overhead. I tell them that I am putting myself in the role of a five- or six-year-old writer trying to figure out how and what to write. First, I draw my picture while discussing what I am thinking about as a writer. I call this my "picture writing." Then I compose one or two sentences that explain my illustration. I call this my "word writing." While writing, I involve the children in helping me spell, stretch out words, put space between words, decide on end marks, etc. I do use temporary spelling during this demonstration because I want the children to become comfortable using temporary spelling as beginning writers. Marie Clay describes temporary or invented spelling as "a powerful strategy for encouraging children to use the sounds they hear in words they are trying to write, and finding letters for those sounds they hear. Since Charles Read first discovered some preschool children who were inventing their own spelling system by this means, it has been recognized as a way [for children] to become more independent as writers" (1991, 111).

I make this temporary spelling message explicit during the first lesson and future sessions by saying, "I don't expect you to know how to spell all the wonderful words inside your minds when you are five and six years old, and learning how to spell words using 'temporary spelling' will help you. You'll learn how to spell many, many words in standard spelling this year also, but temporary spelling will help you in the meantime." (One of my first formal writing lessons with first-grade children is on temporary spelling, which I discuss in Chapter 11.)

After my writing demonstration, the children and I discuss topics they might want to write about. As we brainstorm ideas, I draw a picture cluster on the overhead, writing one or two words beside each picture so they can use this as a spelling resource while they write. I ask the children to think about these topic suggestions for a minute so they can choose the idea that is best for each one of them. They aren't limited to these suggestions; rather, I tell my group to write about something that is important to them. I also suggest that they start with a picture, then finish their entry by writing their words. I know that many of the children will only "write" pictures that day. Part of my work during quiet-writing time in the beginning weeks of school is to help children record sentences in their writing tablets about their illustrations so that they begin the process of connecting print to picture ideas.

For the first entry, the children stay together on the floor, writing in their tablets with their anthologies underneath for support. After this, they will write at their tables so that I can circulate to assist individual children during this time. I rarely write in my own journal during the beginning weeks of quiet writing with first graders because these are golden instructional minutes. Instead, I often model my entry on the overhead before they begin their writing so they see me in action as a writer. As the children develop their understandings about writing, spelling, and composing messages, I eliminate these "writing an entry" demonstrations and use this time for writing minilessons and doing demonstrations on conventions, craft, and genre. Figure 9–1 is a sample of a first-grade child's writing tablet entry.

Second-Grade Writers

With second-grade writers, I also start quiet-writing time sometime during the first week. Again, I want my young writers to develop good quiet-writing habits early and learn the routine of starting our writing workshop time with ten minutes of quiet writing. When the children choose their notebooks from the sea of notebook colors, their first task is to write their names on adhesive labels, first in pencil, then in a permanent black marker, and attach the labels to the upper right-hand corner of their notebook. Occasionally I collect notebooks and when I return them, I want names to be legible and in a predictable place.

My introductory session to notebooks is mainly procedural with a taste of writing. With my last second-grade group, we started in this way:

The children gathered on the floor around the overhead with their writing notebooks and pencils and I began by showing them how to set up their first entry by writing the date in short form (9-1-95) and how to skip a line before starting their writing. I require this "date/line space" format so that their writing is not crammed together on the page, making it difficult to read. Later, when the children begin continuing entries from one day to the next, I show them how to write the date in the margin so we know how many days they've worked on it. I then showed them how they could write on every line, or skip a line between the written lines. On the first day, they had a choice. Sometimes I require line spaces because it makes it easier for editing work, but it isn't necessary for every entry. This first entry was meant to help the children get back into their writing by noticing, observing, and thinking.

Next I talked with my group about what to write. I posed several questions for the children to think about:

- What is important to you?
- What have you noticed lately?
- What are you wondering about?
- How is second grade?

After a few moments of quiet, I asked them to talk with a friend or two sitting next to them about what they were thinking or what they might write

FIGURE 9–1   *Roni's first-grade writing tablet entry*
"Jana might come over to my
home! and have cake and ice cream
with my cousins."

about. After a short discussion time, I asked the children to share their own writing ideas or a friend's ideas with the group. I began a cluster on the overhead as they took turns calling out ideas. When one child offered an idea, the rest waited for me to finish writing it before another person made a contribution. I was in charge of compiling their ideas; they were in charge of giving ideas in a clear, organized way without everyone talking at once. Contributions came quickly and soon we had a variety of ideas for the children to work with, although they were not confined to these topics when they began their own writing. The items on our cluster that day follow:

- family
- places to go
- today
- clouds
- starting second grade
- vacation
- universe
- Pluto
- favorite books
- becoming a writer
- school year
- friends
- pets
- something that happened

After we finished our list of possible writing ideas, the children began writing their first entry while I wrote in my own school journal. For this first session, we stayed together, gathered on the floor, notebooks in our laps, finding our thoughts at the end of a busy week, searching for the words and spellings to write them down. After this first writing session, the children wrote in their notebooks at their tables. In the quiet, I discovered that Heidi was crying. Our conversation went something like this:

Janine: Heidi, come close to me. What's wrong? Why are you crying?
Heidi: I don't know what to do. I've never done this before.
Janine: Did you do any writing last year in your first-grade classroom?
Heidi: Yes, but it was different.
Janine: That's OK. You're learning new things in here. What do you think about a lot, Heidi?
Heidi: Horses. My family.
Janine: Perhaps you can write about one of those. You can always draw a picture first if that helps you with your thinking. There isn't a wrong way to do this, Heidi, really. Are you OK with this now?
Heidi: Yes. (Her head was still down. I wasn't convinced.)
Janine: I'll check in with you in a few minutes and see how you're doing. I suggest starting with a drawing. You're a wonderful artist, Heidi. Your drawing can be your words today.

Heidi settled, I returned to my writing notebook to capture the gist of our first writing session. While heads were bent over notebooks, I heard Timmy whisper to Tracy, "How do you spell Las Vegas?"

"Use temporary spelling. I'm writing, too," Tracy replied.

I glanced over at Heidi and she seemed more at ease. She had written "My Family" in her notebook. I was surprised she had started. I could see she was a tentative writer.

After fifteen minutes of quiet writing, I asked the children to form groups of two or three and share their writing. (See Figure 9–2.) I walked among them while they read aloud their entries so that I could get a sense of their writing topics. They were as varied as the children themselves. There were several entries about family pets and August vacations. Priscilla had written about her favorite books, Eddie about his growing excitement that he was going to his first San Diego Padres game with his father, and Nhi about her mischievous hamster. Adrienne wrote about her two dogs, circling those words that she was uncertain how to spell. Her entry follows:

Today I got tow dogs and won's a girl and won's a boy and the girls name is Athena. The boys name is Horcelis and Horcelis Navr bits Athena all was bits but I love hor still. And I tat the dogs haw to sit and bork and they do it cas they are smort and they like me They like my sister too My mom loves the dogs so moch that she all was fieeds tham.

(*Today I got two dogs and one's a girl and one's a boy and the girl's name is Athena. The boy's name is Hercules and Hercules never bites. Athena always bites but I love her still. And I taught the dogs how to sit and bark and they do it because they are smart and they like me. They like my sister too. My mom loves the dogs so much that she feeds them.*)

Tracy compared first *and* second grade in the same classroom, Elizabeth wrote about the loss of her grandfather, and Lisa chose to write a brief commentary on her older brother:

9-1-95

My brother is werd very werd. He can Belly danss, and sometimes me and my sister call my Brother Steffaney Because He akse like a Girl some times.

(*My brother is weird, very weird. He can belly dance, and sometimes me and my sister call my brother Stephanie because he acts like a girl sometimes.*)

I also took a moment to check in with Edward that day since this was his first writing entry in English after spending two years in a Spanish literacy classroom. He did have a complete thought written:

Me and family going to Disneyland for 3 years.

This was a good benchmark in terms of evaluating what he could already do as a writer in English. I was surprised he was able to compose even that sentence. The unusual syntax was typical of second-language writers. Time, daily writing, interactive writing instruction, and collaborating with fellow writers would help him immensely. I discuss Edward's writing development in Chapter 13.

SUSTAINING QUIET WRITING

As the children and I continue this ten-minute period of quiet-writing time throughout the year, I alternate between writing in my own journal, circulating around the room to do an overall check of how my writers are doing, and sitting beside one of my struggling writers, like Christina or Edward, and giving them individual attention and instruction. (See Chapter 13 for a discussion on struggling writers.) After our quiet-writing time is over, we gather as a group to organize ourselves for the start of our workshop time. I usually don't allot time for whole-group or partner sharing of writing notebook entries; rather, this is one of the options the children have during our workshop time.

As I observe my young writers at work in their notebooks during quiet-writing time, I also gather minilesson ideas. I look for their confusions, struggles, or successes and use these as teaching opportunities for the entire

FIGURE 9–2
Jana and Kaley: sharing
writing notebooks

class. For example, I did a minilesson on "sentence spacing" after reading Brenda's entry in her notebook after our field trip to the San Diego Zoo. She wrote:

I had fun at the zoo.
   I saw grafds I like the zoo a lot. it is a lot of fun. . . . The zoo is very pesifole
   and very fun.
   I like the ahnimols a lot.
   They are cool.
   (I had fun at the zoo. I saw giraffes. I like the zoo a lot. It is a lot of fun . . .The zoo is very peaceful and very fun. I like the animals a lot. They are cool.)

When I read Brenda's entry, I noticed a pattern in her writing. She was writing one sentence per line, or what she perceived to be one sentence per line, then starting on the next line with her new sentence. I could see she was making a transition, developing her conceptual understanding of punctuation when writing, and perhaps writing one sentence per line was helpful to her. I decided to do a minilesson with the entire class on how to put a little extra space between sentences after end marks instead of starting the next sentence on a new line.

The minilessons that I glean from writing notebooks usually focus on conventions of writing and spelling. Minilessons that deal with ideas, content, and genre are developed from individual writing projects or whole-group writing projects. (See Chapter 12 for minilessons during writing workshop.)

Topics for entries in notebooks during quiet-writing time vary widely among the children. How they arrive at these topic ideas is an individual process, but one that I help along. I listen closely to children as they talk about the stuff of their lives, and often I will say to them, "You really need to write about that in your notebook during quiet-writing time." When Victor's mom talked with us about Victor getting his leg run over while playing by the side of the road in their neighborhood, we were all dismayed. I wondered what words would find a resting place on the pages of their notebooks that morning. I peered over hunched shoulders during quiet-writing time to read the children's entries, and discovered that several had chosen to write about the stuff of Victor's life. Cynthia wrote:

1-10-96 Abawt Victor
   Victorwas a grat firend he mad os lafe a lot. he was vary smart I washe thes naver hapande to hem and I hop he gats wale sone
   (About Victor: Victor was a great friend. He made us laugh a lot. He was very smart. I wish this never happened to him and I hope he gets well soon.)

Kayalani wrote:

Today Mis. Janine fand awt that Victor got his fot ran ovr. . . . I almost crod would you croy?

(Today Ms. Janine found out that Victor got his foot ran over. . . . I almost cried. Would you cry?)

The children understood the injustice. The driver's actions lacked all human decency and I wanted them to understand this. I worried about their ability to feel compassion and recognize injustice when they were inundated with aggressive images on TV or experienced it "live" in their neighborhoods. At that point in our year, distressing events that had made their way into our discussions ranged from stabbings over Barbie dolls, to a small child being shot by a gang when her parents turned down the wrong street in L.A., to being frightened by the sound of gunshots on New Year's Eve, to Victor's leg being run over and a driver not stopping to see if he was injured. They were all disturbing, and I didn't want the children to accept this as an appropriate way to live. Writing notebooks provide a place to not only write about weird brothers, baseball games, and favorite books, but also about outrage and injustice.

In addition to encouraging children to write about their lives, I "find" topic invitations when I take my daily walk. I bring in little things that catch my eye along my walking route because I enjoy sharing them with the children. Every spring in Southern California, the southern magnolia and jacaranda trees have wonderful blossoms, and I loved bringing those in to share and display in our science/discovery area. In the spring of the year with my second graders, I discovered a Venus's flytrap on a Sunday visit to the Wild Animal Park and brought it to school. Many of the children had never seen a plant like this and weren't familiar with the way it "catches" its nourishment. Of course there wasn't a fly or small insect to be found that day, so I took the end of a paper clip and triggered the little hairs on one of its leaves so the children could see its reaction to "dinner." They were tickled with the feeding habits of this mysterious plant and for several days many wrote about it during our quiet-writing time. Timmy wrote:

4-8-96 Miss Janine got us a venus fly trap and Im going to chay flys for it and Im going to feid it. Halp

(Miss Janine got us a Venus's flytrap and I'm going to chase flies for it and I'm going to feed it. Help!)

Venus's flytraps, southern magnolias, and jacaranda blossoms are invitations to write—not assignments. When I share items like this, I say something like, "You may want to write about this in your notebook today or sketch a quick drawing of it if you don't have something else on your mind." I "drop" invitations constantly in hopes that my group will begin viewing the world as writers, simmering with writing ideas until they have notebooks and pencils in hand.

Writing topics and invitations come from other places, too. When we were preparing for our field trip to see the Ms. Frizzle Exhibit at the Natural History Museum in San Diego, Lisa wrote several entries about our upcoming adventure, writing this final entry in her notebook before we left:

6-19-96

The day after tomorrow we are going to the: *Magic School bus the Living Seas Museum.* I hope it's fun, but I just know it will. I'm going to where some fish—or funny like, Mrs. Frizzle. We are going to see: *In the time of the Dinosaurs, On the Ocean floor, Inside the Earth's Crust, Inside the Human body, Lost In the Solar System,* and things like that. the End!

I also have the children take their writing notebooks with them when we go on field trips. When we attended a production of Winnie-the-Pooh at the California Center for the Performing Arts in Escondido, we had time to sketch the set in our notebooks before the production started. After the performance, many of the children wrote about it in their notebooks on the bumpy bus ride home. We later incorporated these entries into oil pastel drawings that we did to capture our theater experience. David's entry follows:

1-24-96

I like it wan the pig wus runeing bak and fort. it was funeor wan he wus Dancing. tar plan wus tat piglit wus supos to luke like Babe Row but he dadt luke like ham.

(*I liked it when the pig was running back and forth. It was funnier when he was dancing. Their plan was that piglet was supposed to look like Baby Roo, but he didn't look like him.*)

Entries in writing notebooks often continue after we return home from field trips. Upon our return from our trip to the San Diego Zoo, Cynthia wrote in her notebook:

I thot the zoo wos fon. . . . My lags got tiurd because Janine sad we wer goeg too woke a lat and she wos riut I like it wan Mes. Janine is riute. . . . Janine do you think that the goats dropping stinks? I do it stinks bad to me did you see the giraffe they were big. I like the monkeys I wonder what they were eating? I seen a goat pregnant the Zoo wos fun

(*I thought the Zoo was fun...My legs got tired because Janine said we were going to walk a lot and she was right. I like it when Ms. Janine is right! Janine, do you think that the goat's droppings stink? I do. It stinks bad to me. Did you see the giraffes? They were big. I like the monkeys. I*

wonder what they were eating? [I've] seen a goat pregnant. The Zoo
was fun.)

Since our quiet-writing time occurs directly after shared reading (the
children have their notebooks and pencils ready on their tables for a smooth
transition), I also encourage responding to the books we read during shared-
reading time. At one time, I had the children keep a separate reading journal
for their reading responses, but eventually I discovered that writing notebooks were a wonderful place for this, plus it was one less journal to keep
track of. Entries were especially vivid when we were reading *Lassie Come-
Home* (Wells 1995). Cynthia's empathy for Joe, his family, and the indecent
power of poverty was evident in her entry. She wrote:

Abawt the book cold Lassie come-home

   A few das ago. we startad a book kold Lassie come-home it is
abawt. a boy and has parants. and there dag name'd Lassie they
ware so por that they had to sale the dag I no naw they fal becosae
I hade a dag one'c and we hade to sale it I stad in my badroom for
12 days and I only came awt to eyt and to jrak and to go to the
bath room some time's I wlode go awt siad to get some frash ara
the End

   (About the book called Lassie Come-Home:

   A few days ago we started a book called Lassie Come-Home. It is
about a boy and his parents and their dog named Lassie. They were so
poor that they had to sell the dog. I know how they feel because I had a
dog once and we had to sell it. I stayed in my bedroom for twelve days
and I only came out to eat and to drink and to go to the bathroom.
Sometimes I would go outside to get some fresh air. The End.)

During this ten-minute quiet-writing time, I see children playing with
poetry, working out disagreements between friends, imagining magic holes
that turn girls into princesses, grieving that a grandmother didn't die in peace,
describing accidents such as toes getting caught in doors when "the only things
left is blood and almost muscle," or in Priscilla's case, planning the details of her
dolphin characters, Liz and Lizey, for her fiction story. (Figure 9–3.)

   The children do use their writing notebooks for other purposes besides
entries during quiet-writing time. They also write in their notebooks during
minilessons and writing-workshop time. The children are always welcome
to continue writing in their notebooks during our workshop time. When we
are working on shorter whole-group writing projects, for example, poetry or
autobiographical paragraphs, the children often work on planning and
drafts in their notebooks. When we are working on writing pieces from the
class, e.g., letters, or a piece for the classroom, e.g., a tour guide for open
house, I ask the children to write/plan their thoughts in their notebooks
before we gather as a whole group to work on a draft together. In this way,

the notebook becomes a gathering place, a planning place, a thinking place, and a drafting place, as well as a quiet-writing place.

   Some of the most memorable entries in the children's writing notebooks occurred during the spring of our second-grade year when a hummingbird appeared in the bushes outside our classroom window in mid-April. We first discovered its presence when we returned from recess, and we *had* to take a moment to quietly observe this tiny bird flitting nervously back and forth from the trees to the bushes. The hummingbird rewarded our efforts at being still, as it landed on a bush for several seconds, allowing us to get a closer

FIGURE 9–2
Priscilla's notebook entry: planning fictional characters

look. It was a moment that demanded an entry in our notebooks. Rachael wrote:

> 4-15-96—today we saw a HummingBird it was beautiful. It came closir and closir and it went back and forth back and forth.
>
> *(Today we saw a hummingbird. It was beautiful. It came closer and closer and it went back and forth, back and forth.)*

Brenda wrote:

> today I sall a hmmingbred it look like it had a totseetow on boy was it fliing so fast it flw bake and foth, hey wint to this tree and that tree
>
> *(Today I saw a hummingbird. It looked like it had a tuxedo on. Boy was it flying so fast. It flew back and forth. He went to this tree and that tree.)*

Cynthia wrote:

> tow Day after snace, we saw a hamming Bird I cad tall that it was . a garl Maybe the rast of the clas cad not tall bot the resan way I cad tall that it was a garl is it had a paec stomack and a garen back and I thick it had blue ies I loved the hamming Bird.
>
> *(Today after snack we saw a hummingbird. I could tell that it was a girl. Maybe the rest of the class could not tell but the reason why I could tell that it was a girl is it had a pink stomach and a green back and I think it had blue eyes. I loved the hummingbird.)*

Rosanna wrote:

> today after ressaiss there was a huumingbrid it was amazing I was astonished I thik Miss Janine was to I liked it so much I didn't get the coler of it's eys it was beautiful it was sod of gray
>
> *(Today after recess there was a hummingbird. It was amazing. I was astonished. I think Miss Janine was too. I liked it so much. I didn't get the color if its eyes. It was beautiful. It was sort of gray.)*

I loved reading the children's entries that day. Rachael's and Brenda's entries were lyrical, like poetry. I heard the lines from *Love You Forever* (Munsch 1986) in Rachael's writing with her repetition of "back and forth, back and forth." I wondered if she was aware of this influence on her writing, or if she had simply internalized the rhythm of the words. Rosanna had borrowed straight from the pages of *Rumpelstiltskin* (Parkes 1986) when she wrote that the hummingbird was "amazing" and that she was "astonished." In fact, after I had finished my own entry that day and was peering over small writing shoulders, Rosanna had stopped me and asked if I would please write the standard spelling for *astonished* and *amazed* so that she could add them to her dictionary. Good literature feeds the soul and pages of young writers. I continually look for this "literature influence" in the children's writing.

Our feathered friend did not leave us after making its first appearance in the bushes outside our room. Thanks to the keen eyes of two fifth-grade girls, we discovered an amazing sight just two days later: a hummingbird nest. It was nestled on the branch of one of the bushes outside our classroom door. That morning during quiet-writing time, I wrote the following entry in my journal:

> We have discovered that the little hummingbird has built a nest in our bushes. Now we know why the little hummingbird has been around here so much. It's so tiny. It's made out of seeds and feathers. I didn't realize they would be so tiny. I'm hoping the little bird lays eggs. I hope we haven't contaminated it with our presence and our smell.

It appeared that we had a trusting mama hummingbird in our midst, as the morning after we had admired the architectural work of "our" hummingbird (by this time we felt like she belonged to Room 12), she presented us with the gift of one milky-white egg in the middle of her nest. It felt like a miracle. We couldn't believe our good fortune of having a mother hummingbird build her nest and lay a perfect jelly bean–sized egg so close to us. None of us had ever experienced the beauty of this before.

We decided not to wait for our writing time to capture the events of "The Little Hummingbird: Day 3" in our writing notebooks. The children and I piled inside, hung backpacks on the backs of chairs, grabbed notebooks and pencils from cubbies, and settled into crafting our thoughts and sketching drawings. We couldn't start our day in an ordinary way when something extraordinary had greeted us that morning. Lisa wrote:

> We looked in a littil (*little*) tree and soue (*saw*) a hummingbird's nest. The day before we soue (*saw*) the hummingbird that belong to the nest.
>
> the end
>
> P.S. How much does a Hummingbird weigh? And how much does it's eggs weigh?

Priscilla wrote this entry in her notebook:

> This morning we saw a humming biard's egg. I was amazed.
>
> Qustuns I have about the Humming bird.
>
> 1. how big will it be when it haches
> 1. how long will it tack to hach

(*This morning we saw a hummingbird's egg. I was amazed.*

Questions I have about the hummingbird:

> 1. *How big will it be when it hatches?*
> 1. *How long will it take to hatch?*)

The day after the arrival of the first egg, we discovered a second egg in the nest, nestled next to the first egg. The second egg seemed a little close to the edge, but we were quite adamant about not disturbing it and trusted that the mama hummingbird knew what she was doing. We weren't going to interfere with her incubation process. However, we were a little concerned that she wasn't tending her eggs as closely as she should be, because we hadn't seen her warming her eggs yet. We thought perhaps she was using the same trick as the goose in *Charlotte's Web*—letting the sun do some of the work for her—only she didn't have any straw to fluff over her eggs in her absence. Hmmm . . . did we have a young mother on our hands?

The next Monday, we finally saw the mother perched on her two little eggs. We tiptoed by her into our classroom so as not to disturb her peace of mind. She had important work to do, and we wanted her to do it. Jonathan wrote this entry in his notebook that morning:

> I like the hummingbird a lot and the first time I saw it I was shocked and whan I saw the two eggs I was amazed and I like the Humming-bird a lot and the moma sat on her eggs
> (*I like the hummingbird a lot, and the first time I saw it, I was shocked. And when I saw the two eggs, I was amazed. And I like the hummingbird a lot. And the momma sat on her eggs.*)

By the time the hummingbird events had unfolded, it was the beginning of our last week of school before our May vacation. The timing couldn't have been worse. We needed information and began researching hummingbirds. We located "hummingbirds" in the life science section of our Encarta CD so that we could research some of our questions, as well as find out if there were any chance those little eggs would humor us and hatch before we left. We discovered that a hummingbird only lays two eggs—even that seemed monumental for such a petite feathered vertebrate—and that it usually takes about two weeks for the eggs to hatch. Unfortunately that was about five days too many for us at this point. We were beside ourselves with worry. Would our little nest and jewel eggs survive without our watchful eyes?

Sadly enough, when we returned to school at the end of May, we discovered that our mama hummingbird, her little nest, and jewel eggs had not survived. Peggy Duffield, one of our Reading Recovery teachers, had kept an eye on the little nest while we were gone, and I shared her note with the children our first morning back together. She explained that there had been no sign of the mama bird during the entire first week of May, and that on May 14, everything had disappeared altogether. No hummingbird. No nest. No eggs. Peggy wrote, "No clue as to where or why."

My kids were quiet. It wasn't the "welcome back" any of us wanted. We all felt like Room 12 had lost something precious. And, it was also the last of the children's entries about our little hummingbird. Figure 9–4 shows one of Victor's hummingbird entries in his writing notebook.

REFLECTION

Just as quiet reading is daily time for my young readers to revel in the pages of good books, practice their reading, and lead "readerly lives," quiet writing

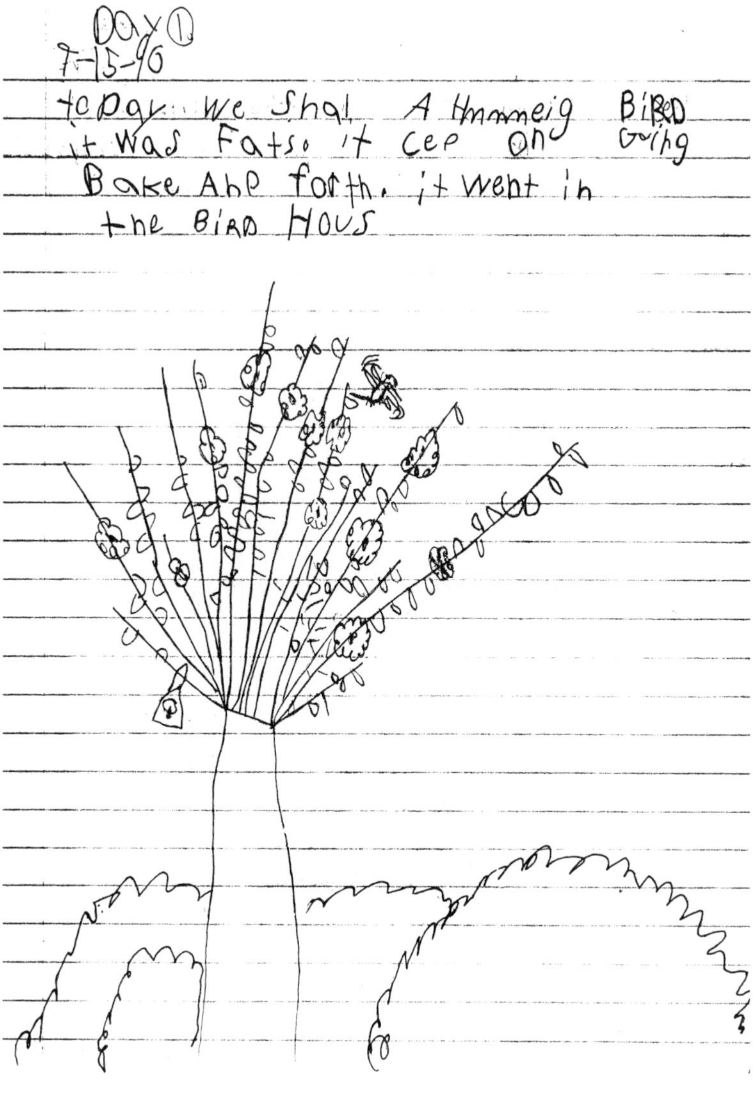

FIGURE 9–4
Victor's hummingbird entry in his writing notebook

is an oasis of time for my young writers to compose what they notice and wonder as they begin to lead "writerly lives." Like quiet reading, it is a time in our classroom when everything else stops, we become a community of writers, and the only business of our classroom is to write. It is a chance for every writer, regardless of development, to practice writing without the worries of form and correctness.

Along with quiet writing, writing notebooks give children a place to collect their thoughts and comment on their world. It is a space where noisy words can learn to wait their turn so that quiet words can yell for attention. Notebooks also provide a "room" in which to . . . explore the solar system, plan sleepovers, experiment with story characters, dream about owning a house with one hundred rooms, imagine a lost world of dinosaurs, believe in the miracle of hummingbirds, and cry over missing nests and eggs, or lost dogs that never come home. It is a place where Priscilla and other children can write about "something that I have in my body. . . . (that) I think about inside."

Writing notebooks and quiet-writing time help children slow down, notice more, and live better lives.

10 | JOURNALS

Getting a journal is like
buying shoes. You have to
find the one that fits.
And you are the only person
who can tell if it pinches.
—*Jean Little "My Journals"*

3-21-96

Dear Mom,

I can't wait until I go to Priscilla's House and Nancy's House and we will play game's. Do not forget, it's my birthday. I love you.

Love, Jana

Dear Jana,

We did not forget it was your birthday. You had such a big party Sunday, we thought you were *too* tired to remember that it was really today. We'll have Jennifer sing to you. Ha, ha, ha!

Love Mama

FAMILY JOURNALS

When I began teaching at Bobier Elementary, I developed the idea of a family journal because I didn't know my school community, and was looking for ways to connect our classroom to the children's families. I had long been doing weekly letter journals with my students and decided to extend this concept to having the children write weekly letters to their families in a separate journal. I believed that in addition to connecting our classroom to children's homes, writing weekly letters would give my young writers a meaningful purpose and audience for their writing, which are two of my prime considerations when shaping writing opportunities.

I introduced family journals at Back-to-School Night, showing families what the journal would look like, and answering questions they had about writing back to their children. I always stress that they print instead of writing in cursive and write simple reply letters because eventually I want the children to be able to read these themselves. My goal is to help parents understand how to be supportive of the process, to let them know that writing back to their children each week is important, and that this journal will help their children become confident writers and readers. I also include a letter of explanation in the journal (Appendix 10–1) so families can read this when the journal arrives home. Lastly, I tell families that I hope family journals will become treasured memory books for their children.

Preparing Journals

All of my classroom journals, family journals included, are made with folded 9×12" covers, with blank $8\frac{1}{2} \times 11$" paper inside. I like small journals for many reasons. They are easy to make, carry, and store, and they fit nicely in small hands. I include the following pieces in family journals:

- cover: 9×12" tagboard folded in half, covered with 11×14" brightly colored butcher paper
- cover artwork: handprint painting by the children—Left hand on back cover, right hand on front cover
- inside front cover: Letter to families explaining family journals
- inside pages: ten pieces of blank $8\frac{1}{2} \times 11$" paper
- inside back cover: description of the cover artwork

I not only like practical journals, but also artistic journals, so the children create the covers for every journal we have in our classroom. The children do the artwork on the butcher paper that is then taped to the tagboard cover. (See Appendix 5–1 for diagram.)

Besides journal covers being a wonderful art project, I believe children like their journals more, and do a better job of caring for them when they've had a part in creating them. A list of some of my favorite ways to do cover artwork appears below.

- handprint painting
- sponge painting
- string painting
- marble painting
- bubble painting
- scrunched paper painting
- straw painting
- spray bottle painting
- potato prints
- leaf prints
- thumbprints with ink pad (create your own creatures and designs)
- crayon/marker/colored-pencil illustrations

Once covers are made, and the pieces are in order, I staple journals in the center with a long-neck stapler, then place clear, book-binding tape on the folded spine of the journal for reinforcement. This usually keeps journals in one piece. If not, I run a second piece of clear, book-binding tape over the staples on the inside center page of the journal. Assembling journals in this fashion is a job that I save for family helpers for home projects. I make a model of one journal, include all of the supplies needed for assembling journals, place everything in a large bag, and send the project home to those parents who have indicated on their Family Help survey that they would like to do home projects to assist with our classroom world. I've always had willing helpers.

Getting Started

I usually introduce family journals during our second week of school. I like Thursdays for family journals because the children have been immersed in our classroom world for the better part of a week, so there are several interesting classroom news items to write about. However, I don't require that children write about classroom news; anything that is important in their world is fair game for their letters. I also like Thursdays because the children can share their journals with their families, families can write back, and children can return journals to school Friday morning. On Thursdays, we devote our entire writing workshop to our family journals, as it usually takes the entire forty-five minutes to complete the process.

First-Grade Writers

When I introduce family journals to beginning first-grade writers, I focus on letter format and the "simple act" of composing. When I embark on this first writing session with my first graders, I know that they are at various stages of writing development. Some know all of the letters and sounds, and others do not. Some understand the concept of a word, how to spell simple words, and how to develop a thought into a sentence, while others do not. Some have already written letters to distant friends or relatives, while others have never done any of this. Given this, I believe that family journals offer the kind of literacy opportunity, regardless of writing development, that Frank Smith describes in this way:

> Children who come to school already members of the club, who regard themselves as the kind of people who read and write, should find expanded opportunities in school for engaging in all the activities of club membership. Children who have not become members before they get to school should find the classroom the place where they are immediately admitted to the club. (1988, 11)

With my last group of first-grade children at Bobier, I spent two days starting family journals with them. Our two-day process follows.

Day One The first day, I gathered my group around me during shared reading and read aloud from some of the family journals that children from the previous year had loaned to me. I wanted them to hear what children had written about and how their families had responded. I showed them the difference between the children's letters at the beginning, the middle, and the end of the year. To ease the worries of some of my ESL children, I purposefully included Virginia's journal because it was a wonderful example of Virginia's English development. Virginia had immigrated from China, and her first language was Mandarin. I shared three letters from her journal. This was one of Virginia's letters at the beginning of our year:

Dear Family,

Mom and Dad
What is Cat play?

Love, Virginia

In March, which was the middle of our year, she composed this letter to her mom:

Dear Mom:

did Alvan wear green today mom?

Love Virginia

In July, at the end of our school year, Virginia wrote:

Dear Mom,

Today me and Steven was going to the classroom I saw a caterpillar and Steven tell me to care (*carry*) it into the classroom to saw (*show*) Janine and now we have 2 caterpillar.

Love, Virginia

After sharing several journals, I ended our session by telling the children that we would be starting our family journals the next day, and that their job was to think about what we could write in our first letter since we would be composing it together. I asked them to think about these four questions as they searched for ideas:

- What is important to you?
- What questions do you have for your family?
- What could you write about in our classroom world?
- What have you seen recently that was interesting to you?

Why this introduction to family journals the day before we actually start writing? I call this "steeping time." First, children become familiar with the concept of a family journal by seeing other children's journals and second, it gives them some time to think and prepare for our first letter. My thoughts center on the time a new process deserves, quality of work, and the attention span of little ones. The double task of acquainting them with family journals *and* composing a letter is too much for one session with beginning first-grade writers.

Day Two   The next day, at the start of our writing time, we gathered around the overhead to compose our first letter. We compose this first letter together as a class in a shared-writing/guided-writing format, as I find it is the most explicit way to help children with the initial letter to their families. The children had pencils, their new family journals, and their anthologies, which doubled as lap desks. The night before I had made two marks on the first blank page of each journal: a small dot so they would know where to write the date and a little square so they would know where to write the greeting. I make these small marks on the first pages of their journals to help the children organize page space for letter writing. At the beginning of the year, my first graders write on unlined paper. Drawing lines with a ruler to tidy up the writing comes later. My overhead transparency was set up with these same two marks.

First, I asked my group to find the little dot on their papers and put one finger on it. Then, I showed them how to write the date in short form (9-7-96) right after this dot. Next, I asked them to find the little square, and we wrote our greeting after that: *Dear Family.* I chose to do a simple greeting at this point, with everyone writing the same one. As the year progresses, I help children personalize their greetings to specific family members.

We had been immersed in reading Roald Dahl's book *Fantastic Mr. Fox* (1985), and that came out as a favorite topic for our letter. We negotiated our first sentence, *We are reading Fantastic Mr. Fox,* and began to compose together:

Janine: Our first word is *we.* Does anyone know how to spell *we?*

Tracy and Holly: w-e.

Janine: Great. Now we just need to make that a capital "w" because it starts a sentence.

Our next word is *are.* Anyone know *are?* It's a little tricky and it's one that I want you to learn in standard spelling this year, so I am going to spell this one out for you: a-r-e. We need to put a finger space in between the words *We* and *are* so that it is easy to read. So far, our letter reads: *We are.* The next word is *reading.* Let's stretch it out and write down the sounds we hear. We'll use temporary spelling for this word.

Children: Rrrreeeeddddding.

Janine: Good. What's at the beginning?

Children: "R."

Janine: Put a finger space between *are* and the /r/ that starts *reading.* Now, keep stretching it. What do you hear in the middle?

Children: /e/.

Janine: Write that down next. Stretch it out again: r–e–ddddd–ing.

Children: "d."

Janine: So far we have "r-e-d." Now for the ending. Three letters make that sound: /-ing/. You will hear those letters a lot in words: *ring, sing, bring, thing* . . . (I did a minilesson on the /-ing/ pattern during the next day's shared-reading session.)

Janine: So far we have written *We are reading...* in this sentence. Now to finish our first sentence: *We are reading Fantastic Mr. Fox.* Where would we be able to look in our classroom to find out how to spell *Fantastic Mr. Fox*?

Children: It's on the cover of the book. It's on our daily schedule in the pocket chart. (It was good to know they were noticing print!)

Janine: Great. Let's retrieve the book so we can "scrounge for print" and copy it right off the front cover. That's another way we can help ourselves as writers when we are working through the spellings of words.

Now, let's read what we've written so far, starting with *Dear Family.* Use your finger or your pencil eraser to follow along as we read together:

Dear Family,

We are reading Fantastic Mr. Fox.

This type of dialogue continued as we composed the rest of our letter to our families. Our finished letter read,

Dear Family,

We are reading Fantastic Mr. Fox. Bunce doesn't clean out his ears. OOOO!

We love this book.

Love, (name)

The entire composing process took about thirty minutes. Once again, children paired themselves on the floor so that those who felt they might need the helping hand of a "teacher" close to them were guided by children who felt they indeed could be teachers during this time. I wrote carefully on the overhead so the children could follow along, consulting my writing for letter formation, spellings, how to put a finger space between words, and how to form end marks. We shared the task of choosing the ideas together for the letter (shared writing), and I guided them through the actual composing of the text (guided writing). For some children, the process was manageable, and for others, it was challenging. I expected both. However, I still believed the demonstration beneficial for all the children, whatever level they happened to be at in "our club."

We read through our letter together, then discussed how to match our drawings to what had written. For example, I told them it would confuse the reader to see a picture with rainbows and flowers when we had written about a fox. With that reminder, most of the children went to their tables to complete their illustrations. Those who needed extra assistance with finishing their letters stayed at the overhead with me for a few minutes until their writing was completed.

Once again, while the children were drawing their illustrations, we stopped to take walks around the room and view one another's work. I brought the children together at various times—I call this a "fishbowl"—to demonstrate simple crayon/drawing techniques that would assist them in their work:

- how to shade properly
- how to use space well
- how to outline with a darker crayon and color in with a lighter crayon
- how to consult the book to help with the drawing of a character
- how to bring the sky right down to the horizon

I do these minilessons during work time because I want to encourage exploration, viewing each other's work to inspire our own, and developing pride in the way that we complete every piece of work in our classroom, even when it is a simple illustration in our family journals.

If I value the concept of family journals, then I also have to value every piece that is part of the process. The way I hold this work in my hands, the way I treat it with care, respect, and purpose, all translate into how the children treat their process and product throughout the entire year. I plan the process before I work with the children. I explore, experiment, and reflect as I go through the process with them. This first work session, from composing the letter to finishing illustrations, usually takes about an hour and a half. I devote this kind of time to family journal letters for approximately the first month so that children develop good work habits with this journal. After that, I move into a different type of modeled writing process, which is described below.

Second-Grade Writers

I begin family journals with second-grade writers in the way that I eventually handle this process with first graders. Again, I focus on letter format and composing thoughts into sentences in the introductory lesson, but in a slightly different way. The following is a description of the way I started family journals with my second graders.

I began our family journal writing time with my own letter to my husband, Michael. I wrote on a large sheet of chart paper so that the children could view my writing as I composed my letter. I drew a line down the center of the chart paper to create two sides: one side for the illustration and the other side for the text of the letter. I started my illustration while the children were busy getting their pencils and two helpers were passing out our new family journals. After everyone was settled, I began my "think-aloud" writing to Michael: "First I need to write the date in short form in the top right-hand corner, *9-7-95*, then my greeting to Michael, down and to the left of that: *Dear Michael* . What kind of punctuation mark do I need after my greeting?"

"A comma," the children said to me. They knew greetings to letters, and they knew commas. They had done this every week during their first-grade year.

"I've been thinking about what I want to write to Michael, and mainly I've just been very busy getting a new school year started with all of you, so I think I'll write about that to him.

"*Dear Michael,* (I reread) *We have been very busy starting our new school year.* That ends my first sentence. I need to put an end mark there. I'm just going to end it with a period.

"*At first it was a little strange to call them second graders! The first day I called them first graders!* I think an exclamation point is more appropriate at the ends of these two sentences. It was tricky getting used to calling you second graders!

"*It took me ten years to move to second grade. My kids think that is a LONG TIME!* I really want to emphasize long time so I'm going to write those two words in capital letters. That will get my point across even better. OK, now where am I? I think I need to reread and see how it all fits together at this point:"

9-7-95
Dear Michael,
We have been very busy starting our new school year. At first it was a little strange to call them second graders! The first day I called them first graders! It took me ten years to move to second grade. My kids think that is a LONG TIME!

"Yes, I think that makes sense. Now I need to finish off my letter. Besides, I'm almost out of room. I think I will let Michael know that Back-to-School Night will be here soon. I'll end with that: *Soon it will be Back-to-School Night and my class wants to do a Bubble-Bath Play!*

"Now for my closing: *Love You.* What punctuation mark comes after my closing?"

"A comma," the children responded.

"Good. You remember. Now for my name: *Janine.*

"There. I think that completes my letter and now it's your turn to write to your families. Please open your journal to the first two pages so that you can start setting up your letter. As soon as you have the date and your greeting written, I will excuse you to continue your writing either on the floor or at your table. Please make sure you have your letter completed before you start your illustration."

I walked among my group as they were setting up their journals, excusing those who had finished properly, reminding others to include commas after their greetings, or nudging a few who needed to erase and write more neatly so their families would be able to read letters with ease. I always keep my group gathered close to me during this setup time so that I can help monitor the start of the process. Once the children had the date and greeting written, they found their own places to finish composing their letters, then drew their illustrations to complement what they had written.

I asked for a quiet-writing time as the children composed so that they could keep their thoughts in order as they wrote. If they needed spelling assistance from one of their neighbors, they knew how to ask: "Excuse me, do you have time to help me spell a word?" This had been modeled and reminded since the beginning of their first-grade year. Several of the children had "scrounge for print" papers and were up at my chart letter that I'd written to Michael, copying the standard spelling of a word or words they needed for their own writing. Brian Cambourne developed the term "scrounge for print"; I also use the term in our classroom to refer to small pieces of paper kept in baskets on the children's tables for copying down the conventional spellings of words around the room, then taking them back to their table to assist them in their writing. By now, the children knew several ways to be resourceful in figuring out spellings as they wrote, including these strategies:

1. Stretch out the sounds and write them down—temporary spelling.
2. Scrounge for print in the room.
3. Ask a friend for help. Ask up to five friends.
4. Ask Ms. Janine or another adult for help.

Even though several were "scrounging for print" at my letter, the children were writing their own letters with their own ideas. I discovered that some of them were writing about Back-to-School Night, but they were composing with their own words, only using my letter for a word resource when they needed it. My modeled writing was an important demonstration, but this was my letter, and we had spent the previous year discussing that copying my letter did not make it their letter. No one writes thoughts and ideas in exactly the same way, and they needed to write from inside their own heads.

As I looked around, the children seemed confident now as they composed their own letters. It was a leap in proficiency from their beginning efforts as first-grade writers. Edward, an ESL student, and Heidi, one of my struggling writers, needed help composing their letters, so I asked Edward to begin with his illustration so I could assist Heidi with her letter. I helped Edward compose his letter when I finished with Heidi.

The next morning, while we were settling in during morning-work time, several brought their family journals to me so that I could read what their families had written back to them. This was a common practice in our classroom. Victor, Lee, Lisa, and Kayalani had all written about our upcoming Back-to-School Night. Lee's letter follows:

9-7-95

Dear (aunt's name),

We are doing a Bubble Bath play. Do you want to come?

Love, Lee

Dear Lee,

What on Earth is a Bubble Bath Play. I dont know what it is but I am shure I would like to see it as long as you are a part of it!

Eddie's letter to his family showed he was still enthralled with the small-group castle study he was involved in at the end of our first-grade year:

9-7-95

Dear Dad,

Janine said me and Jonathan and Victor can Biuld a castle for the castle gruop on tap of paper. And we have a castle Book that sous how to Biuld, a castle.

Love, Eddie

(*Janine said me and Jonathan and Victor can build a castle for the castle group on top of paper. And we have a castle book that shows how to build a castle.*)

Dear Eddie,

I hope you and your friends work as a team and complete your castle model. Remember to be patient with each other, and not let those little mistakes that happen make you guys upset at each other.

Keep up the good work.

P.S. Your writing is getting better.

Dad

Editing Family Journals

With second-grade writers, I focus mainly on editing their letters with them, because in general, they have far fewer struggles with composing and spelling than first-grade writers. However, I still give composing and spelling assistance to second graders who need it. When I had my last second-grade group, JoAnn, my assisting teacher, worked in our classroom during our family journal time, and our goal was to each meet with sixteen writers for a quick edit on their letters. My purpose for this weekly editing session was to continue the work of teaching the conventions of writing in a purposeful context, without overwhelming or frustrating my young writers. During these two-minute conferences, JoAnn and I concentrated on these things:

- clarity: Does the letter makes sense; does it have proper syntax?
- punctuation: Does the child use end marks—commas, apostrophes, capital letters, etc.—properly?
- standard spelling: Does the child correctly spell high-utility words and unusual words that are used frequently?
- letter form: Does the letter have a clear greeting, body, closing?

Our process unfolded in this way:

As the children worked at their tables, JoAnn and I first helped those children like Heidi, Juanita, Edward, Christina, and Tanya who still needed composing help. Then, as children finished their letters, we quickly went into our editing work. The children kept their pencils in hand, making the appropriate corrections while we talked with them, pointed things out, and

FIGURE 10–1 *Eddie's family journal letter*

generally worked through their letters from greeting to closing. The key was to match the editing to the child so that it was helpful. Depending upon the child, my editing process followed this structure:

- clarity: I read or the children read their letter aloud quickly to double-check that it made sense. We cleared up any meaning and syntax issues first.
- punctuation: I developed a punctuation resource sheet (Appendix 1–2) that the children and I referred to when we tackled punctuation. The children kept this resource sheet paper clipped to the inside back cover of their journals. We concentrated on these items:
  - making sure there was a comma after the greeting
  - making sure the first word of the first sentence started with a capital letter
  - making sure there were appropriate end marks after sentences; I often had to read the body of the letter aloud so the children could hear where end marks were needed
  - making sure there was a comma in the closing
- spelling
  - We automatically corrected any high-utility words that were on the first one hundred list. We would then turn to the back inside cover and write the date and misspelled high-frequency words under it, reminding the children to check this list when writing future letters because we wanted to get those words "cleaned up."
  - We corrected any unusual words that the children had written more than one time in their letters OR any words that might be hard for family members to decipher in the temporary spelling form and wrote them on the list in the back inside cover of the journal.

Trying to meet with all of the children before lunchtime kept JoAnn and I on our toes, but for the most part, we were able to manage it. If children finished both their letters and illustrations and were waiting for one of us to edit with them, they left their journals open at their tables, participated in one of the choices in our room—listening center, computer, quiet reading in the classroom library or at their table, or reading bigbooks at the easel—and we would call them over for their editing session when we were ready. This system worked well for everyone. We didn't have to do crisis classroom management—hurrying to get to everybody before someone finished—and the children were able to use their time in productive ways versus having to wait around for us. This kept our work environment purposeful and focused. I believe children with "time on their hands" eventually have difficulties; children who receive help in structuring their time eventually become learners who can direct themselves.

Sustaining Family Journals

Writing letters to our families is a sacred Thursday writing ritual in my classroom throughout the year. After our first guided writing session, we always follow this format:

1. We gather as a whole group so the children can watch and listen to me as I write my letter to Michael (modeled writing).
2. We set up journals with date and greeting.
3. We continue writing and illustrating at tables with composing and editing assistance from fellow students, me, or any other adult in the room.

The children's letters are as individual as the children themselves, although our classroom world seems to find its way into much of their correspondence. Classroom news is always the topic of my weekly letters to my husband, so that probably influences the children's topic choices. Classroom news generally consists of:

- books we are reading
- unit studies
- special school events
- upcoming field trips
- anything else that is noteworthy

Writing home about books is always a favorite. After I shared James Marshall's version of *The Three Little Pigs* (1996), Jana wrote this letter to her family:

Dear Mom,

Janine read a book called *The Three Little Pigs* and it by James Marshall. Janine says he's a great writer and I agre with her. The part I like is Mind your own business hank you said the pig. James Marshall died.

Love, Jana

Dear Jana,

Your class sure gets a chance to read some interesting stories.

Love Mama

(*Janine read a book called The Three Little Pigs and it's by James Marshall. Janine says he's a great writer and I agree with her. The part I like is, "Mind your own business, thank you," said the little pig. James Marshall died.*)

When we were immersed in our ocean exploration study and I was reading the book *Ocean: The Living World* (Greenaway, Gunzi, and Taylor 1994) to my class, Rosanna wrote this letter to her mom:

3-14-96

Dear Mom,

Today Janine read a book and ther was this fish and the name of it was called Lettuce Slug. It is vere intersting.

Love, Rosanna

P.S. You see how it looks in my ilustasin.

P.P.S. It is only 1" but I am going to draw it biger. and it is a boy and gile

(*Today Janine read a book and there was this fish and the name of it was called Lettuce Slug. It is very interesting.*

P.S. You see how it looks in my illustration.

P.P.S. It is only 1" but I am going to draw it bigger. And it is a boy and girl.)

Dear Rosanna,

I am glad you enjoy Mrs. Janine's stories the picture you made is beautiful. Keep up your good reading and listening.

Love Mom

When we started our space exploration study, Lisa wrote this letter to her mother:

Dear Mom,

Yesterday we stardid our Space Exploration. What little do you know about space? I only know one thing about space and that is the stor's are big ball's of Gass Brning millions of miles away. Love, Lisa

(*Yesterday we started our Space Exploration. What little do you know about space? I only know one thing about space and that is the stars are big balls of gas burning millions of miles away.*)

Her mother responded with this letter:

Dear Lisa,

I know that there is no air or gravity in space. I know that light travels through space. The planets in our solar system orbit around the sun. Space is a very fascinating subject! I have always liked outer space. (I remember seeing the moon landing on TV as a child!)

Love, Mom

Many children also write to their families about their five-, six-, seven-, and eight-year-old lives that are separate from our school world. I learn a lot about my first and second graders through these letters. Rachael wrote the following letter to her little sister when she had "sister things" to clear up with her:

Dear Katie,

I like you when you are nise to me but when you are mean to me I get made and when you hreat me I get relly relly made. Love, Rachael

(I like you when you are nice to me but when you are mean to me I get mad. And when you hurt me, I get really, really mad.)

Rachael's mom wrote back for her little sister, which had become a practice in their family:

Dear Rachael,

I like you when you're nice to me but when you are mean to me it makes me sad so I am mean back to you to let you know how it feels. You are mean to me first. From now on let's just be nice, not mean. Love, Katie

Priscilla was obviously struggling with lost connections and separations when she wrote this seven-year-old honest and touching letter to her mother:

Dear Mom,

Why did my dad devaut you when he davaut you how old was I was I 3 or like about 2. Mom tell me in your letter. Please write back very soon.

love, Priscilla

(Why did my dad divorce you? When he divorced you, how old was I? Was I three or like about two? Mom, tell me in your letter. Please write back very soon.)

Priscilla's letter ached for reassurance. I admired the way her mother responded with a little information and a lot of love:

Dear Priscilla,

Your father divorced me before you were born, but it doesn't matter because I love you very, very, very much.

Love, Mom

Adrienne wrote this letter to her mom when she was wondering if her grandma was coming for a visit:

9-7-95

Dear Mom,

Today my sister told me tha my grandma was comeing tomorow and im happy cas I love hor and she's lonly. That's why I whont toe with hor Thats why I love her so moch.

(*Today my sister told me that my grandma was coming tomorrow, and I'm happy because I love her and she's lonely. That's why I want to be with her. That's why I love her so much.*)

Adrienne's mom didn't write back to her that week, which isn't uncommon with family journals. When children return their journals to school and there aren't reply letters in them, I remind them to remind their families to read their letters and write back to them. Occasionally, I write notes home or call families if "no response" becomes a pattern.

I ask my ESL children to write to family members or neighbors who can read and write back to them in English. This always worked out for the children in my classroom, although if it hadn't, I would have paired them up with fifth-grade writers at our school, and those students would have become part of their "extended family" for the year. I found it interesting that for many of my ESL families, the English writing of parents and siblings developed over the course of the year as they corresponded with their first or second graders in their family journals. Sylvia always wrote to her older sister because she could write back to her in English, although occasionally, Sylvia's father would write back to her in Spanish. At Christmas time, Sylvia wrote the following letter to her dad:

12-14-95

Dear Dad,

Merry Christmas because you buy me toys when it is Christmas so you buy my little sister to and I am buying for presents and for my mom

Love, Sylvia

Her father's response follows:

HOLA SYLVIA

GRASIAS POR IR ALA ESCULA ESPERO QUE SIGA LLENDO Y SE SIG PORTANDO BIEN CON SU MAESTRA-USTD ES MI HIJA MAS INTELIGE.

FELIZ NAVIDAD Y ANO NUEVO LE DEZA SU PAP QUE LA QUIERE.

My friend and colleague, Rose-Yvonne Urias, translated Sylvia's father's "sweet note" for me, and her translation follows:

Hi Sylvia,

Thank you for going to school. I hope you will keep going and continue to behave yourself with your teacher (be good to your teacher, obey, etc.) You are my intelligent daughter. Merry Christmas and Happy New Year wishes from your father who loves you.

Even though Sylvia's father wrote back to her in Spanish, his reply was accepted and celebrated in our classroom.

LETTER JOURNALS

Letter journals are a place for the children and I to write to each other, and share bits and pieces of our lives once a week. This journal doesn't have a fancy name; the children and I simply call it "My Journal." I have enjoyed keeping this type of journal with young children for many years. Joanne Hindley, who currently teaches at the Manhattan New School in New York City, first inspired me to start a journal like this when I was teaching in Oregon. I had the opportunity to study with Joanne when she conducted a summer writing course in a neighboring district. After she shared some of her journals with us, I decided that I wanted to nurture similar written relationships with my students.

I have continued this type of journal in the years since that time with only minor changes: shape, size, and "look" (adding the children's beautiful, artistic covers), and writing back to the children right in the journal rather than on a Post-it note pressed onto the page. I have also deepened my beliefs about why I think this journal is significant not only to young writing lives, but also to the classroom community in general.

First, this journal has become a place where the children and I have quiet, weekly conversations with each other that might not otherwise occur. I read journals and know how to greet children in the morning; "Leticia, how is your little sister after her surgery?" or "Chris, how was horseback riding this weekend?" I remember letters so that I can mention ideas to children when they are stuck and can't think of one thing to write about: "David, what is your new Lego building project at home?" or "Jana, what family events are scheduled for this weekend?"

Secondly, I have also decided that my letters to the children have two audiences. First, and most important, they are for the children. Second, and perhaps equally important, they are for their families. In reading through these letters, I want their families to gain an understanding of who I am as their child's teacher, and how I am a part of their child's life at school. I also want the letters to communicate that I believe my effectiveness as a teacher depends upon my relationship with their child. My hope is that these letters will provide a view of the way their children and I interact with each other, as well as the importance I place on relationships in my work. I want them to know how much I value and celebrate the individual personalities of their children. I learn so much about the children, and they learn a lot about me as we write to one another and read one another's letters.

Finally, I believe this journal is not only about relationships, but it also meets the criteria for "real writing" because it involves

- a real writing situation—a letter
- a real audience—their teacher
- a real response—from their teacher
- a real reason—sharing our lives, asking questions

Preparing and Getting Started

I add letter journals to our writing routine during either the third or fourth week of school, after we have established family journals. Letter journals are constructed in the same manner as our family journals, with this letter from me taped to the inside cover of each journal:

Dear ___,

This is your journal for writing to me every week. You may write anything you wish in it. You may ask me a question, or tell me about something that you are doing at home. You might want to write about your pet, or how you're feeling today. You may want to write to me about your favorite food (or foods!), or what flavor of ice cream you like. (My favorite flavor is vanilla!) Or, just write down anything special that you would like to share with me. I will read your journal and write back to you every week. Remember to put it in the journal tub when you bring it back to school so that I am able to write back to you before you take it home the next week.

I begin letter journals with first- and second-grade writers in the same manner in which I start family journals. I also have the children write their first four letters to me in class (over the course of a month) so that they have help composing their beginning letters and understand the process of writing to me. I focus on the following items during this month of guided letter writing:

- setting up the letter with date and greeting
- finding my name for standard spelling if the child can't remember how to spell it (inside letter, front cover)
- drawing lines with a ruler to keep the writing neat and legible (mid–first grade and second grade)
- deciding what is important and interesting to write about
- working through spelling and punctuation while writing the letter
- using a proper closing
- rereading the letter to see if it makes sense
- completing an illustration on the opposite page to go with the letter

After a month of writing their journal letters in class, the children begin composing their letters to me as part of their homework responsibilities on Tuesday evenings and turning journals in to me Wednesday mornings. This gives me the rest of the week to read, then write my letters back to them. I have the children write their letters to me at home for two reasons. First, I don't want two days of our writing time consumed by two different journals. Second, I hope the children's families will become involved with the composing process, helping their young writers at home as they write their letters to me, while paying attention to writing conventions, spelling, and handwriting. With first-grade writers, I send home a piece I've written titled "Handwriting Assistance" so families can help their children work on neat, legible handwriting in the context of composing their letters, much like I do in the classroom (see Appendix 10–2). In practice, not all families helped their children in this way, or at all, but there were many who valued this time with their children. Children who didn't complete this responsibility at home, for any number of reasons, wrote to me during our morning-work time or their recess if they chose to.

Like family journals, letters vary widely, although a majority of the children's letters are about "their worlds" and not our classroom world. Letters range from roller-skating adventures to favorite foods. With my last group, Kaley spent a month writing about her upcoming birthday party, and Brenda composed beautiful poetry about trees:

10-10-95

Dear Janine

trees talke when the wind blows
trees move when the wind blows
trees whisper when the wind blows
trees grow when the rain falls down

a poem for you love Brenda

I wrote back to her:

10-12-95

Dear Brenda,

Your poetry is so very beautiful. I loved it when you read it to me
this morning and told me how you sit outside and watch the trees
and write your poetry. You have such a wonderful way of telling me
about it. You are a poet, Brenda. You think and write poetry. I do
hope you write more of your poems to share with me.

Love, Ms. Janine

Jana detailed episodes at home with a pesky younger sister, and Tracy
wondered about becoming a great artist:

Dear Janine,

I like writeing to you a lout to! This is a question Do you think that
I'll be a geat art's? I think I will be a famous art's.

Love, Tracy

(*I like writing to you a lot too! This is a question: Do you think that I'll be
a great artist? I think I will be a famous artist.*)

My response to Tracy follows:

3-8-96

Dear Tracy,

. . . In answering your question about being a great artist, I think
you will be a great artist if you want to be. It will take a lot of practice, discipline, and going to a good art school. You can work on it
now by drawing a lot. I know you love to do that, so it shouldn't be
hard for you to draw a lot.

I will help you find the information about where Eric Carle and Tomie dePaola went to Art Institutes. What type of artwork do you want to do?

Love, Ms. Janine

Nhi wrote countless entries about her mischievous hamsters, and Lee wrote joyful letters about learning how to swim in her grandmother's pool:

9-19-95

Dear Janine,

My swimmiing poul is up to my hin and with my flotes I can jump in to the wotr and I flot and if I jump strat up I wil go undr the wotr but the flotes pl me up.

Love, Lee

(*My swimming pool is up to my head and with my floaties I can jump into the water and I float and if I jump straight up I will go under the water but the floaties pull me up.*)

I wrote back to her:

9-21-95

Dear Lee,

Wow! I didn't know your pool was that deep. That's a bigger pool than I thought it was, my dear. I'm glad you wear a floatie to keep you up and pull you up when you jump straight up. Are you learning how to swim?

Love, Ms. Janine

Sometimes events make their way into children's journal entries that unfortunately are part of our world and that children have to cope with now. An event that occurred during my last year at Bobier was one that my second graders called "The Street of Killers." Kayalani led a discussion about this tragic news story during our class meeting one morning toward the end of September. The children's discussion, which I recorded in my journal, follows:

Kayalani: I was looking through the newspaper and I saw on TV, a three-year-old girl went into L.A. and (Kayalani read the heading of the newspaper article she was holding) "Wrong Turn onto Street of Killers." People surrounded the car. One guy shot, and it hit a little three-year-old girl, and she died.

(Brenda immediately said she knew about this, too.)

Kayalani: The guy kept trying to go, and they kept surrounding the car, and they shot the little girl who was in her mom's lap.

Joseph: Can I see (the newspaper picture)?

Kayalani: (reading from newspaper) One was five. The girl was . . . What does that say, Tracy?

Tracy: Stephanie.

Kayalani: Yeah. Steph was five.

Brenda: Yeah, and she had blond hair and red cheeks.

Kayalani: No, she didn't have red cheeks, but regular cheeks.

Tracy: Kay, I think we need to move on.

Kayalani: Ms. Janine's going to read this.

Tracy: I don't think we have time.

Kayalani: Janine, what do you think?

Janine: I think this should be decided by the children.

Kayalani to group: Do you want Ms. Janine to read it?

Group: Yeah. (I proceeded to read Kay's newspaper article.)

Rosanna: Is that real?

Janine: Yes.

Rosanna: Where was that?

Janine: Los Angeles. Two hours north from here.

Rosanna: I'm going to tell my mom not to go there. It's dangerous.

Janine: These people didn't want to be there either. They just took a wrong turn.

Tracy: That's why we live in Vista. Vista doesn't have gangs. Most gangs are in Oceanside and that's far away, a little bit. My brother hangs around with some gang friends but he isn't in a gang. It's safe here in Vista.

Edward: My mom told us not to go with strangers. She said we need to go to Vista. It's safe here.

One of the children: I'm glad Edward is here. I don't want him to be dead.

I realized how much the event had affected Kayalani when I read her next journal letter after school:

Dear Janine, on the TV I wocht the Nows and on the Nows there was a 3 yorod gral got shot I was scard wan. I sol it you will se it wan it is are clas meding

Love Kay Evans

(*Dear Janine, On the TV I watched the news and on the news there was a three-year-old girl got shot. I was scared when I saw it. You will see it when it is our class meeting. Love, Kay Evans*)

Beside her letter, Kayalani had drawn an illustration that she had labeled "Street of Killers." It made me ache to see this in a seven-year-old's journal. (See Figure 10–2.)

I wrote back to Kayalani:

Dear Kayalani,

I was very dismayed to hear about the shooting of the little girl in L.A. I think it was horrible. I think you did a very good job sharing this information with the kids. I'm proud of you, Kayalani, for caring so much about other people and bringing in news to share with us. How are you feeling? Is there anything else you would like to do? Please let me know.

Love, Ms. Janine

How sad it is that events like this find their way into children's journals, and how unsettling it is when I find myself attempting to write reassuring letters back to them. I didn't have conversations about events like this with my classmates or write about them to my teachers when I was a young girl

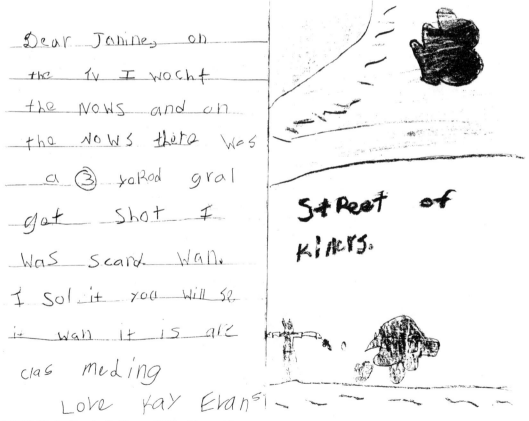

FIGURE 10–2 *Kayalani's "Street of Killers" journal letter*

attending elementary school in North Dakota. Discussions and letters like these remind me I am teaching in a much different time than the one I experienced during my own elementary years.

REFLECTION

In my classroom, family journals and letter journals play a significant role in the children's writing development. Both journals help children develop their skills and confidence as writers. I expect my students to become writers during their first-grade year and become better writers during their second-grade year, and they do—with time, consistent writing, and instruction. I remind them that in order to be understood, they must pay attention to the conventions of writing and spelling when they compose their letters. Eddie's dad did the same for Eddie when he sprinkled these comments into his responses to him:

- Your punctuation is getting a little better; we will keep working on it.
- Eddie, your punctuation and grammar is getting better! We'll keep working on it, and later you will even be showing me more rules that I didn't know about.
- P.S. Try to make capital letters a little BIGGER.

With journals, the stakes are high. The children are writing to people they love, and the people who love them back keep nudging them, over time, to write clearly.

In addition to developing writing skills, these journals also nurture relationships. In a school where I wondered if people felt like they were part of any significant community, I hoped that written conversations in journals would provide one way to create a feeling of "belonging." During my four years of teaching at Bobier, I found that a majority of the children and their families treated our journals with seriousness and care. What we wrote about mattered to them. They wanted to be part of "our club" in Room 12.

It is good to find journals that fit "just right."

11 | DEVELOPING A WRITING WORKSHOP

In the workshop children write about what is alive and vital and real for them—and other writers in the room listen and extend and guide, laugh and cry and marvel.

—*Lucy Calkins,* The Art of Teaching Writing: New Edition

At the beginning of April during my last year at Bobier, one of our second grade class meetings began with considerable debate about the size of the new albino alligator on display at the Wild Animal Park. Rachael had gone out to view this extraordinary reptile when the exhibit first opened and said it looked smaller than what she'd expected, only about "one yard" long. The next day, she revised her original announcement. Attempting to balance four rulers in two hands, she proceeded to demonstrate to our class that she thought the albino alligator was about four feet long.

"I read in the most recent ZooNewz that it's supposed to measure seven feet long," I told Rachael and the rest of the class. "Rachael, you could write to the Education Department at the Wild Animal Park and ask them. If you're really interested in finding this out, that would be the best place to research your answer."

Rachael was our resident animal lover and already had ambitions of growing up and becoming a baby-animal doctor. We knew she was already an expert at small-animal burial, having conducted a lovely burial for her moth, Hairy. Like David and his dreams of being a space engineer, I could see this as Rachael's life work because she loved reading about different animals in books and magazines and often expressed her love for animals in her letters to me, such as this one:

Dear Janine,

What's your favit Ainomole? my favit Ainomole is evry Ainomole

Love, Rachael

(*What's your favorite animal? My favorite animal is every animal.*)

After our class meeting conversation that day, Rachael decided she couldn't rest until she knew the size of that albino alligator, and soon she and Leticia began composing a letter to the Wild Animal Park education staff during our writing-workshop time. When they finished, they read their letter to me while I typed it on the computer, so that we could send both their letter and a typed version of it. Their letter follows:

Room 12 Bobier Elementary
220 West Bobier Drive
Vista, California 92083

April 8, 1996

The Zoological Society of San Diego
P.O. Box 551
San Diego, California 92112–0551

To whom it may concern:

We are second graders at Bobier Elementary. We have questions about the albino alligator:

Question 1: How old is the albino alligator?

Question 2: How long is the albino alligator right now: Does it get 7 feet long?

Please write back as soon as you can. We are waiting for your answer.

Sincerely,
Rachael and Leticia

By the end of the month, Rachael and Leticia had received a response from the Education Department at the San Diego Zoo, and they reported to the class that the albino alligator was indeed seven feet long. After a science lesson on how light hitting the water can distort the size and shape of an object with Mrs. Flaherty, our science lab teacher, Rachael decided this must have been the problem when she first viewed the alligator, and that it would have been easier to judge its length had it been on land. Mystery solved.

Writing-workshop time in my classroom provides time for children like Rachael and Leticia to write letters to the Education Department at the San Diego Zoo and pursue other writing projects that are important to them. Writing workshop also gives me the time I need to guide children through writing projects that I feel are important for them to experience as young writers. I use our workshop time to instruct and mentor children as writers, model what good writers do, demonstrate how writers solve problems, monitor progress, influence developing attitudes about writing, and live among my young writers as a fellow writer. I find that my current workshop time with young writers is much more complex than my beginning practices in which we used this time to primarily write and publish books. Because of my desire to have children "dig deeper" as writers and actually do less publishing, this period of time continues to be the most difficult balancing act in my classroom.

SCHEDULING WORKSHOP TIME

Establishing, sustaining, and scheduling a productive writing workshop with primary children is challenging. "How we structure the workshop," writes Lucy Calkins, "is less important than *that* we structure it" (1994, 188). However, I've done a great deal of experimenting with the *how* of scheduling a writing workshop so that children have time to pursue individual projects and I have time to lead children through specific writing projects that I know are important to their development as writers. Currently I design my weekly writing schedule in this way:

Monday	Tuesday	Wednesday	Thursday	Friday
Quiet Writing	Quiet Writing	Quiet Writing	Family Journals	Quiet Writing
	Minilesson or Lesson (when needed)	Minilesson or Lesson (when needed)	• Janine models letter	Minilesson or Lesson (when needed)
	Teacher-Led Writing Project OR Unit Study Journal	Individual Writing Projects OR Unit Study Journal	• Children write letters. • Janine, Children edit letters.	Individual Writing Projects

My goal is balance. First, because I value quiet writing, I include time at the beginning of our workshop for the children to write quietly for ten to fifteen minutes, four days a week. After quiet-writing time, we gather as a whole group for a minilesson or a longer writing lesson based on the children's writing needs. At most, I do this four times per week, although I rarely conduct lessons that frequently; two lessons per week is average.

Since I also believe it's important for children to have time to work on individual projects of their choice, I schedule two days per week, Wednesday and Friday, for children to have the opportunity to do this.

Last, I schedule time for delving into teacher-led writing projects—for example, poetry, fiction, memoir, or informational storybook—two days per week, which in my case, is Monday and Tuesday. I use teacher-led project time to give explicit instruction about a particular genre and extend the children's writing knowledge and abilities. If we are immersed in a unit study, I also use "teacher-led project" time for children to write entries in their study journals.

I monitor curriculum and writing demands every week, and on Mondays, the children and I discuss the schedule for that week's writing-workshop time and make decisions about how our writing week will look based on our needs as writers.

Often, we have writing notebooks, a teacher-led writing project, individual projects, and unit study journals in progress at the same time. When we are immersed in a teacher-led writing project, I encourage the children to continue working on it during the one or two days they have individual writing–project time. Some children choose to do this, and others wait until the next week when we have our regularly scheduled time for that writing project again. Our workshop is busy.

I am flexible about this weekly writing schedule—to a point—in terms of scheduling individual and teacher-led writing projects. If I think we need to devote most of our writing time to our unit study journals or a teacher-led project that we're working on, I consult with the children to see if they're willing to abandon individual-project time that week. This usually occurs more toward the end of projects when we're trying to wrap things up. However, I never dispense with family journals on Thursdays. The children's communication with their families is too important to schedule inconsistently.

PREPARING MATERIALS

The children have these materials for our writing-workshop time:

- writing tablet or notebook: Children use this for daily quiet-writing time and occasionally for planning and/or drafts of teacher-led projects. The children store their tablets/notebooks in their cubbies.
- double-pocket folder: Children use this to store writing projects that are in progress. I prefer a double-pocket folder to a file folder because items do not fall out as easily. The children either purchase folders or use folders that I provide. They write their names on folder labels and place the labels on the upper right-hand corner of the folders. The children store these folders in their cubbies.
- student portfolio: Children use this to store drafts of both individual projects and teacher-led projects. Portfolios are stored alphabetically in hanging file folders in two plastic tubs so the children have access to them and can file their drafts easily.
- dictionary: I copy and assemble a small paper dictionary for each child. It includes the high-frequency words, number words, months of the year, colors, etc. The children store their dictionaries in their cubbies.

- table resources: These are small versions of our class-made alphabet, which I re-create and photocopy; letter/number formation card; the first one hundred high-frequency words, organized alphabetically; and a punctuation resource card. These resources are laminated and stored in a plastic bin on each table.

In addition to these materials, the children have access to different types of paper and other writing supplies including pencils, erasers, paper clips, tape, scissors, glue sticks, staplers, staple removers, rulers, colored pencils, markers, crayons, adhesive labels, and Post-it notes. These supplies are stored in a central area in our classroom. (I discuss additional materials available to children in Chapter 1.)

GETTING STARTED

With primary children, I spend six to eight weeks easing into a full-fledged writing workshop. First I introduce writing tablets or notebooks, and we spend our entire workshop time writing our entries and sharing them with one another. During the second week of school, I introduce family journals and begin establishing this Thursday routine. During the third week, I introduce "My Journal," which is a weekly letter journal between each child and me. Eventually, the letter journal will become a "homework journal," but I like to work with it in the classroom for about a month before the children start taking it home to write to me one evening per week.

Conducting Temporary Spelling Lessons

With first-grade children I also do several lessons on "temporary spelling" during this first month of writing. A temporary spelling lesson that I did with my last group at the beginning of their first-grade year follows:

I asked the children to choose a partner and spread out on the floor facing my large sheet of chart paper. Each pair had a big piece of butcher paper and crayons for writing. I explained to them that I wanted them to learn a method for spelling words even when they weren't sure of the spellings. "You are still little," I told them. "I don't expect you to know how to spell all of the wonderful words you have in your head for your writing, but I still want you to use those words, so this is a way to do that."

I chose the first word to spell. "Let's start with *camel*," I said. "Say it with me slowly: *camel*. What do you hear at the beginning? (/c/ and /k/ were the responses.) You and your partner decide which letter you're going to use. They are both good choices because both of them can stand for that sound. I'm going to use /c/. What's next? Stretch out the word so you can hear the next part. (/a/ was the response). Great. Stretch it out again. (/m/ was the response.) Stretch it out again. (/l/ was the response.) Nice job. We've just spelled *camel* with temporary spelling. We wrote down the sounds we heard in *camel* in the order we heard them. Now, you and your partner need to draw a little picture of a camel next to the word so that you remember what it is. When you're finished, draw a circle around it. What's another word that you would like to spell this way?"

We continued this lesson for another fifteen minutes, spelling and drawing pictures to remember the words we had spelled. At the end, I gave them the word *camera* and asked them to work out the spelling with their partners. After that, we compared the different ways they had spelled it: camra, kamra, cmra. I reminded the children that temporary spelling is *temporary*, that sometimes they will spell the same words differently in their early writings, and that's OK.

I find this a helpful spelling lesson for beginning writers, and I do this several times with them during the first few weeks of school. I like to do "color charts" with my young writers in which they choose a color—green, for example—and we spell objects using temporary spelling that are generally that color, such as grass, plants, lime jello, etc., drawing pictures to go with the words so the children can recall the words easily. At Bobier, we hung our temporary-spelling color charts for our Back-to-School Night with an explanation about our writing lessons. Mary O'Neill's *Hailstones and Halibut Bones* (1989) is a wonderful book to weave into these beginning color/spelling lessons.

With my last second-grade group, I also scheduled my first teacher-led writing project during the first month of school as we worked on autobiographical paragraphs to display with our portraits for Back-to-School Night.

Creating Little Books

Another writing project that I share with both first- and second-grade children during the beginning weeks of school is composing "little books." Little books are blank books of four to eight pages ($3\frac{1}{2} \times 8\frac{1}{2}$"), stapled together in the center. I share models of little books that children have written previously, whether they be about butterflies, the sun, the ocean, or flowers, and discuss the process of creating books like this. I invite the children to write little books about things that are important to them. With first-grade children, we often write the first book together so the children have experience composing together before composing alone or with a partner. We do not edit or recopy these little books.

During these first weeks of writing workshop, I prefer to go slowly with the children. I delve into beginning writing projects and lessons thoroughly so that when we do move into working on individual writing projects, the children understand routines, use of time and materials, and have a beginning understanding of the focus and depth I want them to have in their writing work. The only way I know how to do this is by giving time and attention to these beginning types of writing.

At the end of six to eight weeks, I develop a list of the types of writing the children have been involved in since the start of the year. Typically, these items appear on the list:

- writing-notebook entry
- letter
- little books
- autobiographical paragraph
- story writing

It is at this point, when I feel the children have enough writing knowledge for their own individual projects, that I "open up" our workshop time and schedule one or two days per week for children to begin individual projects. As I continue to involve the children in teacher-led projects, we add them to the list of writing possibilities for their individual-project time. As the year progresses, the children's list of writing choices generally includes

- letter
- little book
- poetry
- writing notebook
- classroom newsletter article
- autobiographical piece
- informational storybook
- any other important writing project that they discuss with me

The following chart shows my process of establishing writing-workshop routines in the beginning weeks of the school year:

Week 1	Week 2	Week 3	Week 4	Week 5 and on . . .
• writing notebooks	___continued___	_____	_____	_____
	• family journals	___continued___	_____	_____
		• letter journals	___continued___	_____
	• first grade: start temporary spelling lessons • second grade: start first teacher-led project: "About Me" paragraph	• continue mini-lessons or lessons_____	___continued___ • little books	• start "Official Workshop Schedule;" establish individual-project time: • status-of-the class

Week 1	Week 2	Week 3	Week 4	Week 5 and on . . .
				• list of choices • writing note-book (cont.) • letter • little book • "About Me" piece • continue adding to project list after completing teacher-led projects
				• establish "Special Classroom Projects" list: • letters • notices • bulletins
				continue teacher-led projects
				begin unit study journal entries

MANAGING INDIVIDUAL WRITING PROJECTS

Organizing Young Writers

At the beginning of the writing workshop when children are working on individual projects, I use the same status-of-the-class (Atwell 1998) proce-dure and form that I use at the start of our partner-reading time when I check in with my young readers to see what they are reading each day. This takes place after quiet writing and my minilesson if I've chosen to do one that day. I do a status-of-the-class because I want to know what projects the children are choosing for themselves before they scatter to work as writers, and I want the children to hear what other writers are doing. Often children will collaborate on a project when they hear another person is doing something similar. I encourage collaboration as long as children remain productive. I've discovered that working together creates enthusiastic writers and wonderful pieces of writing.

I do this status-of-the-class procedure for another reason. I know that most of the time the children will not be able to finish their writing projects during one writing session and will have to store works-in-progress in their double-pocket folders. This is fine with me. Once I have written their project choice on my clipboard, I have it for future reference when I check in with them the next time we are working on individual projects. For example, when Rachael told me she was starting a new piece about her dog, Bobby, I discovered that the last time we were immersed in individual projects she was working on a little book about the ocean. When I asked her about that project, she replied that she had forgotten about it. Thus, I was able to remind her about her first project. I want the children to make decisions regarding writing projects, but I need to do it in a structured, manageable way for my own teaching work.

There are always a few children who have difficulty deciding on a topic and form for a writing project. When I do my status-of-the-class, and I encounter children who can't decide on a project, I ask them to wait on the floor, think, and listen to the what the other children are doing; then I talk with them at the end. Sometimes children hearing what others are doing is all that is required to trigger an idea. Other times, children are ready to write after I offer suggestions based on what I know about them and their lives. If neither of the above helps, I ask children to talk with other writers. This involves walking around the room to see what others are doing and talking with them to see if they have suggestions or would be willing to have a fellow writer work on a project with them. Finally, to help young writers get into the habit of looking for writing ideas, I am always on the lookout for writing opportunities, saying to children, "You know, that would be a great writing project during writing workshop. You may want to think about doing that." Again, I use the concept of "simmering time," as I remind the children to view the world as writers and be on the lookout for writing opportunities in their young lives.

In addition to the list of writing projects that the children can choose from, I keep a running list of "special writing projects" that need our attention. These projects range from letters to notices, to bulletins, to posters, to anything that comes up in the life of our classroom that needs our written attention. Thank-you letters frequently land on this list. We write letters to every person, group, or business who contributes to the life of our classroom in some way. We thank field trip drivers, guest speakers, teachers who lend us books, families who do home projects, those who contribute time and/or materials, people who contribute special resources for a unit study; the list goes on. Children create bulletins announcing a 5-cent increase in the price of milk and juice in the cafeteria or that sandals are forbidden footwear on the playground. Children also compose notices announcing upcoming events such as picture day or special assemblies, which I copy for them to take home in their school folders.

As I or the children become aware of items that need to be written, we write them on a list in our writing area. Then, at the start of our individual-project time, I remind the children that we have classroom writing projects that need someone's attention. I list off the projects and ask for volunteers; often the children collaborate on these projects. I do this before taking the status-of-the-class so that children get situated with these projects first. Some of the classroom writing projects that my group of second graders worked on during the year are listed below.

- letter of inquiry to Mr. Lacey about his telescope
- description and explanation of Rachael's fish chart
- descriptions of leaf collections
- a letter to Kayalani's aunt asking two questions:
  1. Which came first—the Milky Way Galaxy or the Milky Way Candy Bar?
  2. Where did the name the Milky Way come from?
- a letter to Seymour Simon asking the same questions as letter to Kayalani's aunt
- classroom newspaper/magazine
- thank-you letter to Ms. Stern's father for space materials
- thank-you letter for our computer
- thank-you letter to the Dairy Council
- thank-you letter to Mrs. Cordero—Reading Rainbow: The Milkmakers
- letter to the cafeteria: Where's the lettuce?
- thank-you letter to Mr. Nicholas: the swallows book and newspaper article
- bulletin posting new juice and milk prices
- thank-you letter to Mrs. Browning—*Just Grandma and Me* CD
- thank-you letter to Mrs. Garcia: ice cream sandwiches!
- thank-you letter to Mr. Rodriguez: glove puppets
- "Cows in the Classroom" photo and story poster
- letter to Mr. Lacey and Mike West: OK to bring telescope on Wednesday, April 17
- letter to Mrs. James: What are you and your fifth graders building by your classroom?
- letters to Mrs. Jones' fifth-grade students in eastern Washington

Managing the Writing Time

Once the children have checked in with me and are immersed in their individual or collaborative projects, my job is to help as many young writers as possible. This is my conferencing time, my instruction time, my mentoring time, my busy time. During my conferences with them, I help children:

- plan their writing
- work through their writing if it doesn't make sense
- give a direction to their writing if they're "stuck"
- compose words and sentences if it's difficult for them

- edit their writing
- publish their writing by typing at the computer if it's quick—otherwise I do this after school
- by listening

I am always looking for ways for children to help themselves and one another partly because it will help them learn and partly because I have quite a large class. I remind them to reread drafts as they write or to share their work with other writers for their responses. With their permission, I use their work in minilessons to demonstrate what they are doing or how they are solving writing problems, or to celebrate something outstanding in their writing. Minilessons—or full lessons if they are longer—allow me to "conference" with my entire class, so I don't feel the pressure to handle every writer's needs individually. I never meet every young writer's needs every day. It's impossible. What I aim to do is meet as many needs as I possibly can over time. Good writers develop over time. I don't expect good writing to happen overnight.

Cows in the Classroom

When David, Joseph, and Eddie were working on a "Cows in the Classroom" photo story, my conferencing time with them led to two class lessons in which these three young writers shared what they were writing, how they were working on it, and what problems they were solving along the way. "Cows in the Classroom" is a mobile dairy classroom sponsored by the Dairy Council of California, with the purpose of bringing a cow and calf to school sites to show children a bit of farm life and acknowledge the benefits of drinking milk. During the presentation, the children had written notes and sketched drawings in their writing notebooks, and I had taken pictures. Once the photos were developed, David, Joseph, and Eddie had volunteered to team up and work on a photo story to display in our classroom. Their idea was to display the photos on a large piece of tagboard, then write a narrative piece to go with it. I anticipated interesting dynamics from these three working together, and I wasn't far off in my initial assessment.

Their first hurdle was learning the art of collaboration. First they wrestled with who was going to write which part. When I joined them, they had three different pieces in progress, none of which had a stellar beginning. They each had good parts in their writing, but they needed to meld these pieces together to create a decent beginning. So, during my conference time with them, my task was to help them write a complete beginning out of three separate beginnings.

After much discussion, referring to our journal entries from that day, and a fair amount of wrangling between the boys on what information should or should not be included, we ended up with a beginning that was satisfactory to everyone. We had so many arrows and markings from one draft to the next that the boys asked me to type it on the computer so that we could make sense of it:

On Friday, March 15, Mr. Maat from the Dairy Council of California brought cows to our school. First he showed us the heifer and the heifer's name was Becky Neeka. When he opened the trailer, we were amazed. The heifer was big. Everyone said, "Wow!" Then he talked about it with us. He said,

"The heifer has four stomachs and you can see the hip bone from the back. The cows weighs 1,200 pounds and it is 2 years old. She can have a baby once a year starting at two years old. She eats 20 pounds of hay each day. She drinks 40 to 50 gallons of water a day."

Now work on

1. Milking the cow
2. The milking machine
3. The bull calf

I typed the "Now work on" portion at the bottom to remind the boys in what order to work on the rest of the narrative. I also wrote this next sentence, "Then Mr. Maat showed us how to milk the cow . . ." on a lined sheet of paper so that they could pick up as a group without my direction. The boys and I went through this process with the class in a writing lesson so everyone could see the work that had gone into crafting their beginning.

David, Joseph, and Eddie did a similar second lesson with the class after they finished the last part of their photo story, concentrating on how they had worked on the flow of the information so that it made sense. Their ending follows:

Then Mr. Maat showed us how to milk the cow. You put your thumb on top of the teat and you put the other four fingers around the teats and pull it down and squeeze. The milk is warm when it comes out. You can also use a milking machine and not your hand. Mr. Maat talked about the milking machine. Then he told us how to use it.

Then Mr. Maat took out the bull calf and we got to pet the bull calf. The bull calf had an infection on its front leg. The bullcalf was white and black. We were amazed. Everyone said, "Wow!" again.

The End

This was a challenging writing project for these boys. After expending so much energy on this project, I didn't think they were quite up to the thank-you letter we needed to write to the Dairy Council, and fortunately Lee was willing to take on this task as one of her writing projects. Her letter was short and precise:

March 27, 1996

Dear Mr. Maat,

Thank you for bringing the cows. I didn't know cows have four stomachs. I didn't know cows had four teats, too.

Sincerely,
Lee

Mrs. Camarino's Baby

The children learned about the art of interviewing when four girls on our classroom newsletter team decided to interview JoAnn Camarino, our assisting teacher. At the beginning of our third term of school, the children discovered that Mrs. Camarino was expecting a baby, and this event was clearly the breaking story in our second-grade newspaper world. I helped the team members with their interview preparation. Their process follows:

Preparing for the Interview:
- brainstorming and deciding upon appropriate and on-topic interview questions
- writing questions on a piece of paper with enough space to write Mrs. Camarino's responses
- deciding who would ask which questions before the interview
- practicing reading/asking the questions
- deciding who would write the responses
- setting up the interview time and place: our classroom at one of the tables during writing workshop

Conducting the Interview
- asking questions clearly
- asking for spelling/writing assistance if needed: the group or Mrs. Camarino
- thanking Mrs. Camarino for her time

Writing the Interview Article
- writing a draft of the interview with questions and responses
- meeting with Janine for revision and editing (if needed)
- meeting with Mrs. Camarino to read the final draft of the article
- meeting with Janine for typing the interview in newspaper format

Publishing the Interview
- including the article in the classroom newsletter
- giving Mrs. Camarino a copy of the newsletter with her interview

Throughout this interview project, the team shared its work during minilessons with the class so that the other children would learn how to conduct and write interviews. (A wonderful resource for helping children conduct thoughtful interviews is Paula Rogovin's book, *Classroom Interviews: A World of Learning.* See Appendix 7–1)

The girls' final interview article follows:

An Interview with Mrs. Camarino

By Roni, Jana, Elizabeth, and Priscilla

Mrs. Camarino is going to have a baby so we decided to interview her for our first newspaper article:

Girls: How are you going to choose your baby's name?
Mrs. Camarino: From a book of names and help from our friends.
Girls: What are you going to name your baby?
Mrs. Camarino: Maybe Jordan or Alexandra.
Girls: Are you ready to have your baby?
Mrs. Camarino: YES!
Girls: When are you going to have your baby?
Mrs. Camarino: About August 10.
Girls: Are you excited to see your baby?
Mrs. Camarino: I am very excited to see my baby.
Girls: Do you have an extra room for the baby?
Mrs. Camarino: No. We're planning to buy a house and Elyssa (Mrs. Camarino's oldest daughter) and the baby will share.

Bringing Individual Projects to Completion

Because the children's individual projects are varied, completion of projects takes many different forms. Letters need to be delivered or sent to the person or group they're intended for. Many times, I type an "adult draft" to send with their "child draft" to make reading easier for the receivers—particularly if they're not used to reading children's temporary spellings. It seems to respect both worlds.

Poetry is either rewritten by hand or typed by me, then illustrated and matted for display in our classroom.

Little books are stored in a basket in our classroom library so that children can read them during our quiet-reading time.

Longer books that the children write and edit with me are typed and bound by me, then illustrated by the children. We have another basket in our classroom library for these books so the children can read them during our quiet-reading time also.

We do, or try to do, whatever the project requires in terms of completion for an audience. If I type a project, I ask the children to make a good-faith effort to check their punctuation and spelling before I sit down to do final editing with them before typing it for them after school. They complete a "Writing Conference Checklist" to prepare for our final conference (Appendix 11–1). My editing conferences are not long with primary children. My goal is to address capitals, end marks, quotation marks, and the spellings of three to five words. By this point, I have seen the draft several times (if it's a longer project), so I don't belabor it.

I don't do much editing with my young writers until the content of the piece is clear. Getting a piece to that point is the focus of my first few conferences with them, then the editing follows. I also work diligently on editing during family journals and teacher-led writing projects, so I don't feel like I have to "teach everything there is to know about writing conventions and spelling" during these individual-project conferences. It's not productive with primary children. It is interesting to note that by the end of second grade, I had several children who needed only minor editing help to bring their shorter pieces to standard form in both writing conventions and spelling.

Sharing and Response

Children share their work with one another in an ongoing process throughout our workshop time. I used to end every writing workshop with a whole-class sharing time that consisted of children reading their published books to the class. We still take time to share and celebrate finished pieces either at the beginning or end of our workshop time, but it is no longer the majority of our

FIGURE 11–1
*Priscilla and Jonathan:
peer editing*

sharing time. Instead, I encourage children to share often while they write (Figure 11–2) and invite them to share their works-in-progress during a minilesson or lesson. My goal is to have writers question and respond to one another's writing while they are in the process of writing. As a writer, I find this equally, if not more helpful than when I seek response after I've finished a piece.

When Priscilla's dog, Bea, ran away from home, she decided to make several "missing dog" posters to post at school. First, she shared her poster with us because she wanted our response before writing a letter to our principal asking him if she could post them. This was the design of Priscilla's poster:

Missing Dog
Date Missing 2/23/96
[pen and pencil drawing of Bea]
Her name is Bea
1340 Palomar

When Priscilla shared her missing dog poster with us, the children felt that she needed to include more information. I jotted down their suggestions as they gave them to her:

- What color? Brown, a little dirty.
- How tall? One foot.
- Phone Number? The children decided it would be better not to include this information, as other children might do prank phone calls which her mom wouldn't like. I seconded this line of thinking. Instead they suggested she write her name and Room 12.

FIGURE 11–2
Lisa, Adrienne, and
Christie discussing writing

Lisa then offered to help Priscilla compose her letter to Mr. Lacey asking for his permission to hang posters around the school. This was their finished letter:

3/11/96

Dear Mr. Lacey,

May I put up poster's in the school? Becuse my dog ran away or somboddy (*somebody*) stold (*stole*) her. I am worried about where she is. It bothers my hol (*whole*) family.

Love, Priscilla

Our principal responded with this letter:

Dear Priscilla,

Thank you for writing to me. Yes, you may put up posters to help you find your dog. I hope Bea comes home soon.

Sincerely, Mr. Lacey

The children asking Priscilla to include more information in her missing dog poster and Lisa offering to help Priscilla compose her letter to our principal are two examples of children paying attention to one another as writers and offering helpful responses during a sharing session. However, I find that this kind of "responsive sharing" is difficult for young children to do in the beginning weeks of a writing workshop. They tend to view sharing as a read-aloud time. They sit politely, smile, and wait for the next person to share. I find that one of my biggest tasks with young writers, and one of the things I always tackle when we are listening to one another, is showing children how to dig in to the writing and respond to it so it is helpful to the writer.

I show my group how to respond to writers by asking them why they want us to listen to a piece, asking what they are wrestling with, asking questions about the writing, or by making comments or asking questions such as: "Would you read that again, I'm not clear," or "I love how you described that," or "How did you think of exactly those words, they're perfect!" I think of this as responsive conversation. I don't have a prescribed set of questions or responses. Rather, I work to *listen* as a fellow writer and teacher of writing and either question, affirm, ask for clarification, or give my opinion if I'm asked for it. I didn't know how to "live" this way among my young writers and respond in this manner to their writing efforts until I was doing a lot more writing myself and reflecting upon what is helpful and not helpful to me in my writing life. As I continue to work on authentic, helpful responses with my young writers, I hope that at some point I will see them spontaneously seeking out responses from one another during our workshop time, *while* they are writing, as a natural part of their process and work. I also listen for them to do this with me when I am wrestling with a piece in front of them. When I was muddling through my fiction piece and couldn't figure out how to resolve a friendship problem between my three sea otter characters, Hickory, Acorn, and Willow, Brenda said, "You know, I feel sorry for Acorn. She's stuck in the middle between Hickory and Willow, and she just wants to be friends with them both. It's just like me when I wanted to take two friends camping and they both liked me but they didn't like each other . . ."

It was the response I needed that day. I had been losing sleep over what to do with these three otters because I wanted to portray a "real ending" to a friendship problem that exists for millions of seven- and eight-year-olds, and not a "they lived happily ever after" ending that seemed like an easy escape to finishing my piece. It was the biggest "aha" for me that day in terms of how the right response at the right moment can be so helpful to a writer. I never expected it to come from an eight-year-old. It changed my view of "sharing and response" with young writers forever.

When a response like this happens, I know we are really living as a classroom of writers. I listen for this active "writing talk," which is the talk I model and engage my writers in when they share in front of the whole class. I tell my young writers that good writing talk is like good book talk, and that I expect them to be wide awake and to listen carefully to help a writer when a writer seeks help. It takes a long time for a writer to understand what type of response is helpful and who to go to for response. I take the time to communicate this to first- and second-grade writers in hopes that they will become sophisticated and selective in this part of their work also.

Teaching Minilessons During Individual Project Days

Although many of the minilessons or lessons that I do, either by myself or with other children, are based on the projects they are working on, I also focus on the conventions of writing during this time. Approximately every two weeks, I conduct an "editing lesson" with the children. I type four or five sentences from some of their drafts, minus all conventions, and we edit these sentences together, marking the page with our corrections. Gathered around the overhead, I work on a transparency and the children work on their own papers. I find it is one way to remind and reteach about spelling, punctuation, and capitalization and keep it in the context of the children's writing. Figure 11–3 shows Nhi's editing sheet.

The following list is a compilation of some of the conventions of writing and spelling minilessons that I teach and reteach when we gather as a group at the start of our workshop time, although it is by no means exhaustive.

Lessons About Conventions of Writing
- punctuation: comma, period, question mark, exclamation point, apostrophe, quotations marks, colon, ellipsis

- Periods are small dots, not the size of a cloud.
- The dot of an *i* is a small dot, not the size of a cloud.
- Commas, periods, and the bottom period of exclamation points and question marks rest on the line and are close to the last word of the sentence.
- capital letters: used for names of important people, places, things, holidays
  - we don't write capital letters in the middle of words unless a capital letter is needed (e.g., McDonald's).
- abbreviations: Mr., Ms., Mrs., Dr.
- contractions: apostrophe replaces missing letter(s)
- plural *s* vs. possessive *s*: "I see two *dogs*." versus "That is my *dog's* bone."
- when to use *a* versus *an*
- date in "short form" is written 9-20-96 or 9/20/96
- spacing: put enough space between words and between sentences so that words and sentences don't run together
- handwriting: writing neatly so drafts are easy to read

Editing Review

Name: _Nhi Nguyen_ Date: _7/10/96_

"Elizabeth said to her, "Will you be my friend?"

the girl said to her, "Yes I will. my name is marie."

"What is your name?" said elizabeth?

"that's a beautiful name," said marie.

she said, "I am getting too sick to take care of the both of you."

Well done.

she cried and suddenly her mom woke up and said, "What's all the racket?"

FIGURE 11–3 *Nhi's editing sheet*

Frequent Spelling Lessons/Reminders

- high-frequency words
- to, too, two versus toe, tow
- their, there, they're
- witch, which
- write, right
- are, our
- and, an
- quiet, quite
- off, of

PLANNING TEACHER-LED WRITING PROJECTS

Teacher-led projects are my opportunity to broaden children's writing horizons. Before the year begins, I map out which projects I want to do with the children so that I can plan enough time for them. I do the following writing projects with first-grade children:

- letters
- little books
- story with beginning/middle/end
- Christmas cards
- informational storybook
- poetry: Mother's Day/Father's Day
- scientific drawings
- three writing samples

I do the following writing projects with second-grade children:

- autobiographical paragraph
- holiday cards
- informational book
- poetry: Mother's Day/Father's Day
- concertina books
- fiction
- memoir
- scientific drawings
- three writing samples

Each project is different and quite structured in terms of the way I take the children through it. My goal is to "get them inside" each particular genre so they know what is required to write in that genre. It is a process of planning, teaching through minilessons and lessons, conferencing, and using wonderful children's literature to highlight the aspects of that genre. Projects like autobiographical paragraphs or holiday cards can take three to five days. Projects like informational storybooks or fiction stories can take four to six weeks, because we don't work on them every day. I try not to rush the work because if the children truly understand what's required in that genre of writing, they will be able to work on a similar project when they have individual writing–project time.

I worked through an autobiographical paragraph project with my second-grade group when we were preparing for our Back-to-School Night because I wanted them to craft a short paragraph about themselves to display with their portraits. Our process follows:

I had been mulling over how to help my second-grade writers craft this piece of writing when I happened to read Jack Prelutsky's autobiographical information in his poetry book *New Kid on the Block* (1984). The style of writing was a perfect model for our own work, although I realized the description he wrote of himself was now dated. For my first project lesson, I reintroduced the book to the class and read "About Jack Prelutsky" from a transparency that I had made. He wrote:

> JACK PRELUTSKY,
> bearded and
> hazel-eyed,
> lives in
> Albuquerque,
> New Mexico.
> When he is
> not writing
> irresistible poetry
> for children,
> he is . . .
> singing a song, tuning a guitar,
> rearranging a growing collection of
> frog bric-a-brac, inventing and
> playing odd word games, taking
> photographs, going bananas on his
> computer, doodling, building slightly
> cockeyed shelves, making nutty
> things out of metal, paper, or plastic,
> cooking an edible, winding a wind-
> up toy, fixing his bicycle, munching
> chocolate chip cookies, flying from
> here to there, visiting schools and
> libraries to share his poetry, reading quietly,
> thinking out loud, and
> wondering what in the world he's
> going to do next . . .

The second time through, we examined it for the critical information that Jack Prelutsky included and composed a list:

- name
- hair color
- eye color
- where he lives
- interesting and funny things about himself

We decided we would write our own pieces including similar information; however, the children also wanted to add age and family information.

I composed my draft in front of my group on the overhead, talking through what I was thinking about as a writer, weaving in the critical information we had agreed should be in our paragraph:

Janine Chappell Carr

I live in Oceanside. I am a thirty-one-year-old teacher with blondish-brownish hair and greenish-bluish eyes! When I am not with my thirty-two second graders at school, I am . . . walking to my Broadway music tapes and singing out loud, talking to my flowers, sending letters, sticking my nose in a book, or giving Michael a hug. . . .

After I finished, the children remained gathered around me with their writing notebooks and began composing their first drafts. I wanted to keep my writers close for the first draft. It was a short piece and I didn't want the commotion of children returning to their tables to write, then returning to the floor for sharing and discussion. I reflected in my journal during their ten-minute quiet-writing time:

> . . . I want the children to write an "About Me" piece to put up with their pencil portraits. . . . I suppose I could have shown more examples. I'm going to grab Bruce Degen and Joanna Cole's bios in the Magic School Bus . . . Dinosaurs. Then ask the children to either continue with theirs or try a different style. Finally, when they think they have what they want, I'll ask them to rewrite it on a blank paper to turn into me for typing. Right now I wish I had a computer in the room. If they were all great readers I would ask them to get books and inspect the bios. . . .

At the end of our ten-minute quiet-writing time, I asked the children to share with one or two other children around them. I listened to children closest to me. Once finished, four children—Priscilla, Tracy, Lisa, and Elizabeth—volunteered to read their first drafts to the entire class. I was eager to have them read aloud and discuss their first drafts as a group so that we could then go back and review our own pieces with new information, discussion, and hopefully different writing eyes. I asked the children to listen for at least one line that captured them during the readings. As it turned out, the sharing session wasn't quite as successful as I'd hoped.

Priscilla had to reread hers because we couldn't hear her, as she kept holding her notebook in front of her face. However, the group chose her line "When I'm not writing, I'm eating chocolate chip cookies or chocolate milk shakes or chocolate milk" as a standout sentence. Adrienne tried to dig deeper into Tracy's piece by asking her what she does when she picks on her brother and Tracy didn't want to answer the question. With Lisa, we noted the age comparison she did between her and her sister: seven and fourteen. Elizabeth received chuckles from the group with this sentence: "I am the girl whose brother had a birthday and got Winnie-the-Pooh underwear."

After the four writers shared their paragraphs, I shared the few books from our classroom library that I had collected quickly during their quiet-writing time, pointing out the biographical information on the authors and illustrators. I invited children to spend part of their writing time studying these or other books as they worked on their pieces for their portraits. We also decided that the children could ask me or another friend to read the biographical information if it was too difficult for them to read.

That night, before leaving, the children turned in their writing notebooks so that I could read their first drafts. I wished I'd had time to skim through all of them as they worked, but I hadn't. Too many needed assistance with reading, spelling, and forming ideas. I pored over them after school, considering the results of our process. During my reading time:

1. I wrote notes on a Post-it about features in the writing that I thought would be noteworthy to discuss the next day at the start of our writing time:

   - this is about you—not a lot about your family
   - need help organizing info. from name to age to eye color to hair color to where live to things I like
   - no phone numbers
   - use Tracy's as an example

2. I separated the writing notebooks into two stacks: One stack included those children who seemed to be well on their way and could continue without my assistance. The second stack included those children I felt were having difficulty and needed help. I would meet with this second group after our whole-group lesson at the start of our writing time the next day.

Continuing and Finishing the Project

The second day of our writing project, we gathered around the overhead projector again as a whole group. I talked with the children about my process of going through their drafts and what I noticed in their pieces. I went through my Post-it note of recommendations and asked them to pay particular attention to these items as they worked on their drafts again. I reread my piece, reminding them that writers need to reread their work before they can pick up with their thoughts again. Earlier that morning, I had asked Tracy if she would be willing to share her piece with the group again, this time on the overhead, so that we could examine her actual writing. She agreed, and it seemed helpful to the others to see her organized, clear ideas, and the neatness of her work, even in draft form. (See Figure 11–4.)

Before I excused them to start with their writing again, Kayalani expressed some concerns about spelling. She was worried about spelling every word correctly. I reminded her, and the rest of the group, to focus on clear ideas in this draft. We agreed they could use temporary spelling, ask a friend, or draw a line for the word and get it later to help with spelling problems while they were composing. I also reminded them I would type their drafts for this particular display and correct misspellings when I did this. My

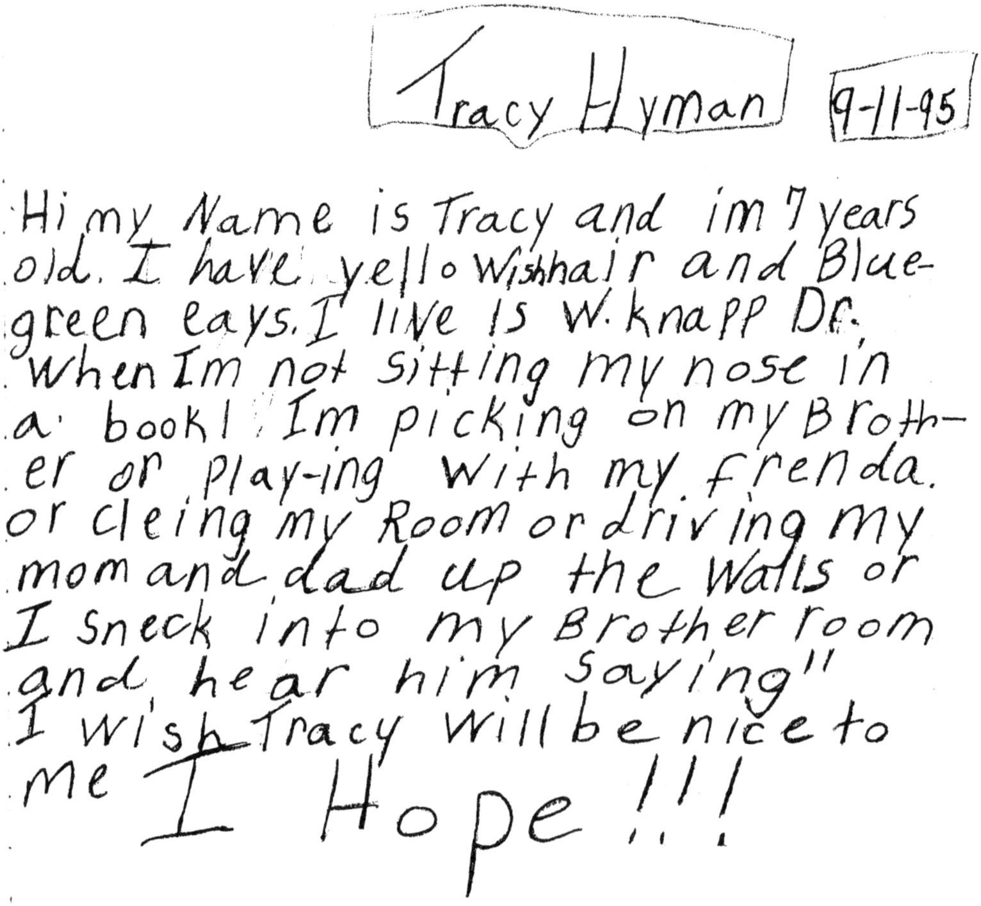
Tracy Hyman 9-11-95

Hi my Name is Tracy and im 7 years old. I have yelloWishhair and Blue-green eays. I live is W. knapp Dr. When Im not sitting my nose in a book Im picking on my Broth-er or play-ing with my frenda. or cleing my Room or driving my mom and dad up the Walls or I sneck into my Brother room and hear him saying" I wish Tracy will be nice to me I Hope!!!

FIGURE 11–4 *Tracy's autobiographical paragraph*

advice to "use your best judgment and thinking" seemed to alleviate Kay's worries, as well as the worries of a few others.

First, I excused to their tables the children who were "well on their way" so they could begin immediately. Some wanted to start over, whereas others wanted to tinker with their drafts from the previous day. I gathered the remaining small group close to me and began tackling their difficulties with them. These items needed the most attention: trying to make sense, figuring out what to do, and solving spelling problems. I nudged each one along, excusing them to write at their tables as they solved problems. I didn't want them to be stuck. I needed to get them moving forward, and I hoped that the community of writers at their tables would be helpful after my initial problem-solving time with them.

Many of the children managed the writing project well during the next two writing sessions, finishing their final drafts and rewriting them with their best spelling and punctuation before turning them in to me. Even Christina, who struggled as a writer, had finished the process. She still had difficulty with her handwriting, but her thoughts were clear, and she had written them by herself. I was proud of her.

> Hi, my name is Christina. I am 7 yers old. My hair is yellow. My eye are blue. My mom is the best. I like to do school work.
> (*Hi, my name is Christina. I am 7 years old. My hair is yellow. My eyes are blue. My mom is the best. I like to do school work.*)

While a majority of the class was successful with this writing project, Lee, Edward, and Heidi had the most difficulty. Lee continued to have trouble focusing on her work. I excused her to another area of the room to work by herself because she couldn't concentrate on her work at her table. She doodled, talked with the other children, looked around the room—everything except tackle her writing. Working without others around seemed to help, but in the end she didn't seem to even try writing a complete draft:

> I live in CA LoFonya Vista Old 7 Hair Color Blond Eye Color Brawne

I could tell she wasn't invested or interested in the process. Lee seemed to either be all hot or all cold on projects. I asked her to work on putting each one of her thoughts into a sentence instead of just writing a list. She knew how to do this. In the end, she dictated her final draft to me, which read:

> I'm seven years old. I live in Vista. My hair color is blond and my eye color is brown. My cousin, Sam, runs around in her underwear! I have five people in my family.

Edward was working hard in his notebook. His first draft showed his process of continuing to work through English syntax:

I live and Vista I yd lif playen and I Nintendo I ym old 7 Miy color of mi jar is brown miy bird pocd and nos. Bidr poc my and nos too.

I asked Edward to read his writing to me. He actually read his piece with more correct English syntax than he had written. I repeated it to him in the way that we would read it in English:

"I live in Vista. I like playing Nintendo. I am 7 years old. My hair color is brown. My bird punched my nose. My brother punched my nose too."

He wanted the last part changed to "My bird punched me in the nose. My brother punched me in the nose too." I didn't write it with him in his notebook this time—I simply remembered it for retyping. I should have, though. As I worked with Edward throughout the year, I began to realize how much this strategy helped him. Rewriting in English, below his first entry, became part of our yearlong practice not only in his writing notebook, but also in his journals.

REFLECTION

After two years of writing work with my last group of children at Bobier, I listed the types of writing they had tackled as young writers. These included:

- daily functional: jobs, sign-ups, sign-ins, lunch menu, bathroom, etc.
- journals: response, correspondence, research, question, clarify thinking
- notebook entries: collecting ideas, developing writing fluency
- poetry: composing and shaping poems
- informational storybook: expository writing; nonfiction
- autobiographical paragraphs: sharing information about themselves
- cards: formal and informal to family and friends
- letters: inquiry, thank-you, get-well, problem-solving, general correspondence
- invitations: Back-to-School nights, Open House nights, special programs
- tour brochures: Open House nights
- captions/summaries: newspaper articles, math projects
- labels: science/discovery area, other areas of the room
- notices: posted on class bulletin board
- concertina book: summary of story and narrative of field trip
- writing samples: benchmark assessments showing growth as a writer
- Myself As a Reader/Writer: self-evaluation in preparation for school conferences
- sharing clues: description of sharing object
- book talk forms: bibliographic information, summary of book, and favorite part
- interviews: family and school members for class projects

Granted, not every type of writing was done during the course of the writing workshop, but I realized that writing permeated every crack and crevice of our classroom life. Daily life simply required that the children write in some form or another.

Lucy Calkins writes, "Writing is lifework, not deskwork" (1991, 7). I think this is also true for five-, six-, seven-, and eight-year-old writers. I believe that a writing workshop gives primary children a place to capture the needs, wants, and workings of their lives and write about them. It is a time when Edward can "use his mind to make books," and a place where Rosanna can write a reassuring letter to her sick grandmother in the hospital (edited letter):

Dear Grandma,

How are you feeling? I feel really sorry. I know you still can't walk but I will always love you. Even if you have an operation, I will always love you. No matter what you do or where you go, I will always love you forever and ever.

Love,

Rosanna

It is also a place where Adrienne can write real dialogue between her two fiction characters, Lottie, an octopus, and her mother—dialogue that in all likelihood took place between Adrienne and her own mother (edited draft):

. . . In the middle of the night, Lottie woke up and said,

"Mommy, when you were a little girl did you have any problems with your friends?"

"Well," said Lottie's mother, "when I was a little girl I had a best friend and her name was Becie. And one day a new girl came and Becie always played with her but never played with me. Why?" said Lottie's mother.

"Because when Adrienne and I were playing tag, another octopus came up and her name was Lisa. When Lisa came, Adrienne asked her if she wanted to go to her house and Lisa said, 'Yes,' so they went to Adrienne's house and left me there all alone, and I was sad."

"Why don't you just tell Adrienne how you feel?" said Lottie's mother.

"I'll try," said Lottie. "But whenever I try to tell her something, Lisa always gets in the way," said Lottie sadly.

"How does Lisa get in your way?" said Lottie's mother.

"She always pulls her away just to show her something, or she pushes me away and talks to Adrienne," said Lottie.

"Well, maybe Adrienne and Lisa aren't the right friends for you," said Lottie's mother.

"They're the right friends for me. It's just Lisa that's in the way. Anyways, I think Adrienne doesn't like me anymore," said Lottie.

"Adrienne likes you. Maybe it's just the way Lisa's treating her and she's having a hard time," said Lottie's mom. "Just get a little rest. Maybe that will help you. . . ."

Finally, writing workshop is a place where Priscilla can write poetry to express her sadness when "missing dog posters" don't help, and her little dog, Bea, never returns home (edited draft):

My Dog

My dog is missing.
I loved her so.
I used to cuddle up to her
when she cried.
I still cry
because I miss her so very much.
Because she's my dog
forever more.

12 | MONITORING PROGRESS

I love . . . the look of words
the weight of ideas that popped into my mind
I love the tracks
of new thinking in my mind.

—Maya Angelou, "I Love the Look of Words"

On Chris' first day of first grade, his mother and little brother stayed with him until the morning bell rang so they could walk him from the playground to our classroom door. A towhead with beautiful blue eyes, Chris held onto his mother's hand and was reluctant to say good-bye.

"Chris is a little nervous about starting school and being in school all day," his mother said to me. "He's been carrying your letter around for a week."

I bent down to reassure Chris that I knew all about first-day-of-first-grade worries, and I told his mother and brother they were welcome to stay with us for awhile if that would help. Chris didn't say a word. He just nodded "yes," and held onto his mother's leg.

A few days later, when Chris completed his first writing sample, I realized that he was what I call a "young" first grader. Not only had he written his name backward, but he had also reversed most of the letters. His picture wasn't focused on one topic, and he didn't attempt any writing, unlike other young writers such as Rosanna, who had labeled hers "6 Flags Magic Mountain," which she had copied from our chart of possible writing topics.

As I got to know Chris, I learned that, with an August birthday, he was also chronologically younger than most of his classmates. He'd had an impatient kindergarten teacher, he'd suffered through the divorce of his parents, and he now lived with his mother, who had opted for welfare support so she could parent her two boys during the day and go to school at night.

Given both Chris' school and home histories, I worried about his literacy journey. Particularly after his first writing sample, I wondered how long it would take for him to become a writer. However, he surprised me. By midyear, Chris was comfortable composing his thoughts using both temporary and conventional spelling. In April, his midyear writing sample looked like this:

I went. too, meik Donellds, And my Brother, fel in ther bolls I jommt, in ANd hlpt him, my kosin kamd, too, wy went dan the slid it wos fon,

(*I went to McDonald's, and my brother fell in their balls. I jumped in and helped him. My cousin came too. We went down the slide. It was fun.*)

I studied his writing sample and noted several positive aspects to his writing. Chris had:

- made a good topic choice because it was from personal experience
- focused his writing on one topic
- written complete thoughts
- exhibited an awareness of punctuation and was exploring how to use it
- spelled sixteen words conventionally, which calculates to a spelling accuracy rate of 55.1 percent

These were items that Chris needed to work on:

- leaving more space between words
- learning the conventional spelling of /we, was, fun/
- eliminating capital letters from the middles of words unless it's needed
- ironing out reversals: N, s
- using punctuation and conventional spelling

At the end of Chris' first-grade year, he wrote the following piece for his writing sample:

> I Love,d vacashIn Becus.
>   I got to see my Gramo.
>   and the're is a revre there.
>   and the revre leds to a Bech.

Like before, Chris' topic choice was terrific, as well as his ability to stay focused on that topic. First-grade writers are notorious for jumping topics in one piece of writing because oftentimes conversations at their table trigger a memory, and suddenly that becomes part of their piece—regardless of what they were originally writing about! Chris' handwriting was larger and more legible at the end of the year, which was an improvement from his midyear sample. He was still reversing the letter /s/ in his writing, and there was only one capital letter in the middle of the word "vacash In." Overall, even though it was another short piece in comparison to the work of other first-grade writers, I felt that Chris had made good progress during the year. Lucky for me, I had Chris as a second grader, so I was able to monitor his writing progress another year.

At the beginning of his second-grade year, Chris composed this piece for his writing sample:

> My Gandmoe's Birde's ore Rilee Fony. She has a perockt and a yloe Birde. and somtims I get Mad at them.
>   (*My grandma's birds are really funny. She has a parakeet and a yellow bird, and sometimes I get mad at them.*)

When studying his sample, I was interested to see the overgeneralization of the "apostrophe s" rule, as he was using it for most of his plurals.

Many second-grade writers go through this phase. Chris continued to use temporary spelling with ease, and for the most part, his high frequency word spellings were conventional, except for the word *are*, which became a spelling goal for him.

For his midyear writing sample in second grade, Chris decided to write an informational piece instead of a personal narrative piece. He wrote:

Crocodiles

Crocodiles Have pawrful Jos. and sleep whith the'r mouth opin whith the'r dady's in the'r Mouth.

(*Crocodiles have powerful jaws, and sleep with their mouth open with their babies in their mouth.*)

In terms of positive characteristics in his writing, Chris had:

- experimented with a different genre of writing on his own
- titled his piece
- focused on one topic and seemed to know something about it
- written neatly and legibly
- shown a spelling accuracy rate of 47 percent
- shown a more developed understanding of punctuation usage

I noted the following as "needs work" areas in his writing:

- use of apostrophes: overgeneralizing "apostrophe rules" and now doing "apostrophe r"
- writing /d/ for /b/
- spelling goals for high-frequency words: *with* and *their*
- still using capitals at the beginning of words in the middle of sentences

At the end of two years, Chris wrote this piece on travel for his final writing sample:

Travlle,

I love too travlle on plane trane and bus. I loved it wen i was a baby and i love it rite naw and i well love it for ever. Janine love's to travlle too. the end

(*I love to travel on plane, train, and bus. I loved it when I was a baby, and I love it right now, and I will love it forever. Janine loves to travel too. The end.*)

Chris' writing development was a measured process. He didn't have writing spurts; rather, his pace was slow, but steady. Throughout my two years with him, I observed that he needed a lot of time to complete his writing, although I never considered him a struggling writer. As I reviewed his last writing sample, I ruefully noted that he continued to write /i/ for the word *I*, even after countless lessons that the word *I* is written with a capital letter. However, I thought he had made great strides as a developing writer over the course of two years. Over time, things like capital letters in the middles of words, not enough spacing between words, and letter reversals had managed to work themselves out. More complicated issues like punctuation and spelling still needed attention, but those were manageable. Chris still needed to tend to the details of writing conventions and spelling, but he was able to compose pieces that were interesting and clear, which is at least half the work in becoming a good writer. Although he never composed "volumes" like many of the other children, at the end of two years, Chris had made considerable progress since his first writing picture efforts at the beginning of first grade.

WRITING SAMPLES

In my classroom, writing samples are an important part of the way in which I monitor the children's writing progress. I consider my daily observations of their writing work in notebooks, journals, and teacher-led and individual writing projects an informal means of assessment, and writing samples a formal measure of progress. I study both daily writing work and writing samples to monitor how the children's writing knowledge and skills are developing in order to determine what they need next to move them forward as writers.

I collect four formal writing samples a year. Three samples, beginning, midyear, and year-end, are required by the district for the children's district language arts portfolio. I have the children compose the fourth sample for our school conferences, which occur during the fourth month of school, so families can view a current writing sample during the conference.

Since I have a choice, I give the children an open-ended prompt, "Write about something that is important to you," instead of a literature prompt. I do this because I believe writers can only write thoughtfully and well about things that are important to them. These writing samples are one-draft samples; they are not revised, edited, or rewritten because the purpose is to see what the children can do on their own as writers.

I prepare a form for each writing sample so that samples are clearly marked. An example follows:

First Grade
Beginning of the Year Writing Sample
Name:_____Date:_____

For first-grade children's first writing sample, I draw a box for a picture and leave space underneath for their writing if they attempt to write anything. Many of the children only draw a picture or label the picture with a string of letters, or one or more words in conventional and/or temporary spelling. For midyear first grade through year-end second grade, I prepare the forms with lines.

At the beginning of second grade with my last group, we conducted the writing sample process in this way:

First, we discussed the purpose of the writing sample (to show what you can do as a writer), and brainstormed possible writing ideas. I reminded them to write about something that was important to them, something they could provide a lot of information about, or something they had noticed that was interesting to them. After that, the children discussed possible topics among themselves before we talked about them as a whole group. I made a "cluster chart" of their ideas during our whole-group discussion. A listing of the items that appeared on our chart follows.

Beginning Year Writing Sample (9-18-95)

- birthdays
- school: second grade, family helpers
- house: what you do!
- new things: bike
- animals: dog, cat, pets, bird, fish
- Lee's swimming pool and what she does
- family: cousin having a baby, baby sister
- favorite books
- someone you love
- me!
- fun places: Six Flags Magic Mountain, Disneyland
- trips

After our brainstorming session, the children and I reviewed my expectations for the writing sample. These included:

- choosing a good topic for you; one that you know a lot about
- rereading often as you write
- writing neatly
- doing your best with spelling; search out spellings on your own
- writing neatly
- doing your best with punctuation

After this introductory work, the children returned to their tables to begin writing. Those children who were still searching for an idea stayed on the carpet so we could discuss possible topics until they discovered one that seemed "just right." Once they had an idea, they, too, returned to their tables to begin their writing work.

While the children composed their thoughts, I walked around giving general assistance and encouragement, but not specific help; I reminded them to work slowly and thoughtfully. When they finished, they had two choices: quiet reading or writing in their writing notebooks. The room needed to stay calm and quiet for our entire writing session in order to respect the time needs of all writers. I didn't want anyone to feel rushed or distracted with his or her work.

Studying Writing Samples

After the children complete their writing samples, I study them to determine how they are progressing as writers. First, I lay out any previous samples that I have—for example, by second grade, I have both kindergarten and first-grade samples—and make general comparisons. I look for patterns of growth over time. Visually, I can see the differences immediately just by scanning them.

At the beginning of first grade, when the children are new writers, I assess the significant characteristics in their writing samples so I can determine their levels of written language development. They fall into one of two categories: emergent writer or early writer. The characteristics that I assign to these levels of development follow:

Emergent Writer

- picture only
- picture and "string of letters"
- picture and label

Early Writer

- picture and sentence with temporary and/or conventional spelling
- one topic with a few supporting sentences
- beginning use of punctuation

I actually make a class composite sheet of the children's writing development after this first writing sample so that I can refer to it throughout the year. The following shows the writing development of my last group when they entered first grade, which was a typical starting profile for every class that I taught at Bobier:

emergent: picture only: 22 children
emergent: picture and label copied from chart: 5 children
early: picture and sentence with temporary spelling: 3 children

In my last group, Lisa seemed to be a child that was born a writer. I soon discovered that like Barbara Esbensen, she could find the longest stories living in the shortest pencils. As I reviewed her first-grade writing samples, I was struck by her early understanding and use of writing conventions, along with what appeared to be a natural "writing voice." For her beginning year first-grade sample, she had drawn a picture of a castle and written the word *Disneyland*, underneath it (with the *y* reversed), which she had copied from our brainstorming chart.

By midyear, Lisa was writing clearly, using more standard spelling than temporary spelling, and exhibiting a well-developed understanding of punctuation. She wrote:

I Was Very Very sick. I oMost throwup on My bed. My teppuchre was 103.9. but today Aftr school I'm going to the Doctrs office.

(*I was very, very sick. I almost threw up on my bed. My temperature was 103.9, but today after school, I'm going to the doctor's office.*)

At the end of our first-grade year, Lisa's cats, whom I had come to know and love through journal letters, were the focus of her last writing sample. She composed this wonderful piece:

I Love cats. I Love my cats. I have four kittens, There mother, and our other cat. I like cats a Lot. the only cats I Hate are tom cats. Cats are my life. I Love them Because one of my cats act like a man. his name is Pepey. He likes Atalein food. I Love him very very much.

(*I love cats. I love my cats. I have four kittens, their mother, and our other cat. I like cats a lot. The only cats I hate are tomcats. Cats are my life. I love them because one of my cats acts like a man. His name is Pepey. He likes Italian food. I love him very, very much.*)

As my young writers begin composing longer pieces, or enter "the writing stage" (Traill 1993), my system of assessment becomes more detailed, and I focus on three broad areas—form, fluency, and correctness—when I study their daily writing and writing samples to determine how they are developing as writers. (Leanna Traill's continuum of written language development is also a helpful resource and can be found in her book, *Highlight My Strengths* 1993.) My rubric for monitoring progress follows:

Studying Children's Writing Development Form

- topic choice
  - Is it something the writer knows a lot about?
  - Does the writer provide enough information?
  - Does the writer stay focused on the topic?
- genre choice (usually second grade)
  - Is this a surprise genre choice for this writer?
  - Is this a good choice for this writing sample or piece of writing?
- organization of space and format
  - Is there enough space between words and sentences?
  - Is the writer writing in a conventional format: left to write, top to bottom?

Fluency

- language and word choice
  - How much does the writer write?
  - Is it sufficient for the topic choice and genre?
  - Does the writer use "good words"; is it language that captures the reader?

Correctness

- punctuation
  - Does the writer attempt or include any punctuation?
  - What level of punctuation knowledge does the young writer exhibit: beginning, developing, proficient?
- handwriting
  - Is the piece legible and neat?
  - Is the handwriting uniform?
  - Are there letter reversals?
  - Are there capital letters mixed with small letters in words?
- spelling
  - What is the percentage of conventional spelling in the sample? How does this compare to previous samples?
  - Does the temporary spelling make sense and show a developing understanding of our spelling system?

After a quick review of any previous writing samples I have (in Lisa's case, her first-grade samples) I study the current writing sample more closely using this rubric. I don't use the rubric to score the paper, rather to get a sense of how the children are developing as writers in each of these areas. For example, Lisa wrote this piece for her beginning second-grade writing sample:

I am so, so, so glade that my grandma mite come home today or Wednesday. Yesterday me and my mom went to visit my grandma. My mom is very happy too.

(*I am so, so, so glad that my grandma might come home today or Wednesday. Yesterday me and my mom went to visit my grandma. My mom is very happy too.*)

When I studied Lisa's writing using this rubric, I rated her as being proficient in topic and genre choice, organization of space and format, and handwriting. I gave her a "developing well" rating in language and word choice, punctuation, and spelling. In two of Lisa's first-grade samples, she had not used a comma between the words *very very* and in this piece she showed a new level of understanding by including commas between the words *so, so, so*. Her understanding and use of punctuation at the beginning of second grade was quite sophisticated. She was a solid early writer.

When Lisa completed her midyear writing sample in second grade, her spelling accuracy rate was 98.6 percent, an increase from an 84 percent spelling accuracy rate in her first-grade midyear writing sample. She wrote:

I love school because it is very, very fun And all my friends are here to play with me. And there names are: Elizabeth, Snow, Christina, Christie, Mary, Rosanna, Nhi, Sonia, Joseph, almost everyone in the class and some in different classes, too. Even someone that go's to a different school her name is Joy and her little sister Marry. All my friends are my best friends. This is a true story. The Fnd.

As I studied her sample, it was clear how much Lisa knew as a writer. She continued to choose personally relevant topics and write about them with ease. Her handwriting and organization of space were consistently excellent, and she continued to increase her knowledge and use of punctuation. In this piece she used end marks, commas, capitals, and a colon correctly. She was still working through the appropriate use of an apostrophe, but it wouldn't take her long. I determined that Lisa was exhibiting the characteristics of an early fluent writer because of her level of proficiency in each of the areas on my rubric.

At the end of second grade, Lisa wrote this piece for her final sample:

In May or July I went to a pool party. To my friend Candace's pool party, it was fun. But then when the big kids got there it was'nt fun. Because some of them cept on pling on me to the dep end were I coud'nt swim at all.

(*In May or July I went to a pool party, to my friend Candace's pool party. It was fun. But then when the big kids got there, it wasn't fun because some of them kept on pulling on me to the deep end where I couldn't swim at all.*)

In this piece, Lisa had her "apostrophe s" rule correct at the end of *Candace's*, but apostrophes in contractions were still challenging. She knew apostrophes were needed in words like *wasn't* and *couldn't*, but she didn't have the placement right yet—almost there. I didn't think this piece captured her usual writing voice—it seemed more like a retelling—but it was the end of a busy two years, and we were tired. When I considered the body of writing work that she had done during our two years together, I could see that Lisa had developed into an extraordinary young writer. Figure 12–1 shows samples of Lisa's two-year writing development.

ESL WRITERS

Chris and Lisa are two examples of writers who have very different writing journeys, but nonetheless make steady progress as writers. I find, however, that I must monitor the progress of ESL children even more closely. I don't overmonitor, or even "overworry," because more than anything else, ESL children need *time*. One noticeable difference in their writing development from children whose first language is English is that it generally takes much longer for them to use correct syntax in their writing, although this too depends upon each child. Most young children show syntax confusions as they begin to write because they are still learning proper English forms and usage rules in their speech. However, in my experience, ESL children generally show syntax confusions longer than other children. Many of these confusions are ironed out over the course of one or two years, and a few are not. In general, ESL children require five to seven years to become proficient in their second language (Escamilla 1994). A teacher only has a year or two of that five- to seven-year journey. I try to keep that in perspective as I work with ESL children, while maintaining high expectations for their progress.

Monica was one of several Mexican American children in my classroom who spoke Spanish at home and English at school. Both of Monica's parents spoke Spanish, but her older high school sister spoke Spanish and English. She was also surrounded by several cousins in her neighborhood, and one in our classroom, who spoke English, so she was immersed in her second lan-

FIGURE 12–1
*Lisa's writing samples:
overview of development*

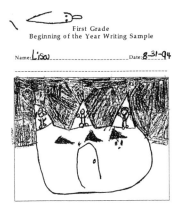

First Grade
Beginning of the Year Writing Sample

Name: Lisa   Date: 8-31-94

Disneyland

End of Year Writing
First Grade

Name: Lisa Pearce   Date: July 12, 95

I love cats I love my cats. I have
four kittens, There mothers are our other
cat I like cats a lot the only cats I
hate are tom cats. Cats are my life.
I love them Because one of my cats
act like a man. his name is Pepey.
He likes Atalein food. I love him very very
much.

Mid-Year Writing
First Grade

Name: Lisa Pearce   Date: 1-10-95

I Was Very Very
Sick I o Most throwp
on My Bed. My teppuchre
WaS 103.9. but to day
Aftr School I'm going to
the Doctrs office.

Spelling Accuracy
95.6%

Second Grade
Mid-Year Writing Sample

Name: Lisa D. Pearce Date: 11/96
I love school beccue it is
very, very fun And all my friends are here to play with me
And there names are: Eliza
beth, Snow, christina, christie, Mag
Rosanna, Nhi, Sonia, Joseph, almost
everyone in the class and so
me in different classes, too
Even someone that goes to a
different school her name is
Joy and her little sister marry.

guage. At her father's request, Monica usually spoke only English at school, and not Spanish. She was a quiet girl, and I had to seek out daily conversation with her; otherwise, I knew I wouldn't hear from her.

At the beginning of first grade, Monica drew a picture of herself surrounded by flowers and wrote SEAWORLD underneath. My guess was that she simply chose a word at random from our chart of possible writing topics and wrote it on her paper. In any case, the text didn't match the picture.

During the next four months, Monica, along with all of the other children, was immersed in daily writing of some type: journals, quiet writing, teacher-led or individual writing projects. Whenever possible, I helped Monica compose her thoughts in English in a guided writing format, much like I did with our first whole-class journal letters (see Chapter 10). It helped her to hear how to compose her thoughts in English and to receive help forming the letters and words in English. When she completed her midyear writing sample, I could see that Monica was making progress as a writer in her second language:

> I Love wn I spn Nogi at my Grandma And my mom to pks my like sister to she lik my grandma And my sister to And we lik my Grandma And I Dot hf a papa Im sade pk my papa Die Snd Im ve rsade pk my papa Die And Im ve sade pk my papa die and my mom es sade to and sister to and my brother to and my Dad to pk et was my mom dad and my dad is sade to and Im ve sade and my sister too. . . .
>
> (*I love when I spend [the] night at my grandma's, and my mom too because my little sister too, she like my grandma, and my sister too, and we like my grandma, and I don't have a papa. I'm sad because my papa died and I'm very sad because my papa died. And I'm very sad because my papa died, and my mom is sad too, and my sister too, and my brother too, and my Dad too because it was my mom's dad and my dad is sad too, and I'm very sad and my sister too. . . .*)

As I read through Monica's writing sample, I could see that Monica had chosen to stay with a familiar theme: her family and in particular, the loss of her Pap (her grandfather). I knew about the loss of Monica's Papa from previous pieces she had written in her writing notebook and journals, but her writing sample was one more reminder that this ache was still with her. Lucy Calkins asks, "How can we expect children to write well when we don't know their stories?" (1991, 13). Even in a formal writing sample, I first read for the stories of the children's lives. Once I am inside their worlds, then I work to help my young writers learn how to write their heartfelt stories with clarity and power.

Using my rubric, I rated Monica's writing sample in the following way:

- Topic Choice and Genre Choice: well done; stayed focused on the topic
- Language and Word Choice: repetitious; mostly familiar words; perhaps should try poetry as a way to express her sad feelings about her Papa
- Organization of Space and Format: proficient; nice spacing between words

- Punctuation: not developed; no punctuation in the writing
- Handwriting: proficient; using capitals in the middle of sentences
- Spelling: developing; two goals—*because, like*; writing Pks or PK for *because*; dropping the /e/ from *like*

Monitoring Syntax

In addition to the above areas, I also add another item to my rubric with ESL children: syntax. I study how their understanding of English syntax is developing in their writing, because it generally mirrors how they are speaking English. In studying Monica's sample, you will note that she doesn't use the past tense of *die*, which throws off the flow of the reading if you are an English speaker, but at that time, it matched her use of present and past tense forms when she spoke English.

Nhi, my student from Vietnam, had an interesting nuance in her speaking and writing of English, in that she would read or write *say* for *said*. Edward was even a little different in that he would pronounce *said* with a long /a/ sound when sharing his writing. I tackle small syntax issues like these when I work individually with ESL children—not in front of the whole group because I don't want to embarrass them, and I want them to continue to be risk-takers in their second language. I point out the correct English form gently, but matter-of-factly, saying something like, "Monica, in English, we would say *died* instead of *die* in this case. You need to add a /d/ on the end of the word when you write it in your sentence: I'm sad because my papa die*d*."

Sometimes I elaborate and have ESL children practice with me, first in speaking, then in writing. For example, when I was working with Edward on his pronunciation of *said*, I said something to this effect: "Edward, we say the word *said* with an /e/ sound in the middle, not an /a/ sound. Can you hear the difference? Say it with me. *Said*. Now, let's look at the spelling of the word. It's tricky because it has /ai/ in the middle, and it makes you think it's an /a/ sound. Practice saying it in your head or out loud when you need it in your writing."

With Nhi, I explained the difference between *said* and *say* in this way: "Nhi, in English, we pronounce this word, *said*, not *say*. Can you hear the difference? Look, it has a /d/ on the end of the word, and that letter stands for the /d/ sound. When you write the word *said*, say it to yourself quietly, and put that /d/ sound on the end."

During the year, I begin to hear the children do a similar "correcting and explaining" process with one another, in much the same way that they hear me doing it. Remarkably, they seem to accept these gentle form and usage lessons from one another quite willingly, and from what I observe, without frustration, discouragement, or embarrassment.

At the end of our first-grade year, Monica wrote about her "papa" again, only this time, she referred to him as "grandpa." Her piece follows:

I mest my grandpa? Because He wus My Bast grandpa! Because. He waus! niss-cin-of? And He! yost. to. Biy? tos. He wus. cin of niss But?

He dect. no. theat! The-cat-wus. ded-Bcasue? He-wus-Bese-wohing-My-litl? sister-But-Hes-cat? wus-ded-Bcasue. My-grandma-dect! fed-my-grandpa. Cat-Bcause-She-wus? cid-fo-mein-But. She es not mein? lot Bcause she es. nis naw.

(*I missed my grandpa because he was my best grandpa because he was nice, kind of. And he used to buy toys. He was kind of nice but he didn't know that the cat was dead because he was busy watching my little sister. But his cat was dead because my grandma didn't feed my grandpa's cat because she was kind of mean. But she is not mean [a] lot because she is nice now.*)

As I studied Monica's writing sample to determine her progress as a writer, two things struck me. First, her English syntax was essentially correct except for her last sentence. Second, whereas her midyear writing sample had no punctuation, her year-end sample was full of punctuation marks. A notable pattern was that at the end of each line she had placed either an exclamation point or a question mark. In between that, she had sprinkled lots of periods and dashes between words. She didn't realize that the marks should have been on the page for a reason, and not simply "sprinkled in" at random.

Monica had progressed from "no understanding" of punctuation to a "developing understanding." Her next goal would be to refine her use of punctuation.

Since Monica was part of my last group at Bobier, I was able to monitor her writing development for two years. With many ESL children, my work never feels complete in a year. At the beginning of second grade, Monica wrote about her bird for her writing sample:

My brar bid becus my sister wus at scool. And my big sister. wus clening the bach room and my brd jup. don of the cach And wet. to the Big Brar name Bobe and the Brar. name Bobe sep on the Brar and wen I cam hom we my cusen. I wus lecing for my bast brar and i told my big sister wer is my brdr she told me he dad I wus sad and wen my Dad cam. hom I cid becus my brar did I am sel. sad so es my dad but. my. Dad sad I am going to diy you a nw wun.

(*My bird died because my sister was at school. And my big sister was cleaning the back room and my bird jumped down off the couch and went to the big bird named Bobe. And the bird named Bobe stepped on the bird, and when I came home with my cousin I was looking for my best bird, and I told my big sister, "Where is my bird?" She told me, "He's dead." I was sad, and when my dad came home I cried because my bird died. I am still sad. So is my dad, but my dad said, "I am going to buy you a new one."*)

Again, there were several positive aspects to Monica's writing in terms of topic and genre choice, language and word choice, organization of space and format, and handwriting. The two areas that needed the most attention in Monica's writing at this point were spelling and punctuation. High-frequency words that needed attention included *because, when, was, down, off, went, I, is, new, one.* She also required instruction on adding "quiet e" to the ends of words like *home* and *come.* Monica had worked on most of these high-frequency words previously as part of her weekly spelling work; however, she wasn't remembering them. I wanted her to practice more and consult our high-frequency word cards more when she was doing her daily writing.

Punctuation was still random for Monica, although she had far less punctuation in this piece than her last first-grade writing sample. She seemed to be developing a better conceptual understanding of punctuation; however, she still wasn't sure how to make it "fit" into her writing.

I found two notable items in terms of Monica's syntax: she hadn't included an /s/ on the end of *he,* so that it read *He dead* instead of *He's dead*; and she hadn't included a /d/ on the end of *name* so it read . . . *the big bird name Bobe* instead of . . . *the big bird named Bobe.* In my experience, leaving off endings is a common problem with ESL learners, whether it's in the context of present tense, past tense, or possessives. Again, I simply correct and explain gently, but matter-of-factly, so they clear up these small issues when speaking and writing in English.

Monica showed improvement in her spelling accuracy in her second-grade midyear writing sample. For this piece, she wrote:

> My little stsire. Birthday is to Day. And she trns 6 And. We are going to Making a poned on SaturDay Because we cant mak one for her to Day And My MoM said at we only. culd have some presed And [Celina] said ats OK. with her And MoM said OK too. So did my dad. And I did too.
>
> *(My little sister's birthday is today. And she turns six. And we are going to make a pinata on Saturday because we can't make one for her today. And my mom said that we only could have some presents and [Celina] said that's OK with her and mom said OK too. So did my dad. And I did too.)*

Monica's spelling accuracy rate on this piece was 86.4 percent, in comparison to a 61.6 percent spelling accuracy rate on her first-grade midyear writing sample. I calculate the spelling accuracy rate on the children's midyear samples because I send home a copy of this writing sample and the spelling information with the children's report cards. To calculate the spelling accuracy rate, I divide the number of words spelled conventionally by the total number of words in the writing sample.

At this point, Monica's writing development included the following interesting items:

- She wrote *making* instead of *make,* which was the incorrect form for her sentence.

- She didn't include the "quiet e" at the end of words like *make*.
- She didn't include an /s/ ending on *sister's* and *presents*, so she had an incorrect form of each word in the sentence.
- She dropped the /th/ digraph from the beginning of *that's*.
- She still didn't understand rules of punctuation and used punctuation marks randomly.

All of the above became writing goals for Monica, which I monitored when I sat beside her to work with her on a current piece of writing.

The last piece of writing that Monica did in our classroom was a letter of introduction to her new third-grade teachers, written on the last day of school. Her letter follows:

Dear Ms. Gillogly, And Ms. Lopez

As you get to Now me you will see what I look like And I will get to Now Both of you And I can't wait until we met And I am excited Because you are going to Be my Now Teacher And I hope you halp Me Teach a lot

Tack you.

Love, Monica.

(*As you get to know me, you will see what I look like, and I will get to know both of you, and I can't wait until we meet, and I am excited because you are going to be my new teacher, and I hope you help me teach a lot. Thank you.*)

Yes, there were still difficulties, mainly in the areas of spelling and punctuation, but I found the progress she had made in her second language remarkable. She had started her first-grade year drawing herself in a field of flowers, with the word SEAWORLD written underneath, and at the end of two years, she was writing a charming letter of introduction to her upcoming third-grade teachers. I was proud of her accomplishments, not just as an ESL writer, but as a young writer, period. Figure 12–2 shows samples of Monica's two-year writing development.

COMPARISON OF TWO YEARS' WRITING GROWTH

At the end of my two years with my last group of students at Bobier I asked myself, "How much have these children grown as writers over the course of two years?" I remembered that most of the children's beginning first-grade writing samples were picture only with no words and little or no attempt to label or write with temporary spelling. I looked through all of the children's writing samples and compared where they had started as writers to where they had progressed. Most of my young writers showed growth similar to Rachael's—beginning first grade as emergent writers and developing into early fluent writers by the end of second grade. Those children who seemed to have extraordinary language skills, like Lisa, progressed from

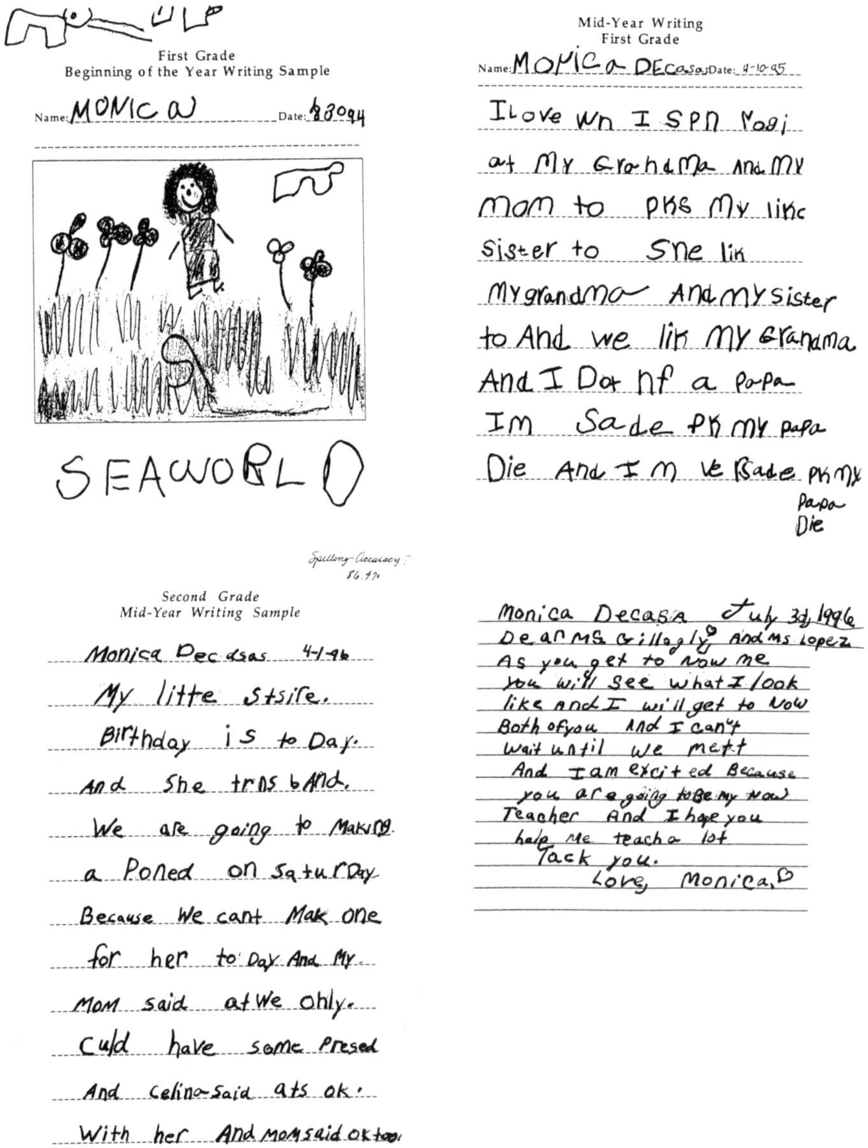

First Grade
Beginning of the Year Writing Sample

Name: MONICA   Date: 9 80 94

SEAWORL O

Second Grade
Mid-Year Writing Sample

Monica Dec dsas   4-1-96
My litte stsire.
Birthday is to Day.
And She trns bAnd.
We are going to Making
a Poned on saturDay
Because We cant Mak one
for her to Day And My
Mom said at We ohly
Culd have some Presed
And Celino said ats ok.
With her And mom said ok too.

Mid-Year Writing
First Grade

Name: MONICa DECasas Date: 4-10-95

ILove wn I SPn rosi
at My Grahama And my
mom to pks my liRe
sister to Sne liR
mygrandma And my sister
to And we liR My Granama
And I Dot nf a PaPa
IM Sade PK my papa
Die And I m Ve Bade PKmy
papa
Die

Monica Decasa July 3d, 1996
Dear MS crillogly And ms lopez
As you get to now me
you will see what I look
like and I will get to Now
Both ofyou And I can't
wait until we mett
And I am excited Because
you are going to Be my New
Teacher And I hope you
help Me teach a lot
Tack you.
Love, Monica.

FIGURE 12–2   Monica's writing samples: overview of development

being emergent writers at the beginning of first grade to being fluent writers by the end of second grade.

I also developed a list of what I observed to be the children's writing instructional needs upon entering third grade. A summary of this list follows:

Form

- developing ideas
- rereading for meaning
- shaping a piece so it doesn't ramble
- providing better focus for a piece

Fluency

- using transitional words to start sentences
- developing English syntax (ESL students)
- writing frequently

Correctness

- using correct punctuation
- exhibiting clear handwriting
- spelling: using resources
- spelling: learning high-frequency words
- spelling: learning vowel patterns

Just as I tracked the children's reading development over a two-year period with anecdotal notes and running records, the children's writing samples were evidence of their growth as writers, with some of my writers more skilled and confident than others. After sitting beside them while they wrote every day and studying their written work for two years, I felt like I knew "the insides" of these children as writers, much like I knew them inside and out as readers. I believed these children knew how to express themselves and communicate effectively through the written word, which is why we want children to become writers in the first place.

REFLECTION

Monitoring the progress of young writers calls for consistent analysis of their written work and then using that information to help them work out their confusions or fill in gaps in their writing knowledge whether it be in the areas of topic and genre selection, language and word choice, organization of space and format, punctuation, handwriting, spelling, or syntax. Above all, writing development must be assessed in the context of the children's personal writing (Traill 1993).

In the process of assessing children's writing development in the context of their personal writing, I have never been able to find the time to write quick anecdotal notes about their writing progress while assisting them, which is my practice during reading conferences. Generally, my pencil is busy alongside theirs as we work together to construct clear, thoughtful pieces and iron out problems and confusions about the conventions of writing. Whereas reading aloud is fleeting, and there is no visual proof—thus the need for anecdotal notes or running records during conferences—writing leaves a paper trail and gives me the evidence I need to determine what my young writers know and where they need to go. Perhaps I will change my practice at some point in time and decide that I must take notes as I sit beside my writers. However, I found it impossible to record anecdotal notes at Bobier with thirty-two primary writers who often needed active composing assistance. Their written work provided me with enough information to monitor their progress and move them forward.

I rely on the children's entire body of written work, not just writing samples, to document their writing progress. I do "quick studies" of their daily writing work as I sit beside them, analyzing the same areas that I do in their writing samples. I examine the children's writing closely because the details of their writing help me make decisions about how to propel them forward. I realize that children do not develop as writers in exactly the same ways, so I look for general patterns in their writing development and knowledge, and I note the specific confusions so I can help them.

Children learn the "how-to's" of writing over time as they immerse themselves in their writing, share their work, hear good models of writing, see other writers at work, read good literature so they know what good writing sounds like, and perhaps most important, learn how to monitor their own writing progress. I've already made my case for why it's important for children to learn how to monitor themselves as readers, and I believe that helping children learn how to monitor themselves as writers is equally important. Again, I listen for "my talk" to become "their talk" when they are composing, sharing, and responding to one another. I want young writers to be able to criticize and celebrate their writing efforts long after they've been in my classroom.

At the end of our second-grade year, Rosanna, another gifted writer in our classroom, chose to write a short memoir piece for her final writing sample. She wrote:

When I was five I baly lernd how to spell my name. My mom say's to prackti's some more. So I trid my best. and trid, and trid, one day my mom saide get a pies of paeper. then she said I will tell you how to spell it. And write it down. And say it five time's so I did wat she saide then she took it away and gave me another peper. And gess wat I finely spelld my name. My mom and my dad and sister and my ator sister were all prord of me and so was I!

(When I was five, I barely learned how to spell my name. My mom says to practice some more. So I tried my best, and tried and tried. One day my mom said, "Get a piece of paper." Then she said, "I will tell you how to spell it, and write it down, and say it five times." So I did what

she said, then she took it away and gave me another paper. And guess what? I finally spelled my name. My mom and my dad and sister and my other sister were all proud of me and so was I!)

Like Rosanna's mom, I am there to nudge my young writers to practice, write it down, and try their best. As they do this, I watch, study, and talk with the children about their efforts. It is the dual processes of *observation* and *instructional conversation* that tell me how to help them next, so that like Rosanna, they learn, do well, and feel proud of themselves as writers.

13 | STRUGGLING WRITERS

His attempts to write tell us something of the things he is noticing in print, although we must always remember that his eye may perceive more than his hand can execute.

—*Marie Clay*, Becoming Literate

Children who struggle to become writers do so in different ways. In this chapter I profile two young writers, Christina and Edward, who needed closer instruction to help them manage the process of writing. As with the three struggling readers I profile in Chapter 8, I chose these two students because (1) I felt they represented the many children I've worked with who have initial writing struggles and (2) they show my levels of success as a writing teacher. I can recall students who, like Christina, had trouble with several parts of the composing process and made only moderate gains with close instruction, while other young writers made wonderful gains with the same type of individualized help. Other struggling writers were like Edward, who experienced difficulties with the conventions and nuances of a second language until he had acquired enough knowledge to propel himself forward at a steady pace. Again, my intent is to show the interactions and close instruction that I used with Christina and Edward as a template for working with struggling writers in the midst of a busy classroom. My goal was to lend my hand to their pencils as a way to help them execute what their eyes perceived and their minds imagined.

CHRISTINA

When Christina started first grade, she drew a picture of Six Flags Magic Mountain (two mountains; one with five flags, and the other with one flag) for her first writing sample. Underneath her picture she wrote: "6 Fa." That was Christina's attempt at copying "6 Flags Magic Mountain" from the chart of possible writing topics we had brainstormed for our first writing sample.

In April, Christina wrote the following piece for her writing sample:

I like wan weY are PaTing, are DiNoSAURs, Foring clae But Wan We. arE PaTing are, DiNOSAURS I was TheKing. of we Kan. go TO ThE PoK For are Fe. . .

(I like when we are painting our dinosaurs firing clay, but when we are painting our dinosaurs, I was thinking if we can go to the park for our field trip.)

240

Most beginning writers have to work through their share of difficulties when they are learning how to compose their thoughts, so I wasn't overly concerned about Christina's writing development at this point in time. When I observed Christina writing and studied her writing attempts, I noticed these difficulties, which are common in first grade:

- trouble focusing while writing
- trouble forming letters neatly
- difficulty with pencil grip—her hands would sweat a lot when she wrote
- difficulty with stretching out words and using temporary spelling
- mixing capital and lowercase letters in words
- incomplete sentence structure

But I became concerned about Christina's writing development during the second half of our first-grade year because she wasn't "taking off" as a writer. Whereas most of the other children were settling into their writing work and developing a beginning level of proficiency with composing, spelling, and punctuation, Christina seemed mired in the same difficulties. Weekly, I helped her compose her journal letters, notebook entries, and special writing projects, while my classroom aide worked with her on letter formation, thinking these kinds of instruction would make the difference. However, for Christina's year-end writing sample, she wrote a simple, patterned piece:

> I love my Dog
> I love my Fash (*fish*)
> I like my Dog
> I like my Fash (*fish*)
> I love my sar (*sister*)
> I like my mom
> I like my Dad
> I like my FrEs (*friends*)
> I like my Hos (*house*)

It was a predictable piece of writing for Christina. She often wrote about her family members, her dog, Bear, and her love for everyone in her family. She was especially close to her father because he was at home due to a disability, so he was responsible for most of his two daughters' care. Christina's mother worked full time at Wal-Mart. I knew Christina loved composing pieces about her family, but I wanted her to expand her writing horizons.

Handwriting Difficulties

My work with Christina continued in second grade wherein she started the year by writing this entry in her notebook:

9-11-95 I Do Not like my head wrating (*I do not like my handwriting.*)

It was clear that Christina needed to work on her handwriting problem because it was making the composing process labored and frustrating to her. With the extra assistance of JoAnn, our second-grade Basic Skills teacher. who worked in our classroom for approximately ninety minutes a day, four days a week, I set about giving intensive handwriting help to Christina. Using a composition book for a handwriting journal, JoAnn worked individually with Christina approximately three days a week, ten to fifteen minutes per session. Christina practiced these things in her journal when she met with JoAnn:

- first and last name
- upper- and lowercase letters of the alphabet
- one or two letters that were giving her difficulty (intensive practice)
- writing a sentence of her choice

JoAnn concentrated on the following items with Christina as part of her handwriting instruction:

- positioning of the paper
- gripping pencil properly
- sitting up properly to write
- using conventional and temporary spellings of words when Christina was writing her sentence so that she would be comfortable with both types of spelling when composing on her own

Composing: Interactive Writing

In addition to intensive handwriting instruction, I worked closely with Christina when she was composing. I would sit beside Christina and first ask her to tell me what she wanted to write. Once she was able to compose her thoughts orally, we would tackle them in writing. For example, at the beginning of our second-grade year, I helped Christina compose the following journal letter to me (edited draft):

9-19-95

Dear Janine,

I like the school. It's the best school in [the] world. I don't want to go to a new school.

Love, Christina

In terms of instructional help, I focused on both composing the message and spelling the words:

- *Dear Janine*: I reminded Christina where to look in her journal to find the standard spelling of these two words; I asked her what type of punctuation was needed after the greeting of a letter.

- *I like the*: Christina knew the standard spelling for these words.
- *school*: I helped Christina with the conventional spelling by stretching it out and having a discussion with her that went something like this:

J: What sound do you hear at the beginning?
C: /s-s-s-s/.
J: What letter stands for that sound?
C: /s/.
J: Good. Do you need an upper- or lowercase /s/?
C: Small /s/.
J: Why?
C: Because it's in the middle of the sentence.
J: Stretch out the word with me again. What do you hear next?
C: /k-k-k-k/.
J: What letter stands for that sound?
C: /k/.

FIGURE 13–1   *Christina's journal letter*

J: Yes, but it isn't that letter in this word. What other letter stands for that sound?

C: /c/.

J: Good. (If she hadn't known, I would have said to her, "/c/ is another letter that stands for that sound.")

J: Do you need an uppercase or lowercase /c/?

C: Small /c/.

J: Why?

C: Because it's in the middle of the word.

J: The next letter is tricky because it's a silent letter. You don't hear it in the word. It's an /h/. Now for the middle of the word. Stretch it out with me again. What makes that /oo/ sound?

C: /u/?

J: Good choice. It's a different vowel. I'll help you. It's two /o/'s. Other words that have that pattern are *noodle, poodle,* and *pool.* They all have that /oo/ pattern in the middle. What do you hear at the end? Stretch it out so you can hear it.

C: /l-l-l/.

J: What letter?

C: /l/.

J: Great. You've spelled it in conventional spelling. It's a tricky word but one that you should learn how to spell this year so you can write it quickly.

After this spelling minilesson, Christina and I went back to the work of composing, first rereading what she had written (*Dear Janine, I like the school.*), then continuing with her message. Rereading while composing is something I do repeatedly when I help all young writers because they often forget to do this and end up with a piece that doesn't make sense. Before we continued with the writing, I asked Christina to repeat the next part of her message to remind herself what she was working on. Our composing continued in this way:

- *It's:* I helped her with the contraction, reminding her that *it's* stands for *it is.*
- *the:* Christina knew in standard spelling.
- *best:* Christina was able to stretch it out and spell it conventionally; I told her it was a word that's "spelled like it sounds."
- *school:* Christina scrounged for print in her letter because she had just written this word.
- *in the:* Christina knew both words in standard spelling.
- *world:* I helped her with the standard spelling in the same way I helped her spell *school.*
- *I:* Christina knew in standard spelling.
- *don't:* I helped her with the contraction although we missed inserting the apostrophe.
- *want:* I helped her with the /nt/; beginning writers have difficulty hearing /nt/, /nd/, and /ng/ endings.
- *to go to a:* Christina knew in standard spelling.
- *new:* I helped her with the standard spelling.

- *school*: Christina copied it from where she'd written it previously; I asked her what end mark she wanted to use to signify to me—her reader—that it was the end of the sentence.
- *Love, Christina*: I reminded her that the closing needed a capital letter; I asked her what type of punctuation was needed between *Love* and her name.

This type of guided, interactive writing is similar to the "writing a story" procedure developed by Marie Clay as part of her Reading Recovery program (1993b, 28–31). I find it an extremely helpful strategy with children like Christina who need close instruction in:

- deciding on an idea for writing
- forming the letters and words to write the idea
- spelling high-frequency words
- developing an awareness of spelling patterns in more difficult words
- recalling the idea while writing
- rereading to check for meaning

It may seem like it would take a great deal of time to do this type of interactive writing with a child, but I can usually manage a letter the length of Christina's in five to seven minutes. I am brisk, but caring with my instruction. Especially with those children who have trouble focusing while writing, I model how to take care of the business of writing in a timely manner.

I also consider this "composing time" spent with writers like Christina an investment for future writing sessions. I don't have the luxury of time to help all of my struggling writers every day. When I do sit beside them, my goal is to promote problem solving and resourcefulness by questioning and suggesting ways to solve problems so that again, "my talk" when I am working with them hopefully becomes "their talk" when they are working on their own. As a last resort, I give spellings or take more control of the composing than I would like to if I sense frustration on their part or if I need to move them along more quickly because time is running out.

There are other factors I consider when I engage in explicit instruction of this nature. Several thoughts flash through my mind when I kneel or sit down beside a struggling writer, including

- How much time do I have?
- Who else needs time today?
- How long is the text/message that the child wants to compose?
- If it is a longer message, do I need to help them compose the first part and let them finish as best they can while I leave to work with another child, then ask them to check in with me when they're finished?
- What do I know about this particular child as a writer, and how much conventional versus temporary spelling should I pursue? Within reason, I require my writers to spell all high-frequency words conventionally.

With Christina, this form of guided, interactive writing proved to be helpful. By the middle of our second-grade year, Christina was showing better progress as a writer. She wrote this letter to me in April in her journal:

Dear Janine

I like the Venus Fey Trap a lot Now that the venus Fey Trap has a dinner it might ned a glass of water

Love Christina

I wrote back:

4-17-96

Dear Christina,

I really smiled at your letter. I think you have just the right idea, my dear. One would think it might need some water. I actually need to remember to water it a lot because it likes soggy soil. I will show you how much water and you can water it. Would you like the job?!

Love, Ms. Janine

Christina hadn't included a stitch of punctuation in her writing, but I thought her idea and "languaging" were wonderful. It was a departure from her patterned writing of "I like my mom . . . I like my dad . . . ," which was the hallmark of her previous efforts.

The same week that Christina wrote to me about the Venus's flytrap, she decided to write to her mom about the little hummingbird outside our door in her family journal. Her letter follows:

4-18-96

Dear MoM,

I like The little. Humming-bird Egg in The, tree.

Love, Christina

PS DonT, Forgot to WRite Back.

Her mom responded with this letter:

Dear Christina,

I didn't know you had a Hummingbird egg in the tree at school, I Love hummingbirds thats why I have the feeder up at home.

Love Mom

I helped Christina compose her letter that day, and it was a classic example of her writing struggles. To start off, the lines she had drawn on her paper to help her organize her writing were done haphazardly. She hurried the writing, then when I asked her to correct some of the letter formation, she erased several times until the paper was smudged and difficult to read. Overall, her focus was scattered that day and it showed in her writing efforts (see Figure 13–2).

What I did appreciate about both Christina's Venus's flytrap letter to me and her hummingbird letter to her mom was that she seemed to take more risks with her language and word choice, and both pieces were a departure from the same "patterned feel" that her previous work exhibited. However,

FIGURE 13–2   *Christina's family journal letter*

Christina returned to what was familiar to her when she composed her second-grade midyear writing sample. She wrote:

> I love my mom a lot I. wish that she was here right now I love hri a lot The End
>> (*I love my mom a lot. I wish that she was here right now. I love her a lot. The End*)

When I calculated her spelling accuracy rate it was 95.2 percent, but again, I didn't see much risk taking in the kinds of words that she used, or in the topic or word choice. In terms of punctuation, she had only included one punctuation mark, a period, which was not in the proper place. However, her handwriting was neat and legible, and her writing was well-organized on the page. I considered that progress for Christina.

I received another glimpse of Christina as a writer when she completed a "Myself As a Writer" survey for our parent-teacher-student school conferences. (See Chapter 15 for information on this survey.) I had to help Christina complete her survey because after watching her initial attempts to record her thoughts, I could see she was having difficulty. Her responses to the statements on the survey follow:

1. My favorite kind of writing: poetry
2. What I love about writing: I like writing
3. What I find challenging about writing: (Christina didn't answer this question and couldn't think of anything when I asked her if she wanted me to write for her.)
4. When I am having a problem writing a word this is what I do: I ask a friend for help.
5. Someday I would like to write about: Animals I would like to write because they are nice. You can feed them.
6. This is how I feel about myself as a writer: I feel grat I am hape of me I am doing a grat job (*I feel great. I am happy for me. I am doing a great job.*)

I was surprised with her responses to statements 3 and 6. It appeared that Christina didn't perceive herself as a struggling writer because, in her own words, "I feel great. I am doing a great job." I was ready for her to list "a million challenges" when it came to writing—"hard to think of ideas, hard to spell, hard to write neatly, or hard to organize the writing on the page" came to my mind—but she didn't.

After two years of being immersed in a writing classroom, Christina progressed to a certain point but was never able to compose with ease. She had received consistent instruction, but writing was still difficult for her. Clearly she had progressed from her first picture-only writing sample to being able to write her thoughts by herself, but her writing hadn't reached what I consider second-grade proficiency. Christina seemed unconvinced that writing was worth all of the hard work and never gave it the attention that she gave to her reading.

Edward, who had been in a bilingual kindergarten and first-grade classroom, was then moved to my English-only classroom by his parents at the start of his second-grade year. He had his own interesting set of struggles as a writer, which are often typical of ESL children. He could already read and write in Spanish, so he was able to transfer some of his Spanish knowledge to writing in English. Whereas Edward made quick progress reading in English—I never considered him a struggling reader—writing posed more challenges for him. Essentially, as I studied his English writing development and listened to his oral language development, I found they mirrored each other. Edward's first writing sample follows:

> myn bird jaf I boby bird and da bird Poc my and dI nos and a mom
> and dad Poc my di nos and dad bird poc my anda mIrnin. my dad
> cah o bird jay was a lyto bird and ma brador lov jam.
> (*My bird have a baby bird and the bird punch me in the nose and a
> mom and dad punch me in nose and dad bird punch me in the morning.
> My dad catch a bird he was a little bird and my brother love him.*)

In order to understand Edward's writing knowledge, a person has to know something about the Spanish language. I don't speak Spanish, but by observing my Spanish ESL children and studying their writing samples with wonderful bilingual teachers at Bobier like Rose-Yvonne and Leo Urias, I was able to learn how to "read" their beginning writing efforts, and thus learn how to help them.

For example, in Edward's piece, he consistently used /j/ for /h/ because /j/ is the letter that makes the /h/ sound in Spanish. This was the number one alphabetic confusion for him to work out. Other typical ESL confusions that I noted in his piece, then worked on with him in future written work included:

- representing the /ch/ digraph with a /c/
- using /y/ for the /e/ sound in *me* and *he*
- using /d/ for the /th/ sound in *brother*
- general confusion with vowel sounds: using /a/ for *me*, *him*, *he*, which he spelled j-a-y; using /ir/ for the middle of *morning*; using /o/ for the word /a/
- being unaware of the /-ing/ ending: using /-in/ for the ending of *morning*
- hearing *in the* as one word: *anda*

Every week, either JoAnn or I helped ESL students like Edward with their writing, using the same interactive writing strategy that I used with Christina. When we started our letter journals in our classroom, I helped Edward compose his first letter to me. I started by asking Edward what he wanted to write to me, and he responded with the following:

"Dear Janine,

We can play with the Legos because I love the Legos.

Love, Edward"

Edward's sentence contained all high-frequency words except the word *Legos*. I wanted him to learn the standard spelling of high-frequency words, so I helped him with these words in different ways that included:

- *we, can, I*—"spelled like it sounds" words: I helped Edward stretch out the sounds in the words so he could spell them.
- *play*: I stretched out the word in two segments—/pl/ and /ay/, commenting on the /pl/ partner letters and the /ay/ pattern.
- *with*: This is an interesting word for all beginning writers, not just ESL writers. I often work through *with* in this way:
  - /w/ sound: This is tricky because when primary children voice the sound of /w/, they think it's represented by a /y/. (Say the /w/ sound then the letter /y/ to yourself and you will see your mouth forms a /y/ for both.) I reminded Edward that the letter /w/ made the sound we were hearing.

FIGURE 13–3 *Edward's journal letter*

- /i/ vowel: This was challenging for him, so we looked at our alpha-bet resource card on the table and discussed the two sounds of /i/— /i/ like in *igloo* and /i/ like in *ice cream*.
  - /th/ digraph: I always refer children to the words *the* and *Thursday* when we discuss this digraph and remind them that /th/ are two let-ters that "hold hands" to make that sound.
- *the*: Edward knew this word in standard spelling.
- *Legos*: This is not a high-frequency word; I wondered how Edward would solve his problem, and I reminded him he could either stretch it out or "scrounge for the print" in the room. He decided to find the word on the Legos bin in the classroom, copy it onto a "scrounge for print" paper, then write it in his journal.
- *because*: I reminded Edward that he could use the high-frequency word resource cards on the table to help himself and pointed out the word *because* under the /B/ section. He copied this word from the card and I commented on the "quiet e" at the end.
- *love*: Edward knew this word in standard spelling.

This kind of instructional spelling conversation, as well as a lot of rereading while composing, helped Edward as a writer not only with this first letter, but in much of his writing throughout the year.

Instructional Spelling Conversation

Sometimes I feel like I am a broken record when I help writers like Edward stretch out words again and again and again, helping them "keep their place" with the phoneme sequence—small units of sound in spoken words (Moustafa 1997)—as they listen and write what they hear. I call this work "instructional spelling conversation" when I sit beside my students and help them in this way.

I have noticed with many young writers, not just strugglers, that the process of stretching out a word slowly and hearing and writing the sounds in a left-to-right sequence is difficult for them. Recently, my observations were confirmed when I read the results of several research studies compiled by Margaret Moustafa in her book *Beyond Traditional Phonics* (1997). The studies she cites looked at children, their perception of phonemes, and their difficulty manipulating phonemes. The surprising results were that most kindergartners—83 percent of those tested—could not analyze spoken words into phonemes most of the time, and 30 percent of the children tested at the end of first grade could not do this either (1997, 12). Moustafa applied the research results to children's process of learning letter-sound correspon-dence as it relates to learning how to read, but clearly the results can also be applied to understanding children's writing development. In watching my young writers, particularly struggling writers, I found that the process of stretching out words, listening for phonemes, and writing "what they hear" in left-to-right sequence was an extremely difficult task, and one that required a lot of instructional attention.

I have discovered that sitting beside my young writers and stretching out the words with them as they compose does seem to help. They often hear the sounds better and are more successful translating these sounds into letters and words. However, I also know that it is more difficult for children to learn how to stretch out the words themselves and listen for the sequence of sounds so they can either write the word conventionally or write a good approximation of the spelling. The only way I know how to help them is to model the process that I would like them to begin doing for themselves. As when I was helping Edward with the word *with,* or Christina with the word *school,* I give "clues" as children work on the spellings of words, and I resist telling them the letter(s) unless it becomes necessary. I keep one of our picture alphabet resource cards right in front of them as we work, so we can refer to it for letter-formation and letter-sound help. Below is a list of "clues" I often give to the children as I help them analyze the phonemes they hear then translate them into letters and words on their papers:

- "This word has a quiet letter on the end."
- "Another letter besides /k/ makes the /k/ sound. Do you know what it is?"
- "Another letter besides /s/ makes the /s/ sound. Do you know what it is?"
- "Another vowel makes that sound. Do you know what other vowel it could be?"
- "That vowel wouldn't make that sound. Do you know what other vowel it could be?"
- "Yes, it is that vowel/consonant. What other vowel/consonant could it have been? How did you know it was this one?"
- "It's that /-er/ ending. What two letters make that ending?" (er)
- "It's that /e/ ending that's not an /e/. Do you remember what other letter often makes that /e/ ending? It's like the end of Timmy (child's name in the classroom that ends with a /y/)."
- "Three letters make that /-ing/ ending. Do you know what they are?" (ing)
- "Three letters make the /-ink/ sound. Do you know what they are?" (ink)
- "Three letters make the /-est/ ending. Do you know what they are?" (est)
- For digraphs: "Those two letters hold hands and make one sound. Do you remember those two letters?"
- For blends: "Those are partner letters and you say them together. Do you hear the two letters you are blending together?"

Essentially, I try to do this spelling process in a questioning/discovering way rather than supply the information. I find that all young writers, not just struggling writers, benefit from this type of instruction. If it's a difficult sequence of sounds to separate and hear, I give the correct information, saying something like this, "This is tricky to hear and these are the letters in this part of the word." Sometimes I accept their close approximations and say, "You are very close and it's a difficult part in the word to hear all of the letters. We're going to leave it in temporary spelling in your writing today."

As JoAnn and I continued our weekly interactive writing instruction with Edward in his writing notebook, family journal, and teacher-led or individual writing projects, we often explained confusions that resulted when he tried to transfer his knowledge of Spanish to his English writing. By the middle of the year, not only was there progress in Edward's English syntax, but his writing was much neater and better organized on the page, and his spelling accuracy had improved. His midyear writing sample, with a spelling accuracy rate of 80.3 percent follows:

Crocodiles

Crocodiles ar big and good They it people if you get food They ar good wit you and if you don't let get some food He et you up and you be cie and gor mama be not hape and gor dad be not be hape and I not got to be in the Zoo.

(*Crocodiles are big and good. They eat people if you get food. They are good with you and if you don't let [them] get some food he eat you up. And you be cry and your mama be not happy and your dad be not be happy and I not got to be in the Zoo.*)

Again, Edward's writing mirrored his oral language development, but he was showing consistent progress. Language confusions in this piece that needed instructional attention included

- *are*: There is a quiet /e/ on the end of *are*.
- *eat*: /ea/ is the vowel pattern at the beginning; not /i/.
- *with*: The /th/ ending digraph still has not ironed out from his first writing sample.
- *he'll*: He needed to use the contraction *he'll* instead of the word *he*.
- *cry*: He was unaware of the /cr/ blend at the beginning; *sad* would be a better word in this context.
- *your*: He represented the beginning /y/ sound with a /g/.
- *happy*: He used an /e/ at the end instead of /y/.
- *your mama be not happy*: He needed to understand the correct English form—*your mama won't be happy.*
- *I not got to be in the Zoo*: He needed to understand the correct English form—*I won't get to [go] to the Zoo.*

It wasn't a matter of sitting down beside Edward and pointing out all of the confusions in his writing and trying to remedy or correct them. Rather, I noted these syntax and spelling problems when I studied his writing, and I looked for opportunities to "fill in the gaps" in his knowledge when I worked with him. It took repeated demonstrations on my part and repeated practice on Edward's part as he worked on his writing pieces each day.

As with Christina, I was interested in how Edward perceived himself as a writer, and I studied his midyear "Myself As a Writer" survey closely. His responses are listed below:

1. My favorite kind of writing: Stories
2. What I love about writing: because is bere (very) good and helpe (help)
3. When I am having a problem with my writing this is what I do: I sc a frined or I sc Jenine (*I ask a friend or I ask Janine*)
4. When I am having a problem writing a word this is what I do: Sound out the words and ask Janine
5. Someday I would like to write about: Superman and birds and horses and Foggy
6. This is how I feel about myself as a writer: I fil (*feel*) good and awesome

Even with the difficulties of learning how to write in his second language, Edward was intact. It was good to see that he felt "awesome" about himself as a writer when I knew that it was hard work for him.

Throughout the second half of our school year, Edward continued to immerse himself in his writing. JoAnn and I continued to meet with him to clarify syntax and alphabetic confusions that were a normal part of the process in learning how to speak, read, and write in his second language. Toward the end of the year, Edward composed two wonderful pieces of poetry that I believed were a celebration of his growth as an ESL writer. The first poem was written for his mom for Mother's Day, and the second poem was written for our class poetry book. Both of Edward's rough-draft poems, which he wrote independently, follow:

> Mom.
> I love you more
> Then the Erthe.　　　(*than the Earth*)
> and The moon.
> And the sun.
> You love flowers mom.
> Yes, yes, I love you.

> My swing gose　　　(*My swing goes*)
> up and Down
> around to the ground
> Then gose to the sky　(*Then goes to the sky*)
> my swing my swing
> is my favorite game
> my swing.

Another piece that shows Edward's writing development is a letter that he wrote to his dad toward the end of the year:

June 16, 1996

Dear Dad,

I love you but im sad becasue my mom is gowin to Mexico.

Love, Edward

The last two pieces that Edward wrote unassisted in our classroom were his year-end writing sample and his letter of introduction to his third-grade teachers. Edward's lingering syntax confusions are more apparent in his writing sample than his letter, but both pieces show his progress as an ESL writer:

Wen I went fish I got a big fish and my Dad sad you got a big fish Edward I only got a littel fish Then he sad the one ho ges a big fish and you go home Then i got 19 littel fish and my Dad said you only got littel fish wat are you gana do . . . wel I got a big fish now so I got home and my dad was ciaig so I sad Look this fish ar for you . . . I love you Edward so wigo fish so he said Littel Edward you ar nice

(When I went fishing, I got a big fish. And my Dad said, "You got a big fish, Edward. I only got a little fish." Then he said, "The one who gets a big fish and you go home." Then I got nineteen little fish and my Dad said, "You only got little fish. What are you going to do?" Well I got a big fish now so I got home and my Dad was crying so I said, "Look, these fish are for you." "I love you, Edward, so we go fish." So he said, "Little Edward, you are nice.")

7/30/96

Dear Mrs. Lopez, and Mrs. Gillogly hi my neme is Edward I wana now if Mrs. Lopez is my techer or Mrs. Gillogly if the two of you ar my techer ol be happy bat Mrs. Janine is move in to Washington I wish you are good lake Janine.

Love Edward,

(Dear Mrs. Lopez and Mrs. Gillogly,

Hi. My name is Edward. I want to know if Mrs. Lopez is my teacher or Mrs. Gillogly. If the two of you are my teachers I'll be happy. But Mrs. Janine is moving to Washington. I wish you are good like Janine.)

There is a footnote to Edward's writing development however, because Edward did write to me after my husband and I moved to Washington. Even six months later, everything in his writing had improved: handwriting, spelling, syntax, punctuation, and organization of the writing. His letter follows (see Figure 13–4):

Dear Janine

I Love my house me and my brother share are room. Linda she Has a room for Her on I Love to now what Do you got for Chrismas.

Love Edward.

(I love my house. Me and my brother share our room. Linda, she has a room for her own. I love to know what do you got for Christmas.)

ESL children who, like Edward, struggle initially as writers, can make good progress if given time, explicit instruction, and daily writing opportunities. I teach closely when I know it's necessary, in hopes that I can eventually remove myself from the middle of their composing process—although I often find myself teaching closely all year. One year is a small part of a second-language acquisition process that can take five to seven years, and I try to keep it in perspective as I help ESL children attain some level of confidence as writers.

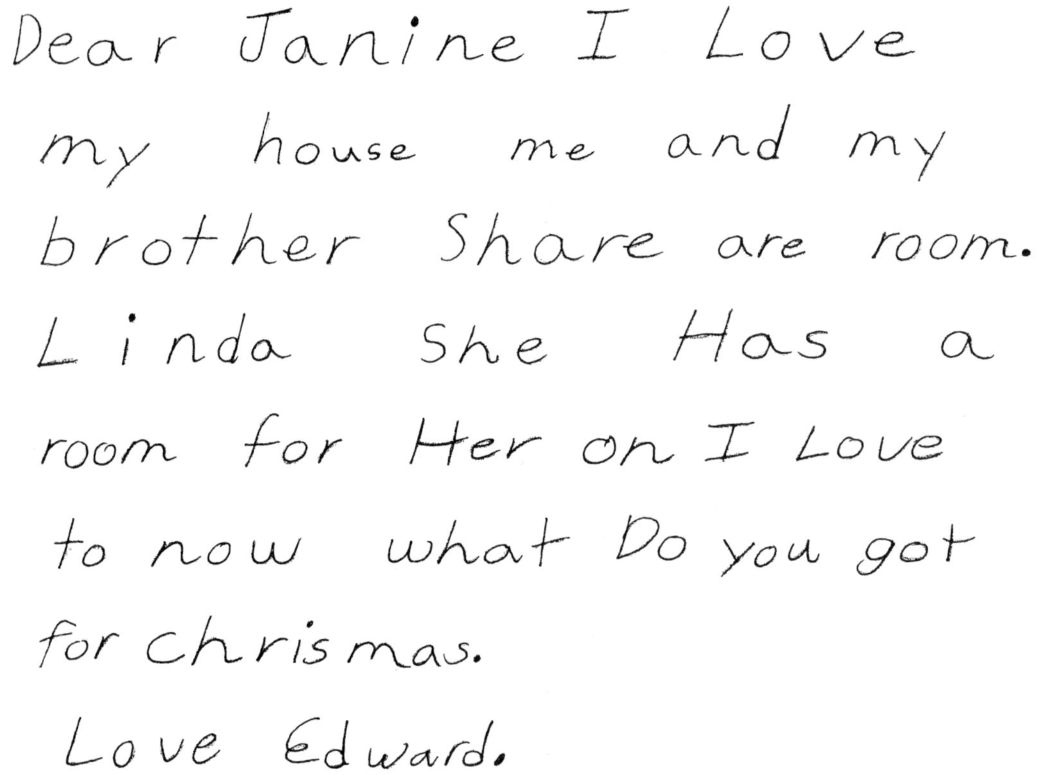
Dear Janine I Love my house me and my brother Share are room. Linda She Has a room for Her on I Love to now what Do you got for chrismas.
Love Edward.

FIGURE 13–4 *Edward's letter*

Young children who struggle to become writers show their frustrations on the page in front of them in different ways. Pages that are blank or pages that have smears, smudges, syntax, or spelling confusions all represent writers in need of a mentor. The only way I know how to work with struggling young writers like Christina and Edward is to give them more time and closer instruction in the form of guided, interactive writing assistance. During this time of close instruction I focus on these strategies:

Composing Strategies

- selecting topic and genre: figuring out what's important to them or what they know a lot about
- saying what they want to write out loud so they can hear their thoughts before writing them
- recalling the idea while writing
- rereading to check for meaning
- reading to another person to check for clarity and meaning
- placing punctuation: reading their writing out loud to determine where punctuation marks should go

Handwriting Strategies

- positioning the paper correctly
- using a comfortable pencil grip
- sitting in a comfortable position that lends itself to legible writing; for these children it generally means sitting properly at a table
- knowing when to use capital letters and small letters
- reminding themselves to check letters they reverse: e.g., /b/ and /d/
- keeping capital and small letters a uniform size

Spelling Strategies

- stretching out words to hear left-to-right sequence of sounds for temporary spelling
- giving spelling "clues" while helping children stretch out words
- learning high-frequency words so they are at the "tips of their pencils" when they are writing
- knowing how to use print resources in the room to find the conventional spelling of words
- developing an awareness of spelling patterns, particularly onset and rime, to help them tackle unfamiliar words and more difficult words

My teaching part in this journey does feel significant because for most children, primary classrooms are the seeds and beginning blossoms of literate lives. I have an inner sense of urgency to succeed with children who struggle. I don't think of them as "only" five-, six-, and seven-year-olds;

rather, I feel the weight of their twenty-five-, thirty-six-, and forty-seven-year-old lives hanging in the balance.

At the end of one especially long, tiring school day, I remember saying to my principal that the complexities of teaching are humbling, and I don't always feel I have done justice to the work that's needed. I particularly feel this with children who struggle as writers and readers and can't quite seem to get their hands to execute what their eyes perceive and their minds imagine. It's difficult, but necessary work, to help these children make sense of something that doesn't.

14 | SPELLING

*My spelling is wobbly. It's good spelling but it wobbles
and the letters get in the wrong places.*

—A. A. Milne, Winnie-the-Pooh

Toward the middle of my last year at Bobier with my second graders, I wrote
this entry in my journal after helping the children set up their spelling folders for the week:

> The kids are really starting to play with words and patterns and
> notice words within words. Kaley is checking on the spelling of her
> cat's name and has written it on a piece of paper to take home
> tonight. Joseph spontaneously brought over the dictionary for me
> to check a spelling. Classroom is quiet and working today. Very
> nice. Elizabeth did a Spelling Demons chart for next week. Fin-
> ished in good time.

We live in a society where spelling does matter. I know that the more I
care about a piece of correspondence or other writing, the more I pay attention to my spelling. In my primary classroom, I do teach spelling. I actually
treat spelling as a "field of study" and expect my students to use spelling as a
tool to help themselves as writers, knowing full well that having a strong,
high-frequency writing vocabulary will also assist them as beginning readers.

I am always searching out information and perspectives on the role of
spelling in young children's early literacy development, and I have found
that the research of Sandra Wilde and Richard Gentry and Jean Wallace
Gillet have been the most helpful in terms of thinking through and setting up
my spelling program. In a *Primary Voices* article titled "What Is Our Responsibility in Helping Children Learn to Spell?" Sandra Wilde writes, "Spelling
curriculum and instruction need to reflect the knowledge base of the
teacher, the developmental levels and needs of the students, and the desires
of the community" (1996, 2).

She continues,

> It might be useful to consider the variety of ideas in the educational commu-
> nity about helping children learn to spell. I had considered using a term like
> spectrum or continuum, but realized that the picture is more complex; we
> no longer see spelling curriculum as limited to formal programs focusing on

word lists, but rather a menu of possible activities and processes, with varied points of view on the value of each of them. Four areas stand out: invented spelling, spelling in the writing process, word lists, and spelling patterns. (1996, 4)

As I read through Wilde's brief description of these four areas, I analyzed my own spelling program and decided that my beliefs and practices reflect these aspects of her continuum:

Wilde's Area and Continuum	My Spelling Practice
• Invented Spelling: encourage as needed, or encourage but move to standard spelling as soon as feasible	• Invented Spelling: encourage but move to standard spelling as soon as feasible
• Spelling in the Writing Process: work with students as needed, or work from a scope-and-sequence plan	• Spelling in the Writing Process: work with students as needed
• Memorizing Words from Lists: words fitting spelling patterns, high-frequency words, curriculum-related words, self-selected words, or not at all	• Memorizing Words from Lists: words fitting spelling patterns, high-frequency words, curriculum-related words, self-selected words
• Spelling Patterns: work with students as needed, or work from a planned series of patterns	• Spelling Patterns: work with students as needed
• Time: regular time on spelling with emphasis on teaching as much as possible, or less frequent time with more left to incidental learning.	• Time: a balance of both ends of the continuum: regular time on spelling with emphasis on teaching as much as possible, along with a great deal of incidental learning as teaching opportunities continually present themselves in our reading and writing discussions

I don't believe there are "either/or"s in my spelling program, but rather I think it reflects a combination of many principles. My approach to spelling is one of immersion in both formal and informal work. The intent of this chapter is to discuss my formal, individualized spelling program, which includes memorizing words from lists, studying spelling patterns, and spending regular time on spelling.

My individualized spelling program focuses on helping young children develop a writing vocabulary of high-frequency words so that these words are at the tips of their pencils when they are composing. I use Gentry and Gillet's developmental spelling assessment to help me determine when first-grade children are ready for an individualized spelling program. I start children on formal programs when they have reached the phonetic or transitional phase of spelling development, so first-grade children start their individualized spelling work at different times of the year.

I also use Gentry and Gillet's list of the "Five Hundred Words Most Frequently Used by Children in Their Writing" for my first and second graders' core list of "school words" that they work on in their spelling folders each week. Gentry and Gillet discuss both the developmental spelling assessment and the high-frequency word lists in their book, *Teaching Kids to Spell* (1993).

SPELLING FOLDER PREPARATION AND ORGANIZATION

I purchase heavy, tagboard file folders with metal clips at the top to organize the children's spelling work. This type of folder requires a double-hole punch and is similar to the folder I use for the children's literacy portfolios. I want the children to be able to work individually with their spelling words, so I need an efficient system that lends itself to this process.

On the left side of the spelling folder is a sheet that lists the first one hundred of Gentry and Gillet's five hundred high-frequency writing words (Gentry and Gillet 1993). First-grade children usually start at the beginning of this list, although they often know how to spell the first five words—*a*, *the*, *and*, *I*, *to*—when they start their individualized spelling work.

Second-grade children work from this list also. At the beginning of their second-grade year, I assess them on their spellings of these first one hundred words. We circle the words that the children know how to spell conventionally. The children start with those words remaining on the list. When the children finish the first list of one hundred words, we add the second one hundred high-frequency words to their folders. In my last group, Tracy, a capable speller, was able to work through three hundred of the five hundred words on this list by the end of second grade.

Organized on the right side of the spelling folder is a form for the children to write their weekly spelling words and a sheet to mark each of the weekly spelling check scores. The children write the next five words from their high-frequency word list on the left side of the form, and the other five words are their personal choice. The children choose at least two of their self-selected words from their writing notebooks; the remaining personal choice words can be from our classroom, from home, or "from inside their heads." Figure 14–1 shows the inside of one child's spelling folder.

FORMAT OF OUR WEEKLY SPELLING WORK

The children's weekly spelling work is a four-part process:

- word-study lesson
- spelling folders setup

- weekly practice
- Friday spelling checks

The first two parts of the process, conducting word-study lessons and setting up spelling folders take place on Monday. The third part, practicing spelling words, occurs—or is supposed to occur—Monday through Thursday evenings as part of their homework; and the fourth part, performing spelling checks, takes place on Friday.

Step 1: Conducting Word-Study Lessons

Word-study lessons evolved from my study of the children's spelling errors on their weekly spelling checks. The intent of this formal word-study lesson and informal lessons when the children set up their spelling folders is to help the children actively construct knowledge about our spelling system. By studying the children's misspellings and comparing them to the conventional spellings, I thought that with some discussion, we could clear up some of the letter patterns that were causing difficulty. It also seemed likely that if one child was struggling with a particular letter combination in a word it was a good possibility that others were or would be in the future.

For example, when I studied Priscilla's spelling of *want*, I found she was overgeneralizing the /wh/ pattern that occurs at the beginning of question

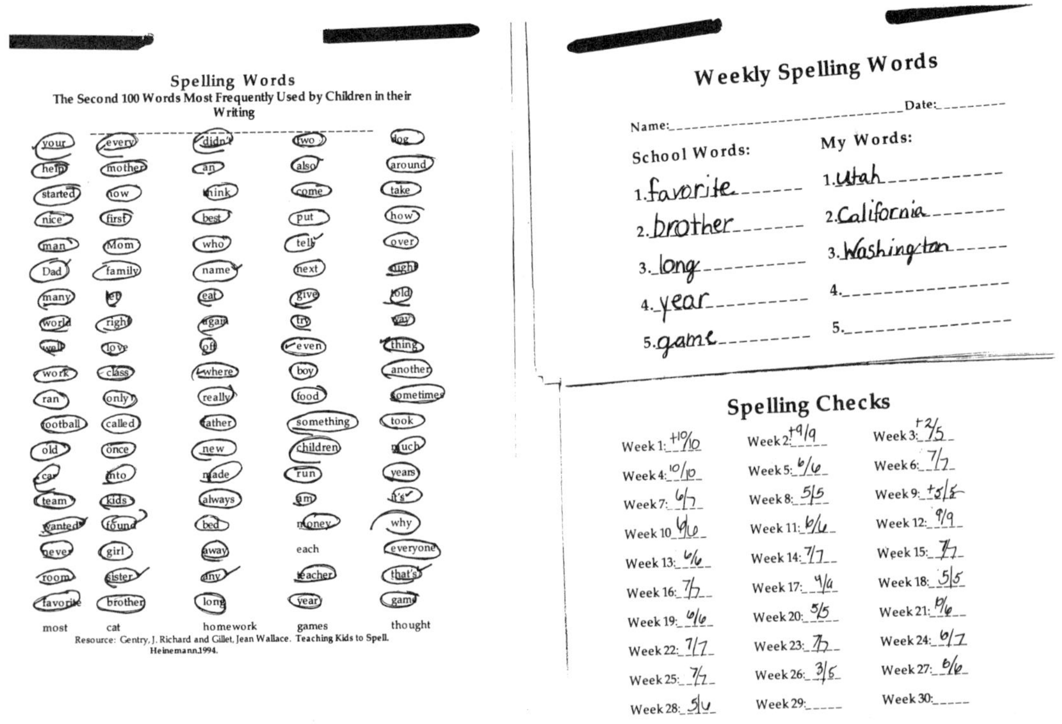

FIGURE 14–1   *Roni's spelling folder*

words. Kaley's spelling of *hose* for *house* was a perfect opportunity to compare and contrast the /o/ and /ou/ letter patterns in words, using word family listings to clarify the patterns. The word *because* is always a demon for young children, as they often rely on the phonetic spelling /bekuz/ or /becuz/ instead. So, by capitalizing on the difficulties or confusions of a few, I hoped I would benefit all. These kinds of observations led me to teach a ten-minute whole-group word-study lesson before the children set up their spelling folders on Mondays. I organize the lesson in the following way:

Friday night after school, I copy the children's spelling errors from their spelling checks onto a large piece of chart paper, separating them into two groups. The first group, which I write in one color, includes those "demons" that are from the high-frequency word lists. The second group, written in another color, are those "demons" from the children's own personal word lists. I leave plenty of room on the chart paper for a word-work area for me to use when the children and I discuss the spelling patterns and challenges. I don't write any of the children's names next to the words missed; rather, I see it as an opportunity to study those words with everyone, regardless of who already knows how to spell them and who is still struggling with them.

On Monday morning, at the start of our forty-minute spelling session, I gather the children around the chart paper, then launch into my lesson, showing them the underlined parts of the words that seem to be causing the most confusions. As we discuss the difficulties and examine word patterns together, I write more examples on the chart paper to illustrate how that pattern occurs in other words. Some of the words listed are my examples, and others are offered by the children. A completed word-study chart from one of my lessons with my group of second-grade spellers appears below.

Spelling Demons/Word Study
10-23-95

w<u>ha</u>t	<u>a</u>re	bec<u>au</u>se	w<u>an</u>t
	<u>a</u>rmy		
	<u>a</u>rk		
w<u>here</u>	<u>b</u>lue	c<u>ould</u>	h<u>ouse</u>
<u>there</u>	<u>b</u>lack	w<u>ould</u>	m<u>ouse</u>
	<u>b</u>lubber	sh<u>ould</u>	
	<u>b</u>locks		

/dr/: <u>dr</u>aw <u>dr</u>agon <u>dr</u>oop <u>dr</u>ain <u>dr</u>op <u>dr</u>ape <u>dr</u>ank <u>dr</u>ool <u>dr</u>ag <u>dr</u>um <u>dr</u>eam

This chart doesn't represent all of the discussion and brainstorming that occurred that morning; however, our conversation focused on the underlined portions of those words. The blend /dr/ was included on the chart because the word *draw* had cropped up as a difficult word in one of the children's writing notebook entries. My goal is to keep this lesson short, ten minutes at the most. After the lesson I leave the word-study chart in plain view when the children begin working on their own spelling folders so they can refer to this resource as needed.

With my last group, after I finished my word-study lesson, my second graders started presenting their own word minilessons. Their instruction often focused on "words within words." Some of the word/spelling strategies that children presented are listed below. The underlined portion of the word indicates where the children focused their instructional discussion with the class.

Joseph: <u>four</u>, <u>heating</u>
Priscilla: ho<u>me</u>, thi<u>nk</u>, ti<u>me</u>
Elizabeth: L<u>isa</u>, sp<u>elling</u>, <u>off</u>, <u>Mickey</u>, <u>mark</u>er, <u>mitten</u>, Har<u>old</u>
Edward: spelling strategy—When unsure of a word, he writes the word on scrap of paper first before writing it down on his "good paper." Word examples: wonder, people, died, for, put, "mani" for many, you, bank.
Rosanna:

- Sunday (Sun day)—compound word discussion; adding to compound word chart in the room
- Timmy/Lacey—rhyming element with different endings /-y/ and /-ey/
- vio<u>let</u>

Because I started to notice that my second graders were misspelling many of the same high-frequency words, I tallied over a four-month period how many times we reviewed these words during our word-study lessons. From a teacher-research standpoint, I was interested in knowing which words were "true demons" for my young spellers so that I could remind them to take an extra minute to spell them correctly when they wrote. The "top twenty" spelling demons that we posted in our classroom are listed below. The underlined portion(s) of the words indicate the consistent trouble spots for the children.

fri<u>e</u>nds	<u>k</u>now	v<u>e</u>ry	w<u>here</u>
bec<u>au</u>se	c<u>ou</u>ld	wha<u>t</u>	fr<u>o</u>m
th<u>ei</u>r/th<u>ere</u>	th<u>ey</u>	wh<u>o</u>	<u>other</u>
wa<u>nt</u>	h<u>e</u>lp	wh<u>en</u>	ab<u>out</u>
s<u>ome</u>	<u>a</u>lso	ag<u>ai</u>n	

During this same period of time, I also kept track of the children's misspelled personal words, to see what letter patterns and idiosyncrasies were posing difficulties for them. A sampling of some of these personal words appears below, and again, the underlined portion of each word indicates where instructional discussion occurred with the children. Note how much of the discussion focused on vowels:

p<u>e</u>nc<u>i</u>l	plan<u>e</u>t	t<u>e</u>nt	<u>eigh</u>t/ate
<u>p</u>teradact<u>y</u>l	bookm<u>a</u>rk	<u>e</u>qu<u>a</u>tions	tep<u>ee</u>
m<u>ea</u>nt/m<u>i</u>nt	Feb<u>r</u>uary	sp<u>e</u>lling	booksh<u>e</u>lf
spil<u>l</u>	w<u>oo</u>d	emp<u>t</u>y	c<u>a</u>rt
Ind<u>i</u>an	cup<u>b</u>oard	p<u>e</u>rfect	h<u>ea</u>rt
fr<u>owned</u>	w<u>aste</u>/w<u>ais</u>t	ma<u>chi</u>ne	m<u>a</u>rching

After studying children's trouble spots, I can often anticipate where their spelling difficulties will occur. Vowels and vowel patterns are often the culprits; however, I don't overteach them because it takes time for young children to construct "vowel knowledge" of our spelling system—time spent reading, writing, discussing, and learning these spelling nuances.

Being aware of these trouble spots helps me when I conduct my word-study lessons with the children. I focus on the "sound(s) they think they hear in the word," then show them the actual letter or letters that represent that sound. Knowledge of these spelling difficulties is also uppermost in my mind when I sit down to help the children when they write. I can generally predict the problem areas when they work through spellings, and so it is a matter of waiting to see what teaching opportunities might present themselves. I am always ready to engage in linguistic conversation.

Step Two: Setting Up Spelling Folders and Practice Sheets

After my word-study lesson, Monday's spelling session is mainly procedural, with the children setting up their spelling folders and practice sheets for the week. First, children write the five school words I expect them to practice and learn on the form on the right side of their folders. These five words come from the words that aren't yet circled on the list of one hundred words on the left side of their folders. Each child's five words are different depending upon their assessment at the end of their first-grade year or beginning of their second-grade year. When I set up spelling folders for the first time, I put a little check mark by each of their five words so they can find them easily. I want them to go in the order of the words, from the most frequent to the least frequent of the first one hundred, and not pick and choose all over the page.

They then write these same five words on the left-hand column of a white, trifolded "Look, Say, Cover, Write, Check" sheet that I prepare and copy for the children. Wide-ruled notebook paper works just as well. This sheet has enough space for four nights of practice—Monday through Thursday—with each word practiced twice every night. (See Figure 14–2).

After children write five school words in their folders and on their practice sheets, they choose up to five of their own spelling words. If they choose five, then they have a total of ten words to practice throughout the week. The number of words children choose for themselves depends upon each individual child. I often recommend the number of "choice words" based on what I know about each speller. For personal words, I talk with the children about choosing words from their writing notebooks, around the room, and books they are reading, or words inside their heads that they want to learn how to spell.

While the children write their spelling words, I bustle around the room helping them. Particularly with first graders, any additional help, whether from a family volunteer, older student, classroom aide, or assisting teacher, is appreciated. With my second-grade group, JoAnn, my assisting teacher, worked with the children during this time also, which helped immensely. If the children can find the word(s) in the room themselves, they are expected to locate and write the standard spellings. If they can't find the words, then I write the words for them, giving a word minilesson in the process.

For example, Cynthia chose these five personal spelling words one Monday when we were setting up our spelling folders: *Jupiter, spaceship, name, face, flower*. As Cynthia told me her words, I wrote them on one of the small scrap papers at our table. As I wrote the words for her, I showed her some of the interesting patterns in each word:

1. Jupiter: Capital J; the word it; the /-er/ ending
2. spaceship: compound word; /c/ has the /s/ sound; quiet /e/ at the end of space; /sh/ digraph at the beginning of ship
3. name: quiet /e/ at the end
4. face: /c/ has the /s/ sound like in space; quiet /e/ on the end like in name
5. flower: /fl/ pattern at the beginning; /ow/ pattern in the middle; /-er/ ending like in Jupiter

That same day, when I stopped to work with Kaley, two of her school words were came and back. I listed word families for came and back and underlined the rime portion of each word so she could see the patterns:

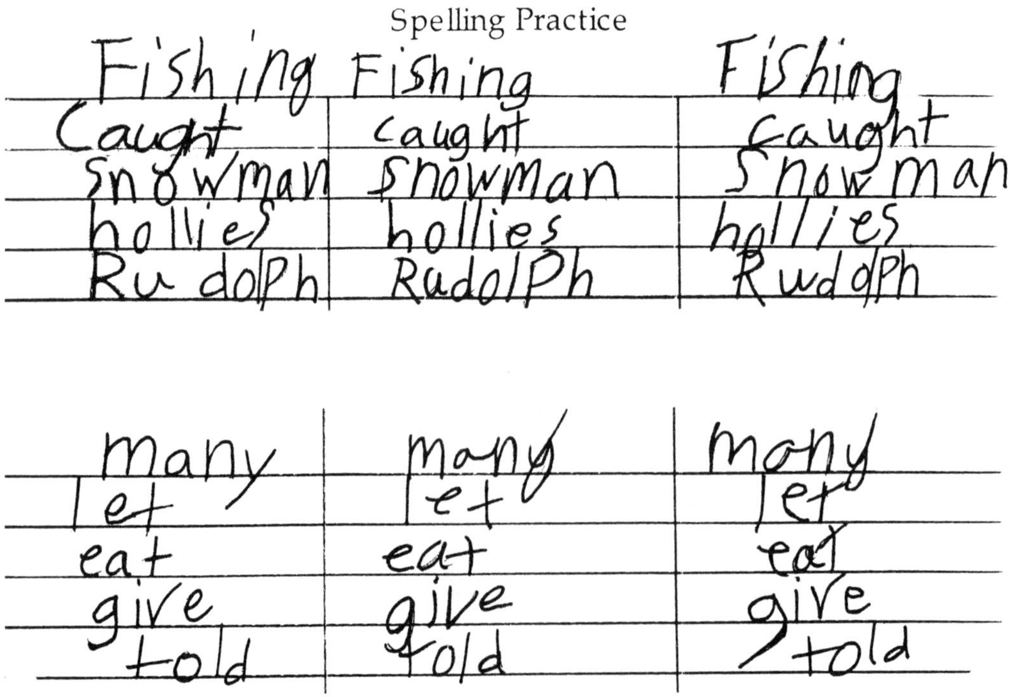
Spelling Practice

Fishing	Fishing	Fishing
Caught	caught	caught
Snowman	Snowman	Snowman
hollies	hollies	hollies
Rudolph	Rudolph	Rudolph

many	many	many
let	let	let
eat	eat	eat
give	give	give
told	told	told

FIGURE 14–2 *Eddie's spelling practice papers*

c<u>ame</u>	b<u>ack</u>
l<u>ame</u>	p<u>ack</u>
d<u>ame</u>	s<u>ack</u>
m<u>ame</u>	att<u>ack</u>

I list the words in columns like these so that children can see that the only change in the words is the onset, or the first letters. The only exception in this case is the word *attack* because the onset contains three letters instead of one. It was an interesting word to include for this reason.

It just takes a quick minute to study words and make comparisons while the children set up their spelling folders; yet, I believe it is important conversation to have with them. My goal is to help the children recognize the consistencies in our language so that words aren't so mysterious to them when they are writing and reading.

After the children write their personal words in their folders, they write them on a *green* trifolded practice paper. Different-colored practice papers help them—and me—keep things straight.

The last step in this setting-up process is to have spelling folders and practice papers checked by me or anyone else assisting in the classroom at this time. I find that children sometimes scramble the letters when they write the words on their practice papers. Since conventional spelling is the goal, I need to make sure they aren't practicing temporary spelling. With a quick look down each practice sheet, I check to see if the words are written correctly and neatly, then initial the outside of their practice papers so families know—and I know—that I checked them at school.

After the children finish their spelling setup, they place their spelling folders in our plastic spelling tub and tuck their practice sheets inside their school folders to take home. I always schedule spelling setup during the last thirty to forty minutes before lunch so that the children tend to business and complete their work. Those who finish early have these choices available to them in the classroom:

- quiet reading in the classroom library
- enjoying one of the book/tape sets
- reading bigbooks at the easel
- reading nightly reading book
- writing in your writing notebook

Setting up spelling folders on Monday mornings works well, as it takes the place of our partner-reading time. The children don't take books home over the weekend, so they don't have partner reading. Our Monday morning language arts routine follows:

housekeeping
class meeting
quiet reading
shared reading
morning recess

writing
spelling: word study lesson and folder setup
lunch

Step Three: Practicing Spelling Words

The children practice their spelling words Monday through Thursday nights as part of their homework. I teach the children the routine at school the first week we have spelling practice so that they understand how to do this at home. I show parents how the children are to practice at our Back-to-School Night so that they can assist with the process also. In addition to this, I send home an informational letter describing the spelling program, practice steps, and ways to encourage and help the children as spellers, so that families understand the program and my expectations. (See Appendix 14–1.) The children go through the following steps for their spelling practice each evening:

1. Look at the word.
2. Say it and spell it out loud.
3. Cover it with your hand.
4. Write it down in the next column.
5. Check it with the original word to see if it is correct.
6. Do this a second time in the last column on the practice sheet.

I first learned this Look, Say , Cover, Write, Check practice strategy with trifolded paper from Lynda Palmer, a wonderful junior primary teacher at Aberfoyle Hub School in Adelaide, South Australia. Pinnell and Fountas also outline this spelling practice strategy in their book *Word Matters: Teaching Phonics and Spelling in the Reading/Writing Classroom* (1998).

I monitor weekly practice closely. Those children who do not practice at home during the week practice at school instead. I create an extra set of practice papers and either have them practice by themselves before school or during morning-work time. If a classroom helper assists with practice, then it's done whenever a moment presents itself. In my last group, I averaged five to six children who practiced at school every week because they didn't practice at home.

Step Four: Performing Friday Spelling Checks

Friday morning is our routine spelling check day. With my last group, I was fortunate because Rachael's mom and JoAnn were able to do individual spelling checks. If I didn't have this help, I would have paired my second graders as spelling partners, as they were quite capable of giving each other their spelling checks with some assistance from me. With first-grade children, I would have requested help from older students at my school. With my second graders, I conducted Friday morning spelling checks in this way:

During housekeeping, the children turned their spelling practice sheets in to the homework tray so that Rachael's mom and JoAnn could staple their spelling checks to them once they were completed. Having both pieces together gave me the opportunity to check children's home spelling practice and compare it to how well they had done on their spelling checks.

After our morning recess, Rachael's mom and JoAnn began doing spelling checks during shared reading and writing workshop. They worked at one of our tables so that the children could go to them individually and complete their spelling checks. They followed this routine with each child:

1. They gave the child the words one at a time. Rachael's mom and JoAnn looked at the list of words (prepared on Monday) in their spelling folders.
2. They corrected spelling checks and conducted a short spelling minilesson with the child on words that had been missed. (See Figure 14–3.)
3. The child circled school words that they had spelled correctly on the list of high-frequency words on the left side of the folder. He or she did not circle misspelled words, as the student would need to practice them for another week.
4. Rachael's mom and JoAnn made small check marks next to the high-frequency words that the child would work on the next week. (Up to five, depending upon the number of high-frequency words spelled correctly that week.)
5. They wrote spelling check scores on the form on the right side of the folder and also on a class summary sheet for me so that at a glance, I could review the entire class' spelling check scores.
6. They then asked that child to quietly tell the next person it was time for his or her spelling check.

Getting through the entire class took both of them until lunchtime—about an hour and a half—because they spent considerable time with these children talking with them about their spelling, unusual word patterns, how they were doing, and how they could work just a little harder at times.

Later, after school, I looked through the children's spelling checks to see how they had done. For example, when I studied my second grader's first spelling checks, everyone had done well except for five children: Tanya, Adrienne, Crystal, Jana, and Leticia. Tanya, Crystal, and Leticia did not come as a surprise to me, but Adrienne and Jana did. Knowing the children's learning histories, I did the following:

1. I wrote notes home about Jana's and Adrienne's spelling checks, reminding them to study better during the week. We were still getting into the routine of school and this seemed like a blip for them.
2. On Monday during spelling time, I talked with Tanya, Crystal, and Leticia about decreasing the number of school words the next week to two or three words, and I asked them to choose only one word of their own to learn. I believed they were trying to learn too many words. I also planned extra spelling practice for them with JoAnn during the week.

My goal for *all* of the children is to increase their writing vocabularies. I believe strongly in this type of spelling program, but I have needed to rework it at times for some children so that they, too, will be successful.

SPELLING CHALLENGES

Another piece that I added to my spelling work with my second graders is something that we called "spelling challenges." I began doing this when I noticed the children seemed to be making a shift into more sophisticated word territory.

We started adding spelling challenges to our weekly word-study charts when we encountered some unusual words during our ocean exploration study. While we were reading *Ocean: The Living World* (Greenaway, Gunzi, and Taylor 1994) and *The Magic School Bus on the Ocean Floor* (Cole and Degen 1992), we were introduced to words like *omnivore, carnivore, herbivore, iridescent, agile, caudal fin, dreamily, burrow, anatomy, continental shelf, regenerate, submarine,* and *intertidal*. These words demanded that we stop to study their spellings because they rolled around in our mouths in such interesting ways and were such hearty words for second-grade minds. Thus, I decided to add words like these that popped out at us while we were reading,

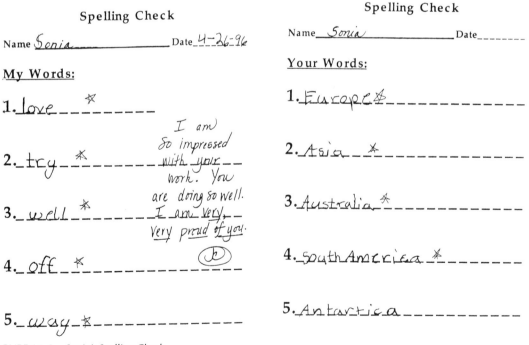

FIGURE 14–3   *Sonia's Spelling Check*

to our current word-study chart for the children to consider as "spelling challenges" when they set up their spelling folders each week.

Perhaps the one word that generated the most excitement among my second graders was the Hawaiian word for trigger fish: *humuhumunukunuku-apuaa*. We first encountered the word during shared reading while we were reading *The Magic School Bus on the Ocean Floor* during our ocean study. The children were so taken by the length of the word and the unusual pronunciation that we had to study it further. I showed the children how to segment the word into syllables to make the spelling of it more manageable: *Humu humu nuku nuku a pu aa*. After introducing the word that day, several children decided to tackle it as a spelling challenge. I remember how Nhi spent three weeks studying this word before she finally spelled it correctly on her spelling check. We were both thrilled!

Another piece that I added to second-grade spelling folders that year was a list of the state names by region. Several children started consulting our U.S. map for state names for their personal word lists, so I developed a resource for them to work from in their spelling folders. I prepared these three items, two-hole punched them and added them behind the children's high-frequency words lists:

- list of state names by region
- map of the U.S. with state names
- map of the world with continent names

Working on the state names was optional for my second graders and not everyone chose to do this. Those that did choose to do this added state/continent names to their personal spelling lists each week. On Friday, during spelling checks, we circled the state names that were spelled correctly on their state lists, and the children also highlighted them on their maps. This same routine applied to the continent names. I had the children keep both records of their progress, highlighting names on both the list and map, because it was one more way for them to learn the geography of the United States and the world.

TRANSFER TO DAILY WRITING

When it comes to children learning word lists, there are always lingering questions as to whether they will remember the conventional spellings and use them in their daily writing work. My general perception is that the degree of transfer from spelling checks to daily writing varied among children. It seems that some children are able to hold the spelling of a word "forever" after only a quick glance or practice session; others need the weekly practice to "cement" the conventional spelling; and a few others can practice diligently, do well on the weekly spelling checks, and then never transfer the conventional spellings to their daily writing work. These children don't seem to recall that they have ever studied conventional spellings of high-frequency words.

Toward the middle of our second-grade year at Bobier, I studied the children's conventional spelling in their writing samples and daily writing work and grouped my spellers into three categories: high, medium, and minimal transfer.

It was encouraging to see that the "high transfer" group was the largest, although percentage-wise it was 55 percent, or just over half, of my class. Ten children, or 32 percent of the class, had what I considered a medium level of transfer between their study and the use of high-frequency words in their writing, and four of the children, or 13 percent of the class, fell into the category of minimal transfer. Interestingly enough, three of the four children in this category also struggled as readers. David was a mystery to me because he was finally blossoming into a good reader, but his spelling was not improving. He wasn't developing spelling awareness, and it was affecting his writing tremendously. He could read it, but nobody else could, save for someone with a practiced eye at reading invented spelling.

Throughout the rest of our year together, I reminded David and the other children to be more resourceful spellers by consulting the high-frequency word cards in the baskets on their tables and checking their dictionaries, the room, and with a friend when they were writing. Also, I spent more time on spelling during family journal editing and during the spelling portion of their writing conferences. These were small, daily ways of giving their high-frequency word awareness a boost. The idea was to help these children pay more attention to their spelling when their spelling history showed that they didn't.

REFLECTION

I try to keep spelling in perspective as I help primary children develop "word knowledge" that will assist them as readers and writers, knowing that they are young and that the English language can be confusing and full of contradictions. I want them to understand that spelling helps a writer communicate more effectively, especially in a language like English that is filled with homonyms, such as *to*, *too*, and *two*. My goal is for the children to begin "living like spellers" each week, searching out and simmering with words. I want them to know that I think they are up to the task of increasing their conventional spelling in their daily writing. And I also want them to get in the practice of gathering ordinary or unusual personal words. Essentially, I want them to pay attention to their spelling. Sandra Wilde writes,

> We need to destigmatize spelling, to help students realize that being a good speller is a combination of doing enough reading so that you've seen a lot of words in print over and over again, and taking the time to develop strategies like taking an extra second to get a word right or learning how to use a dictionary. Let's work hard to help students become better spellers, but let's also help them realize that society places far more emphasis on spelling

than it deserves (in what other area of life do we expect 100% perfection?) and that your self-respect should never be dependent on whether you know how to spell *because*. (1996, 10)

During my one or two years with a group of children, I hope they develop a love for the "look of words," and actively work on adding ordinary and extraordinary words to their writing vocabularies. I also hope that at some point my students will understand that they wield power in their pencils when they are able to write their ideas clearly with words that are spelled correctly. In our society, it will either create or destroy opportunities for them, and in many cases, it will determine how the rest of the world responds to them. And even though I know there are certain contexts in which I agree with Rabbit's statement, "Spelling isn't everything and there are days when spelling Tuesday simply doesn't count" (Milne 1926), I also know there are times when spelling is everything, and that spelling instruction does count for something.

15 | PORTFOLIOS: BUILDING A LITERACY HISTORY

When we appreciate the depth of children's understanding—how they start from the most fundamental and difficult questions about literacy, when we understand how much they need to know and do manage to learn beyond what is in our . . . lesson plans, we become more aware of the many ways in which we teach.

—*Glenda L. Bissex,* Partial Truths

After Jana's first-grade midyear school conference, her mother wrote a short letter to me in Jana's Note Book thanking me for "a most informative school conference." She appreciated the "collection of information" that Jana and I had presented to her and felt that she had learned a lot about Jana as a learner as well as had her concerns about Jana's reading development addressed. Jana was the fourth child in her family to attend elementary school, and her mother had attended many teacher conferences, but she seemed especially appreciative of this type of school conference experience.

The "collection of information" that I presented to Jana's mother during the first-grade conference was in the form of a literacy portfolio. In this portfolio, I had compiled Jana's "literacy history" since the start of the school year. This portfolio included early literacy and math assessments, along with personal and family information. Leanna Traill describes portfolios as "an objective overview of a child's attitudes, interests, strengths, and instructional needs . . . that present a cohesive, informative profile of a child's progress in literacy learning. It is a professional account of learning to share with the learner, parents/caregivers, colleagues, principals, and administrators" (1993, 60).

When I first started teaching, each child's "portfolio" was a collection of samples and papers in a construction-paper folder that I shared with families at conference time. Since these humble beginnings, I have experimented with portfolios every year, and have finally settled upon three portfolios that the children and I use consistently in our language arts and math work. One portfolio is my "teacher assessment portfolio" and houses each child's literacy and math assessment information. The second portfolio is a "self-evaluation portfolio," which is maintained by each child and contains reading, writing, and art surveys, samples, and artifacts. The third portfolio is a "student math portfolio," which again, is maintained by each child and stores math work and projects. The two portfolios that I discuss in this chapter are the teacher assessment portfolio, and the students' language arts self-evaluation portfolio.

Assessing children's literacy understanding is important, ongoing work throughout the one or two years that I am their reading and writing teacher. It also creates a fair amount of paperwork that has to be compiled and organized for easy access so that I can look through it quickly, note progress over time, and share it with families during school conferences or with colleagues if I have concerns about a child's reading and writing development. Not only do I have to decide which surveys, assessments, and samples are important for determining what each child "does and does not know," but I also have to decide how to organize everything. To that end, I have developed the following system for my teacher assessment portfolios:

The folder that I use for each child's assessment portfolio is actually called a "classification folder" and can be purchased at any office supply store. I buy the folders that have two additional dividers in the middle, so the folder actually has six sections. Each section has two metal prongs at the top, so it is necessary to two-hole punch papers before inserting them onto the prongs. I like this folder for several reasons:

- It is made of a heavy tagboard so it is durable.
- I can reuse the folder year after year if I write the student's name in pencil on a file label.
- It is easy to add papers to throughout the year.
- It resembles a medical/dental/loan folder in which staff members compile a patient's or client's history.
- It is a professional, organized way to share information with families and colleagues.

The following table lists the sections of this portfolio; which surveys, samples, and assessments are included in each section; and when assessments are administered or items are completed during the school year so that I can evaluate a student's progress and make good instructional decisions. I should also note that when assessments are readministered, e.g., letter/sound, or when new samples are added, e.g., writing samples, they are always placed on top of the previous items, so that the current information always appears first.

Organization of Teacher Assessment Portfolio

Section	Surveys, Samples, Assessments	When Administered or Completed
Section 1: Personal Information	• Who Am I? Survey (resource: Fisher 1991) • typed biography from Who Am I? survey • child's self-portrait • child's family portrait • family expectations sheet	• within the first six weeks of school • Back-to-School Night

Organization of Teacher Assessment Portfolio

Section	Surveys, Samples, Assessments	When Administered or Completed
Section 2: Letter/ Sound Work	• letter/sound assessment (resource: Clay 1993a)	• within the first six weeks of school; repeated every three weeks until child shows mastery of letters/sounds
Section 3: Reading Assessments	• running records (resource: Clay 1993a)	• beginning, middle, and year-end
	• cassette tape of child reading; I enclose it in a Ziploc bag, two-hole punch the top, and attach it to the metal prongs	• only if I have taped the reader
	• Concepts About Print (resource: Clay 1993a)	• within the first six weeks of school; administered only if I am concerned about a child's knowledge in this area
Section 4: Writing Assessments	• writing samples	• beginning, middle, and year-end
	• letter formation sample	• within the first six weeks of school; repeated until handwriting is fluent and legible
	• hearing and recording sounds in print (resource: Clay 1993a)	• within the first six weeks of school; administered only if I am concerned about a child's ability to hear and record sounds in words
Section 5: Spelling	• developmental spelling assessment—to determine when to start individual spelling program (resource: Gentry and Gillet 1993)	• first grade: within the first eight weeks of school
	• first one hundred high-frequency words (resource: Gentry and Gillet 1993)	• end of first grade: within the last three weeks of school OR • second grade: within the first three weeks of school

Section	Surveys, Samples, Assessments	When Administered or Completed
Section 6: Math Assessments	• Math Their Way individual composite record for first/second grade • number writing: 1–1,000 • daily reviews • district math assessments	• assessed beginning, middle, and year-end on math concepts and skills listed • ongoing throughout the year

It is a challenge to find the time to administer these assessments and complete the surveys or projects with the children. Those assessments that have to be administered individually, I do during morning-work time, quiet reading, partner reading, recess, or before or after school if opportunities present themselves. If it is a survey that a parent volunteer, classroom aide, or assisting teacher can administer or complete, then I have them help with the assessment process also. In an ideal classroom world, I would be able to administer all of the assessments and observe children carefully during the assessment task; however, it just didn't happen when I had thirty-two children. I would be the first to say it gets hectic and I often feel like I never have enough time, thus my goal is to keep my systems organized so that I can make the most of the minutes I have. The following table shows how I have managed administering assessments and completing assessment projects with young learners.

Surveys, Samples, Assessments	How Administered	Who Administered, Taught, or Completed
Who Am I? survey	individually—home or school	parent helper, classroom aide/teacher, Janine
child's self portrait and family portrait	whole-group drawing project	Janine
family expectations sheet	Back-to-School Night	parents complete
letter/sound assessment	individually—school	parent helper, classroom aide/teacher, Janine
running records	individually—school	Janine

Surveys, Samples, Assessments	How Administered	Who Administered, Taught, or Completed
concepts about print	individually—school; only if I'm concerned about child	Janine
writing samples	whole group—school	Janine
letter formation sample	whole group—school	Janine
hearing and recording sounds in print	individually—school; only if I'm concerned about child	Janine
developmental spelling assessment	individually—school	parent helper, classroom aide/teacher, Janine
high-frequency words assessment	individually or whole group—school	Janine, parent helper, classroom aide/teacher

Jana's Teacher Assessment Portfolio

My assessment portfolio for Jana is typical of many first-grade children's portfolios. Jana was a steady learner, but experienced occasional bumps in her reading and writing development. Her portfolio opens with a narrative piece that I typed about Jana after conducting an interview with her at the beginning of first grade. The resource I used to conduct this interview was Bobbi Fisher's "Celebrating Me" form in her book, *Joyful Learning* (1991). It reads:

My name is Jana. My birthday is March 21, 1988. I have two dogs, Skippy and Dawg. My mom, dad, two sisters, two brothers, and me are in my family. These are some of my favorite things:
   My favorite book is Snow White.
   My favorite TV show is Full House.
   My favorite color is pink.
   My favorite food is carrots.
   My favorite game is Duck, Duck, Goose.
   My favorite animal is a dog.
   Karisa, Kendra, and Tyler are my friends. I like to collect rocks. When I am inside, I like to play games with my brothers and sisters. When I'm outside, I like to ride bikes with my brothers.
   I am like other people because I have the same color of eyes. I am different from other people because I wear different clothes.
   When I grow up, I want to be a doctor. The most special thing about me is that I like to make my baby sister laugh.

This first section of Jana's portfolio also includes a self-portrait and a portrait of her family that she drew during the first two weeks of school. The final piece in this section is an "Expectations and Entry" survey completed by Jana's mother on our first-grade Back-to-School Night.

Expectations and Entry Survey

Name of Parent(s): Vicky and David
Child's Name: Jana
Telephone Numbers: (home and work)
Age of Child and Date of Birth: 6 years; March 21, 1988
Languages Spoken: English
Health Factors: 0
Family Members: Father: David; Mother: Vicky; Brothers: John and Jason; Sisters: Jessica and Jennifer

Your Expectations of Me

Please take a moment to write down your expectations of me, your child's teacher, for our school year.

1. To teach Jana the first-grade curriculum.
2. To teach Jana to read and to enjoy books.
3. To help Jana learn to cooperate.
4. To teach Jana how school works.
5. To help Jana to enjoy school.

Your Expectations of You

Please take a moment to write down your expectations of you, the parent, for our school year.

1. To make sure Jana gets her homework done.
2. To help Jana with her homework.
3. To listen to Jana when she tells me about her day.
4. To be excited about Jana's work.
5. To help Jana be ready for school by being prepared, eating good foods, and getting enough sleep.

Your Expectations of Your Child—School, Academic, and Social

Please take a moment to write down your expectations of your child during our school year.

1. To learn to read.
2. To finish her first-grade math.
3. To be polite and use good manners.
4. To cooperate with others.
5. To be a good listener.

What do you see as the strengths of your child?

A happy child
Cooperative
Works hard

Likes to show off some . . .
Likes to ask questions

What do you see as areas for growth?

Needs to open up more
Needs to learn phonics—to read

Are there any things that you want me to know about your child that may be helpful?

She's afraid of trying new things—gets very upset at times.

The second section contains Jana's letter/sound assessment completed during the first six weeks of first grade. Jana identified all upper- and lower-case letters correctly and knew the sounds for eighteen of the twenty-six letters. Given her level of knowledge, I chose not to repeat this assessment again during her first-grade year. I was able to observe mastery of the few remaining letter sounds through her writing work.

The third section of the portfolio contains Jana's first-grade running records, taken at the beginning, middle, and end of the year, which are the only assessments in this reading section of her portfolio. I did not administer Concepts About Print at the beginning of the year because I observed that her book and print knowledge were solid. Also, I didn't tape-record Jana reading during the year, so there wasn't a cassette tape to include in this section, either. If I tape-record, it is Concern children only.

The first running record I did with Jana was at the beginning of October, approximately five weeks into our school year. The book she "read" was *Uncle Buncle's House* (Cowley 1996), an emergent reader. Essentially Jana engaged in "memory reading," so I wasn't able to calculate an accuracy rate for her reading. However, she could point to five words in the text (*there, are, in, Uncle Buncle*) when I asked her to do this, so she was developing a sight vocabulary.

The second running record I did with Jana was in April, at midyear. She read *Boring Old Bed* (Cowley 1996), an early reader. The information I calculated and recorded after Jana read to me shows my concern about her reading development at this time:

Running Words: 164
Errors: 29
Error Rate: 1: 5.6
Self-Correction Rate: 1: 16
Accuracy Rate: 82.3%

My comments: Jana is not monitoring herself for meaning; attitude—seems very resistant to working harder; she seems to not want to deal with difficulties as a reader; being served in Reading Recovery program; starting to use initial sounds as a problem-solving strategy, which is an improvement.

Jana's third running record, taken at year-end, was completed by Cathy Smith, our Reading Recovery teacher. The text was *The Dandelion* (Houghton Mifflin series) and was an early level text. With "double teaching effort," Jana had shown significant progress as a reader by the end of the year. This time her accuracy rate was 93 percent, her error rate 1:14, and her self-correction rate 1:1. Cathy wrote these summary statements about Jana on her running record:

> Jana has recently begun to incorporate equal parts m s v [meaning, syntax, and visual]. When she errs, it usually involves the visual. Jana now uses several strategies to solve reading problems. She skips words she doesn't know and comes back to beginning. She seldom shrugs and says, "I don't know!"

The fourth section of Jana's assessment portfolio contains writing assessments and samples. I made copies of her three first-grade writing samples to include in this section because the actual samples go into a district language arts portfolio that is passed on to each teacher through fifth grade.

For Jana's beginning-of-the-year sample, she drew a picture of herself, her mom, and her little sister going to see the movie *The Lion King*. She wrote underneath her picture, *THE MOVIES*, which she had copied from our brainstorming chart.

Jana's midyear writing sample showed quite a leap in fluency, although spelling and vowel sounds still needed considerable attention. She wrote:

> I mit git my ers pest nacs weekenes and I wot git the hop af my mom wil lat me. my mom and dad sid I can. on eitr I git to swam at my ant and I love to go and swam and I wil be lofogs and I wil love being it bcos we like to swim on my dad pon is os in the pol and we scriem ot lod like tos ahhhhhhh! ahhhhhh! ahhhh! I lvoe to swim my baby sister name is Jennifer likecs to sowam like I dow. my ant is name ___hes goi hes ers pesh. I cant wat to git my ers pesh it wil be fon I love to.my dad dos wot to go to the dazrt ane more. I love to go and sowinm bcos my kosin is hape bcos hed love the hos. I love to swom I jip of the diving bod. my dad like to go and jop of it. I love my dad a lot.
>
> *(I might get my ears pierced next weekend. And I want [to] get the hoop if my mom will let me. My mom and dad said I can. On Easter I get to swim at my aunt's and I love to go and swim and I will be—and I will love being it because we like to swim on my dad. [He] pushes us in the pool and we scream out loud like this: ahhhhhhh! ahhhhhh! ahhhh! I love to swim. My baby sister's name is Jennifer likes to swim like I do. My aunt's name—. She's got her ears pierced. I can't wait to get my ears pierced. It will be fun. I love to. My dad doesn't want to go to the desert anymore. I love to go and swim because my cousin is happy because he love the house. I love to swim. I jump off the diving board. My dad likes to go and jump off it. I love my dad a lot.)*

Jana's end-of-the-year writing sample still showed spelling difficulties with high-frequency words. She was a classic example of a child who practiced and did well on weekly spelling checks, but didn't transfer her spelling knowledge to her daily written work. For her last first-grade writing sample she wrote:

My grandma and grandpa wint to Mailed to sal the motre homea I miss my Grandma and Grandpa aLot I kow thay miss! me a haae boch to I all was sahed them a chaneds aLot I coll they aLot Thay coll me aLot to we tock and tock. But thay are back now I git to go to thar hosue to day and maby she will woch me play sochr and all win for her and all give her some of my sochr snack and my Grandpa will git some to I will git aLot of origis to ent ill ent the most cose I hanf to play she all was cms to the games so she can see a rill grla play

(My grandma and grandpa went to Maryland to sell the motor home. I miss my grandma and grandpa a lot. I know they miss me a whole bunch too. I always saved them a candies a lot. I call them a lot. They call me a lot too. We talk and talk. But they are back now. I get to go to their house today, and maybe she will watch me play soccer, and I'll win for her, and give her some of my soccer snack. And my grandpa will get some too. I will get a lot of oranges to eat. I'll eat the most because I have to play. She always comes to the games so she can see a real girl play.)

The last piece in the writing assessments section is Jana's letter formation assessment, which she completed during the first week of school. Like the letter/sound correspondence assessment, I only administered this once during the year because she was able to form all of the upper- and lowercase letters correctly. However, my goal for her was to work on neatness.

The fifth section of the portfolio, which is the last section devoted to language arts—the sixth section is for math assessments and work samples—is for spelling assessments. In Jana's portfolio, this section includes her developmental spelling assessments, which were administered twice before she started her individual spelling work. The table below shows Jana's spelling attempts of the ten words listed in Gentry and Gillet's developmental spelling assessment (1993, 41–48).

Conventional Spelling	Jana's First Assessment: Week 5	Jana's Second Assessment: Week 12
monster	Md	Misd
united	uN	unte
dress	r	grs
bottom	Bt (B reversed)	BPo
hiked	H	Hit

Conventional Spelling	Jana's First Assessment: Week 5	Jana's Second Assessment: Week 12
human	HuM	HMn
eagle	Eo (E reversed)	EGL
closed	oz (z reversed)	cos
bumped	BT	bot
type	TirT	tip
	Level of Development semiphonetic	*Level of Development phonetic*

The last piece in this spelling section was an assessment of Jana's ability to write the first one hundred words most frequently used by children in their writing (Gentry and Gillet 1993). Jana had not worked on all one hundred of the words by the end of the year, so I only assessed her on the seventy-five words she had studied during the second half of her first-grade year. She was able to write fifty-one of the seventy-five words in conventional spelling. The twenty-four words she had not yet mastered at the end of first grade included *was, they, would, when, were, there, went, said, them, because, about, until, people, make, could, very, want, this, homework, good, done, their, back, children.* In studying her spelling errors of those twenty-four words, I discovered Jana relied on phonetic spelling, often using the "sound of a vowel" in her spelling if she was unsure of the conventional spelling, e.g., "thay" for *they.* It was good information for me, her teacher, in terms of where to focus my spelling instruction with her during her second-grade year.

Except for the year-end pieces that I added to Jana's portfolio, this was the "collection of information" that I presented to Jana's mother at our school conference when we met to review Jana's progress and discuss goals for the second half of the school year. The information within the portfolio was critical in terms of my ongoing assessment and evaluation of how Jana was progressing as a reader and writer. The organization of the information allowed me to present "Jana as a learner" to her mother in a professional manner and give "paper proof" of where Jana had started on her literacy journey at the beginning of first grade and the progress she had made since that time.

SELF-EVALUATION PORTFOLIOS

I didn't work much with the concept of self-evaluation portfolios until my last year at Bobier, when I was teaching my group of second graders. There were several reasons I wanted to explore self-evaluation portfolios. First, I wanted the children to reflect on their work as readers and writers because I believe the process of self-evaluation is critical to children's success as learners. Second, I wanted my group to use their portfolios to conduct their mid-year school conferences with their families. Third, I wanted the children to have a place to save drafts of important writing work and projects. With these goals in mind, I embarked on helping my second-grade readers and writers create their own self-evaluation portfolios.

The children used file folders to house their "collection of information." These folders were filed in alphabetical order in hanging file folders, and were stored in large plastic tubs on the floor, labeled "Children's Portfolios." The children had two portfolios in their hanging file folders—their language arts portfolio and their math portfolio. I stored my teacher assessment portfolios in two tubs on a shelf in my teacher area. The children needed to have easy access to their portfolios because they filed items in them throughout the year.

Myself As a Reader and Writer Forms

At midyear, when school conferences were drawing near, I created two self-evaluation pieces for the children to complete: Myself As a Reader and Myself As a Writer. When I sat down to craft the evaluation forms, it was a process of mulling over what I wanted the children to consider about themselves as readers and writers so they could present this information to their families during their conferences. Both evaluations appear below, along with the questions I asked myself that led to composing the statements I wanted the children to respond to:

Myself As a Reader

1. My favorite author:

   • Are the children searching out favorite authors and books?
   • Are they connecting to these authors and returning to them?

2. What I love about reading:

   • Are the children developing healthy attitudes about reading?
   • How do they view the act of reading?

3. What I find challenging about reading:

   • What exactly do the children find challenging as they continue to develop as readers?
   • Do the challenges have similar characteristics depending upon the level of development of the reader?
   • How can I use this information for my teaching?

4. When I am having a problem figuring out a word this is what I do:

   • How do the children cope with word difficulty?
   • What strategies do they believe they use?
   • How does that compare with my assessments of their reading behaviors?

5. A book that I want to read some day is:

   • Are the children looking forward as readers?
   • Are they "living like readers" and always keeping the next good book in mind?

6. This is how I feel about myself as a reader:

- How do the children perceive they are doing as readers?
- What is their "reading barometer" telling them?

7. I want to read to you from this book: (Children have to choose excerpts to read from a book of their choice.)

- How can the children show their families in our formal conference how they are doing as readers?
- How can I offer suggestions for home instruction?

Myself As a Writer

1. My favorite kind of writing:

- Have the children already developed a love for a particular genre of writing?
- Are the children thinking about the different kinds of writing?

2. What I love about writing:

- Are the children developing healthy attitudes about writing?
- How do they view the act of writing?

3. What I find challenging about writing:

- What exactly do the children find challenging as they continue to develop as writers?
- Do the challenges have similar characteristics depending upon the level of writing development?
- How can I use this information for my teaching?

4. When I am having a problem with my writing this is what I do:

- What do the children do when they can't decide on a topic and are searching for an idea?
- What do the children do when they are trying to figure out the style and form of the piece?
- What do the children do when their writing doesn't make sense?
- What do the children do when they get "stuck" and can't figure out where to take their piece next?

5. When I am having a problem writing a word this is what I do:

- How do the children cope with spelling difficulty?
- What strategies do they believe they have?
- How does that compare with my assessments of their spelling resourcefulness?

6. Someday I would like to write about:

- Are the children looking forward as writers?
- Are they "living like writers"—collecting ideas, noticing their world, simmering with topics to write about?

7. This is how I feel about myself as a writer:

   - How do the children perceive they are doing as writers?
   - What is their "writing barometer" telling them?

8. A sample of my writing:

   - How can the children show their families in our formal conference how they are doing as writers?
   - How can I offer suggestions for home instruction?

My second graders completed the self-evaluations over the course of two days during our writing time. First, I explained why I felt these were important pieces to complete for our conferences, then I read through the surveys so the children could begin thinking through their responses. After the children understood how they were to evaluate themselves, we began working through the evaluations as a whole class, statement by statement, some children waiting patiently for others who needed a bit more time, or sometimes going ahead if they had their ideas ready and were confident about what they wanted to write. At times, I wrote the standard spelling for various words on the overhead as they were requested by the children. In between that, I worked on my own evaluation forms, so that I could share them with the children as we worked.

When we were working on the "Myself As a Reader" evaluation, the children asked for additional help with completing the fourth statement: "When I am having a problem figuring out a word this is what I do." They said something to this effect: "We'll tell you the different ways that we solve problems and you list them on the overhead. Then, we'll write down the ones we use on our own papers."

A thought occurred to me as I considered the children's completed list of problem-solving strategies that day. I felt it was a list that deserved its own chart in our room as well as on refrigerators at home. So, I decided to type their list of problem-solving strategies and include it with report cards so that families would have it at home. Families had received similar information in journals, anthologies, and newsletters, but it was one more way to remind families of problem-solving strategies beyond "sound it out." For the most part, I retained the same language that the children used, only clarifying when I thought it might aid understanding. The finished list follows:

Problem Solving Hard Words

We brainstormed this list of ways to figure out hard words when we are reading. Please keep this handy when you are reading and helping at home.

1. Put in another word that makes sense.
2. Start over; take another run at it.
3. Sound out the word/letters.
4. Ask an adult.

5. Ask a friend.
6. Cover part of it and see if that helps to figure it out.
7. Skip it and come back to it.
8. Look at the picture.
9. Look in another book to remember the word.

My Favorite Books List

Another piece that the children completed for their portfolios was a list of their favorite books. My goal was for the children to show a list of books they had grown to love, then share the importance of these books with their families during conferences.

The form is simple: "My Favorite Books" is the heading, with lines drawn for name and date, and more lines, numbered one through ten, for the children to list their top ten favorite books at that moment in time. The idea is for children to write the title of their absolute favorite book on line number one, then rank their remaining choices after that.

We set our tubs of books around the room with enough space for children to walk through, mingle with them, and write titles on their papers. We also discussed the fact that they didn't have to list ten books on their paper if they didn't feel they had ten favorites; that is, if they only had four favorite books, then they only had to list four. In between helping children with the task, I worked on the impossible task of compiling my ten favorites.

Portfolio Sharing: A Rehearsal

With the above materials ready in the children's portfolios, along with any additional writing pieces and artwork samples they had collected during the first half of the school year, my group had one final "to-do item" to prepare for their conferences. I felt they needed a rehearsal in order to be able to share their portfolios with their families with confidence. So, before the first conference took place, we practiced sharing our portfolios with one another.

First we gathered around Juanita and Sonia, and I gave them some pointers—slow down, speak a little louder, point to the items as you read, etc.—while they shared their portfolios with each other. The children were to share the contents of their portfolio in this order:

- Myself As a Reader
- My Favorite Books
- Myself As a Writer
- writing samples/projects
- artwork

After the children watched my work with Juanita and Sonia, they found partners, chose a place in the room to sit together, and began sharing their portfolios with each other. I spent my time walking among the children, listening in as they presented to each other, giving tips for a better presentation when I felt they were needed. After this first round of sharing, the children found new partners and shared their portfolios a second time. The children were eager to share their portfolios with each other and this seemed to build even more anticipation for meeting with their families.

Jana's Self-Evaluation Portfolio Presentation

When Jana shared her portfolio with her mom during her midyear school conference, she started with the front cover of her portfolio, showing her mom the pencil portrait she had drawn at the beginning of the school year and reading the autobiographical paragraph she had written to display with her portrait:

> My name is Jana. I'm seven years old. My hair color is brown. My eye color is brown. I'm in second grade. I play soccer a lot. My cousin's name is Peter. I live in Vista, California. I have six people in my family not including me. My teacher's name is Janine Chappell. My sister Jennifer drives me bananas. I love drawing a lot. I have two dogs.

Next, Jana shared her "Myself As a Reader" piece, reading it aloud to her mother:

Myself As a Reader

1. My favorite author: Marc Brown
2. What I love about reading: I love to imagine things that arnt in the book. I love just reading It is fun. to Read I thek (*I love to imagine things that aren't in the book. I love just reading. It is fun to read I think.*)
3. What I find challenging about reading: Log wodes because thar chalging (*Long words because they're challenging.*)
4. When I am having a problem figuring out a word this is what I do: (1). Asc sowon. (*Ask someone.*) (2). Come back to it. (3). Sound out the word. (4). Put in a word that makes sense. (5). Start over. (6). Ask Janine or a friend. (7). Skip it and come back to it. (8). Look at the picture.
5. A book that I want to read some day is: Pee Wee Scouts Cookies and Crutches
6. This is how I feel about myself as a reader: good because I lene now words wale I read difrit book's it hope's me be a beter reader. because book's make me laf (*Good because I learn new words while I read different books. It helps me be a better reader because books make me laugh.*)
7. I want to read to you from this book: *Mad About Madeline*.

After Jana read an excerpt to her mom from her *Madeline* book, she presented her list of favorite books.

My Favorite Books

1. *Mad About Madeline*
2. *Me First*

3. *Nate the Great*
4. *Just a Mess*
5. *Franklin is Messy*
6. *Arthur Babysits*
7. *Max's Chocolate Chicken*
8. *Me too!*
9. *The New Baby*
10. *You Be Good and I'll Be Night*

These items completed the reading portion of Jana's portfolio, and next she presented her writing work to her mom. She began with the "Myself As a Writer" piece, again reading it aloud to her mom:

Myself As a Writer

1. My favorite kind of writing: journal and poetry
2. What I love about writing: I love to writing about things
3. What I find challenging about writing: Spelling Deminds (*Demons*)
4. When I am having a problem with my writing this is what I do: Look in the classroom
5. When I am having a problem writing a word this is what I do: I asc my famly or my friends or Janine (*I ask my family, or my friends, or Janine.*)
6. Someday I would like to write about: Poetry and animals world and about people and the sun and rain
7. This is how I feel about myself as a writer: good some days and bad some days.

I still smile at Jana's response to how she felt about herself as a writer. It seems that all writers, whether seven or forty-seven, have good and bad days with their writing.

Next, Jana shared her space informational book writing project with her mom. First, she showed her the planning work she had done before she started composing, then her rough draft, and finally her finished, published book. It had been a long writing project in our classroom—taking an entire month—as it was the culmination of our space exploration study. Jana's final typed draft follows:

Page 1: Hi, I'm Jana. I like Saturn and the sun and the stars. Saturn is a planet. The sun and the stars are hot.

Page 2: Saturn's rings are not solid. They are made of rock and dust and ice. Saturn's rings are magnified under a magnifying glass and you can see the rock and stone. On Saturn's rings you would have to run really, really, really, really, really, really fast.

Page 3: Saturn is the sixth from the sun and it might be cold since it's the sixth planet. Almost farther than the planet Pluto.

Page 4: How hot is the sun? Is the sun hotter than your oven or your stove or your washing machine?

Page 5: Are there two suns in space now with the new planet? If there is a new planet in our galaxy it would be interesting to find out.

Page 6: This is a star that is near the sun. But, it is hot. The sun is just a star.

Page 7: The sun is made out of one big star and it's orbiting around the moon but the planets orbit around the sun.

Page 8: Saturn's rings are magnified under a magnifier glass and you can see the rock and stone.

Jana completed her portion of the conference that day by presenting her math portfolio to her mother in the same way she had shared her language arts portfolio. After that, I shared my teacher assessment information in reading, writing, spelling, and math, with a brief look at Jana's report card at the end. Vista Unified has a developmental continuum report card for the primary grades, so it was a matter of transferring the information from my assessments to the district report card. With my completed assessments, it was actually quick work.

Jana and the other children continued to add items to their self-evaluation portfolios throughout the second half of our school year. The children always saved drafts of any teacher-led writing projects we had worked on, as well as any other pieces they were proud of. I reminded them of my criteria—that they had worked hard and were proud of their efforts—often. By the end of the year, Jana had filed these additional pieces in her portfolio:

Writing Work

- Mother's Day poem
- Father's Day letter
- field trip concertina book: rough draft and final draft
- poem for our class poetry book: *Poems We'll Treasure Forever*

Artwork

- guided drawing: ocean animals
- pencil drawings: "Sun in Art" project
- zoo mural
- Winnie-the-Pooh oil pastel drawing

Both Jana's Mother's Day poem and Father's Day letter were touching pieces that she had written as gifts for her mom and dad. When I read her Mother's Day poem, I could see she was trying to find her place with her mom now that a little sister was commanding more of her mother's time and attention:

> Mom
> I miss having all the fun.
> But I know it's even funner
> with Jennifer on Mother's Day.
> 'Cause Jennifer is my little sister
> that I love everyday, even on Mother's Day.
> But I love you, too, on Mother's day.
> Actually, I love you both.
> I love you.

Jana also had a wonderful relationship with her adventurous father, and she wrote about this in her "memory letter" to her father for Father's Day:

Dear Dad,

Happy Father's Day! I rember (*remember*) when we whent (*went*) to the desert and you helped me go up to the hill. It was fun and skary (*scary*). I love you a lot more then Easter and all the holiday's! I love you. Love, Jana

I valued Jana's portfolio because it gave her a place to reflect on who she was as a reader, writer, and person, and also a place to collect writing pieces that were significant to her. Perhaps most important, Jana's portfolio was a celebration of the reader and writer she had become during the two years that I was her teacher. Jana valued her portfolio because like Kate Bloomfield, it was her way of saying to her family, "Hey World, here I am!"

STUDY OF ROOM 12'S SELF-EVALUATION PORTFOLIOS

At midyear, after the children completed their "Myself As a Reader" and "Myself As a Writer" evaluations for their portfolios, I spent time studying their responses. First, I studied individual evaluations because I was interested in how the children perceived themselves as readers and writers. Second, I compiled the information from all of the evaluations so I could look for trends in their responses. From a teacher-research standpoint, I was looking for patterns that might be illuminating in terms of my own teaching, perhaps showing me where I had and had not spent enough time in my teaching. When I have the time, I like to examine information in this way because it shows me where to focus my teaching with the children, both on a whole-group and an individual basis. I have to compile the information on paper because otherwise I can't "see" trends in the responses.

On the "Myself As a Reader" evaluations, I discovered that one of the most intriguing patterns was the children's responses to how they figured out problem words. At that point in time, I had grouped my readers and writers into my three "monitoring progress" categories (see Chapter 7) in this way:

- No Concerns: 10 children
- Mild Concerns: 14 children
- Concerns: 6 children

These were the questions I considered when I decided to examine this information closely:

- Would there be similarities and/or differences in the types of strategies used between the three groups of children?
- Would each group have a distinct reliance on one or two strategies and would these be the same or different strategies between groups?

- Do the strategies the children perceive themselves using match the strategies I observe them using?

I listed the responses from our "Problem Solving Hard Words" list, tallied the responses, and figured out the percentage of children in each group who had indicated they used each strategy. When I studied the compiled information, I discovered the two predominant strategies among all three groups were "Sound out the word/letters" and "Ask Ms. Janine or a friend." My most fluent readers were much more comfortable substituting with a word that makes sense than either of the other two groups. Were they able to cope better with the work of sustaining meaning, substituting a word that was "close" so that they could move on, where perhaps the other two groups were still focused "on getting each word right"? I was interested in watching this reading behavior among the Mild Concerns and Concerns groups of readers. I felt I needed to devote more instructional time to this strategy.

The strategies "Skip it and come back to it," and "Look at the picture" were two strategies that I felt the children needed to use more than their responses indicated they were. Again, both needed more instructional time from me during shared reading and reading conferences. I also wanted my Mild Concerns group to use the "start over/take another run at it from the beginning of the sentence" more than the results indicated they were. I had been working on this rereading strategy extensively with my Concerns group readers, and it appeared half of these children were internalizing this strategy.

Overall, I desired a better balance of all strategies used, save for "look in another book," which seemed time-consuming and difficult for young developing readers. If the children were having difficulty with the word in this book, I doubted they would be very successful locating and figuring it out in another book—a previous page, yes—but a different book was the last strategy I would concentrate on with them. The results of my study were revealing. Time to adjust my instruction, again.

When I studied the children's "Myself As a Writer" evaluations, I noticed another interesting pattern in their responses to how they work through spelling difficulties (writing problem words) in their writing. As I did with the "Problem Solving Hard Words" study, I listed the responses from our "Writing Hard Words" list, tallied the number of children who indicated they used them, then figured out the percentage of children in my No Concerns, Mild Concerns, and Concerns groups who used each strategy.

When I studied my compiled data, the most interesting pattern I noticed was the resourcefulness of my No Concerns and Mild Concerns writers in that a majority of the children in both of these groups relied on themselves to work through their spelling dilemmas by either using temporary spelling or finding the word in our classroom. On the other hand, my Concerns group was not as confident in these two strategies, as the least amount of children in this group used them in comparison to the other two strategies they employed. My No Concerns group turned to me the least, with even more of the children in that group turning to their friends for help first. About the same number of children in my Mild Concerns group and Concerns group solved their problems by asking someone else for the spelling. I had work to do in terms of pushing them along and helping them develop confidence and skill in tackling challenging words by using their own resources.

I was amazed at how much I learned not only about the children, but also about my teaching when I studied and compiled their responses on their self-evaluation forms. I saw their responses as little mirrors of how I had been involved in their learning lives day after day, and I became even more aware of the "how" and "in what ways" my teaching was influencing them, as well as in what areas I had and had not been spending my time. This small teacher-research project was a way for me to understand my readers and writers better, as well as improve my own teaching practices.

REFLECTION

Both my teacher assessment portfolio and the children's self-evaluation portfolios are living, breathing collections of samples and observations that show growth over time. They don't collect dust. I refer to and add items to my assessment portfolios daily. The children have access to their self-evaluation portfolios at all times so that they can add pieces or look back on pieces during the course of their work. These portfolios reflect the lives of these young learners because they are the learners. Portfolios have color and texture in comparison to report cards, whether they are traditional reporting forms or developmental continuums.

The "paper proof" that children are indeed moving forward as readers and writers is helpful to teacher, children, and families. When we live with these young learners every day, whether at home or in the classroom, we sometimes forget exactly where the children started in their literacy journeys. Portfolios capture this "living history" and show how the children are "growing up" as readers and writers.

These portfolios are also the backbone of my parent-teacher-student conferences. I view these midyear conferences as "state of the child" conferences in which we celebrate the growth of the learner while also setting goals for further progress. Both my teacher assessment portfolio and the children's self-evaluation portfolios show evidence of their development in reading, writing, thinking, and learning. The self-evaluation portfolios provide a way for young children to present themselves as learners so that they are the centerpiece of the school conference.

When I think of my second-grade students sharing their portfolios with their families, I remember my conference with Priscilla and her mother and how they discovered they shared a common love of poetry and left my classroom carrying an armload of poetry books because they wanted to spend the rest of the evening reading poetry together. I also recall Edward, and how I admired and appreciated the way he assisted his parents' understanding of his portfolio by reading and speaking to them in both Spanish and English. I remember how Nhi helped her mother in similar ways, except she brought her older brother with her so that together, they could translate Nhi's portfolio into Vietnamese so her mother would understand who Nhi was as a reader and writer. And sadly, I recall how Tanya's mother cried when Tanya read aloud her memories of a father who had died when she was in kindergarten.

Whereas portfolios helped me appreciate the depth of children's understandings and questions about literacy, they also helped me appreciate the children's lives. As I listened to my young readers and writers share their portfolios with their families, I felt their diversity, strengths, struggles, and celebrations. And finally, these portfolios helped me see the many ways, spoken and unspoken, in which I teach.

EPILOGUE

Hope is the thing with feathers
That perches in the soul,
And sings the tune without the words,
And never stops at all . . .

—Emily Dickinson, "Hope is the thing with feathers"

At the end of E.B. White's *Stuart Little*, the reader discovers that Stuart, a little boy mouse who has been on a quest throughout the entire story, is ready to set forth yet again:

> Stuart rose from the ditch, climbed into his car, and started up the road that led toward the north. The sun was just coming up over the hills on his right. As he peered ahead into the great land that stretched before him, the way seemed long. But the sky was bright, and he somehow felt he was headed in the right direction. (1945, 131)

After teaching children at Bobier Elementary for four years, and my husband teaching at Washington Middle School in Vista Unified for five years, we decided it was time to move on, and headed north to the state of Washington, which is my home state.

Teaching at Bobier was a mixture of celebration and frustration, laughter and tears, anger and admiration, both at the school and classroom level. Yes, there were days when I tired of working through child, family, and school problems. In my classroom, there were hassles every week. "Life in classrooms is an intense social experience," writes Ralph Peterson. "At best, it is elbow-to-elbow living" (1992, 1). I remember well the times when it was closer than elbow-to-elbow living. Even though we strived to live by the motto "Think deeply, speak gently, love much, laugh a lot, work hard, give freely, and be kind," which was posted and illustrated by one of the children, there were moments and days when we forgot our motto.

Despite the problems, I never used, nor believe in, a system of assertive discipline or rewards to "manage my class." In a conversation about his thought-provoking book *Punished By Rewards*, Alfie Kohn states, "You show me a school . . . where students are working with one another in a caring environment to engage with interesting tasks that they have some say in choosing, and I'll show you a place where you don't need to use punishments or rewards" (1995, 16). My goal was to create an active, thoughtful classroom and to help children care. I emphasized communication and also reminded children that they were responsible to a larger group. Each time I helped children solve their problems, I learned how to do this work better.

At the end of my four years, saying goodbye to my colleagues and the children and their families was difficult. I pondered how to come to "the end." I wondered how to wrap everything up, tie it with a bright-colored ribbon, and proclaim my work was finished. I contemplated an ending that held the promise of new and different beginnings.

In the end, Rachael's and Jana's mothers organized a potluck dinner, which was a new experience for several children, so that our classroom community could come together one last time and celebrate our two years of learning together. It was a remarkable evening with approximately 130 people in attendance. During my principal's closing remarks, he said that one word came to mind as he looked out at the children and their families, and that was "community."

The children and I brought our classroom living to an end by writing and publishing our own poetry collection, titled *Poems We'll Treasure Forever*, which we read to one another on our last day of school. Good-byes were tearful but graceful, with Jana handing out pink tissues from a box of Kleenex that she had brought to school that morning. When the bell rang that day, it was hard to say, "Let's go home," as I stood at the door, looking at the faces of these children that I had come to love so much.

When my husband and I arrived in Washington, our mailbox was full of letters from Room 12 kids. Priscilla wrote to tell me that she was writing a book about our two years together and was in need of title ideas. Lisa wrote in one of her letters, "I weigh 60 pounds. I lost two pounds . . . I go to Tanya's house almost everyday, and we always play school because we loved how you tote (*taught*) us. So now we play school EVERYDAY!"

Rachael wrote long letters describing how all of the "Room 12 kids" were doing as grown-up third graders, and Jana sent a postcard of Shi-Shi and Bai-Yun, so that I would know the long-awaited giant pandas had finally arrived at the San Diego Zoo. "Rats," I wrote back to her. "I missed them."

Now, everyone's lives have moved on, and I receive only occasional correspondence from the children. At one point, I received a letter from Sonia in which she wrote:

Dear Janine,

I have ben thro lots of truble because my uncol died on Wenday. And my ante has ben very sat these days. She has not eaten yet or these other days. Because she is very, very sad about this prolam. but where tring to help her alot. but were stil tring to be happy so she could be hersalf againg.

(*I have been through lots of trouble because my uncle died on Wednesday. And my aunt has been very sad these days. She has not eaten yet or these other days, because she is very, very sad about this problem. But, we're trying to help her a lot. But, we're still trying to be happy so she could be herself again.*)

I lingered over Sonia's letter because I could still hear the melody in her words, as well as her compassion and care. I could feel her troubles and started searching in my mind for a poem to send to her, hoping that long-distance words would help. I could hear the strength of Sonia's voice, and the voices of Bobier children came rushing back at me.

"The early lilacs became part of this child," writes Walt Whitman. Eloquently he speaks of the white and red morning-glories, the song of the phoebe-bird, the noisy brood of the barnyard . . . in essence, the world that became part of this curious child as he went forth into the world. In my classroom at Bobier, I hoped that well-loved books, favorite journals, a visiting hummingbird, shared laughter, a tissue to wipe tears, evenings with families, field trips near and far, missing dog posters, a kind word, spelling *humuhumu-nukunukuapuaa*, burying a dead moth, grieving the loss of a parent or grandparent, all things big and little, seen and unseen, spoken and unspoken . . . would become part of these children "for many years or stretching cycles of years," just as these children became a part of me, and changed me forever.

If I could capture what my years at Bobier convinced me of as a teacher, it would be how important it is to trust that all children have a tremendous need to learn about and make sense of their worlds, and that all children possess a deep inner desire to become readers and writers. Day after day inside the walls of Room 12 and beyond, I discovered that these quite ordinary children had extraordinary minds and abilities. I learned how critical it is to first begin with what children know, understand, and don't understand in their worlds, then as a mentor, work alongside them and reveal the endless possibilities for their lives as readers, writers, and learners.

My Bobier years also convinced me that all children deserve equally rich learning environments in every school across America. Lamentably, we are far from that. When state budgets don't provide for all schools to have fresh paint, trees, flowers, grass, and bushes, essentially those items that make life sweet, pleasurable, and beautiful, and children endure buildings and books that are worn out both inside and out, we are not providing equal education in our public schools. There are very few places of business in this country that would allow their establishments to look like many elementary schools do, Bobier included, much less expect their employees to work well without the necessary materials, resources, and training. We can and must do better for our "Bobier children" and our "Bobier schools" that are everywhere.

I have also come to understand how deeply the art of teaching lives within me and how much I love living among schoolchildren in a caring classroom community that values good books, sharp pencils, reams of blank writing paper, kind words, high expectations, talk, laughter, quiet, and time—time that allows us to make lasting, cherished memories. I realize now that I will always view the world as a teacher of young children.

There was a day in first grade, when the children and I were gathered together, that Tracy shared with us that she'd had a really bad day the day before. The discussion that followed held the seeds of what I hoped these children would carry within them as they went forth into the world. It also convinced me, once again, of the importance of being a thoughtful mentor in the lives of young children and creating an opening for their voices. Their conversation, which I captured in my journal, follows:

Tracy: Yesterday I had a really bad day. I put my backpack down, and people were pushing. That really hurt my feelings, and Quartressa's feelings were hurt. Some were grabbing at the tub at P.E. and pushed me. That really hurt my feelings.

Kayalani: Treat a girl . . .

Eddie: with respect.

Kayalani: . . . Not a piece of dirt.

Tracy: Or a boy.

Kayalani: Like to animals. Feed it, be nice to it.

Tracy: If you really want to hold that basket, just go up to them and say, "Please may I hold that?" If they say, "No," just walk away. Otherwise it hurts people's feeling. If you push someone . . .

Rosanna: Say, "Move out of the way?"

Tracy: Some of you know better.

Brenda: Like Adrienne, she's always nice. She never pushes people.

Priscilla: Like my little sister. She poured soda on my head. Then she got scared and ran to the kitchen. When she fights with me, then I push her back.

Tracy: You shouldn't push when you fight. I could see you smiled, Priscilla. So sometimes it's not so bad.

The children continued for a few moments with similar "empathy stories" and how you should treat people. They were quiet for a moment, and then Tracy turned to me, in all seriousness, and said, "Janine, it's like you. You grew up with a great mind. You grew up with the power to teach people. You have the power with feelings."

They are some of the most exquisite, and humbling, words I have ever heard. They are words that bring me back to my original premise that knowledgeable, loving teachers—who take the time to establish strong classroom communities and make connections with children's families—are essential when it comes to helping all children, regardless of race or wealth, develop literate voices so that they may go forth into the world with strength and compassion.

APPENDIX 1–1
Writing Resource:
Alphabet Card

Our Alphabet		A, a apple	B, b bird
C, c cat	D, d dragon	E, e elephant	F, f fish
G, g galoshes	H, h house	I, i Igloo	J, j jeep
K, k kangaroo	L, l lion	M, m Marisela	N, n Nest
O, o octopus	P, p pig	Q, q queen	R, r Robby
S, s sun	T, t tent	U, u underground	V, v vest
W, w windmill	X, x fox	Y, y yellow	Z, z zigzag line

Created by
Room 12 First Graders

APPENDIX 1–2
Punctuation Resource

Copies of this punctuation resource card are laminated and placed in the children's "resource basket" (one per table) to assist them when they write. Other resources in the basket include alphabet cards, letter formation cards, and high-frequency word cards.

End Marks: Use at the end of a sentence.
. **period** We are in second grade.
! **exclamation point** We are in second grade!
? **question mark** Are we in second grade?

Comma: Use when you want to take a little pause.
Dear Janine,
Love, Janine
We bought carrots, tomatoes, and lettuce.

Quotation Marks: Use when characters are talking.
"Not I," said the goose.
"Not I," said the cat.
"Not I," said the dog.

Capital Letters:
1. Names: Janine Chappell
2. Places: Bobier Elementary School
             Vista, California
3. Important Things: the Statue of Liberty
4. Beginning of Sentences: We go to school at Bobier Elementary.

APPENDIX 1–3
Before-School Student Letter

Dear _____

Hi! I am writing to say hello to you before our school year starts on Monday, August 29, 1994. I hope that you are ready for school to start again. I am anxious to meet all of you. I am wondering what you are like, what you are interested in, and what you have been doing during your vacation. I know that at least a couple of you have had brothers or sisters in my classroom, so you already know all about me. For the rest of you, I will tell you a little bit about myself in my letter.

I liked to be called Janine. If you would rather call me Ms. Janine, that would be fine too. I am married and my husband's name is Michael Carr. He teaches seventh graders at Washington Middle School. He has red hair! We have been married almost two years and we do not have children—only nieces and nephews.

I love to sing and play the guitar and we will do that on the first day of school. I also love to read and I will have many, many favorite books to share with you every day. I am anxious to hear about your favorite books. Please bring a favorite book to school the first day if you have one you would like to share. You will be reading every day at school and at home. That really is the best way to learn how to read—by reading.

I also love to walk, plant flowers in the garden, and travel. In the past few years I have traveled to Australia, New Zealand, England, Scotland, Wales, and Ireland (which are countries in our world that are a long distance from where we live in California), and many places in the United States. We will be spending a lot of time looking at the world and U.S. maps in our classroom.

Before our first day of school, I would like you to talk with someone in your family about what is interesting to you and what you would like to learn more about. Last year we studied about plants, the human body, our solar system, and many other things. I'm quite interested in what you want to study about.

Please wear comfortable clothes to school. Every day we play outside and two days a week, we have P.E. Girls, it is best to wear tennis shoes and play clothes instead of dresses and fancy shoes. If you choose to wear a dress, please wear or bring a pair of shorts to wear underneath. We will be painting the first day of school also, so choose your clothes carefully.

If possible, please bring these supplies with you on Monday. We will talk about other supplies that you will need that day:

1 White Pillowcase: we will be making book bags out of these. The pillowcase can be new or used. If it is a used pillowcase, please make sure it is sturdy and clean as you will be carrying a book home for reading every night in it. If you have an extra pillowcase and want to bring it to share with a friend, please do. Some children may not have a pillowcase to bring. Thank you.

A Backpack: For carrying items between home and school every day.

2 Double-Pocket Folders: With pockets on the bottom, please, not on the side.

I look forward to seeing all of you on Monday, August 29th. I will be meeting you on the playground, so I will see you then. I hope you have lots of fun playing these last couple days of vacation. I can't wait to see your smiles and faces. See you Monday morning.

Love From Your First-Grade Teacher,

Janine Chappell Carr

PS. You may want to bring a morning snack to eat at recess time. Being in school for a full day takes some getting used to, and a morning snack helps a lot. I usually eat an orange, or banana, or a graham cracker.

APPENDIX 1–4
Before-School Family Letter

Dear Families,

I am writing to welcome you and your child to my first-grade classroom. This is my ninth year of teaching first- or second-grade children and every year I learn more by being with five-, six-, and seven-year-olds. I hope that you enjoyed reading my letter to and with your son or daughter. I like to connect with them before school starts so that I'm a bit more familiar to them.

During the first week of school your child will be taking home information about my program. This will help you understand my beliefs about teaching and learning with young children. The beginning of the year is hectic, with what seems like a lot of information to read, but I promise you, once the routine is set, everything evens out.

Although I don't require that you purchase the items I mentioned in your child's letter, if you are able to, it would be helpful. In my classroom newsletter, CONNECTIONS, I will inform you of additional needs as they come up. Although we will be making book bags for the classroom library books that go home every evening for reading, it is still helpful for your child to have a backpack for safe travels for folders, book bags, and other items.

The first day of school tends to be hectic. I want to explain the school's procedure so that you know what to expect when you bring your child. If you are dropping your child off at school between 8:00 and 8:20 A.M., s/he will line up in the picnic table area and the teacher on duty will walk everyone out to the playground at 8:20, where they will play until 8:35 when the bell rings. If you arrive after 8:20 A.M. and are dropping off your child, s/he will need to walk to the playground and will play until the bell rings. If you want to stay with your child on the playground, I will be outside at 8:20 with a sign with my name on it so that you know who I am and the children know where to assemble. Please introduce yourself to me if you choose to stay with your child.

Parent help is very important to our classroom during the year. The first need I have is help with sewing book bags if you are a person who has this skill. We tie-dye book bags the first week of school, so pillowcases need to be cut in half and sewn very quickly. If you are able to donate a set of 54" shoelaces, that would help us, too, as we use these as the drawstrings for the book bags. Assembling journals is also a huge project during the first couple of weeks of school, so please let me know if you have any spare time to help us. I will connect with you immediately.

Last, I look forward to a year of making memories, laughter and smiles, writing books, singing songs, being involved in projects, and reading books that are so good you just can't put them down. I simply look forward to a year of life and learning with new first-grade children and with you, their families.

Best Wishes From Your Child's First-Grade Teacher,

Janine Chappell Carr

APPENDIX 1–5
Family Help Survey

Dear Families,

The following list contains ways that you can help us in our class-room. Please read through the survey and check those items that you would like to help with. Please return this form to school as soon as possible. We need your help! This will be my first of many thanks to you.

Best Wishes,

Janine Chappell Carr

In-Class Help:
_____ Help with our individualized spelling program on Friday mornings

_____ Read with children

_____ Take pictures of class events and activities

_____ Supervise walking field trips or long-distance field trips

_____ Share a hobby or tell about your job

_____ Help children publish their writing work

_____ Type children's written work for final projects

_____ Assist with school celebrations

_____ Can be called on as needed for any type of classroom help

_____ Other:

At-Home Help:
_____ Cutting and sewing book bags out of pillowcases. We need help with this immediately!

_____ Assembling journals. I will show you how to prepare journals and will provide all of the supplies. We need help with this immediately!

_____ Type children's written work into final projects/books.
_____ Cover paperback books with contact paper for our class-
room library. I will show you how to do this and will pro-
vide all of the supplies.
_____ Assemble class-made bigbooks for our classroom library.
_____ Can be called on as needed for any type of home project
_____ Other:

•

Your Name: _____

Child's Name: _____

APPENDIX 1–6
Classroom Newsletter

CONNECTIONS

Room 12 Parent Newsletter..................................*September 5, 1995*
Bobier School Phone: 724-8501

Welcome to 2nd Grade in Room 12

Welcome back to school and to our second year together as a learning community. Already we have our first week behind us. It was wonderful to see all of the children last Monday with their new haircuts, school clothes, and shoelaces that are miles long--but not as long as they seemed on them last year as first graders! I hope that you had an enjoyable "August Vacation". When I asked the children if they had been reading during our month off, most of them said YES! I was very pleased to hear that. Even on our first day of school I had planned for our Quiet Reading time together, and the children settled into finding old favorites and new books in our classroom library very quickly. It feels very good to be back together again. As always, I am available if you have questions or concerns that need to be addressed. Our Note Books are being assembled by the Rowland Family, so they will be in service soon so that we have a book for our correspondence. I will get back to you promptly when you call or write a note. Welcome Back.

by Miss Lisa Pearce

School Supplies

Really, not a lot is needed for school supplies at this point in the school year. Most of the children have their 2-pocket folder for their School Folder that goes between home and school every day. I have provided a folder for the children who have not brought one of their own. **Pencils** are also needed at school by the children. Many are bringing several to school and keeping them in their cubby. The school has a 25 cent pencil machine that many children seem to enjoy buying pencils from, so that is a possibility also. Some of the children also like to have the following supplies, but they are not absolutely necessary as we do have sharing supplies at school:

Crayons
Markers
Colored Pencils
Eraser
Ruler
Glue Stick
Spiral Notebook for a Home Writing Notebook:
> (About 100 sheets, wide ruled--Also, some of the children are wanting
> to cover their writing notebook at school that I have provided with
> wrapping paper because that is what I do with mine, so you may
> hear a request from your second grader to bring wrapping paper to
> school for this reason!)

Dates to Remember...

Tuesday, September 5, 1995 - Green Track PTA Gift Wrap Fund-raiser Begins
> Watch for information in your child's School Folder.

Friday, September 8, 1995 - Grandparent's Lunch Day at School--If a
> Grandparent is attending, we would like them to arrive at our
> classroom by 11:30 a.m. as we leave for lunch at approximately
> 11:35 a.m. We look forward to seeing grandparents that day!

Friday, September 8, 1995 - Trumpet Club Book Orders Due

**Thursday, September 14, 1995 - Bobier's Back to School Night for
> Green Track**

See you soon at Back to School Night.
Warmly, Janine Chappell and Second Grade Children

APPENDIX 1–7
Daily Homework Letter

First Grade

For the first two weeks of the school year, I send home a daily homework letter so that both the children and their families understand what their responsibilities are. I also include information about what will be happening the next day in school as well as continuing to relate my expectations in regard to the completion of homework and supporting young learners at home. At the end of two weeks, I change to a weekly homework schedule that is sent home with the children on Monday (in their school folders) and returned by them on Friday. I like the daily homework letters as a way to "ease" children and parents into the responsibilities and routines of our classroom.

Monday's Homework
August 29, 1994

Dear First Graders,

You have two assignments tonight! This is the first assignment: I would like you to collect a few photographs of yourself and your family. Please bring up to five pictures. You will be sharing these with your friends in our classroom tomorrow, so it is important that you bring them to school. Please let your family know that we will need to keep them in our classroom for about two weeks.

The second assignment is to draw and write something about your first day of school. If you would like your family to help you write, that is fine too. Please bring both assignments back to school in your folder.

See you in the morning! You have computer and library time tomorrow afternoon.

Love,

Ms. Janine

Second Grade

Homework
Thursday, August 31, 1995

Dear Second Graders,

This is your last night of homework for the week. I can hear you cheering! It hasn't been too bad this week. I know, I know, it still feels like summer.

Tonight you have a classroom book to read in your book bag. Please read it carefully with someone in your family so that you are ready to read it to your partner tomorrow. Practice, practice so that you are a fine reader. **Remember to bring your book and book bag back to school tomorrow.**

The second item is to browse through the two new book club orders that are in your school folder and see if there is a book or two that you would like to order. There are lots of good books, but I recommend these books if you and your family are thinking about ordering:

Arthur's First Sleepover	Incredible Dinosaurs
Picnic at Mudsock Meadow	Reading Rainbow Library
Henry and Mudge	Trees
Spectacular Stone Soup	Chrysanthemum
Incredible Little Monsters	Swamp Angel
Timothy Goes to School	Frederick
Lyle, Lyle Crocodile	Jack and the Beanstalk
Another Mouse to Feed	Muggie Maggie
Miss Rumphius	The Fortune Tellers
*Arthur Adventure Club (Looks great!)	
The Great Kapok Tree	

If you and your family would like to order books from the Trumpet Club, please have your money and order back to school by Friday, September 8, 1995. The Scholastic book order will be going home with you when we receive it in the mail. Enjoy.

Love from your teacher,

Ms. Janine

APPENDIX 1–8
Weekly Homework Forms

My Weekly Homework
First Grade: Room 12

*Reminder: Prepare for your book talk or your sharing day if it is this week, please. Thank you.**

Name:_____

(Write your first and last name please. Thank you.)

Monday	Tuesday	Wednesday	Thursday
Nightly Reading: Read your book to someone in your family and ask them to sign your nightly reading folder. **Reading Journal:** Write a letter to me, someone in your family, or a character in the book you read. Drawing is optional! **Spelling Practice:** Children who have started spelling have information in their spelling books.	**Nightly Reading:** Same as Monday. **My Journal:** Read what I wrote to you in your journal and write back to me. Draw an illustration too. **Do your best work!** **Spelling Practice:** Use your Look, Say, Cover, Write, Check papers to practice your words.	**Nightly Reading:** Same as Monday. **I Can Read Anthology:** Read your anthology to someone in your family. **Math:** Your math assignment is: (Written by me each week). **Spelling Practice: Study hard: spelling check tomorrow.**	**Nightly Reading:** Same as Monday. **Family Journal:** Read your journal to someone in your family and ask them to write back to you. **Handwriting Work:** Complete your handwriting. **Write neatly!**
_____ (Parent Signature)	_____ (Parent Signature)	_____ (Parent Signature)	_____ (Parent Signature)
_____ (Your Signature)	_____ (Your Signature)	_____ (Your Signature)	_____ (Your Signature)

Weekly Homework: Room 12—Second Grade
September 18–22, 1996

Monday: 9-18
1. Nightly Reading: 20 min.
   • Families, please sign home/school
     reading logs
2. Spelling Practice

Tuesday: 9-19
1. Nightly Reading: 20 min.
   • Please sign reading logs
2. Spelling Practice
3. Journal to Ms. Janine

Wednesday: 9-20
1. Nightly Reading: 20 min.
   • Please sign reading logs
2. Spelling Practice
3. Math: Check school folder

Thursday: 9-21
1. Nightly Reading: 20 min.
2. Spelling Practice
   • Spelling check tomorrow
3. Family Journals   Weekly Attendance: _____
   • Families, please write back
     to the children in their
     journals. Please print!   A Note from Your Teacher:

Weekly Sign-Off:

_____

Child

_____

Parent

APPENDIX 1–9
Second-Grade Curriculum
1995–1996
Janine Chappell Carr—Room 12—Bobier Elementary

I expect second-grade children to:

- read for twenty minutes each evening; quiet read and partner read each day at school
- record books read in their reading log and evaluate themselves on their reading and listening; families sign book each evening
- write and respond in their three journals (journal to Janine, family, and math) each week
- keep a spelling list and practice consistently
- participate in whole-group unit study explorations, research, and projects
- complete one independent unit study and one small-group unit study
- write in their writing notebooks at least three times per week; children will complete formal writing projects throughout the year
- develop competence and confidence in math concepts and skills
- set goals, accept responsibility, and evaluate themselves as learners
- be compassionate, respectful, good thinkers, problem solvers, readers, writers, and learners

Throughout the year the children will be immersed in reading, writing, speaking, and listening experiences that relate to these expectations. Unit study themes will be based upon the interest of the children as well as the curriculum framework for second-grade children. The children will also be immersed in a wide variety of children's literature: fiction, nonfiction, biographies, autobiographies, chapter books that I read to them, and informational storybooks. Videos, guest speakers, and field trips will also be used to engage children in their learning experiences. Field trips tentatively planned for this year include: a theater production (Winnie-the-Pooh at the Escondido Performing Arts Center in January), the Wild Animal Park, the Natural History Museum (Magic School Bus exhibit), and the Palomar College Planetarium for our first unit study on the solar system.

In second grade, these are the major content themes that will be interwoven throughout the year:

Science: Energy and Patterns of Change
- Energy and matter exist in many forms and can be observed and measured.
- The sun, air, and water interact to create weather.
- All organisms go through life cycles.

Social Studies: People Who Make a Difference
- people who supply our needs
- our parents, grandparents, and ancestors, from long ago
- people from many cultures, now and long ago

Math: Strategies
- Number Relations: 1–100; strategies for memorizing addition and subtraction facts; multiplication and division concepts
- Data Analysis, Measurement, and Probability: collecting information, reporting information, measuring with a ruler, likely or unlikely projects in probability
- Patterns, Logical Thinking, Geometry, and Visual Thinking: How many ways can we do things?; investigation of sides, faces, and edges in geometry

Art
- Aesthetic Perception: becoming more aware of the visual and touch properties of artworks and other objects in our environment
- Creative Expression: creating art based on their imaginations and on places, activities, and situations they know
- Art Heritage: learning about the importance of art in different cultures and that artists can influence others through their art
- Aesthetic Valuing: reflecting on experiences with works of art and feeling free to express their preferences in art
  The children will be doing a lot of drawing in art this year, as it is a favorite area of exploration of mine also.

We would appreciate parent support with resources and materials throughout the year during our unit studies. Information and requests will appear in our CONNECTIONS newsletter. We welcome any expertise or area of interest that you would like to share with us throughout the year also.

I look forward to an exquisite year of learning together.

Janine Chappell Carr
Room 12; Bobier Elementary School
220 W. Bobier Drive
Vista, California 92083
School Phone: 724-8501

APPENDIX 2–1
Favorite Chapter Book Read-Alouds

Blume, Judy. 1980. *Super Fudge*. New York: Dell Publishing.

———. 1992. *Fudge*. New York: Dell Publishing

Butterworth, Oliver. 1956. *The Enormous Egg*. New York: Little, Brown and Company.

Cameron, Ann. 1988. *The Most Beautiful Place in the World*. New York: Alfred A. Knopf.

Caudill, Rebecca. 1966. *Did You Carry the Flag Today, Charley?* New York: Henry Holt and Company.

Cleary, Beverly. 1954. *Henry and Ribsy*. New York: William Morrow and Company.

———. 1965. *The Mouse and the Motorcycle*. New York: William Morrow and Company.

———. 1970. *Runaway Ralph*. New York: William Morrow and Company.

———. 1975. *Ramona the Brave*. New York: William Morrow and Company.

———. 1977. *Ramona and Her Father*. New York: William Morrow and Company.

———. 1979. *Ramona and Her Mother*. New York: William Morrow and Company.

Dahl, Roald. 1961. *James and the Giant Peach*. New York: Alfred A. Knopf.

———. 1964. *Charlie and the Chocolate Factory*. New York: Bantam.

———. 1985. *Fantastic Mr. Fox*. New York: Alfred A. Knopf.

Estes, Eleanor. 1944. *The Hundred Dresses*. New York: Harcourt Brace Jovanovich.

Gannett, Ruth Stiles. 1948. *My Father's Dragon*. New York: The Trumpet Club.

Gardiner, John Reynolds. 1980. *Stone Fox*. New York: Thomas Y. Crowell.

Grahame, Kenneth. 1938. *The Reluctant Dragon*. New York: The Trumpet Club.

Lowry, Lois. 1988. *All About Sam*. Boston: Houghton Mifflin Company.

McLachlan, Patricia. 1985. *Sarah, Plain and Tall*. New York: HarperCollins.

Park, Barbara. 1982. *Skinnybones*. New York: Alfred A. Knopf.

White, E. B. 1945. *Stuart Little*. New York: HarperCollins.

———. 1952. *Charlotte's Web*. New York: HarperCollins.

APPENDIX 3–1
Making Bigbooks

I have discovered that making my own class bigbooks with the children is an inexpensive way to build a collection of quality, well-loved bigbooks for my shared-reading time and classroom library. I use butcher paper for the pages of my bigbooks because it is usually in good supply at school. The steps for constructing a bigbook follow:

Step 1: Unroll a length of butcher paper (36" width).

Step 2: Fold the butcher paper in half so the width of the paper is now 18". I do this on the floor. It helps if a child or another adult assists.

Step 3: Cut the folded butcher paper into 14" lengths on a paper cutter. The finished pages will be 14 × 18". I double the pages because it increases durability and strength of the page.

Step 4: Punch two holes on the open (not folded) edge of the butcher paper. I do this because the folded edge is easier for the children to turn. Since I don't laminate the inside book pages (laminating film is an expensive resource), I often fold clear book-binding tape around the folded edges of the pages.

Step 5: Glue artwork and text to front and back covers and inside pages. I generally laminate the front and back covers.

Step 6: Assemble bigbook with two metal book rings.

Open Edge

Folded Edge

Hole punches for rings

Clear, book-binding tape folded around edge

APPENDIX 3–2
Favorite Bigbooks
Listed by Publisher

Nellie Edge Resources, Inc.
PO Box 12399
Salem, OR 97309-0399
1-800-523-4594

*Bigbooks include black-line masters for little books

Edge, Nellie. 1988. *I Can Read Colors.* Salem, OR: Nellie Edge Resources, Inc.

———. 1994. *I Can Spell Cat.* Salem, OR: Nellie Edge Resources, Inc.

Edge, Nellie, ed. 1988. *Songs and Rhymes for a Rainy Day.* Salem, OR: Nellie Edge Resources, Inc.

Edge, Nellie and Friends. 1994. *I Can Read More Colors.* Salem, OR: Nellie Edge Resources, Inc.

Hamilton, Arthur. 1988. *Sing A Rainbow.* Salem, OR: Nellie Edge Resources, Inc.

Paton, Sandy, and Caroline Paton (adapted by). 1988. *The Opposite Song.* Salem, OR: Nellie Edge Resources, Inc.

Pavelko, Virginia, and L.B. Scott (adapted by). *Five Little Speckled Frogs.* Salem, OR: Nellie Edge Resources, Inc.

Raffi and Debi Pike. 1988. *Goodnight, Irene.* Salem, OR: Nellie Edge Resources, Inc.

Reynolds, Malvina. 1988. *Magic Penny.* Salem, OR: Nellie Edge Resources, Inc.

Traditional. 1988. *Down by the Bay.* Salem, OR: Nellie Edge Resources, Inc.

———. 1988. *Finger Plays and Action Rhymes.* Salem, OR: Nellie Edge Resources, Inc.

———. 1988. *Five Little Pumpkins.* Salem, OR: Nellie Edge Resources, Inc.

———. 1988. *Jack-O-Faces.* Salem, OR: Nellie Edge Resources, Inc.

———. 1988. *Make Friends with Mother Goose.* Salem, OR: Nellie Edge Resources, Inc.

———. 1988. *Mary Wore Her Red Dress.* Salem, OR: Nellie Edge Resources, Inc.

———. 1988. *My Aunt Came Back.* Salem, OR: Nellie Edge Resources, Inc.

———. 1988. *Oh, A-Hunting We Will Go.* Salem, OR: Nellie Edge Resources, Inc.

———. 1988. *One Elephant Went Out to Play.* Salem, OR: Nellie Edge Resources, Inc.

———. 1988. *Over in the Meadow.* Salem, OR: Nellie Edge Resources, Inc.

———. 1988. *Peanut Butter and Jelly.* Salem, OR: Nellie Edge Resources, Inc.

———. 1988. *Teddy Bear, Teddy Bear.* Salem, OR: Nellie Edge Resources, Inc.

———. 1988. *The Wheels on the Bus.* Salem, OR: Nellie Edge Resources, Inc.

———. 1991. *Make Friends with Mother Goose Volume 2.* Salem, OR: Nellie Edge Resources, Inc.

———. 1994. *I Love the Mountains.* Salem, OR: Nellie Edge Resources, Inc.

———. 1994. *Playmate.* Salem, OR: Nellie Edge Resources, Inc.

Rigby
PO Box 797
Crystal Lake, IL 60039-0797
1-800-822-8661

Belanger, Claude. 1988. *The T-Shirt Song.* Crystal Lake, IL: Rigby.

———. 1997. *I Like the Rain.* Crystal Lake, IL: Rigby.

Davidson, Avelyn. 1990. *The Lion and the Mouse.* Crystal Lake, IL: Rigby.

Drew, David. 1987. *Tadpole Diary.* Crystal Lake, IL: Rigby.

———. 1988. *Hidden Animals.* Crystal Lake, IL: Rigby.

———. 1988. *Postcards from the Planets.* Crystal Lake, IL: Rigby.

———. 1989. *Animal Clues.* Crystal Lake, IL: Rigby.

———. 1989. *Caterpillar Diary.* Crystal Lake, IL: Rigby.

———. 1989. *The Life of a Butterfly.* Crystal Lake, IL: Rigby.

———. 1997. *Somewhere in the Universe.* Crystal Lake, IL: Rigby.

Kaufman, William, ed. 1991. *Catch Me the Moon, Daddy.* Crystal Lake, IL: Rigby.

Lawrence, Lucy. 1990. *Fly, Fly Witchy.* Crystal Lake, IL: Rigby.

———. 1997. *I Spy.* Crystal Lake, IL: Rigby.

Noonan, Diana. 1997. *A Crocodile to Tea.* Crystal Lake, IL: Rigby.

Parkes, Brenda. 1986. *Who's in the Shed?* Crystal Lake, IL: Rigby.

———. 1989. *A Farm's Not a Farm.* Crystal Lake, IL: Rigby.

———. 1990. *Rumpelstiltskin.* Crystal Lake, IL: Rigby.

———. 1990. *The Royal Dinner.* Crystal Lake, IL: Rigby.

Parkes, Brenda, and Judith Smith. 1986. *The Enormous Watermelon.* Crystal Lake, IL: Rigby.

———. 1986. *The Gingerbread Man*. Crystal Lake, IL: Rigby.

Powell, Debbie, ed. 1991. *Wiggles and Giggles: Poems to Share*. Crystal Lake, IL: Rigby.

Primary Science Alive Series: Life, Earth and Physical Sciences. Crystal Lake, IL: Rigby.

Smith, Judith, and Brenda Parkes. 1987. *Jack and the Beanstalk*. Crystal Lake, IL: Rigby.

———. 1989. *The Three Billy Goats Gruff*. Crystal Lake, IL: Rigby.

Scholastic

2931 E. McCarty Street
Jefferson City, MO 65101
1-800-724-6527

Ahlberg, Janet, and Allen Ahlberg. 1994. *Each Peach Pear Plum*. New York: Scholastic.

Asch, Frank. 1985. *Bear Shadow*. New York: Scholastic.

Bourgeois, Paulette. 1986. *Franklin in the Dark*. New York: Scholastic.

Brett, Jan. 1991. *The Mitten*. New York: Scholastic.

———. 1994. *City Mouse-Country Mouse and Two More Mouse Tales from Aesop*. New York: Scholastic.

Cameron, Polly. 1961. *"I Can't" Said the Ant*. New York: Scholastic.

Carle, Eric. 1997. *The Very Hungry Caterpillar*. New York: Scholastic.

Cole, Joanna, and Bruce Degen. *The Magic School Bus* Bigbooks. New York: Scholastic.

Cowcher, Helen. 1997. *Antarctica*. New York: Scholastic.

dePaola, Tomie. 1975. *Strega Nona*. New York: Scholastic.

Freeman, Don. 1996. *Corduroy*. New York: Scholastic.

Heller, Ruth. 1989. *Plants That Never Ever Bloom*. New York: Scholastic.

Hoberman, Mary Ann. 1998. *Miss Mary Mack*. New York: Scholastic.

Hutchins, Pat. 1996. *The Doorbell Rang*. New York: Scholastic.

Keats, Ezra Jack. 1995. *The Snowy Day*. New York: Scholastic.

MacMillan, Bruce. 1992. *Eating Fractions*. New York: Scholastic.

———. 1992. *Going on a Whale Watch*. New York: Scholastic.

McCloskey, Robert. 1992. *Make Way for Ducklings*. New York: Scholastic.

McQueen, Lucinda. 1989. *The Little Red Hen*. New York: Scholastic.

Rogers, Paul. 1997. *What Will the Weather Be Like Today?* New York: Scholastic.

Sendak, Maurice. 1991. *Chicken Soup with Rice*. New York: Scholastic.

Slobodkina, Esphyr. 1997. *Caps for Sale*. New York: Scholastic.

Ward, Cindy. 1991. *Cookie's Week*. New York: Scholastic.

Zimmerman, H. Warner. 1996. *Henny Penny*. New York: Scholastic.

The Wright Group
19201 120th Avenue NE
Bothell, WA 98011
1-800-523-2371

Cowley, Joy. *The Mrs. Wishy Washy Collection*. Bothell, WA: The Wright Group.

————. 1987. *The Cooking Pot*. Bothell, WA: The Wright Group.

————. 1996. *Grizzly and the Bumble-bee*. Bothell, WA: The Wright Group.

————. 1996. *Mr. Grump*. Bothell, WA: The Wright Group.

————. 1996. *Quack, Quack, Quack*. Bothell, WA: The Wright Group.

————. 1996. *Silly Billys*. Bothell, WA: The Wright Group.

————. 1996. *The Little Yellow Chicken*. Bothell, WA: The Wright Group.

————. 1998. *Hairy Bear*. Bothell, WA: The Wright Group.

————. 1998. *The Hungry Giant*. Bothell, WA: The Wright Group.

————. 1998. *The Meanies*. Bothell, WA: The Wright Group.

————. 1998. *When I Was Young: Joy Cowley*. Bothell, WA: The Wright Group.

Melser, June. 1998. *Sing a Song*. Bothell, WA: The Wright Group.

Melser, June (retold by). 1998. *Yes, Ma'am*. Bothell, WA: The Wright Group.

Sunshine Science Collection Level 1. Bothell, WA: The Wright Group.

APPENDIX 3–3
Favorite Poetry Books and Anthologies

The following is a list of favorite poetry books that I have in my classroom library. The titles that are starred (*) are resources that I consult often for creating large poetry charts for shared reading.

Behn, Harry. 1994. *Trees*. New York: Henry Holt & Company, Inc.

*Cullinan, Bernice, ed. 1996. *A Jar of Tiny Stars: Poems by NCTE Award Winning Poets; Children Select Their Favorite Poems*. Urbana, IL: NCTE.

*de Regniers, Beatrice Schenk, Eva Moore, Mary Michaels White, and Jan Carr, eds. 1988. *Sing a Song of Popcorn: Every Child's Book of Poems*. New York: Scholastic.

Farber, Norma, and Myra Cohn Livingston, eds. 1987. *These Small Stones*. New York: Harper & Row.

Farjeon, Eleanor. 1996. *Cats Sleep Anywhere*, illus. Anne Mortimer. New York: HarperCollins.

Florian, Douglas. 1994. *beast feast*. New York: The Trumpet Club.

Frost, Robert. 1978. *Stopping by Woods on a Snowy Evening*, illus. Susan Jeffers. New York: E. P. Dutton.

Goldstein, Bobbye S. (selected by). 1989. *Bear in Mind: A Book of Bear Poems*. New York: The Trumpet Club.

Greenfield, Eloise. 1978. *Honey, I Love*. New York: HarperCollins.

———. 1988. *Nathaniel Talking*. New York: Black Butterfly Children's Books.

Harwayne, Shelley, ed. 1994. *Jewels: Children's Play Rhymes*. Portsmouth, NH: Heinemann.

Heard, Georgia. 1992. *Creatures of the Earth, Sea, and Sky*. Honesdale, PA: Wordsong.

Hopkins, Lee Bennett (selected by). 1990. *Good Books, Good Times!* New York: The Trumpet Club.

———. 1991. *Happy Birthday*. New York: The Trumpet Club.

———. 1994. *April Bubbles Chocolate: An ABC of Poetry.* New York: Simon & Schuster Books for Young Readers.

———. 1995. *small talk: A Book of Short Poems.* San Diego: Harcourt Brace & Company.

*———. 1998. *Climb into My Lap: First Poems to Read Together.* New York: Simon & Schuster Books for Young Readers.

*Katz, Bobbi, ed. 1991. *Ghosts and Goosebumps: Poems to Chill Your Bones.* New York: Random House.

Kaufman, William, ed. 1991. *Catch Me the Moon, Daddy.* Crystal Lake, IL: Rigby.

*Kennedy, X. J., and Dorothy Kennedy, eds. 1992. *Talking Like the Rain: A Read-to-Me Book of Poems.* Boston: Little, Brown and Company.

Lee, Dennis. 1991. *The Ice Cream Store.* New York: Scholastic.

Livingston, Myra Cohn. 1985. *Worlds I Know and Other Poems.* New York: Atheneum.

———. 1987. *I Like You, If You Like Me: Poems of Friendship.* New York: Margaret K. McElderry Books.

———. 1994. *Animal, Vegetable, Mineral: Poems About Small Things.* New York: HarperCollins.

*Merriam, Eve. 1988. *You Be Good & I'll Be Night: Jump-on-the-Bed Poems.* New York: Morrow Junior Books.

Milne, A. A. 1924. *When We Were Very Young.* New York: Dell.

Myers, Walter Dean. 1994. *Brown Angels: An Album of Pictures and Verse.* New York: HarperCollins.

Nash, Ogden. 1991. *The Adventures of Isabel,* illus. James Marshall. New York: The Trumpet Club.

———. 1995. *The Tale of Custard the Dragon,* illus. Lynn Munsinger. Boston: Little, Brown and Company.

———. 1996. *Custard the Dragon and the Wicked Knight,* illus. Lynn Munsinger. Boston: Little, Brown and Company.

O'Neill, Mary. 1989. *Hailstones and Halibut Bones,* illus. John Wallner. New York: Doubleday.

Oppenheim, Joanne. 1967. *Have You Seen Trees?* New York: Scholastic.

*Prelutsky, Jack, ed. 1983. *The Random House Book of Poetry.* New York: Random House.

———. 1984. *New Kid on the Block.* New York: Greenwillow Books.

Rogasky, Barbara, ed. 1994. *Winter Poems.* New York: Scholastic.

Room 12 Student Poets. 1996. *Poems We'll Treasure Forever.* Vista, CA: Bobier Elementary School.

Rosen, Michael J., ed. 1992. *Home: A Collaboration of Thirty Distinguished Authors and Illustrators of Children's Books to Aid the Homeless.* New York: HarperCollins.

————. 1995. *A Spider Bought a Bicycle and Other Poems for Young Children.* Selected by Michael Rosen. New York: Kingfisher.

Rosetti, Christina. 1991. *Fly Away, Fly Away Over the Sea.* New York: North-South Books.

Stevenson, Robert Louis. 1992. *Leaves from a Child's Garden of Verses,* illus. Donna Green. New York: Smithmark.

*Szekers, Cyndy, ed. 1987. *Cyndy Szekeres' Book of Poems.* New York: Western Publishing Company.

Thayer, Ernest Lawrence. 1988. *Casey at the Bat*, illus. Patricia Polacco. New York: Scholastic.

Viorst, Judith. 1995. *Sad Underwear and Other Complications*. New York: Atheneum Books for Young Readers.

APPENDIX 3–4
Favorite Children's Literature for a Primary Classroom Library

The following is a list of favorite children's literature that I have in my classroom library. The list is a compilation of my favorite books and the children's favorite titles. This list does not include many of the emergent or early reading titles in my classroom library (e.g., published by The Wright Group or Rigby) as I generally don't consider those titles as favorites, merely "stepping stone books" for young readers. (Irene C. Fountas and Gay Su Pinnell's book, *Guided Reading*, is a wonderful resource for emergent and early titles.) The titles that are starred (*) are my favorite read-alouds. If you are starting or adding to your own classroom library, this list is intended as a resource for you. Of course I believe that a classroom library full of "real books" is far better for young readers than the limited selections found in expensive basal anthologies.

FICTION

Aardema, Verna. 1975. *Why Mosquitoes Buzz in People's Ears.* New York: Dial Press.

———. 1977. *Who's in Rabbit's House?* New York: Dial Books.

———. 1981. *Bringing the Rain to Kapiti Plain.* New York: Scholastic.

Ackerman, Karen. 1988. *Song and Dance Man.* New York: Scholastic.

Ada, Alma Flor. 1994. *Dear Peter Rabbit.* New York: Atheneum Books.

Ahlberg, Janet, and Allan Ahlberg. 1986. *The Jolly Postman.* Boston: Little, Brown and Company.

———. 1991. *The Jolly Christmas Postman.* Boston: Little, Brown and Company.

*Alexander, Lloyd. 1992. *The Fortune Tellers.* New York: Dutton's Children's Books.

Allard, Harry. *The Stupids* series. New York: The Trumpet Club.

———. *Miss Nelson* series. Boston: Houghton Mifflin Company.

Aliki. 1968. *Hush Little Baby.* New York: Simon & Schuster.

*———. 1982. *We Are Best Friends*. New York: The Trumpet Club.

———. 1986. *Go Tell Aunt Rhody*. New York: Simon and Schuster.

Aragon, Jane Chelsea. 1989. *Salt Hands*. New York: E. P. Dutton.

Asch, Frank. 1979. *Popcorn*. New York: The Trumpet Club.

———. 1981. *Just Like Daddy*. New York: Simon and Schuster.

———. 1982. *Happy Birthday, Moon*. Englewood Cliffs, NJ: Prentice-Hall, Inc.

———. 1984. *Skyfire*. New York: Scholastic.

*———. 1988. *Bear Shadow*. New York: Scholastic.

Auch, Mary Jane. 1992. *The Easter Egg Farm*. New York: The Trumpet Club.

*———. 1993. *Peeping Beauty*. New York: The Trumpet Club.

Aylesworth, Jim. 1990. *The Completed Hickory Dickory Dock*. New York: Atheneum.

Baker, Alan. 1990. *Two Tiny Mice*. New York: Scholastic.

Baker, Keith. 1990. *Who Is the Beast?* New York: The Trumpet Club.

———. 1991. *Hide and Snake*. New York: The Trumpet Club.

Barrett, Judi. 1970. *Animals Should Definitely Not Wear Clothing*. New York: Scholastic.

———. 1978. *Cloudy with a Chance of Meatballs*. New York: Scholastic.

Bayer, Jane. 1984. *A My Name Is Alice*. New York: The Trumpet Club.

*Baylor, Byrd. 1978. *The Other Way to Listen*. New York: Charles Scribner's Sons.

*———. 1994. *The Table Where Rich People Sit*. New York: Charles Scribner's Sons.

Bemelmans, Ludwig. *Madeline* series. New York: Scholastic.

Berger, Barbara. 1984. *Grandfather Twilight*. New York: Philomel Books.

———. 1994. *The Jewel Heart*. New York: Philomel Books.

*Birdseye, Tom. 1988. *Airmail to the Moon*. New York: The Trumpet Club.

Blaine, Marge. 1975. *The Terrible Thing That Happened at Our House*. New York: Scholastic.

Borden, Louise. 1989. *Caps, Hats, Socks, and Mittens*. New York: Scholastic.

Bottner, Barbara. 1992. *Bootsie Barker Bites*. New York: The Trumpet Club.

Bourgeois, Paulette. *Franklin* series. New York: Scholastic.

*———. 1986. *Franklin in the Dark*. New York: Scholastic.

*———. 1996. *Franklin and the Tooth Fairy*. New York: Scholastic.

Brandenberg, Franz. 1976. *I Wish I Was Sick, Too!* New York: William Morrow & Co.

Brett, Jan. 1985. *Annie and the Wild Animals*. New York: The Trumpet Club.

———. 1986. *The Twelve Days of Christmas*. New York: The Trumpet Club.

———. 1988. *The First Dog*. New York: The Trumpet Club.

———. 1989. *The Mitten*. New York: G.P. Putnam's Sons.

———. 1994. *Town Mouse Country Mouse*. New York: Scholastic.

Bridwell, Norman. *Clifford* series. New York: Scholastic.

———. 1992. *The Witch Goes to School*. New York: Scholastic.

Briggs, Raymond. 1970. *Jim and the Beanstalk*. New York: Sandcastle Books.

———. 1978. *The Snowman*. New York: The Trumpet Club.

*———. 1994. *The Bear*. New York: Random House Books for Young Readers.

Brown, Anthony. 1988. *I Like Books*. New York: The Trumpet Club.

———. 1989. *Things I Like*. New York: The Trumpet Club.

Brown, Marc. *Arthur and D.W.* series. Boston: Little, Brown and Company.

*———. 1980. *Arthur's Valentine*. Boston: Little, Brown and Company.

*———. 1993. *Arthur's New Puppy*. Boston: Little, Brown and Company.

———. 1995. *D. W. the Picky Eater*. Boston: Little, Brown and Company.

Brown, Margaret Wise. 1942. *The Runaway Bunny*. New York: The Trumpet Club.

———. 1947. *Goodnight Moon*. New York: Scholastic.

———. 1949. *The Important Book*. New York: The Trumpet Club.

———. 1989. *Big Red Barn*. New York: Scholastic.

Brown, Ruth. 1981. *A Dark Dark Tale*. New York: Dial Books.

———. 1988. *Ladybug, Ladybug*. New York: Dutton Children's Books.

Bunting, Eve. 1989. *The Wednesday Surprise*. New York: The Trumpet Club.

———. 1990. *The Wall*. New York: The Trumpet Club.

*———. 1991. *Night Tree*. New York: The Trumpet Club.

———. 1994. *Smoky Night*. New York: Harcout Brace & Company.

*———. 1996. *Secret Place*. New York: Clarion Books.

Burningham, John. 1987. *John Patrick Norman McHennessy—The Boy Who Was Always Late*. New York: The Trumpet Club.

———. 1989. *Hey! Get Off Our Train*. New York: The Trumpet Club.

*Burton, Virginia Lee. 1939. *Mike Mulligan and His Steam Shovel*. Boston: Houghton Mifflin.

———. 1943. *Katy and the Big Snow*. New York: Scholastic.

*Caines, Jeannette. 1982. *Just Us Women*. New York: Harper & Row.

Calmenson, Stephanie. 1991. *Dinner at the Panda Palace*. New York: Harper-Collins.

Campbell, Rod. 1982. *Dear Zoo*. New York: Penguin Books.

———. 1983. *Oh Dear!* London: Pan Books.

Carle, Eric. 1968. *1, 2, 3 to the Zoo*. New York: The Trumpet Club.

———. 1968. *The Very Hungry Caterpillar*. New York: Philomel Books.

———. 1972. *Rooster's Off to See the World*. New York: Scholastic.

———. 1977. *The Grouchy Ladybug*. New York: Harper & Row.

———. 1984. *The Very Busy Spider*. New York: Philomel Books.

*———. 1986. *Papa, Please Get Me the Moon*. New York: Scholastic.

———. 1990. *Pancakes, Pancakes!* New York: Scholastic.

Carlstrom, Nancy. *Jesse Bear* series. New York: Scholastic.

———. 1986. *Jesse Bear, What Will You Wear?* New York: Scholastic.

———. 1992. *Northern Lullaby*. New York: The Trumpet Club.

Carrick, Carol. 1974. *Lost in the Storm*. New York: The Trumpet Club.

———. 1983. *Patrick's Dinosaurs*. New York: Clarion Books

———. 1986. *What Happened to Patrick's Dinosaurs?* New York: Clarion Books.

Charlip, Remy. 1964. *Fortunately*. New York: Four Winds Press.

Cherry, Lynne. 1990. *The Great Kapok Tree*. New York: The Trumpet Club.

Christelow, Eileen (retold by). 1990. *Five Little Monkeys Jumping on the Bed*. New York: Clarion Books.

*———. 1992. *Don't Wake Up Mama*. Boston: Houghton Mifflin Company.

Cleveland, David. 1978. *The April Rabbits*. New York: Scholastic.

Clifton, Lucille. 1971. *Everett Anderson's Christmas Coming*. New York: The Trumpet Club.

———. 1978. *Everett Anderson's Nine Month Long*. New York: The Trumpet Club.

*Cole, Joanna. 1986. *Bony-Legs*. New York: Scholastic.

Cole, Joanna, and Stephanie Calmenson. 1990. *Ready . . . Set . . . Read!* New York: Doubleday.

———. 1993. *Six Sick Sheep: 101 Tongue Twisters*. New York: Scholastic.

Cole, Joanna, and Bruce Degen. 1992. *The Magic School Bus on the Ocean Floor*. New York: Scholastic.

Coleman, Michael. 1994. *Lazy Ozzie*. Auburn, ME: Flying Frog Publishing.

*Coleridge, Ann. 1983. *The Friends of Emily Culpepper*. New York: Putnam Publishing Group.

*Collins, Judy. 1968. *My Father*. Boston: Little, Brown and Company.

*Cooney, Barbara. 1982. *Miss Rumphius*. New York: The Trumpet Club.

———. 1988. *Island Boy*. New York: The Trumpet Club.

———. 1994. *Only Opal*. New York: The Trumpet Club.

Cooper, Floyd. 1998. *Cumbayah*. New York: Morrow Junior Books.

Cowen-Fletcher, Jane. 1993. *Mama Zooms*. New York: Scholastic.

Cowley, Joy. "The Sunshine Series." Bothell, WA: The Wright Group.

———. 1996. *Boring Old Bed*. In "The Sunshine Series." Bothell, WA: The Wright Group.

———. 1996. *Duck and Hen*. In "The Sunshine Series." Bothell, WA: The Wright Group.

———. 1996. *Mrs. Muddle's Mud-Puddle*. In "The Sunshine Series." Bothell, WA: The Wright Group.

———. 1996. *My Sloppy Tiger*. In "The Sunshine Series." Bothell, WA: The Wright Group.

———. 1996. *Nowhere and Nothing*. In "The Sunshine Series." Bothell, WA: The Wright Group.

———. 1996. *Our Granny*. In "The Sunshine Series." Bothell, WA: The Wright Group.

———. 1996. *Ratty-Tatty*. In "The Sunshine Series." Bothell, WA: The Wright Group.

———. 1996. *Uncle Buncle's House*. In "The Sunshine Series." Bothell, WA: The Wright Group.

———. 1996. *The Monster's Party*. In "The Story Box." Bothell, WA: The Wright Group.

Crews, Donald. 1978. *Freight Train*. New York: Scholastic.

———. 1984. *School Bus*. New York: Scholastic.

———. 1991. *Bigmama's*. New York: The Trumpet Club.

———. 1992. *Shortcut*. New York: The Trumpet Club.

*Cutler, Jane. 1993. *Darcy and Gran Don't Like Babies*. New York: Scholastic.

*Cuyler, Margery. 1991. *That's Good! That's Bad!* New York: Henry Holt and Company.

Davidson, Avelyn. 1993. *Ten Little Caterpillars*. Crystal Lake, IL: Rigby.

Day, Alexandra. *Carl* series. New York: Farrar, Straus, Giroux.

Dayrell, Elphinstone. 1968. *Why the Sun and the Moon Live in the Sky*. New York: Scholastic.

Degen, Bruce. 1983. *Jamberry*. New York: Scholastic.

dePaola, Tomie. *Strega Nona* series. New York: Scholastic.

———. 1978. *Bill and Pete*. New York: Putnam.

———. 1979. *Big Anthony and the Magic Ring*. New York: Harcourt Brace Jovanovich.

———. 1981. *The Friendly Beasts*. New York: G. P. Putnam's Sons.

———. 1982. *Strega Nona's Magic Lessons*. New York: Harcourt Brace Jovanovich.

———. 1983. *The Legend of the Bluebonnet*. New York: Scholastic.

———. 1984. *The Mysterious Giant of Barletta*. New York: Harcourt Brace Jovanovich.

———. 1985. *Tomie dePaola's Mother Goose*. New York: G. P. Putnam's Sons.

———. 1987. *Bill and Pete Go Down the Nile*. New York: G. P. Putnam's Sons.

———. 1988. *The Legend of the Indian Paintbrush*. New York: Scholastic.

———. 1989. *The Art Lesson*. New York: The Trumpet Club.

———. 1992. *Jingle the Christmas Clown*. New York: G. P. Putnam's Sons.

Dodd, Dayle Ann. 1992. *The Color Box*. Boston: Little, Brown and Company.

Dodd, Lynley. 1983. *Hairy Maclary from Donaldson's Dairy*. New York: The Trumpet Club.

Domanska, Janina. 1985. *Busy Monday Morning*. New York: Greenwillow Books.

Dorros, Arthur. 1991. *Abuela*. New York: The Trumpet Club.

Ehlert, Lois. 1992. *Moon Rope Un Lazo a la Luna*. New York: The Trumpet Club.

*Emberly, Michael. 1990. *Ruby*. Boston: Little, Brown and Company.

*Everitt, Betsy. 1992. *Mean Soup*. San Diego: Harcourt Brace & Company.

Faulkner, Keith. 1988. *The Snake's Mistake*. Los Angeles: Price, Stern, Sloan, Inc.

Flack, Marjorie. 1932. *Ask Mr. Bear*. New York: The Trumpet Club.

———. 1933. *The Story About Ping*. New York: Scholastic.

Fleming, Denise. 1991. *In the Tall, Tall Grass*. New York: Henry Holt and Company.

———. 1993. *In the Small, Small Pond*. New York: Scholastic.

———. 1994. *Barnyard Banter*. New York: Scholastic.

Fox, Mem. 1983. *Possum Magic*. New York: Scholastic.

*———. 1984. *Wilfred Gordon McDonald Partridge*. New York: Kane/Miller Book Publishers.

———. 1986. *Hattie and the Fox*. New York: The Trumpet Club.

*———. 1988. *Koala Lou*. New York: Harcourt Brace & Company.

———. 1989. *Night Noises*. New York: Harcourt Brace Jovanovich.

———. 1989. *Shoes from Grandpa*. New York: Orchard Books.

*———. 1994. *Tough Boris*. New York: Harcourt Brace & Company.

———. 1995. *Wombat Divine*. New York: Scholastic.

———. 1996. *Zoo-Looking*. Greenvale, NY: Mondo Publishing.

Freeman, Don. 1964. *Dandelion*. New York: Puffin Books.

———. 1978. *A Pocket for Corduroy*. New York: Puffin Books.

French, Fiona. 1991. *Anancy and Mr. Dry-Bone*. New York: Scholastic.

Gackenbach, Dick. 1977. *Harry and the Terrible Whatzit*. New York: Scholastic.

Gag, Wanda. 1928. *Millions of Cats*. New York: Scholastic.

Galdone, Paul. 1986. *Over in the Meadow*. New York: The Trumpet Club.

———. 1987. *Three Blind Mice*. New York: The Trumpet Club.

———. 1998. *The Three Billy Goats Gruff*. New York: Houghton Mifflin.

Gerstein, Mordicai. 1984. *Roll Over!* New York: Crown Publishers, Inc.

Gilman, Phoebe. 1992. *Something from Nothing*. New York: Scholastic.

Ginsburg, Mirra. 1974. *Mushroom in the Rain*. New York: Collier Books.

———. 1981. *Where Does the Sun Go at Night?* New York: Mulberry Books.

Goble, Paul. 1978. *The Girl Who Loved Wild Horses*. New York: Scholastic.

Goode, Diane. 1991. *Where's Our Mama?* New York: Scholastic.

*Graham, Margaret B. 1967. *Be Nice to Spiders*. New York: HarperCollins Children's Books.

Gunson, Christopher. 1995. *Over on the Farm*. New York: Scholastic.

Guthrie, Woody. 1998. *This Land is Your Land*. Paintings by Kathy Jakobsen. Boston: Little, Brown and Company.

Hale, Sara Josepha. 1984. *Mary Had a Little Lamb*, illus. Tomie dePaola. New York: The Trumpet Club.

———. 1990. *Mary Had a Little Lamb*, photo-illus. Bruce McMillan. New York: Scholastic.

Hawkins, Colin, and Jacqui Hawkins. 1987. *I Know an Old Lady Who Swallowed a Fly*. London: Little Mammoth.

———. 1989. *Old Mother Hubbard*. London: Picadilly Press.

Henkes, Kevin. 1987. *Sheila Rae, the Brave*. New York: Scholastic.

———. 1989. *Jessica*. New York: Scholastic.

———. 1991. *Chrysanthemum*. New York: Mulberry Books.

*———. 1993. *Owen*. New York: Greenwillow Books.

*———. 1996. *Lilly's Purple Plastic Purse*. New York: Greenwillow Books.

Hennessy, B. G. 1989. *A, B, C, D, Tummy, Toes, Hands, Knees*. New York: The Trumpet Club.

Herriot, James. 1986. *The Christmas Day Kitten*. New York: St. Martin's Press.

Hill, Eric. *Spot* series. New York: G. P. Putnam's Sons.

Hoban, Lillian. 1986. *The Case of the Two Masked Robbers*. New York: HarperCollins Children's Books.

Hoban, Russell. *Frances* series. New York: Scholastic.

*———. 1969. *Best Friends for Frances*. New York: Scholastic.

Hoberman, Mary Ann. 1978. *A House Is a House for Me*. New York: The Viking Press.

Hoffman, Mary. 1991. *Amazing Grace*. New York: Scholastic.

Holabird, Katharine. *Angelina* series. New York: The Trumpet Club.

Horton, Barbara Savadge. 1992. *What Comes in Spring?* New York: The Trumpet Club.

Houston, Gloria. 1988. *The Year of the Perfect Christmas Tree*. New York: Dial Books.

Huck, Charlotte. 1989. *Princess Furball*. New York: Scholastic.

Hurd, Thacher. 1983. *Mystery on the Docks*. New York: The Trumpet Club.

*———. 1984. *Mama Don't Allow*. New York: Harper & Row.

Hutchins, Pat. 1968. *Rosie's Walk*. New York: Scholastic.

———. 1970. *Clocks and More Clocks*. New York: Scholastic.

———. 1972. *Good-Night, Owl!* New York: Aladdin Books.

———. 1976. *Don't Forget the Bacon*. New York: Mulberry Books.

———. 1985. *The Very Worst Monster*. New York: Scholastic.

Hyman, Trina Schart. 1983. *Little Red Riding Hood.* New York: Holiday House.

Isaacs, Anne. 1994. *Swamp Angel.* New York: The Trumpet Club.

Ivimey, John W. 1990. *Three Blind Mice.* Boston: Little, Brown and Company.

Jensen, Helen Zane. 1985. *When Panda Came to Our House.* New York: Dial Books.

Johnston, Tony. 1985. *The Quilt Story.* New York: G. P. Putnam's Sons.

Jones, Carol. 1990. *This Old Man.* Boston: Houghton Mifflin Company.

Kalan, Robert. 1978. *Rain.* New York: Mulberry Books.

Keats, Ezra Jack. 1962. *The Snowy Day.* New York: Viking Press.

———. 1964. *Whistle for Willie.* New York: Puffin Books.

Keller, Holly. 1988. *Geraldine's Big Snow.* New York: Scholastic.

Kellogg, Steven. 1971. *Can I Keep Him?* New York: Dial Books.

———. 1972. *Won't Somebody Play with Me?* New York: Dial Books.

———. 1974. *The Mystery of the Missing Red Mitten.* New York: Dial Books.

———. 1976. *Much Bigger Than Martin.* New York: The Trumpet Club.

———. 1977. *The Mysterious Tadpole.* New York: Dial Books.

———. 1981. *A Rose for Pinkerton.* New York: Dial Books.

———. 1986. *Pecos Bill.* New York: Scholastic.

———. 1991. *Jack and the Beanstalk.* New York: Morrow Junior Books.

Kent, Jack. 1984. *Joey.* New York: The Trumpet Club.

———. 1985. *Joey Runs Away.* New York: The Trumpet Club.

Kesselman, Wendy. 1980. *Emma.* New York: Dell Publishing.

Kovalski, Maryann. 1987. *The Wheels on the Bus.* New York: The Trumpet Club.

*———. 1990. *Pizza for Breakfast.* New York: Morrow Junior Books.

Kraus, Robert. 1970. *Whose Mouse Are You?* New York: Scholastic.

———. 1971. *Leo the Late Bloomer.* New York: Windmill Books.

———. 1980. *Another Mouse to Feed.* New York: The Trumpet Club.

———. 1985. *How Spider Saved Valentine's Day.* New York: Scholastic.

*Krensky, Stephen. 1995. *The Three Blind Mice Mystery.* New York: Bantam Doubleday Dell.

Kroll, Steven. 1984. *The Biggest Pumpkin Ever.* New York: Scholastic.

———. 1989. *Newsman Ned and the Broken Rules.* New York: Scholastic.

———. 1991. *Princess Abigail and the Wonderful Hat.* New York: Holiday House.

Lear, Edward. 1991. *The Owl and the Pussycat,* illus. by Jan Brett. New York: G. P. Putnam's Sons.

*Leavy, Una. 1994. *Harry's Stormy Night.* New York: Margaret K. McElderry Books.

Lester, Helen. 1986. *A Porcupine Named Fluffy.* New York: The Trumpet Club.

*———. 1987. *Pookins Gets Her Way*. New York: The Trumpet Club.

———. 1988. *Tacky the Penguin*. New York: The Trumpet Club.

———. 1992. *Me First*. Boston: Houghton Mifflin Company.

———. 1996. *Princess Penelope's Parrot*. Boston: Houghton Mifflin Company.

Lester, Julius. 1994. *John Henry*. New York: Scholastic.

Levinson, Riki. 1986. *I Go with My Family to Grandma's*. New York: The Trumpet Club.

Lindbergh, Reeve. 1987. *The Midnight Farm*. New York: Dial Books.

Lionni, Leo. 1960. *Inch by Inch*. New York: Scholastic.

———. 1967. *Frederick*. New York: The Trumpet Club.

———. 1968. *The Alphabet Tree*. New York: The Trumpet Club.

———. 1973. *Swimmy*. New York: Pantheon Books.

———. 1974. *Alexander and the Wind-Up Mouse*. New York: Pantheon Books.

*———. 1991. *Matthew's Dream*. New York: The Trumpet Club.

———. 1992. *A Busy Year*. New York: Scholastic.

Little, Jean. 1991. *Once Upon a Golden Apple*. New York: Viking.

Lobel, Arnold. *Frog and Toad* series. New York: Scholastic.

———. 1975. *Owl at Home*. New York: Harper & Row.

———. 1977. *Mouse Soup*. New York: Scholastic.

———. 1980. *Fables*. New York: Scholastic.

———. 1982. *Ming Lo Moves the Mountain*. New York: Scholastic.

———. 1985. *Days with Frog and Toad*. New York: HarperCollins Children's Books.

Long, Sylvia. 1997. *Hush Little Baby*. San Francisco: Chronicle Books.

MacLachlan, Patricia. 1994. *All the Places to Love*. New York: HarperCollins Publishers.

Marshall, James. *George and Martha* series. New York: The Trumpet Club.

*———. 1978. *George and Martha: One Fine Day*. Boston: Houghton Mifflin Company.

———. 1988. *Goldilocks and the Three Bears*. New York: Dial Books.

———. 1991. *Old Mother Hubbard*. New York: Farrar, Straus & Giroux.

———. 1994. *Hansel and Gretel*. New York: Puffin Books.

———. 1996. *The Three Little Pigs*. New York: Puffin Books.

Martin, Jr. Bill. 1967. *Brown Bear, Brown Bear, What Do You See?* New York: Henry Holt and Company.

Martin Jr., Bill, and John Archambault. 1985. *The Ghost-Eye Tree*. New York: Scholastic.

———. 1985. *Here Are My Hands*. New York: Henry Holt and Company.

Martin, Rafe. 1992. *The Rough-Face Girl*. New York: Scholastic.

Marzollo, Jean. 1990. *Pretend You're a Cat*. New York: The Trumpet Club.

———. 1997. *Home Sweet Home*. New York: HarperCollins.

Mayer, Mercer. 1968. *If I Had a Gorilla*. New York: Rainbird Press.

———. 1968. *Terrible Troll*. New York: Dial Press.

———. 1968. *There's a Nightmare in My Closet*. New York: Dial Press.

———. 1973. *What Do You Do with a Kangaroo?* New York: Scholastic.

Mazer, Anne. 1991. *The Salamander Room*. New York: The Trumpet Club.

McBratney, Sam. 1994. *Guess How Much I Love You*. Cambridge, MA: Candlewick Press.

———. 1996. *The Dark at the Top of the Stairs*. Cambridge, MA: Candlewick Press.

McCarthy, Bobette. 1987. *Buffalo Girls*. New York: Crown Publishers, Inc.

*McCloskey, Robert. 1941. *Make Way for Ducklings*. New York: Penguin Group.

———. 1948. *Blueberries for Sal*. New York: Puffin Books.

McCully, Emily Arnold. 1992. *Mirette on the High Wire*. New York: Scholastic.

McDermott, Gerald. 1972. *Anansi the Spider*. New York: Scholastic.

McKissack, Patricia C. 1988. *Mirandy and Brother Wind*. New York: The Trumpet Club.

McPhail, David. 1985. *Emma's Pet*. New York: Scholastic.

———. 1990. *Lost!* New York: The Trumpet Club.

Miles, Miska. 1971. *Annie and the Old One*. New York: The Trumpet Club.

Miller, Edna. *Mousekin* series. New York: Simon & Schuster.

Minarik, Else Holmelund. *Little Bear* series. New York: Harper & Row.

Mitchell, Joni. 1992. *Both Sides Now*. New York: Scholastic.

Mitchell, Margaree King. 1993. *Uncle Jed's Barbershop*. New York: Scholastic.

Mosel, Arlene. 1968. *Tikki Tikki Tembo*. New York: Scholastic.

Moss, Thylias. 1993. *I Want to Be*. New York: Puffin Books.

Munsch, Robert. 1985. *Thomas' Snowsuit*. Toronto: Annick Press Ltd.

———. 1986. *Love You Forever*. Scarborough, Ontario, Canada: Firefly Books Ltd.

*Murphy, Jill. 1987. *All in One Piece*. New York: G. P. Putnam's Sons.

———. 1993. *A Quiet Night In*. Cambridge, MA: Candlewick Press.

———. 1995. *Five Minutes' Peace*. Cambridge, MA: Candlewick Press.

*Newton, Laura P. 1986. *Me and My Aunts*. Niles, IL: Albert Whitman & Company.

Noble, Trinka Hakes. 1980. *The Day Jimmy's Boa Ate the Wash*. New York: Scholastic.

———. 1989. *Jimmy's Boa and the Big Birthday Splash*. New York: The Trumpet Club.

Numeroff, Laura Joffe. 1991. *If You Give a Moose a Muffin*. New York: Scholastic.

———. 1993. *Dogs Don't Wear Sneakers*. New York: Aladdin Paperbacks.

———. 1995. *If You Give a Mouse a Cookie*. New York: HarperCollins Children's Books.

*Nye, Naomi Shihab. 1997. *Lullaby Raft*. New York: Simon and Schuster.

O'Keefe, Susan Heyboer. 1989. *One Hungry Monster*. New York: Scholastic.

Opie, Iona, ed. 1996. *My Very First Mother Goose*. Cambridge, MA: Candlewick Press.

*Palatini, Margie. 1995. *Piggie Pie*. New York: Clarion Books.

Pare, Roger. 1983. *A Friend Like You*. Toronto: Annick Press.

Parish, Peggy. *Amelia Bedelia* series. New York: HarperTrophy.

———. 1963. *Amelia Bedelia*. New York: HarperTrophy.

Parker, John. 1988. *I Love Spiders*. New York: Scholastic.

Parkes, Brenda, and Judith Smith (retold by). 1986. *The Gingerbread Man*. Crystal Lake, IL: Rigby.

———. 1986. *The Little Red Hen*. Crystal Lake, IL: Rigby.

Parkinson, Kathy. 1988. *The Farmer in the Dell*. Niles, IL: Albert Whitman & Company.

*Paterson, Katherine. 1992. *The King's Equal*. New York: HarperCollins Children's Books.

Payne, Emmy. 1944. *Katy No-Pocket*. Boston: Houghton Mifflin Company.

Polacco, Patricia. 1988. *The Keeping Quilt*. New York: Simon and Schuster.

———. 1988. *Rechenka's Eggs*. New York: Scholastic.

———. 1990. *Just Plain Fancy*. New York: The Trumpet Club.

———. 1992. *Picnic at Mudsock Meadow*. New York: The Trumpet Club.

———. 1992. *Mrs. Katz and Tush*. New York: Dell Publishing.

———. 1992. *Chicken Sunday*. New York: Scholastic.

Potter, Beatrix. 1893. *The Tale of Peter Rabbit*. New York: Frederick Warne.

———. 1917. *Appley Dapply's Nursery Rhymes*. New York: Penguin Books.

*Pulver, Robin. 1992. *Nobody's Mother Is in Second Grade*. New York: The Trumpet Club.

Raffi. *Songs to Read* series. New York: Crown Publishers, Inc.

———. 1988. *The Raffi Christmas Treasury*. New York: Crown Publishers, Inc.

*Raschka, Chris. 1998. *Simple Gifts*. New York: Henry Holt and Company.

Rey, H. A. *Curious George* series. New York: Scholastic.

Robart, Rose. 1986. *The Cake That Mack Ate*. Boston: Little, Brown and Company.

Roop, Peter, and Connie Roop. 1985. *Keep the Lights Burning, Abbie*. New York: Scholastic.

Rounds, Glen. 1989. *Old MacDonald Had a Farm*. New York: Holiday House.

Rylant, Cynthia. *Poppleton* series. New York: Scholastic.

————. 1984. *This Year's Garden*. New York: Aladdin Books.

————. 1985. *The Relatives Came*. New York: Scholastic.

*————. 1996. *The Old Woman Who Named Things*. San Diego: Harcourt, Brace & Company.

————. *Henry and Mudge* series. New York: Scholastic.

————. 1987. *Henry and Mudge in Puddle Trouble*. New York: Aladdin Paperbacks.

————. 1987. *Henry and Mudge: The First Book*. New York: Aladdin Paperbacks.

————. 1989. *Henry and Mudge Get the Cold Shivers*. New York: Aladdin Paperbacks.

Sacher, Louis. 1992. *Monkey Soup*. New York: The Trumpet Club.

San Souci, Robert D. 1989. *The Talking Eggs*. New York: Scholastic.

Schwartz, Alvin. 1984. *In a Dark, Dark Room and Other Scary Stories*. New York: Scholastic.

Scieszka, Jon. 1989. *The True Story of the 3 Little Pigs*. New York: Viking.

*Seeger, Pete. 1994. *Abiyoyo*. Reprint. New York: Simon and Schuster.

Sendak, Maurice. 1963. *Where the Wild Things Are*. New York: Harper & Row.

*Shannon, George. 1992. *Lizard's Song*. New York: William Morrow and Company, Inc.

Sharmat, Marjorie Weinman. *Nate the Great* series. New York: Bantam Doubleday Dell Books for Young Readers.

Sharmat, Mitchell. 1980. *Gregory, the Terrible Eater*. New York: Scholastic.

Shaw, Charles G. 1947. *It Looked Like Spilt Milk*. New York: Scholastic.

Shaw, Nancy. *Sheep* series. New York: The Trumpet Club, Houghton Mifflin.

Sheehan, Patty. 1988. *Kylie's Song*. Santa Barbara, CA: Advocacy Press.

Slawson, Michele Benoit. 1994. *Apple Picking Time*. New York: The Trumpet Club.

Slepian, Jan, and Ann Seidler. 1967. *The Hungry Thing*. New York: Scholastic.

————. 1990. *The Hungry Thing Returns*. New York: Scholastic.

Slobodkin, Florence, and Louis Slobodkin. 1958. *Too Many Mittens*. New York: The Vanguard Press, Inc.

*Slobodkina, Esphyr. 1947. *Caps for Sale*. New York: HarperCollins Children's Books.

Soto, Gary. 1993. *Too Many Tamales*. New York: Scholastic.

*Spier, Peter. 1961. *The Fox Went Out on a Chilly Night: An Old Song*. New York: Doubleday.

————. 1978. *Oh, Were They Ever Happy!* New York: The Trumpet Club.

Stadler, John. 1995. *The Adventures of Snail at School*. New York: HarperCollins Children's Books.

Staines, Bill. 1978. *All God's Critters Got a Place in the Choir*. New York: E. P. Dutton.

Steig, William. 1969. *Sylvester and the Magic Pebble*. New York: The Trumpet Club.

————. 1971. *Amos & Boris*. New York: Penguin Books.

*————. 1990. *Dr. DeSoto*. New York: Farrar, Straus & Giroux.

————. 1990. *Shrek!* New York: The Trumpet Club.

————. 1992. *Dr. DeSoto Goes to Africa*. New York: The Trumpet Club.

*Steptoe, John. 1987. *Mufaro's Beautiful Daughters: An African Tale*. New York: Scholastic.

Stevens, Janet. 1982. *The Princess and the Pea*. New York: Scholastic.

————. 1984. *The Tortoise and the Hare*. New York: Holiday House.

————. 1985. *The House That Jack Built*. New York: Holiday House.

————. 1995. *Tops & Bottoms*. New York: Harcourt Brace & Company.

Stewart, Sarah. 1995. *The Library*. New York: Farrar, Straus & Giroux.

*————. 1997. *The Gardener*. New York: Farrar, Straus & Giroux.

Surat, Michele Maria. 1983. *Angel Child, Dragon Child*. New York: Scholastic.

Teague, Mark. 1994. *Pigsty*. New York: Scholastic.

The Dandelion. Houghton Mifflin Series.

Thomas, Marlo. 1974. *Free to Be You and Me*. New York: Bantam Books.

Thompson, Kay. 1955. *Eloise*. New York: The Trumpet Club.

*Thurber, James. 1994. *The Great Quillow*, illus. by Steven Kellog. New York: Harcourt Brace & Company.

Titherington, Jeanne. 1986. *Pumpkin Pumpkin*. New York: Greenwillow Books.

Tomkins, Jasper. 1982. *Nimby*. New York: Simon & Schuster.

————. 1987. *When a Bear Bakes a Cake*. New York: Simon & Schuster.

————. 1989. *Bear Sleep Soup*. New York: Simon & Schuster.

Trapani, Iza. 1993. *The Itsy Bitsy Spider*. New York: Scholastic.

Van Allsburg, Chris. 1981. *Jumanji*. New York: Scholastic.

————. 1985. *The Polar Express*. Boston: Houghton Mifflin Company.

————. 1988. *Two Bad Ants*. Boston: Houghton Mifflin Company.

Van Leeuwen, Jean. *Oliver and Amanda Pig* series. New York: Puffin Books.

Viorst, Judith. 1969. *I'll Fix Anthony*. New York: Macmillan Publishing Company.

————. 1971. *The Tenth Good Thing About Barney*. New York: Atheneum.

————. 1972. *Alexander and the Terrible, Horrible, No Good, Very Bad Day*. New York: Atheneum.

————. 1978. *Alexander, Who Used to Be Rich Last Sunday*. New York: Scholastic.

————. 1988. *The Good-Bye Book*. New York: The Trumpet Club.

————. 1995. *Alexander, Who's Not (Do you hear me? I mean it!) Going to Move*. New York: Atheneum.

Waber, Bernard. 1965. *Lyle, Lyle Crocodile*. New York: The Trumpet Club.

*————. 1972. *Ira Sleeps Over*. New York: Scholastic.

*————. 1988. *Ira Says Goodbye*. New York: Scholastic.

*Waddell, Martin. 1991. *Let's Go Home, Little Bear*. New York: The Trumpet Club.

*————. 1992. *Can't You Sleep, Little Bear?* Cambridge, MA: Candlewick Press.

————. 1996. *You and Me, Little Bear*. Cambridge, MA: Candlewick Press.

Wahl, Jan. 1987. *Humphrey's Bear*. New York: Henry Holt and Company.

Walsh, Ellen Stoll. 1989. *Mouse Paint*. New York: The Trumpet Club.

————. 1991. *Mouse Count*. New York: The Trumpet Club.

————. 1992. *You Silly Goose*. New York: The Trumpet Club.

Ward, Cindy. 1988. *Cookie's Week*. New York: Scholastic.

Weiss, George David, and Bob Thiele. 1967. *What a Wonderful World*. New York: Atheneum.

Weiss, Nicki. 1990. *An Egg Is an Egg*. New York: The Trumpet Club.

————. 1992. *On a Hot, Hot Day*. New York: The Trumpet Club.

Wellington, Monica. 1992. *Mr. Cookie Baker*. New York: The Trumpet Club.

*Wells, Rosemary. 1975. *Morris's Disappearing Bag*. New York: The Trumpet Club.

————. 1981. *Timothy Goes to School*. New York: Dial Press.

————. 1983. *Noisy Nora*. New York: Scholastic.

————. 1985. *Hazel's Amazing Mother*. New York: The Trumpet Club.

————. 1986. *Max's Christmas*. New York: Dial Books.

————. 1989. *Max's Chocolate Chicken*. New York: The Trumpet Club.

————. 1991. *Max's Dragon Shirt*. New York: The Trumpet Club.

————. 1993. *Max and Ruby's First Greek Myth*. New York: Dial Books.

*————. 1995. *Lassie Come-Home*. New York: Henry Holt and Company.

West, Colin. 1986. *Have You Seen the Crocodile?* New York: Harper & Row.

Westcott, Nadine Bernard. 1987. *Peanut Butter and Jelly*. New York: E. P. Dutton.

————. 1988. *The Lady with the Alligator Purse*. Boston: Little, Brown and Company.

————. 1989. *Skip to My Lou*. Boston: Little, Brown and Company.

————. 1990. *There's a Hole in the Bucket*. New York: The Trumpet Club.

————. 1991. *The House That Jack Built*. Boston: Little, Brown and Company.

Wiesner, David. 1988. *Free Fall*. New York: Scholastic.

————. 1991. *Tuesday*. New York: The Trumpet Club.

————. 1992. *June 29, 1999*. New York: Clarion Books.

Wilhelm, Hans. *Bunny Trouble* series. New York: Scholastic.

*———. 1985. *I'll Always Love You*. New York: Scholastic.

*———. 1995. *Tyrone and the Swamp Gang*. New York: Scholastic.

Williams, Linda. 1986. *The Little Old Lady Who Was Not Afraid of Anything*. New York: Thomas Y. Crowell.

Williams, Sue. 1989. *I Went Walking*. New York: Harcourt Brace & Company.

Williams, Vera B. 1982. *A Chair for My Mother*. New York: Greenwillow Books.

———. 1983. *Something Special for Me*. New York: The Trumpet Club.

———. 1984. *Music, Music for Everyone*. New York: The Trumpet Club.

Winthrop, Elizabeth. 1986. *Shoes*. New York: Harper & Row.

Wood, Audrey. 1984. *The Napping House*. New York: Harcourt Brace & Company.

———. 1985. *King Bidgood's in the Bathtub*. New York: Harcourt Brace & Company.

———. 1989. *Quick As a Cricket*. Wilts: England: Child's Play International Limited.

———. 1990. *Weird Parents*. New York: The Trumpet Club.

Wood, Don, and Audrey Wood. 1984. *The Little Mouse, the Red Ripe Strawberry, and the Big Hungry Bear*. Wilts, England: Child's Play International Ltd.

Wyeth, Sharon Dennis. 1995. *Always My Dad*. New York: The Trumpet Club.

Yektai, Niki. 1987. *Bears in Pairs*. New York: The Trumpet Club.

*Yolen, Jane. 1977. *The Seeing Stick*. New York: Thomas Y. Crowell.

*———. 1987. *Owl Moon*. New York: G. P. Putnam's Sons.

———. 1994. *Old Dame Counterpane*. New York: Philomel Books.

Young, Ed. 1989. *Lon Po Po*. New York: Scholastic.

———. 1992. *Seven Blind Mice*. New York: Scholastic.

Ziefert, Harriet. 1986. *A New Coat for Anna*. New York: Scholastic.

Zion, Gene. 1956. *Harry the Dirty Dog*. New York: HarperCollins.

———. 1958. *No Roses for Harry!* New York: Scholastic.

———. 1960. *Harry and the Lady Next Door*. New York: The Trumpet Club.

Zolotow, Charlotte. 1959. *The Bunny Who Found Easter*. New York: The Trumpet Club.

———. 1966. *I Like to Be Little*. New York: HarperCollins.

———. 1972. *William's Doll*. New York: The Trumpet Club.

*———. 1995. *When the Wind Stops*. New York: HarperCollins.

NONFICTION

Aliki. 1962. *My Five Senses*. New York: The Trumpet Club.

———. 1984. *Feelings*. New York: Scholastic.

———. 1990. *Manners*. New York: Scholastic.

344 | FAVORITE
CHILDREN'S
LITERATURE FOR
A PRIMARY
CLASSROOM
LIBRARY

————. 1993. *Communication*. New York: Scholastic.

Animals in the Wild series. New York: Scholastic.

Arnosky, Jim. 1986. *Deer at the Brook*. New York: Scholastic.

Bates, Katharine Lee. 1993. *America the Beautiful*, illus. Neil Waldman. New York: Atheneum.

————. 1994. *O Beautiful for Spacious Skies*, illus. Wayne Thiebaud. San Francisco: Chronicle Books.

Berger, Melvin. 1985. *Germs Make Me Sick*. New York: The Trumpet Club.

Brenner, Barbara, and Bernice Chardiet. 1993. *Where's That Insect?* New York: Scholastic.

————. 1993. *Where's That Reptile?* New York: Scholastic.

Brown, Laurie Krasny, and Marc Brown. 1990. *Dinosaurs Alive and Well: A Guide to Good Health*. New York: The Trumpet Club.

————. 1992. *Dinosaurs to the Rescue: A Guide to Protecting Our Planet*. New York: The Trumpet Club.

Brown, Marc, and Stephen Krensky. 1983. *Perfect Pigs: An Introduction to Manners*. New York: The Trumpet Club.

Brown, Ruth. 1991. *Alphabet Times Four*. New York: Dutton Children's Books.

Bunnett, Rochelle. 1995. *Friends at School*. New York: Scholastic.

Calmenson, Stephanie. 1993. *It Begins with an A*. New York: Scholastic.

Cheltenham Elementary School Kindergartners. 1991. *We Are All Alike . . . We Are All Different*. New York: Scholastic.

Cooney, Barbara. 1994. *Only Opal*. New York: The Trumpet Club.

Cowley, Joy. 1988. *Seventy Kilometres from Ice Cream*. New York: Richard C. Owen.

————. 1996. *Joy Cowley Writes*. Bothell, WA: The Wright Group.

dePaola, Tomie. 1981. *Now One Foot, Now the Other*. New York: The Trumpet Club.

————. 1989. *The Art Lesson*. New York: The Trumpet Club.

————. 1993. *Tom*. New York: Scholastic.

————. 1996. *The Baby Sister*. New York: G. P. Putnam's Sons.

*————. 1998. *Nana Upstairs and Nana Downstairs*. New York: G. P. Putnam's Sons.

Duke, Kate. 1983. *The Guinea Pig ABC*. New York: The Trumpet Club.

Egan, Christopher, Lorraine Hopping Egan, Thomas Campbell Jackson, and Diane Molleson. 1994. *My First Book of Animals*. New York: Scholastic.

Eye Openers series. New York: Dorling Kindersley.

Eyewitness Junior series. New York: Dorling Kindersley.

Feelings, Muriel. 1971. *moja means one*. New York: Dial Books.

First Discovery Books series. New York: Scholastic.

Fischer-Nagel, Heiderose, and Andreas Fischer-Nagel. 1987. *Life of the Butterfly*. Minneapolis: Carolroda Books, Inc.

Fleming, Denise. 1996. *Where Once There Was a Wood*. New York: Henry Holt and Company.

Florian, Douglas. 1991. *An Auto Mechanic*. New York: The Trumpet Club.

Gibbons, Gail. 1982. *The Post Office Book*. New York: HarperCollins.

———. 1984. *Fire! Fire!* New York: Scholastic.

———. 1987. *Dinosaurs*. New York: Scholastic.

———. 1987. *Trains*. New York: Scholastic.

———. 1990. *Weather Words and What They Mean*. New York: Holiday House.

———. 1992. *Stargazers*. New York: Scholastic.

———. 1993. *Spiders*. New York: Scholastic.

———. 1994. *Emergency!* New York: Scholastic.

Goldish, Meish. 1989. *What Is a Fossil?* Chatham, NJ: Raintree Steck-Vaughn Publishers.

*Greenaway, Theresa, Christiane Gunzi, and Barbara Taylor. 1994. *Ocean: The Living World*. New York: Dorling Kindersley.

Harris, Pamela. 1995. *Hot Cold Shy Bold: Looking at Opposites*. Toronto: Kids Can Press Ltd.

Heller, Ruth. 1981. *Chickens Aren't the Only Ones*. New York: Grosset & Dunlap.

———. 1982. *Animals Born Alive and Well*. New York: Scholastic.

———. 1983. *The Reason for a Flower*. New York: Scholastic.

———. 1984. *Plants That Never Ever Bloom*. New York: Grosset & Dunlap.

———. 1985. *How to Hide an Octopus & Other Sea Creatures*. New York: Grosset & Dunlap.

Hicks, Roger. 1994. *The Big Book of America*. Philadelphia: Courage Books.

Horton, Barbara Savadge. 1992. *What Comes in Spring?* New York: The Trumpet Club.

Isadora, Rachel. 1983. *City Seen from A to Z*. New York: The Trumpet Club.

Kuhn, Dwight. 1993. *My First Book of Nature*. New York: Scholastic.

MacDonald, Suse. 1986. *Alphabatics*. New York: The Trumpet Club.

Machotka, Hana. 1991. *What Neat Feet!* New York: Morrow Junior Books.

Martin, Jerome. 1991. *carrot/parrot*. New York: Simon & Schuster Books for Young Readers.

———. 1991. *mitten/kitten*. New York: The Trumpet Club.

Marzollo, Jean. *I Spy* books. New York: Scholastic.

McMillan, Bruce. 1983. *Here a Chick, There a Chick*. New York: The Trumpet Club.

———. 1991. *Play Day: A Book of Terse Verse*. New York: The Trumpet Club.

Micucci, Charles. 1995. *The Life and Times of the Honeybee*. New York: Houghton Mifflin.

My First series. Dorling Kindersley.

Pallotta, Jerry. 1988. *Alphabet Book* series. Watertown, MA: Charlesbridge Publishing.

Parker, Nancy Winslow, and Joan Richards Wright. 1987. *Bugs*. New York: Greenwillow Books.

———. 1990. *Frogs, Toads, Lizards, and Salamanders*. New York: Scholastic.

Picture Book Biography series. New York: Scholastic.

Pomeroy, Diana. 1996. *One Potato*. New York: Harcourt Brace & Company.

Pratt, Kristin Joy. 1994. *A Swim Through the Sea*. Nevada City, CA: Dawn Publications.

Rehm, Karl, and Kay Koike. 1991. *Left or Right?* New York: Scholastic.

Rice, Chris, and Melanie Rice. 1995. *How Children Lived*. New York: Dorling Kindersley.

Rockwell, Anne. 1982. *Boats*. New York: E. P. Dutton.

———. 1989. *Apples and Pumpkins*. New York: Scholastic.

———. 1989. *My Spring Robin*. New York: Scholastic.

Rounds, Glen. 1989. *Old MacDonald Had a Farm*. New York: Holiday House.

Ryder, Joanne. 1982. *The Snail's Spell*. New York: Scholastic.

Sandved, Kjell B. 1996. *The Butterfly Alphabet*. New York: Scholastic.

Schwartz, David M. 1985. *How Much Is a Million?* New York: Scholastic.

Scieszka, Jon. 1995. *Math Curse*. New York: Viking.

Sendak, Maurice. 1962. *Alligators All Around: An Alphabet*. New York: HarperCollins.

———. 1962. *One Was Johnny: A Counting Book*. New York: Scholastic.

Simon, Seymour. *Science* series. New York: HarperCollins.

What's Inside? series. New York: Dorling Kindersley.

Wildsmith, Brian. 1974. *Squirrels*. New York: Scholastic.

Yolen, Jane. 1992. *Letting Swift River Go*. New York: The Trumpet Club.

———. 1993. *Welcome to the Green House*. New York: Scholastic.

INFORMATIONAL STORYBOOKS

Bjork, Christina. 1985. *Linnea in Monet's Garden*. New York: R&S Books.

*Cannon, Janell. 1993. *Stellaluna*. New York: Scholastic.

———. 1997. *Verdi*. New York: Scholastic.

Carle, Eric. 1987. *A House for Hermit Crab*. New York: Scholastic.

———. 1987. *The Tiny Seed*. New York: Scholastic.

Cole, Joanna, and Bruce Degen. *The Magic School Bus* series. New York: Scholastic

————. 1990. *The Magic School Bus Lost in the Solar System*. New York: Scholastic.

Cowcher, Helen. *Science* series. New York: Scholastic.

dePaola, Tomie. 1975. *The Cloud Book*. New York: Holiday House.

————. 1978. *The Popcorn Book*. New York: Scholastic.

Ehlert, Lois. 1987. *Growing Vegetable Soup*. New York: Harcourt Brace Jovanovich.

————. 1988. *Planting a Rainbow*. New York: Harcourt Brace Jovanovich.

————. 1989. *Eating the Alphabet*. New York: The Trumpet Club.

————. 1990. *Feathers for Lunch*. New York: The Trumpet Club.

————. 1991. *Red Leaf, Yellow Leaf*. New York: Harcourt Brace Jovanovich.

————. 1993. *Nuts to You!* New York: Harcourt Brace & Company.

————. 1995. *Snowballs*. New York: Scholastic.

————. 1997. *Hands*. New York: Harcourt Brace & Company

Frasier, Debra. 1991. *On the Day You Were Born*. New York: The Trumpet Club.

George, William T. *Box Turtle* series. New York: The Trumpet Club.

Owen, Annie. 1990. *Bumper to Bumper*. New York: The Trumpet Club.

Provensen, Alice, and Martin Provensen. 1987. *Shaker Lane*. New York: The Trumpet Club.

APPENDIX 3–5
Favorite Word Play Books

Throughout the year during shared-reading time, I read aloud titles from my trade book and bigbook collection of "word play" books and conduct mini-lessons to engage the children in phonic and language study. The following is a list of some of my favorite word play books that lend themselves to delightful letter, sound, and language pattern explorations with primary children.

Aylesworth, Jim. 1990. *The Completed Hickory Dickory Dock*. New York: Atheneum.

Bond, Felicia. 1996. *Tumble Bumble*. Arden: Front Street.

Carlstrom, Nancy. 1986. *Jesse Bear, What Will You Wear?* New York: Scholastic.

Cameron, Polly. 1961. *"I Can't" Said the Ant*. New York: Scholastic.

Cole, Joanna, and Stephanie Calmenson. 1993. *Six Sick Sheep: 101 Tongue Twisters*. New York: Scholastic.

Degen, Bruce. 1983. *Jamberry*. New York: Scholastic.

Draper, Tani. 1994. *Miss Mary Mack*. Salem, OR: Nellie Edge Resources, Inc.

Dr. Seuss books. New York: Random House.

Edge, Nellie, and Friends. 1994. *I Can Read More Colors*. Salem, OR: Nellie Edge Resources, Inc.

——. 1994. *I Can Spell Cat*. Salem, OR: Nellie Edge Resources, Inc.

Fleming, Denise. 1991. *In the Tall, Tall Grass*. New York: Henry Holt and Company.

——. 1993. *In the Small, Small Pond*. New York: Scholstic.

Harris, Pamela. 1995. *Hot Cold Shy Bold: Looking at Opposites*. Toronto: Kids Can Press Ltd.

Hennessy, B. G. 1989. *A, B, C, D, Tummy, Toes, Hands, Knees*. New York: The Trumpet Club.

Martin, Jerome. 1991. *carrot/parrot*. New York: Simon and Schuster Books for Young Readers.

————. 1991. *mitten/kitten*. New York: The Trumpet Club.

McMillan, Bruce. 1991. *Play Day: A Book of Terse Verse*. New York: The Trumpet Club.

Neville and Butler. 1988. *Green Bananas*. Crystal Lake, IL: Rigby.

Numeroff, Laura. 1993. *Dogs Don't Wear Sneakers*. New York: Aladdin Paperbacks.

Packard, Mary. 1994. *Bubble Trouble*. New York: Scholastic.

Paton, Sandy, and Caroline Paton. 1988. *The Opposite Song*. Salem, OR: Nellie Edge Resources, Inc..

Powell, Debbie, ed. 1991. *Wiggles and Giggles*. Crystal Lake, IL: Rigby.

Shaw, Nancy. 1986. *Sheep in a Jeep*. New York: The Trumpet Club.

————. 1989. *Sheep on a Ship*. Boston: Houghton Mifflin.

————. 1991. *Sheep in a Shop*. Boston: Houghton Mifflin.

Slepian, Jan, and Ann Seidler. 1967. *The Hungry Thing*. New York: Scholastic.

————. 1990. *The Hungry Thing Returns*. New York: Scholastic.

Snow, Pegeen. 1985. *Eat Your Peas, Louise!* Chicago, IL: Children's Press.

Wildsmith, Brian. 1982. *Cat on the Mat*. Oxford: Oxford University Press.

Winthrop, Elizabeth. 1986. *Shoes*. New York: Harper & Row.

Yektai, Niki. 1987. *Bears in Pairs*. New York: The Trumpet Club.

APPENDIX 4–1
Book-Covering Resources and Information

In my classroom, the children take home both my hardcover and paperback books from our classroom library for nightly reading. In order to withstand the love and care of little hands, I use a plastic library covering for the jacket covers of the hardbound books. I order the library covering from Gaylord's Library Supply and it lasts for two or three years. The covering is available in different sizes, although I prefer the 14" size because it covers the range of most book sizes. Ordering information follows:

Gaylord Book Jacket Cover: 14" (100' roll)
Order #: 2914
PO Box 4901
Syracuse, NY 13221
1-800-448-6160

Parents cover all our classroom library paperback books with contact paper that I order from Highsmith Supply Company. I give willing parents a "book-covering inservice" at the beginning of the year, and then as I purchase books throughout the year, I bundle everything up in "home project bags" and send them home to be covered. I generally average three parents who are willing to do this for our classroom and keep young readers supplied with "fresh books." I also place "Please Return to" computer labels inside the front covers of the books to mark them as school or personal property. The Highsmith Information as well as a drawing to assist you with the covering follows:

Highsmith Protecto Film
Item #: L81–54627 (18' × 75')
W5527 Highway 106
PO Box 800
Fort Atkinson, WI 53538–0800
1-800-558-2110

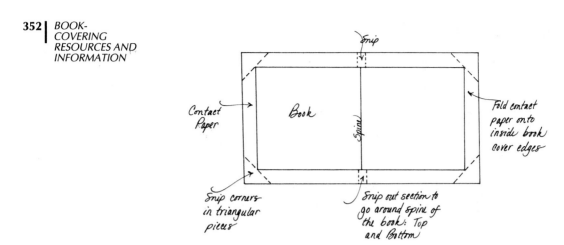

Snip

Contact
Paper

Book

Spine

Fold contact
paper onto
inside book
cover edges

Snip corners
in triangular
pieces

Snip out section to
go around spine of
the book: Top
and Bottom

APPENDIX 4–2
Anthology Introductory Letter

Dear Families,

This is your child's anthology. We call it an anthology in our classroom because it is a collection of several things: songs, poems, cartoons, news, and short stories.

The anthology is an important part of the children's reading materials because the items we will be adding to the notebooks will be familiar to them. Typically, the children will be adding pieces to their anthologies each week. Most of the time we will first read the songs, poems, news, cartoons, and short stories during our shared-reading time so that the children have some experience reading them. I then type and prepare the items for the children's notebooks.

You will discover that most of the items don't have "prepared pictures" and that the children will be doing the illustrations themselves. I prefer that the children do their own artwork so that their pages become "theirs." We generally remember better and have a sense that something is "ours" when we have a personal connection to our work.

The children will be bringing home their anthologies once a week to share with you as part of their nightly reading. Of course they are welcome to take them home more often if you and they would enjoy having it home more. I ask that you please remind your child to tuck it into his or her book bag after you finish reading so that it comes back to school the next day, as the children enjoy their anthologies during daily quiet reading also.

If you notice that your child is having difficulty reading, please help in these ways:

- Read or sing the entire piece *to or with* your child, then encourage your child to read it independently.
- Echo read with your child: You read a line; your child repeats after you. Again, encourage independent reading practice after this.

If you notice that your child is having difficulty with a word, please help problem solve in one or more of the following ways:

- Show your child how to "take another run at the reading": reread starting at the beginning of the sentence or line and see if that helps with the problem word.
- Cover all but the beginning letter or letters of the problem word, and drawing your finger back, help your child sound out the word; once the word problem is solved, remind your child to go back and reread the entire sentence or line so that s/he "holds the meaning together."
- Tell your child to skip it and come back to it. If this doesn't help, then help him or her figure out the problem word another way.
- Remind your child to look at the pictures s/he has drawn, as that may help.
- Give the word!

My rule of thumb with all word problem solving is to help the children figure out the problem the quickest way possible. I don't belabor it. Sometimes it really is best just to tell them the problem word and let them move on with their reading. Let your best "reading instinct" guide you as you help your child.

A last word. Keep the reading pleasurable for both you and your child. Learning how to read is a process and it's important for your young reader to view this process with good feelings. If or when it ever becomes frustrating, it's time to put everything away and get some fresh air instead.

I hope you enjoy the collection the children and I put together this year in the course of our days of reading and learning together.

Best Wishes,

Janine Chappell Carr

APPENDIX 4–3
What's in the News?
September 1–October 7, 1995

Name:_____

U.S. NEWS

1. At the Colorado State Fair, in Pueblo, Colorado, a picture was taken of a little guy "asleep at the wheel" of his wagon.
2. Orville Redenbacher died in September. He developed his own pop-corn out of over 30 different hybrids (kinds) of popping corn. He lived close to us—in La Jolla, California.
3. In Ohio, a Natural History Museum has a dinosaur exhibit where a little two-year-old had to check out the teeth of a T-Rex! Was it a real Tyrannosaurus, Mighty King of Beasts?!
4. Scientists in San Diego are looking at our bat population. They are concerned that it is declining (getting less) because of negative things in our environment.
5. A baby africanized lion was rescued from a breeding farm in Idaho after some of the animals escaped from there. It has a new home in California.
6. Thelma and Louise, a two-headed corn snake at the San Diego Zoo, had 15 babies. They were all born one-headed! The two-headed snake is a freak of nature. The right head is dominant; it eats while the left head looks on. . . .
7. Sports Update: The San Diego Chargers have won two, and lost two. Go Chargers!
8. It's Fall—and it's "leaf-peeping time." The New England States—Maine, Vermont, New Hampshire, Massachusetts, Rhode Island, and Connecticut—are especially famous for their fall leaves.

WORLD NEWS

1. The fossil remains of a new dinosaur have been discovered in Argentina, which is in South America. It is called Carolinii Gigantosaurus. It lived 30 million years before Tyrannosaurus Rex and is the biggest meat eater found so far.

2. In Singapore, a (crazy?) man wants to set a new world record with poisonous snakes. He wants to spend two weeks in a cage with 300 poisonous snakes. Anyone want to join him?!

3. Mt. Ruapehu Volcano erupted in New Zealand. This is the largest eruption of the 9,190-foot mountain in 50 years. Maori elders said it is showing its "mana" or authority, as lord of the other volcanoes in the region.

4. Scientists in Brazil are baffled by a crater that was punched into the tropical rain forest shortly after witnesses reported seeing a bright light streak across the sky. Researchers are uncertain whether the crater, 16 feet wide and 32 feet deep, was left by a meteorite or a piece of comet. One scientist believes it was caused by a block of ice from a comet because the surrounding vegetation (plants) is not burned and the crater's rim is not raised. Another researcher is hoping to find traces of the object that fell from space.

APPENDIX 5–1
Assembling Journals

I enjoy creating small journals with my children each year. We do the art-work together and parents help assemble them at home. I believe the children have more ownership and pride in their journals when we have created them together. The following steps outline our process:

Step 1: Complete artwork on 11 × 14" paper. I use butcher paper or drawing paper, not construction paper.

Step 2: Cut a 9 × 12" tagboard cover.

Step 3: Cover the tagboard cover with the completed artwork in the following manner:

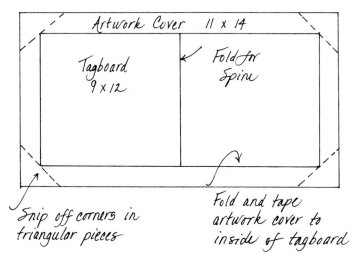

Snip off corners in triangular pieces

Fold and tape artwork cover to inside of tagboard

Step 4: Tape "insert letters" onto the inside front and back covers.

Step 5: Fold paper ($8\frac{1}{2}$ × 11") for the inside pages and staple with a long-arm stapler on the center fold of the cover. I am successful with approximately ten pieces of paper folded in half. I also add a parent informational letter as the first page of the inside journal pages.

Step 6: Cover outside spine with clear book tape for durability.

Step 7: When the journal is full, fold another set of ten pages, staple at center fold, then tape to the first set of pages in the back of the journal. I have also made new journals with the children at this point if there is time and help.

APPENDIX 5–2
Nightly Reading Log Letter

Dear Families,

This is your child's reading log. Monday through Thursday, your child will be choosing books to read at home in the evening. I would appreciate it if you would spend fifteen to twenty minutes reading with him or her and signing and/or adding comments to the reading log.

If your child brings home a new book, these are helpful ways to enter into the reading world with your child:

- LOOK at the cover, pages, and pictures in the book.
- TALK about the cover, the pictures, the story, and any words, ideas or information that might be new to your child.
- ASK what your child thinks and expects the book to be about.
- ENCOURAGE your child's reading efforts.
- SHARE the reading experience.

Sometimes your child may be "trying" a book that evening and it may turn out to be too difficult. If that happens, please take the opportunity to read to your child or let your child read a small amount, perhaps the predictable parts. I will help your child choose a "just right" book the next day at school. Above all, I urge you to show interest in your child's reading and to be patient. Give your child plenty of time to work out words by him or herself.

Sometimes your child will bring home two books: one to read to you and one for you to read aloud. Please make sure your child returns both books the next day in the book bag. Please record the titles of both books in the reading log.

As the year progresses, your child will read increasingly more difficult books. When this happens, these books (especially chapter books) will take more than one evening to read. In the reading log, please help your child record the pages he or she read until your child gets used to doing this on his or her own. It is helpful if you and your young reader review what was read previously so he or she can pick up the information or story with ease.

You will notice that our reading log is also a place for the children to do book checkout and rate their reading and listening during partner reading. After partner reading each day, the children will rate themselves on how they felt they read that day and how they did listening to and helping their reading partner. It is part of the children's ongoing work in keeping track of themselves as learners.

I will check the children's reading logs each week when I meet with them to listen to them read. If I have questions or concerns about your child's reading progress or the reading log, I will get in touch with you promptly. If you have questions or concerns, please let me know and I will discuss them with you. Books, reading logs, and book bags need to be returned to school each day. Thank you for your commitment to helping your child become a strong reader. Enjoy!

Best wishes,

Janine Chappell Carr

---

*With thanks to Lynda Palmer, Aberfoyle Hub School, Adelaide, South Australia for her resourceful "Reading At Home" letter.

APPENDIX 6–1
Book Talk Informational Letter

Dear Families,

The children are going to start giving five-minute book talks in our classroom. There are several reasons I would like them to begin doing this.

First, I believe it is important for the children to begin recommending books to one another, just like we do as adult readers. I do book introductions every day, but I want the children to talk with one another about the books they love, too. I do not want to be the only "librarian" in the room!

Second, I feel it is important for the children to continue to become comfortable speaking in front of our classroom group—even as first or second graders.

Third, it is important for the children to be part of whole-group book discussions as well as those that take place when they are partner reading with each other. Listening to and sharing thoughts with other "book lovers" will continue to encourage our young readers to seek out good books for themselves..

I have attached a form to help the children prepare for their book talks. When the children bring this home, they will be giving their book talk the next day at school. The children need to write their name, the date, title, and author of the book. They do not need to write anything else—I will do that as they give their talks. I would like the children to return this paper on the day of their book talks. The children need to include in their five-minute talk:

- what the book is about
- what the best part is
- a reading of their favorite part or page to us or the entire book if it's short

- Remember the book needs to be at school! The children need to read their favorite part fluently and expressively, so practice is a must!

If you have any questions for me, please let me know through the child's Note Book or when you see me at school. I look forward to wonderful book talks with the children. Thank you as you help them prepare for this.

Sincerely,

Janine Chappell Carr

BOOK TALK

Name: _____

Date:_____

Title of the Book: _____
_____

Author of the Book: _____
_____

What is the book about?

What is the best part? Why?

Read your favorite part or page to us.

How do you think   From your teacher:
you did on your
book talk?

_____

APPENDIX 7–1
Recommended Resources for Primary Teachers

Avery, Carol. 1993. . . . *And with a Light Touch: Learning About Reading, Writing and Teaching with First Graders.* Portsmouth, NH: Heinemann.

Bissex, Glenda L. 1996. *Partial Truths: A Memoir and Essays on Reading, Writing, and Researching.* Portsmouth, NH: Heinemann.

Booth, David, and Carol Thornley-Hall, ed. 1991. *The Talk Curriculum.* Portsmouth, NH: Heinemann.

Calkins, Lucy McCormick. 1994. *The Art of Teaching Writing: New Edition.* Portsmouth, NH: Heinemann.

Cambourne, Brian. 1988. *The Whole Story.* New York: Scholastic.

Clay, Marie M. 1991. *Becoming Literate: The Construction of Inner Control.* Portsmouth, NH: Heinemann.

———. 1993. *An Observation Survey of Early Literacy Achievement.* Portsmouth, NH: Heinemann.

———. 1998. *By Different Paths to Common Outcomes.* York, ME: Stenhouse Publishers.

Dwyer, John, ed. 1989. *a sea of talk.* Portsmouth, NH: Heinemann.

Edwards, Carolyn, Lella Gandini, and George Forman, ed. 1993. *The Hundred Languages of Children.* Norwood, NJ: Ablex Publishing Corporation.

Fisher, Bobbi. 1995. *Thinking and Learning Together: Curriculum and Community in a Primary Classroom.* Portsmouth, NH: Heinemann.

Fountas, Irene C., and Gay Su Pinnell. 1996. *Guided Reading: Good First Teaching for All Children.* Portsmouth, NH: Heinemann.

Fox, Mem. 1993. *Radical Reflections: Passionate Opinions on Teaching, Learning, and Living.* New York: Harcourt Brace & Company.

Fry, Edward. 1994. *Phonics Patterns: Onset and Rhyme Word Lists.* Laguna Beach, CA: Laguna Beach Educational Books.

Gentry, Richard. 1997. *My Kid Can't Spell.* Portsmouth, NH: Heinemann.

Gentry, Richard, and Jean Wallace Gillet. 1993. *Teaching Kids to Spell.* Portsmouth, NH: Heinemann.

Glover, Mary Kenner. 1993. *Two Years: A Teacher's Memoir.* Portsmouth, NH: Heinemann.

Graves, Donald H. 1991. *Build a Literate Classroom.* Portsmouth, NH: Heinemann.

———. 1994. *A Fresh Look at Writing.* Portsmouth, NH: Heinemann.

Harwayne, Shelley. 1992. *Lasting Impressions: Weaving Literature into the Writing Workshop.* Portsmouth, NH: Heinemann.

Heard, Georgia. 1989. *For the Good of the Earth and Sun: Teaching Poetry.* Portsmouth, NH: Heinemann.

———. 1995. *Writing Toward Home: Tales and Lessons to Find Your Way.* Portsmouth, NH: Heinemann.

———. 1999. *Awakening the Heart: Exploring Poetry in Elementary and Middle School.* Portsmouth, NH: Heinemann.

Hickman, Janet, and Bernice E. Cullinan, ed. 1989. *Children's Literature in the Classroom: Weaving Charlotte's Web.* Needham Heights, MA: Christopher-Gordon Publishers, Inc.

Hindley, Joanne. 1996. *In the Company of Children.* York, ME: Stenhouse Publishers.

Holdaway, Don. 1979. *The Foundations of Literacy.* Portsmouth, NH: Heinemann.

Hubbard, Ruth Shagoury. 1996. *A Workshop of the Possible.* York, ME: Stenhouse Publishers.

Hubbard, Ruth Shagoury, and Brenda Miller Power. 1993. *The Art of Classroom Inquiry.* Portsmouth, NH: Heinemann.

Jackson, Margaret. 1993. *Creative Display & Environment.* Portsmouth, NH: Heinemann.

Karelitz, Ellen Blackburn. *The Author's Chair and Beyond: Language and Literacy in a Primary Classroom.* Portsmouth, NH: Heinemann.

Kohn, Alfie. 1995. *Punished by Rewards.* Boston: Houghton Mifflin Company.

Massam, Joanne, and Anne Kulik. 1986. *And What Else?* San Diego, CA: The Wright Group.

McConaghy, June. 1990. *Children Learning Through Literature.* Portsmouth, NH: Heinemann.

Mooney, Margaret. 1988. *Developing Life-Long Readers.* New York: Richard C. Owen Publishers.

———. 1990. *Reading to, with, and by Children.* New York: Richard C. Owen Publishers.

Moustafa, Margaret. 1997. *Beyond Traditional Phonics.* Portsmouth, NH: Heinemann.

Neilsen, Lorri. 1994. *A Stone in My Shoe: Teaching Literacy in Times of Change.* Winnipeg, Manitoba: Peguis Publishers Limited.

Newkirk, Thomas, with Patricia McLure. 1992. *Listening In: Children Talk About Books (and Other Things)*. Portsmouth, NH: Heinemann.

Newman, Judith. 1991. *Interwoven Conversations: Learning and Teaching Through Critical Reflection*. Portsmouth, NH: Heinemann.

Ohanian, Susan. 1994. *Who's in Charge? A Teacher Speaks Her Mind*. Portsmouth, NH: Heinemann.

Peterson, Ralph. 1992. *Life in a Crowded Place*. Portsmouth, NH: Heinemann.

Peterson, Ralph, and Maryann Eeds. 1990. *Grand Conversations*. New York: Scholastic.

Rogovin, Paula. 1998. *Classroom Interviews: A World of Learning*. Portsmouth, NH: Heinemann.

Routman, Regie. 1991. *Invitations*. Portsmouth, NH: Heinemann.

———. 1994. *The Blue Pages: Resources for Teachers*. Portsmouth, NH: Heinemann.

———. 1996. *Literacy at the Crossroads*. Portsmouth, NH: Heinemann.

Smith, Frank. 1983. *Essays into Literacy*. Portsmouth, NH: Heinemann.

———. 1986. *Insult to Intelligence*. Portsmouth, NH: Heinemann.

———. 1988. *Joining the Literacy Club*. Portsmouth, NH: Heinemann.

———. 1998. *The Book of Learning and Forgetting*. New York: Teacher's College Press.

Wilde, Sandra. 1992. *You Kan Read This!* Portsmouth, NH: Heinemann.

APPENDIX 10–1
Family Journal Letter

Dear Families,

This is your child's family journal. This is one of two journals the children will be writing in this year. They will also have a "letter journal" in which they write a weekly letter to me. The children will be writing in their family journals every Thursday during our writing time. When it arrives home on Thursday evening, please read your child's letter and write back! When you do write back, please print clearly and read your letter to your child. This will help the children when they are sharing their family journals during our Friday partner-reading time.

You will notice that your child will have both conventional spelling and what is called *temporary spelling* in his or her letters. As you well know, young children do not know the conventional spellings for all of the wonderful words they want to write. When this happens, I show the children how to stretch out and write down the sounds of these words so that they can include them in their writing. The children will also be working on the correct spelling of the high-frequency writing words (in their weekly spelling work) so that they are "on the tips of their pencils" when they need to write them. As the year progresses, you will notice that their spelling will continue to improve with many words spelled conventionally. However, be prepared to see a mix of spellings in their writing.

I encourage temporary spelling because it allows children to develop as writers. Why, even Christopher Robin used temporary spelling for his signs and messages to his friends in the Hundred-Acre Wood! Please know that whenever we do publish a piece of writing for the general public all spelling and punctuation is corrected.

I ask for your support in accepting your child's temporary spellings as part of his or her writing development and that you be patient, considerate, and respectful when you are deciphering some of the words. If you cannot make sense of something, ask your child to read it to you or tell you what s/he was thinking about when writing the letter. I also ask for your support in writing back to your child each week. These letters are important to the children and they look forward to sharing them.

I appreciate both your "reading and writing time" as you correspond with your young writer. Enjoy!

Warmly,

Janine Chappell Carr

APPENDIX 10–2
Handwriting Assistance

Dear Families,

These are important points to remember when helping young children with handwriting skills:

- **Pencil Grip:** It should be natural, comfortable, and at a correct angle to the paper.
- **Paper Position:** If child is right-handed, the paper should be slanted slightly to the left. If child is left-handed, it should be slanted slightly to the right.
- **Posture:** Young children need to sit up straight so that they have a good view of the paper. Sometimes little ones like to rest their heads on the table, however, it is better if they sit up.
- **Letter Formation:** Children need to form the letters smoothly and correctly. Showing your child how the letters are formed, even putting your hand over his or her hand so he or she can feel the formation of the letter is helpful. The formation of the letter must be fluent and smooth. Sometimes young children have "learned" a very complicated way of making a letter and they need to be taught a different way that is more fluent and easier to do. It is challenging at times.
- **Neatness, Legibility, and Fluency of Handwriting:** The goal for young children is to develop neat, clear, legible handwriting. Your child should strive to use clear handwriting always.
- **Size of Letters:** Show your child that the letters must all be about the same size. Capital and "tall letters" (like /t/ or /h/) are written taller than the small letters. Trying to get the letters even is a process for them and a goal they must work toward.
- **Lines:** Show your child that the letters must touch the line if there is a line to write on. Again, this is a process. Please feel free to draw a line with a ruler if you think it will be helpful. Lines are not always needed nor wanted by young children.

- **Capitalization:** Often children mix capital and small letters in a word as they figure out how all of this works; simply remind your child when to use capital letters and have them make corrections if there are capital letters in the middles of words.
- **Pace:** Remind your child to work at a good pace and not hurry through the writing.

Thanks for paying attention to these "handwriting particulars" when your child is writing at home. Individual help is often the best help and not always possible in a busy classroom.

Best Wishes,

Janine Chappell Carr

APPENDIX 11–1
Writing Conference Checklist

My Writing Conference

Name:_____Date:_____

Have I:

_____Put my piece in order?

_____Read my piece to myself?

_____Read my piece to a friend?

_____Checked for capital letters
      and punctuation?

When I was little i had a dog named Tippy

_____Circled the words I want to check?

(thay)

_____Checked all of the words I can?

(they)

_____Signed up for a conference?

I have ready:

_____My piece of writing

_____My writing folder

_____My dictionary

_____A pencil

APPENDIX 14–1
Spelling Program Letter

Dear Families,

This finds us ready to begin our formal spelling program. As you know, we worked diligently on spelling last year during our first-grade year and we will continue to increase our spelling and word awareness this year through our weekly spelling work and our daily writing time. Our goal is for the children to be resourceful spellers when they are writing and to quickly recognize the high-frequency words when they are reading.

The children will set up their spelling practice sheets on Monday in our classroom and these will arrive home on Monday evening for **four nights of practice.** Throughout the week, the children's practice sheets need to be stored in their school folder and carried back and forth between home and school each day.

Again, your child will have five school words which will be chosen from the list of the five hundred words most frequently used by children in their writing. Some of the words you will recognize if your child worked on them last year. When words appear on practice sheets again this year it means your child has not learned the conventional spellings by memory yet. The children will also have up to five of their own personal words that they can choose from their writing or reading work, our current unit study, or simply from "inside their head." I emphasize to the children to be on the lookout for interesting and unusual words. I help each child decide how many school and personal words seems "just right" for him or her. The most your child will ever have is ten words. Both the school words and the personal words need to be practiced each week. I always love it when the children challenge themselves with words like archeologist, medieval, and Comet Hyakutake. Yes, those were some of the words learned last year by first graders!

The children are to do their "Look, Say, Cover, Write, Check" practice at home Monday through Thursday evenings, practicing each word two times (or more!) each night. Of course it's important for you to be involved in your child's spelling practice. Remind your child to try to see the word in his or her mind as if it's written on a chalkboard before attempting to write it on the practice paper. This helps develop a visual memory for words. Also, any spelling "tricks" that you can share with your child (rhyming patterns or "words within words") are encouraged and helpful. I give similar spelling lessons at school. Even practicing (or singing!) spelling words out loud in the car helps.

We have two people helping us with our spelling checks again this year: Rachael Anderson's mom, Amber, and JoAnn Camarino, our assisting teacher. We are lucky to have their expertise and assistance. The children will turn in their weekly practice sheets on Friday morning and these will be stapled to their spelling checks. This paperwork will arrive home the following Monday as I need to look through everything Friday night after school so I can prepare a chart for my Monday spelling lesson that I do with the children before they set up their spelling folders and practice papers for the new week. It is one of the ways I monitor how each child is progressing as a speller. The second and most important way I monitor spelling development is through the children's daily writing work. I will be in touch with you if I have any concerns. Please let me know if you have any questions or concerns and I will get back to you promptly.

Thanks for the time, support, and effort you continue to give to your child as a reader, writer, speller, and learner. Paying attention to words is helpful to the children in many ways and these are important words for the children to have on the tips of their pencils. Practice, practice, practice! And, enjoy the look and sounds of words with your young reader and writer.

Best wishes,

Janine Chappell Carr

BIBLIOGRAPHY

Angelou, Maya. 1993. "I Love the Look of Words." In *Soul Looks Back in Wonder*, illus. Tom Feelings. New York: Dial Books.

Atwell, Nancie. 1998. *In the Middle: New Understandings About Writing, Reading and Learning*. Portsmouth, NH: Heinemann.

Bissex, Glenda L. 1996. *Partial Truths: A Memoir and Essays on Reading, Writing, and Researching*. Portsmouth, NH: Heinemann.

Calkins, Lucy. 1991. *Living Between the Lines*. Portsmouth, NH: Heinemann.

Calkins, Lucy McCormick. 1994. *The Art of Teaching Writing: New Edition*. Portsmouth, NH: Heinemann.

Clay, Marie. 1991. *Becoming Literate: The Construction of Inner Control*. Portsmouth, NH: Heinemann.

———. 1993a. *An Observation Survey of Early Literacy Achievement*. Portsmouth, NH: Heinemann.

———. 1993b. *Reading Recovery: A Guidebook for Teachers in Training*. Portsmouth, NH: Heinemann.

Dickinson, Emily. 1994. "Hope is the thing with feathers." In *Poetry for Young People: Emily Dickinson*, ed. Frances Schoonmaker Bolin. New York: Sterling Publishing Co., Inc.

Dillard, Annie. 1989. *The Writing Life*. New York: HarperPerennial.

Dwyer, John, ed. 1989. *a sea of talk*. Portsmouth, NH: Heinemann.

Esbensen, Barbara. 1996. "Pencils." In *A Jar of Tiny Stars: Poems by NCTE Award-Winning Poets*, ed. Bernice E. Cullinan. Honesdale, PA: Wordsong Boyds Mills Press.

Escamilla, Kathy. 1994. Lecture during Multicultural Perspectives graduate course. Regis University: Denver, CO, summer semester.

Fisher, Bobbi. 1991. *Joyful Learning*. Portsmouth, NH: Heinemann.

Fry, Edward. 1994. *Phonics Patterns: Onset and Rhyme Word Lists*. Laguna Beach, CA: Laguna Beach Educational Books.

Gentry, Richard, and Jean Wallace Gillet. 1993. *Teaching Kids to Spell.* Portsmouth, NH: Heinemann.

Graves, Bill. 1998. "A Year on Notice: Vernon Elementary School." *The Oregonian* June 8.

Graves, Donald H. 1983. *Writing: Teachers & Children at Work.* Portsmouth, NH: Heinemann.

———. 1991. *Build a Literate Classroom.* Portsmouth, NH: Heinemann.

Holdaway, Don. 1979. *The Foundations of Literacy.* Portsmouth, NH: Heinemann.

Jackson, Margaret. 1993. *Creative Display & Environment.* Portsmouth, NH: Heinemann.

Kohn, Alfie. 1995. "Punished by Rewards? A Conversation with Alfie Kohn." *Educational Leadership* 53(1): 13–16.

Konisberg, E.L. 1996. *The View from Saturday.* New York: Atheneum Books for Young Readers.

———. 1997. "Newbery Medal Acceptance." *The Horn Book* LXIII (4): 404–414.

Kuskin, Karla. 1990. "Being Lost." In *Good Books, Good Times!*, selected by Lee Bennett Hopkins. New York: The Trumpet Club.

———. 1992. "Comfortable Old Chair." In *Home*, ed. Michael J. Rosen. New York: A Charlotte Zolotow Book.

Little, Jean. 1986. "My Journals." In *Hey World, Here I Am!* New York: HarperTrophy.

McCord, David. 1990. "Books Fall Open." In *Good Books, Good Times!*, selected by Lee Bennett Hopkins. New York: The Trumpet Club.

Milne, A. A. 1926. *Winnie-the-Pooh.* New York: E. P. Dutton.

Mooney, Margaret. 1988. *Developing Life-Long Readers.* New York: Richard C. Owens Publishers.

———. 1997. Presentation at the "Year of the Young Reader Conference," Vancouver, WA, April.

Moustafa, Margaret. 1997. *Beyond Traditional Phonics.* Portsmouth, NH: Heinemann.

Neilsen, Lorri. 1994. *A Stone in My Shoe: Teaching Literacy in Times of Change.* Winnipeg, Manitoba: Peguis Publishers Limited.

Owens Renner, Nancy. 1997. *Foucault Pendulum Exhibit.* San Diego Natural History Museum.

Peterson, Ralph. 1992. *Life in a Crowded Place.* Portsmouth, NH: Heinemann.

Pinnell, Gay Su, and Irene C. Fountas. 1998. *Word Matters: Teaching Phonics and Spelling in the Reading/Writing Classroom.* Portsmouth, NH: Heinemann.

Pipher, Mary. 1996. *The Shelter of Each Other: Rebuilding Our Families.* New York: G. P. Putnam's Sons.

Ransom, Kathryn A. 1998. "Reading Report Raises Hopes." *Reading Today: News of the Profession* 15(5) 3–4.

Rief, Linda. 1995. "Staying Off-Balance and Alive: Learning from My Students." In *All That Matters: What Is It We Value in School and Beyond?* ed. Linda Rief and Maureen Barbieri: 5–29. Portsmouth, NH: Heinemann.

Routman, Regie. 1988. *Transitions*. Portsmouth, NH: Heinemann.

Rylant, Cynthia. 1991. "My Grandmother's Hair." In *To Ride a Butterfly,* ed. Nancy Larrick and Wendy Lamb. New York: Bantam Doubleday Dell.

Smith, Frank. 1988. *Joining the Literacy Club*. Portsmouth, NH: Heinemann.

———. 1990. *to think*. Portsmouth, NH: Heinemann.

Taylor, Denny. 1983. *Family Literacy*. Portsmouth, NH: Heinemann.

Traill, Leanna. 1993. *Highlight My Strengths: Assessment and Evaluation of Literacy Learning*. Crystal Lake, IL: Rigby.

Turbill, Jan, Andrea Butler, Brian Cambourne, and Gail Langton. 1991. *Frameworks: Theory into Practice, Revised Edition*. Stanley, NY: Wayne—Finger Lakes Board of Cooperative Education Services.

White, E.B. 1945. *Stuart Little*. New York: HarperCollins.

Whitman, Walt. 1955. "There Was a Child Went Forth." In *Leaves of Grass*. Amherst, NY: Prometheus Books.

Wilde, Jack. 1995. "Share What You Love: An Interview with Katherine Paterson." In *All That Matters: What Is It We Value in School and Beyond?* ed. Linda Rief and Maureen Barbieri: 43–54. Portsmouth, NH: Heinemann.

Wilde, Sandra. 1996. "What Is Our Responsibility in Helping Children Learn to Spell?" *Primary Voices* 4 (November) 2–6.

Winthrop, Elizabeth. 1985. *The Castle in the Attic*. New York: Bantam, Doubleday, Dell.

INDEX